Reading
FAITH & RACE IN
The Asian American Religious Experience

VOL
4
Second
Edition

EDITED BY

JON R. STONE

Kendall Hunt
publishing company

For my former graduate students both here and abroad, including:

Angelo Anagnos, Jordan Almanzar, Henry Bens, Angela Chompff,
Jennifer Dick, Antonio Dillehunt, Philippe Duhart, Jonathan Friedmann,
Javier Gonzalez, Heather Mackey, Jennifer Hoddevik, Shafiel Karim, Daniel Majors,
Ethan Quillen, Jessica Rehman, Vanessa Soriano, Timothy Vizthum, Nikolas Xiros,
and Suzette Zazueta.

Cover image © Shutterstock.com
Buddha with incense and candle.

Kendall Hunt
publishing company

www.kendallhunt.com
Send all inquiries to:
4050 Westmark Drive
Dubuque, IA 52004-1840

Published in the United States of America

Contents

Chapter Sources for Volume Four: The Asian American Religious Experience

Other Volumes in This Series

THE NATIVE AMERICAN RELIGIOUS EXPERIENCE

THE AFRICAN AMERICAN RELIGIOUS EXPERIENCE

THE LATINO/A AMERICAN RELIGIOUS EXPERIENCE

Foreword to the Second Edition of This Series

The need to renew the copyright permissions for most of the selections in these volumes now occasions the publication of a second edition. Since first appearing in 2007, the selections in these four volumes of *Readings in American Religious Diversity* (originally published as one hefty quarto tome!) have been changed only modestly. For the 2012 revised edition, I added only two or three readings to volumes one and two, ones that helped fill-in some of the instructional gaps in the course material. For this second edition, my colleagues and I have decided (reluctantly) to drop several readings—ones that our faculty have tended not to assign—in favor of several newer and fresher ones. In terms of size and substance, the most noticeable additions have been to volumes three and four, which our faculty had deemed a little lean as compared to the first two volumes. And for this second edition, as the editor, I have also taken this opportunity to revise and reword a number of the discussion questions in each volume as well as update the introductory material in each volume to reflect the changes in content (with thanks to Professors Gabriel Estrada, Bradley Hawkins, Sophia Pandya, and Carlos Piar for contributing helpful suggestions).

As I had noted in the *Foreword* to the first edition, it has become a commonplace to speak of America as a religiously diverse nation. From its origins, dating well before the arrival of European settlers, the American continent contained a great variety of peoples, languages, cultures, and religions. The native groups that came to inhabit this vast and varied landscape were of many types, from pueblo dwelling peoples, to those living in the woodlands, prairie, mountain, and coastal regions. During the period of European exploration and colonial expansion, the Americas soon became home to English, French, Spanish, Portuguese, and Dutch settlers. And, after slavery was introduced into the New World, peoples of African tribal descent added their own cultural and religious expressions to the growing ethnic and racial diversity of the land. From many peoples there emerged one nation; from one nation there arose many religious voices. The long conversation—and the spirited debate—over issues of religious and cultural identity continues to this day. What does it mean to be an American? What does it mean to be part of an ethnic or racial community in America? In what ways have religious beliefs and traditional cultural practices informed that meaning or helped shape that identity?

This four volume series presents to students of American religion a collection of primary source materials that serves to illustrate the ethno-racial dimensions of religion in America beyond its usual European expressions. The ethno-racial religious communities featured in this anthology broadly include Native American, African American, Asian American, and an array of Latino communities. A unique feature of these volumes is that their readings come from within the communities themselves, rather than from researchers commenting upon these communities from the outside. Thus, students reading these selections will come to hear the voices and sense the deeply-felt passion, sorrow, frustration, hope, and joy of those individuals who were or are still part of the important conversations at the heart of these four ethno-racial communities' ongoing dialogue and debates within themselves.

More specifically, these primary-source readings are designed to complement the religious and historical materials of the junior-level interdisciplinary capstone course, "American Religious Diversity," which is offered every semester at California State University, Long Beach. For this course, students are required to read religious literature produced by women and men from within at least two of the four ethno-racial communities mentioned above. While many of our instructors have assigned works of fiction, such as short stories or novels, we have found that fictional literature has tended to give our students only a partial picture of the religious dimensions of these communities and the difficulties these groups have experienced in their attempts to maintain traditional beliefs and practices in a predominantly "white" and Protestant culture. Thus, in addition to works of fiction, we have discovered that the diversity of religious experience as well as responses within these communities to discrimination, social dislocation, and loss of traditional culture could be "read" within other types of literature. These include folktales, sermons, letters, speeches, essays and addresses, autobiographies, oral histories and published interviews, as well as immigrant community histories, scholarly treatises, and ethnic denominational self-studies.

Because the course for which these four volumes are designed is taught each semester by six full-time and part-time faculty members, I do not believe that it has been my role as the lead editor of this anthology to instruct my colleagues in how to use these selections. At the same time, because not all of our faculty work in the area of American religious and ethnic history, I think that it is important to provide an outline of themes that emerge from these readings, especially as they show both the similarities as well as the differences in the experiences of these four ethno-racial communities and the role that religious ideas and practices have played within each. Thus, despite differences in their origins and in their specific experiences in the Americas, the literature produced by persons within the Native American, African American, Asian American, and Latino communities share a number of themes which students and instructors can reflect upon and fruitfully discuss. Among these themes is the experience of being outsiders, of social and cultural "otherness," of dislocation, disorientation, and uprootedness, of turning to tradition and relying upon religious institutions for personal and communal support, of the importance of family and the larger ethnic community, of striving after the recognition of basic rights and of one's human worth, of resistance to assimilation and the struggle against the secularizing influences of modern social and cultural life, and of drawing upon mythologies to strengthen one's sense of self and importance in the world.

Owing to all these difficulties and other personal and social experiences, it is profound that, beyond everything, people have continually turned to religion and to traditional expressions of community life for their remedy. There are those who seek succor within a religious community as well as those who adapt themselves and their traditions to meet the exigencies of life as immigrants, as sojourners or as outsiders, in a world where one's experiences are constantly defined by harassment, discrimination, and unrelenting assaults upon one's dignity. But also, and perhaps more importantly, people's experiences have likewise been defined by family, faith, community, friendship, religious mystery, wonder, thankfulness, laughter, and the renewal of the human spirit in the face of adversity.

Of course, while these themes predominate, one can also discern from these readings many lesser and many more contrasting themes. From this quartet of ethno-racial communities, a *discors concordia* or discordant concord can also be heard. The themes and variations that play throughout the pages of this anthology intersect in grand fugal style, and bear witness to the resilience of the human spirit, the signal significance of community, and the central role that religion plays in defining one's place in the world. Religion has been the tie that has bound individuals to their communities, has strengthened those same communities by renewing members' commitments to long-standing traditions, even as those traditions are transformed by the challenges that these and other like communities have had to face.

With respect to the selections themselves: originally it had been the hope of our faculty to include at least 25 readings per volume. But, due to obvious page limitations and higher than expected copyright costs, we have had to limit the number of selections in each volume to about 17–22. Despite these constraints, but not because of them, we decided that it was important to reprint the selected chapters, speeches, essays, and articles in their entirety, unedited, and as they originally appeared in print—coarse language and all. To understand and appreciate the positions and views being advanced or expressed, students need to read these selections *in toto*—two notable exceptions being the journal of Mrs. Jarena Lee and the lengthy chapter from Leslie Marmon Silko, both of which I felt obliged to condense by some 25–30 original printed pages.

Additionally, because the aim of these volumes is to highlight the various types of religious literature produced by members of these four ethno-racial communities, it is evident that not all communities produce the same varieties of literature, neither in the types nor in the same quantity. This difference is most evident in the volume on the Asian American religious experience, in which, to maintain some balance of material among volumes, I have had to include more scholarly and historical types of literature.

Lastly, while this primary-source anthology is primarily intended to meet the interdisciplinary and human diversity requirements of a specific course at Long Beach State, my colleagues and I are also aware of its potential instructional value outside Southern California. Recognizing that instructors and their students at other colleges and universities throughout the United States might likewise find these selections of interest, the volumes are designed to appeal more generally to faculty teaching similar courses in the fields of history, religious studies, ethnic studies, American studies, rhetoric, and comparative literary studies. To help familiarize readers with the four ethno-racial religious communities that comprise this anthology, I have also provided a brief preface or "foretaste" for each volume, along with several suggested questions to help facilitate class discussion. And so that those using this reader may be encouraged to explore further the histories and literatures of these communities, at the beginning of each volume I have included a list of recommended sources for both instructors and students to consult (with credit to Carlos Piar for Volume 3).

Notwithstanding these limitations, my colleagues and I have sought to create an anthology that allows a variety of voices within these communities to be heard, in many cases for the first time under the same cover. Indeed, this text represents a true celebration of the religious diversity that defines the American nation.

Vox manet—the Voice remains (Ovid).

—Jon R. Stone, Ph.D.
Long Beach, Calif.
May 2015

An Addendum to the new title: *Faith and Race in America*

Since 2007, when *Readings in American Religious Diversity* was first published as one large volume of primary source readings, the course for which it was designed has undergone a number of changes. Broadly conceived in 1994 as an upper-level interdisciplinary capstone course examining the multifaceted varieties of religious experiences in the United States, by 2006 this course shifted its focus more directly on the key ways by which religion helped define and preserve the traditional cultures and customs of America's four main racial and ethnic communities: Native American, African American, Latina/o, and Asian American. The course's original unwieldy title, "Religious and Social Ethical Dimensions of American Diversity," was then shortened to "American Religious Diversity." The course reader that accompanied this new focus captured the spirit of that change by giving voice to women and men from within those very communities. But, by 2015, the focus of the course evolved even further by adding greater emphasis on issues of racial justice and gender equality in the United States. With the recent change in the course title to "Faith and Race in America," it seemed natural, if not necessary, to change the title of the course reader as well. But notwithstanding the new title, the essential aim of this collection of readings remains unchanged: diverse voices whose many faiths both affirm communal and inspire individual aspirations to seek after something higher as a nation that is, to quote Ronald Takaki, "peopled by the world."

"Let justice roll down like waters and righteousness like a mighty stream."
(Rev. Martin Luther King, Jr., April 1963, after Amos 5:24)

—Jon R. Stone
Long Beach, Calif.
July 2020

Sources and Selected General Works in American Religious History

Ahlstrom, Sydney E. *A Religious History of the American People.* New Haven, CT: Yale University Press, 1972.

Albanese, Catherine L. *America: Religions and Religion,* 3rd ed. Belmont, CA: Wadsworth, 1999.

Alba, Richard, Albert J. Raboteau, and Josh DeWind (eds.). *Immigration and Religion in America: Comparative and Historical Perspectives.* New York: New York University Press, 2009.

Barkan, Elliott Robert (ed.). *Immigrants in American History: Arrival, Adaptation, and Integration,* 4 vols. Santa Barbara, CA: ABC-CLIO, 2013.

Becker, Penny, and Nancy Eiesland (eds.). *Contemporary American Religion: An Ethnographic Reader.* Walnut Creek, CA: AltaMira Press, 1997.

Butler, Jon, Grant Wacker, and Randall Balmer. *Religion in American Life: A Short History.* NY: Oxford University Press, 2003.

Carroll, Bret E. *The Routledge Historical Atlas of Religions in America.* New York: Routledge, 2000.

Corrigan, John, and Winthrop S. Hudson. *Religion in America,* 7th ed. Upper Saddle River, NJ: Prentice-Hall, 2004.

Ebaugh, Helen, and Janet Chafetz. *Religion and the New Immigrants: Continuities and Adaptations in Immigrant Congregations.* Walnut Creek, CA: AltaMira Press, 2000.

Eck, Diana L. *A New Religious America.* San Francisco: HarperSanFrancisco, 2002.

Gaustad, Edwin S (ed.). *A Documentary History of Religion in America,* 2 vols. Grand Rapids, MI: Eerdmans, 1982–1983.

_____. *A Religious History of America,* rev. ed. San Francisco: Harper & Row, 1990.

Goff, Philip, and Paul Harvey (eds.). *Themes in Religion and American Culture.* Chapel Hill, NC: University of North Carolina Press, 2004.

Hackett, David G. (ed.). *Religion and American Culture: A Reader.* New York: Routledge, 1995.

Handy, Robert T. *A History of the Churches in the United States and Canada.* New York: Oxford University Press, 1977.

Hemeyer, Julia Corbett. *Religion in America,* 5th ed. Upper Saddle River, NJ: Prentice-Hall, 2005.

Lippy, Charles H., Robert Choquette, and Stafford Poole. *Christianity Comes to the Americas, 1492–1776.* New York: Paragon House, 1992.

McDannell, Colleen (ed.). *Religions of the United States in Practice,* 2 vols. Princeton, NJ: Princeton University Press, 2001.

Neusner, Jacob (ed.). *World Religions in America,* 3rd ed. Louisville, KY: Westminster/John Knox Press, 2003.

Porterfield, Amanda (ed.). *American Religious History.* Oxford, UK: Blackwell Publishers, 2002.

Warner, R. Stephen, and Judith G. Wittner (eds.). *Gatherings in Diaspora: Religious Communities and the New Immigration.* Philadelphia: Temple University Press, 1998.

Williams, Peter W. *America's Religions: From Their Origins to the Twenty-first Century,* 3rd ed. Urbana: University of Illinois Press, 2008.

_____ (ed.). *Perspectives on American Religion and Culture: A Reader.* Oxford, UK: Blackwell Publishers, 1999.

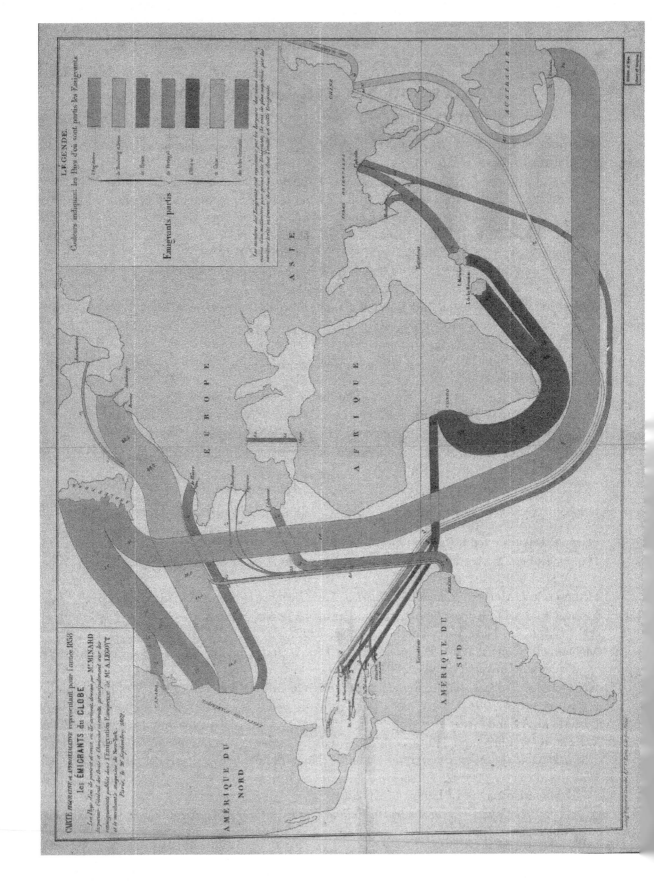

CARTE FIGURATIVE et APPROXIMATIVE représentant pour l'année 1858
les ÉMIGRANTS du GLOBE
par M. MINARD

Paris, le 28 Septembre 1862.

LÉGENDE.
Couleurs indiquant les Pays d'où sont partis les Émigrants.

Émigrants partis

Readings in Asian American Religious Traditions: A Foretaste

Cultural and religious diversity characterize the peoples broadly defined as Asian American. In terms of immigration to and settlement in the United States and elsewhere in the Americas, the first Asian peoples arrived from China in the mid-nineteenth century, followed later by the Japanese, Filipinos, and Koreans, and then by peoples from India and elsewhere in South Asia. By the 1920s, the flow of immigration from Asia became a trickle, due in large part to changes in immigration laws. After these laws were liberalized in the 1960s, new waves of immigrants not only reached the Western Pacific shores, but continued inland beyond the Rockies. After the Vietnam War, larger communities of Asian immigrants began to establish themselves in or near the cities of Boston, Chicago, Pittsburgh, Philadelphia, Houston, and Dallas, as well as Minneapolis and elsewhere throughout the Midwest. Within a generation, these Asian settlements would begin to transform the very character of many suburban American communities.

Historically, the existence of Asian enclaves, such as Chinatowns, Koreatowns, and Little Tokyos, have tended to create concern among long-standing Anglo-American residents. But, the experiences of alien sojourners, if not the ethnic enclaves that they created, were not at all new to Americans. Little Italies, as well as Polish, Jewish, Irish, and Scandinavian neighborhoods, had been carved out of places like Philadelphia, Boston, New York, Chicago, and other major cities across the United States. What was different, however, was the *discontinuity* of cultural and religious traditions that characterized these Asian neighborhoods. Unlike immigrants from Europe, from the standpoint of culture and in most cases religion, Asian Americans were both aliens among as well as alienated from their Anglo-American neighbors. As an example, although both Irish and Chinese immigrants were greeted by harassment and discrimination at nearly every turn, the Irish from Western Europe and the Chinese from East Asia did not inhabit the same cultural or religious worlds, nor did they share similar views regarding the sacred.

Thus, while the readings that comprise this volume bear witness to discrimination, at the same time the Asian American experience has also been defined by cultural misunderstanding, suspicion, race hatred, and by the disruption of family life, as well as by alienation, not simply alienation of the Asian immigrant from "white" Protestant culture, but increasingly of the immigrant or first generation from their progressively Americanized children and grandchildren. To those within the first generation, and to perhaps others, the greatest tragedy of immigration may not have been their heroic struggle to keep their religious and cultural traditions alive like a flickering lamp on a storm-tossed boat, but has been the lack of interest their children have often expressed in tending to such traditions. In this instance, the opposite of faith may not be doubt or disbelief, but indifference.

The difficulty that presents itself in discussing Asian American histories and religious traditions is one of tracing multiple storylines that seldom intersect. Therefore, because of their size and long histories in the United States, for this volume of primary-source readings I have selected the Chinese and Japanese communities as two representatives of the Asian American religious experience generally. In addition, to allow for some comparison of experiences, I have included one brief autobiographical essay by a Filipino-American student from the 1930s as well as two additional readings that give voice to the more recent experiences of immigrants from Southeast Asia. To orient readers to the main reading selections from these two communities, I offer as a "foretaste" the following brief outline of Chinese and Japanese experiences in the United States and the role that religion—Buddhist and Christian—appears to have played historically in defining and maintaining these distinct communities.

Like many immigrants, the Chinese traveled to America seeking fortune. After gold had been discovered at Sutter's mill in California in January 1848, hundreds of Chinese sailed for *Gum Shan/Chin Shan*, or Gold Mountain, to stake their claims. By 1850, there were close to 800 Chinese immigrants in America, most coming from Canton (Guangdong) Province in coastal southern China. Within a decade, there were as many as 35,000 Chinese in the United States. By 1880, that number would climb to over 100,000. While gold had brought the Chinese to California, not all of these immigrants worked the sluices or dug in mines. Some opened businesses, including general stores, laundries, and restaurants. Others fished and shrimped along the Pacific coast and the inland waters. By the 1860s, when mining became less profitable, the Chinese turned to other types of labor. For example, between 1865 and 1869, Union Pacific employed as many as 15,000 Chinese, and a number of Sikhs, to help complete the transcontinental railroad. During this and other periods, harassment of Chinese workers was typical. Anti-Chinese agitation eventually led to passage of the Chinese Exclusion Act in 1882, which suspended immigration of Chinese laborers for ten years. The act was subsequently renewed in 1893, and was in force until its repeal in 1943, when China and the United States were allies against Japan during World War II.

As with most early immigrants, the Chinese did not intend to remain in the United States but saw themselves as sojourners (*luoye guigen*). Those who came were young bachelors or newly married men attracted by the prospect of gaining easy wealth. Few could afford passage for their wives and children but would regularly send a portion of their earnings to their families in China. Most lived in the crowded and squalid conditions of the Chinatowns and low-priced boarding houses. Few, if any, were concerned with establishing long-term communities. In fact, early bachelor immigration patterns, combined with anti-Chinese laws, prevented Chinese men from fulfilling traditional duties to their ancestors. Many, realizing that they might not return to China, arranged for their remains to be returned to their ancestral villages. As Shih-shan Henry Tsai explains, the Chinese immigrant "believed that if his body was buried in a strange land, untended by his family, his soul would never stop wandering in the darkness of the other world" (1986:10). Indeed, to serve the social and religious needs of Chinese immigrants, a number of associations were established. These became known as the Six Companies, and membership was based on family names and on the regional dialect that the Chinese immigrant spoke. Not only did these companies protect the interests of their members, but each company set aside a place for honoring homeland gods. Moreover, leaders of the Six Companies saw conversion to Christianity "as a threat to Chinese culture and Chinese social institutions," and thus sought to dissuade their fellow Chinese from visiting Christian missions. "On a few occasions," writes Tsai, "they made desperate moves, using harassment and social ostracism to discourage the increase of Chinese Christians" (1986:45).

As early as the 1850s, Protestant missionaries had entered the mining camps, intent on converting Chinese laborers. A number of Protestant missionaries, such as William Speer and A.W. Loomis, set up medical clinics, offered English language classes, and published bilingual newspapers. Several others, such as Reverend Otis Gibson, aided the poor, established shelters for run-away prostitutes, and sought to improve the welfare of Chinese immigrants. Though few Chinese were converted, those who did, such as Reverend Ng Poon Chew, would later lament the lawless state of the Chinese American community. Gambling, prostitution, and rampant lawbreaking came to characterize the typical Chinatown. "Opium," Chew warned, "is the devil's curse and device for creating misery" (Chew, in Irwin 1893:51). Sadly, he added, while the churches have brought hope to the Chinese, only a handful have accepted the Gospel. "Many things have to be overcome and endured before a Chinaman can be a Christian. He has to discard all the former beliefs and superstitions and ancestral worship which every Chinaman holds dear; and in addition he has to suffer ill-treatment and separation from his former friends and relatives" (1893:54). Despite the efforts of Chew and other evangelists, the Chinese Americans who did convert—and the number of converts before the 1950s continued to remain small—retained some of their traditional practices, such as honoring their ancestors, following prescribed rituals for weddings and funerals, and visiting Chinese temples to pay "occasional respect to Taoist gods" and, of course, to socialize with fellow sojourners (Tsai 1986:44).

The selection of readings that concern the Chinese religious experience in America document both traditional Chinese and recent Christian expressions. These readings include a turn-of-the-century serialized set of profiles written by Sui Sin Far to correct false impressions and stereotypes of the Chinese, an historical overview of traditional Chinese religious beliefs and practices by L. Eve Armentrout Ma, a social scientific study by Fenggang Yang of Chinese Christian churches as a vehicle for preserving Chinese culture, and an excerpt from Amy Tan's book, *The Kitchen God's Wife,* which examines the continuing, if inconvenient, hold of tradition on a modern Chinese American woman. Also included is a 1937 selection on Chinese temples in the city of Honolulu as well as other pre- and post-war reminiscences published in the regional sociological journal, *Social Process in Hawaii.*

Though economic opportunities had brought the Chinese to America, it was the vast and fertile agricultural lands that attracted Japanese immigrants to Hawaii and the Pacific coastal regions of the United States. But, while most of the Japanese who first immigrated to the United States in the 1880s were young men, one major difference from the Chinese sojourner was that Japanese Buddhist missionaries accompanied the first waves of Japanese immigrants to America. Nearly 90% of immigrants from Japan were Buddhist, and most were members of Jodo Shinshu, a Pure Land sect of Mahayana Buddhism. In fact, it was mostly an accident of history that Jodo Shinshu became predominant among the Japanese in America. First, most Japanese immigrants to Hawaii and California in the 1880s and

1890s—about 60–65%—came from Pure Land regions in southern Japan. Second, Jodo missionaries and priests were among the first to arrive in the United States. Third, those Japanese immigrants who were not originally affiliated with Jodo were drawn to this sect largely because of the opportunity to socialize with other Japanese as well as to fulfill abiding spiritual needs.

The North American Buddhist Mission, later the Buddhist Churches of America (BCA), was officially founded in San Francisco on September 1, 1899. By late December, a second mission had been established in Sacramento, followed in 1901 by a third mission in Fresno and a fourth in Seattle. At that time, the Japanese community numbered just over 2,000. In 1905, the mission headquarters was renamed The Buddhist Church of San Francisco, perhaps to make the English translation of *bukkyokai* ("Buddha's teachings association") more Western sounding. In time, the Buddhist temple/church became a central focus of the Japanese immigrant community, most especially during the period of internment during World War II. As Tetsuden Kashima has observed, "[b]y offering a central locale for the Japanese congregation, through its picnics, religious services, Japanese language schools, Japanese cinema, and so on, the church provided a friendly environment for an ethnic group that often encountered hostility from the society at large" (1977:7).

Interestingly, while the Chinese immigrants tended to define themselves by their families, regions, and dialects, the Japanese located themselves by their generation in America: *Issei* (first), *Nisei* (second), and *Sansei* (third). In addition to generational identities, the transformations that took place within the Japanese community's central organization—the Buddhist church—were principally aimed at holding onto the loyalty of the Nisei, and later the Sansei, who were becoming increasingly more Americanized. For instance, to combat the influences of American culture on the Nisei, the BCA established its own youth clubs and sports leagues patterned after such organizations as the Boy and Girl Scouts and Little League Baseball.

The destruction caused by Imperial Japan's attack on Pearl Harbor in December 1941, and its subsequent offensives throughout Asia and the Pacific in 1942, created heightened suspicion of Japanese communities in America and made them a cause for concern during the U.S. mobilization to defend the homeland from possible invasion. In 1942, President Roosevelt ordered the forced evacuation of persons of Japanese descent from the Pacific coastal regions and their placement in "relocation centers" or internment camps. Of the 110,000 Japanese Americans sent to these camps in desolate areas of the country, 70,000 were Nisei. Even so, whether Issei or Nisei, all Japanese Americans were considered potential saboteurs. During the Relocation period, it is estimated that Japanese Americans lost properties, possessions, businesses, and earnings valued at half a billion dollars. But, despite these losses, one unintended consequence of wartime internment was a renewal of Buddhism among Japanese in the camps. As Gary Okihiro has noted, "the large majority of confined Japanese openly espoused Buddhism, and in some camps, Buddhism gained new adherents" (1985:223). The camps also saw "a resurgence of Japanese folk beliefs and practices," most notably at Tule Lake on the California–Oregon border (1985:230). As Okihiro noted further, "Nisei, who were previously drifting away from Japanese culture, were drawn back to the family unit. Discrimination and the denial of their rights disillusioned many Nisei. They now looked more to their families and ethnic community for security and acceptance" (1985:224).

After the war, rebuilding the Japanese American community was among their first priorities. But, because many Japanese did not return to their previous homes and businesses, and instead settled and worked elsewhere in the United States, Buddhist churches came to be established in cities across middle America, such as Minneapolis, Cleveland, and Detroit.

Accordingly, the additional readings on the Japanese American experience include several personal recollections of Buddhist observances in the temple and in the home (also from *Social Process*) and a number of autobiographical stories by Lydia Minatoya that reflect differences in perspectives among Japanese Americans. What is more, the pieces by Minatoya and the selections from *Social Process* provide interesting examples of generational tensions and testify to the strangely powerful pull that cultural and religious traditions continue to have upon those Japanese whose lives and experiences in modern America would now seem altogether foreign to their immigrant grandparents and great-grandparents. The final two readings represent examples of religious oral histories, one of a Vietnamese Buddhist nun and the other of a former Cambodian Buddhist monk.

Taken together, the readings in this volume—though only a thumbnail sketch of the entire Asian American experience—provide the reader with a glimpse of the role that religion and traditional culture have occupied and continue to occupy in most Asian immigrant communities. These readings likewise give voice to the struggles that all immigrant peoples have encountered as settlers or sojourners in this most culturally and religiously diverse nation in the world today.

Sources and Selected Works in Asian American History, Literature, and Religions

[* indicates works of fiction]

Alumkal, Antony W. *Asian American Evangelical Churches: Race, Ethnicity, and Assimilation in the Second Generation.* New York: LFB Scholarly Publishing, 2003.

Azuma, Eiichiro. *Between Two Empires: Race, History, and Transnationalism in Japanese America.* New York: Oxford University Press, 2005.

Bao, Jiemin. *Creating a Buddhist Community: A Thai Temple in Silicon Valley.* Philadelphia: Temple University Press, 2015.

Bautista, Veltisezar B. *The Filipino Americans from 1763 to the Present: Their History, Culture, and Traditions,* 2nd ed. Naperville, IL: Bookhaus Publishers, 2002.

Bonus, Rick. *Locating Filipino Americans: Ethnicity and the Cultural Politics of Space.* Philadelphia: Temple University Press, 2000.

Buddhist Churches of America (BCA). *Buddhist Churches of America (Vol. 1): 75-Year History, 1899–1974.* Chicago: Nobart, 1974.

_____. *Buddhist Churches of America: A Legacy of the First 100 Years.* San Francisco, CA: Buddhist Churches of America, 1998.

Bulosan, Carlos. *America Is in the Heart: A Personal History*. Seattle, WA: University of Washington Press, 1974.

———— (Epifanio San Juan, Jr., ed.). *On Becoming Filipino: Selected Writings of Carlos Bulosan*. Philadelphia: Temple University Press, 1995.

Burns, Jeffrey M., Ellen Skerrett, and Joseph M. White (eds.). *Keeping Faith: European and Asian Catholic Immigrants*. Maryknoll, NY: Orbis Books, 2000.

Cadge, Wendy. *Heartwood: The First Generation of Theravada Buddhism in America*. Chicago: The University of Chicago Press, 2005.

Carnes, Tony, and Fenggang Yang (eds.). *Asian American Religions: The Making and Remaking of Borders and Boundaries*. New York: New York University Press, 2004.

Cassel, Susie Lan. *The Chinese in America: A History from Gold Mountain to the New Millennium*. Walnut Creek, CA: AltaMira Press, 2002.

Chan, Sucheng. *Asian Californians*. San Francisco: MTL/Boyd and Fraser, 1991.

———— (ed.). *Entry Denied*. Philadelphia: Temple University Press, 1991.

———— (ed.). *The Vietnamese American 1.5 Generation: Stories of War, Revolution, Flight and New Beginnings*. Philadelphia: Temple University Press, 2006.

Chen, Carolyn. *Getting Saved in America: Taiwanese Immigration and Religious Experience*. Princeton, NJ: Princeton University Press, 2014.

Chen, Jack. *The Chinese of America*. San Francisco: Harper & Row, 1980.

Cherry, Stephen M. Faith, *Family, and Filipino American Community Life*. New Brunswick, NJ: Rutgers University Press, 2014.

Cheung, King-Kok (ed.). *An Interethnic Companion to Asian American Literature*. New York: Cambridge University Press, 1997.

———— (ed.). *Words Matter: Conversations with Asian American Writers*. Honolulu, HI: University of Hawai'i Press, 2000.

The Chinese Historical Society of America. *The Life, Influence, and the Role of the Chinese in the United States, 1776–1960: Proceedings, Papers of the National Conference Held at the University of San Francisco, July 10, 11, 12, 1975*. San Francisco: The Chinese Historical Society of America, 1976.

Choy, Bong-Youn. *Koreans in America*. Chicago: Nelson-Hall, 1979.

Daniels, Roger. *Asian America: Chinese and Japanese in the United States since 1850*. Seattle, WA: University of Washington Press, 1988.

———— *Concentration Camps, North America: Japanese in the United States and Canada during World War II*. Malabar, FL: R. E. Krieger, 1981.

*Divakaruni, Chitra Banerjee. *The Unknown Errors of Our Lives*. New York: Anchor Books, 2002.

Do, Hien Duc. *The Vietnamese Americans*. Westport, CT: Greenwood Press, 1999.

Espiritu, Yen Le. *Filipino American Lives*. Philadelphia: Temple University Press, 1995.

————. *Home Bound: Filipino American Lives Across Cultures, Communities, and Countries*. Berkeley, CA: University of California Press, 2003.

Far, Sui Sin (Amy Ling and Annette White-Parks, eds.). *Mrs. Spring Fragrance and Other Writings*. Urbana, IL: University of Illinois Press, 1995.

Farber, Don, and Rick Fields. *Taking Refuge in L.A.: Life in a Vietnamese Buddhist Temple*. New York: Aperture Books, 1987.

Fields, Rick. *How the Swans Came to the Lake: A Narrative History of Buddhism in America*, 3rd ed. Boston: Shambhala, 1992.

Freeman, James M. *Changing Identities: Vietnamese Americans, 1975–1995*. Boston: Allyn & Bacon, 1996.

Fugita, Stephen, and David J. O'Brian. *Japanese American Ethnicity*. Seattle, WA: University of Washington Press, 1991.

Gibson, Rev. O[tis]. *The Chinese in America*. Cincinnati, OH: Hitchcock & Walden, 1877.

Gillenkirk, Jeff, and James Motlow. *Bitter Melon: Stories from the Last Rural Chinese Town in America*. Seattle, WA: University of Washington Press, 1987.

Gonzalez III, Joaquin Jay. *Filipino American Faith in Action: Immigration, Religion, and Civic Engagement*. New York: New York University Press, 2009

Hayashi, Brian Masaru. *'For the Sake of Our Japanese Brethren': Assimilation, Nationalism, and Protestantism among the Japanese of Los Angeles, 1895–1942*. Stanford, CA: Stanford University Press, 1995.

Henkin, Alan B., and Liem Thanh Nguyen. *Between Two Cultures: The Vietnamese in America*. Saratoga, CA: Century Twenty-One Publishing, 1981.

Hing, Bill Ong. *Making and Remaking Asia America through Immigration Policy, 1850–1990*. Stanford, CA: Stanford University Press, 1993.

Hunter, Louise M. *Buddhism in Hawaii: Its Impact on a Yankee Community*. Honolulu, HI: University of Hawaii Press, 1971.

Hurh, Won Moo, and Kwang Chung Kim. *Korean Immigrants in America: A Structural Analysis of Ethnic Confinement and Adhesive Adaptation*. Rutherford, NJ: Fairleigh Dickinson University Press, 1984.

Ichihashi, Yamato. *Japanese in the United States: A Critical Study of the Problems of the Japanese Immigrants and Their Children*. Stanford, CA: Stanford University Press, 1932.

Irwin, Rev. D. Hanson (ed.). *The Pacific Coast Pulpit*. New York: Fleming H. Revell Co., 1893.

Iwamura, Jane, and Paul Spickard (eds.). *Revealing the Sacred in Asian and Pacific America*. New York: Routledge, 2003.

Jensen, Joan M. *Passage from India: Asian Indian Immigrants in North America*. New Haven, CT: Yale University Press, 1988.

Jeung, Russell. *Faithful Generations: Race and New Asian American Churches*. New Brunswick, NJ: Rutgers University Press, 2005.

Joshi, Khyati Y. *New Roots in America's Sacred Ground: Religion, Race, and Ethnicity in Indian America*. New Brunswick, NJ: Rutgers University Press, 2006.

Kanzaki, Kiichi. *California and the Japanese*. San Francisco: Japanese Association of America, 1921.

Kashima, Tetsuden. *Buddhism in America: The Social Organization of an Ethnic Religious Institution.* Westport, CT: Greenwood Press, 1977.

Kibria, Nazli. *Becoming Asian American: Second-Generation Chinese and Korean American Identities.* Baltimore: The Johns Hopkins University Press, 2004.

———. *Family Tightrope: The Changing Lives of Vietnamese Americans.* Princeton, NJ: Princeton University Press, 1993.

Kim, Ai Ra. *Women Struggling for a New Life: The Role of Religion in the Cultural Passage from Korea to America.* Albany, New York: SUNY Press, 1996.

Kim, Byong-Suh (ed.). *Koreans in America.* Memphis, TN: Association of Korean Christian Scholars in North America, 1977.

Kim, Byong-Suh, and Sang Hyun Lee (eds.). *The Korean Immigrant in America.* Montclair, NJ: Association of Korean Christian Scholars in North America, 1980.

Kim, Elaine H., and Eui-Young Yu (eds.). *East to America: Korean American Life Stories.* New York: The New Press, 1996.

Kim, Ilpyong J. *Korean-Americans: Past, Present, and Future.* Elizabeth, NJ: Hollym International Corp., 2004.

Kim, Kwang Chung, R. Stephen Warner, and Ho-Youn Kwon (eds.). *Korean Americans and Their Religions: Pilgrims and Missionaries from a Different Shore.* University Park, PA: Pennsylvania State University Press, 2001.

Kim, Sharon. *A Faith Of Our Own: Second-Generation Spirituality in Korean American Churches.* New Brunswick, NJ: Rutgers University Press, 2010.

Kingston, Maxine Hong. *China Men.* New York: Alfred A. Knopf, 1980.

Kitano, Harry. *The Japanese Americans.* New York: Chelsea House Publishers, 1987.

Kitano, Harry, and Roger Daniels. *Asian Americans: Emerging Minorities.* Englewood Cliffs, NJ: Prentice Hall, 1988.

Kurashige, Lon. *Japanese American Celebration and Conflict: A History of Ethnic Identity and Festival, 1934–1990.* Berkeley, CA: University of California Press, 2002.

Kwon, Okyun. *Buddhist and Protestant Korean Immigrants: Religious Beliefs and Socioeconomic Aspects of Life.* New York: LFB Scholarly Publishing, 2003.

Larson, Louise Leung. *Sweet Bamboo: Saga of a Chinese American Family.* Los Angeles: Chinese Historical Society of Southern California, 1990.

Layman, Emma McCoy. *Buddhism in America.* Chicago: Nelson-Hall, 1976.

Lee, Jonathan H.X., and Jane N. Iwamura (eds.). *Asian American Religious Cultures.* Santa Barbara, CA: ABC-CLIO, 2015.

Lee, Leo O., and R. David Arkush (trans. and eds.). *Land without Ghosts: Chinese Impressions of America from the Mid-Nineteenth Century to the Present.* Berkeley, CA: University of California Press, 1989.

Lee, Li-Young. *The Winged Seed: A Remembrance.* New York: Simon & Schuster, 1995.

Lee, Mary Paik (Sucheng Chan, ed.). *Quiet Odyssey: A Pioneer Korean Woman in America.* Seattle, WA: University of Washington Press, 1996.

Lee, Rose Hum. *The Chinese in the United States of America*. Hong Kong: Hong Kong University Press/Oxford University Press, 1960.

Lessinger, Johanna. *From the Ganges to the Hudson: Indian Immigrants in New York City*. Boston: Allyn & Bacon, 1995.

Lim, Shirley Geok-lin, and Amy Ling (eds.). *Reading the Literatures of Asian America*. Philadelphia: Temple University Press, 1992.

Ling, Amy. *Between Worlds: Women Writers of Chinese Ancestry*. New York: Pergamon Press, 1990.

Ling, Huping. *Emerging Voices: Experiences of Underrepresented Asian Americans*. New Brunswick, NJ: Rutgers University Press, 2008.

Ling, Huping, and Haiming Liu. *Asian America: Forming New Communities, Expanding Boundaries*. New Brunswick, NJ: Rutgers University Press, 2009.

Lorentzen, Lois Ann, Joaquin Jay Gonzalez, Kevin M. Chun, and Hien Duc Do (eds.). *Religion at the Corner of Bliss and Nirvana: Politics, Identity, and Faith in New Migrant Communities*. Durham, NC: Duke University Press, 2009.

Lydon, Sandy. *Chinese Gold: The Chinese in the Monterey Bay Region*. Capitola, CA: Capitola Book Co., 1985.

Lyman, Stanford M. *Chinatown and Little Tokyo: Power, Conflict, and Community among Chinese and Japanese Immigrants in America*. Millwood, New York: Associated Faculty Press, 1986.

Matsuoka, Fumitaka. *Out of Silence: Emerging Themes in Asian American Churches*. Cleveland, OH: United Church Press, 1995.

Melendy, H. Brett. *Chinese and Japanese Americans: Their Contribution to American Society*. New York: Hippocrene, 1984.

Min, Pyong Gap. *Preserving Ethnicity through Religion in America: Koreans Protestants and Indian Hindus across Generations*. New York: New York University Press, 2010.

Min, Pyong Gap (ed.). *Asian Americans: Contemporary Trends and Issues,* 2nd ed. Thousand Oaks, CA: Pine Forge Press/Sage Publications, 2006.

——— (ed.). *Second Generation: Ethnic Identity among Asian Americans*. Walnut Creek, CA: AltaMira Press, 2002.

Min, Pyong Gap, and Jung Ha Kim (eds.). *Religions in Asian America: Building Faith Communities*. Walnut Creek, CA: AltaMira Press, 2002.

Minatoya, Lydia Yuri. *Talking to the High Monks in the Snow: An Asian American Odyssey*. New York: HarperCollins, 1992.

Montero, Darrel. *Japanese Americans: Changing Patterns of Ethnic Affiliation over Three Generations*. Boulder, CO: Westview Press, 1980.

———. *Vietnamese Americans: Patterns of Resettlement and Socioeconomic Adaptation in the United States*. Boulder, CO: Westview Press, 1979.

Nee, Victor G., and Brett de Bary Nee (eds.). *Longtime Californ': A Documentary Study of an American Chinatown*. Stanford, CA: Stanford University Press, 1986.

Ng, David (ed.). *People on the Way: Asian North Americans Discovering Christ, Culture, and Community*. Valley Forge, PA: Judson Press, 1996.

Ng, Franklin (ed.). *The History and Immigration of Asian Americans*. New York: Routledge, 1998.

Numrich, Paul David. *Old Wisdom in the New World: Americanization in Two Immigrant Theravada Buddhist Temples*. Knoxville, TN: University of Tennessee Press, 1996.

O'Brian, David J., and Stephen Fugita. *The Japanese American Experience*. Bloomington, IN: Indiana University Press, 1991.

Patterson, Wayne. *The Korean Frontier in America: Immigration to Hawaii, 1896–1910*. Honolulu: University of Hawaii Press, 1988.

Prebish, Charles S. *American Buddhism*. North Scituate, MA: Duxbury Press, 1979.

Prebish, Charles S., and Kenneth K. Tanaka (eds.). *The Faces of Buddhism in America*. Berkeley, CA: University of California Press, 1998.

Purkayastha, Bandana. *Negotiating Ethnicity: Second-Generation South Asian Americans Traverse a Transnational World*. New Brunswisk, NJ: Rutgers University Press, 2005.

Richardson, E. Allen. *East Comes West: Asian Religions and Cultures in North America*. New York: The Pilgrim Press, 1985.

Root, Maria P. (ed.). *Filipino Americans: Transformation and Identity*. Thousand Oaks, CA: Sage Publications, 1997.

Rutledge, Paul J. *The Role of Religion in Ethnic Self-Identity: A Vietnamese Community*. Lanham, MD: University Press of America, 1985.

———. *The Vietnamese Experience in America*. Bloomington, IN: Indiana University Press, 1992.

San Juan, Epifanio, Jr. *From Exile to Diaspora: Versions of the Filipino Experience in the United States*. Boulder, CO: Westview Press, 1998.

Sano, Roy I. (ed.). *The Theologies of Asian Americans and Pacific Peoples: A Reader*. Berkeley, CA: Asian Center for Theology and Strategies, Pacific School of Religion, 1976.

Saran, Parmatma. *The Asian Indian Experience in the United States*. Cambridge, MA: Schenkman Publishing Co., 1985.

Saran, Parmatma, and Edwin Eames. *The New Ethnics: Asian Indians in the United States*. New York: Praeger, 1980.

Seager, Richard Hughes. *Buddhism in America*. New York: Columbia University Press, 1999.

Shattuck, Cybelle T. *Dharma in the Golden State*. Santa Barbara, CA: Fithian Press, 1996.

Smith-Hefner, Nancy J. *Khmer American: Identity and Moral Education in a Diasporic Community*. Berkeley, CA: University of California Press, 1999.

Spickard, Paul R. *Japanese Americans: The Formation and Transformations of an Ethnic Group,* rev. ed. New Brunswick, NJ: Rutgers University Press, 2009.

Sung, Betty Lee. *Mountain of Gold: The Story of the Chinese in America*. New York: Macmillan, 1967.

Takaki, Ronald. *Strangers from a Different Shore: A History of Asian Americans*. Boston: Little, Brown and Company, 1989.

*Tan, Amy. *The Joy Luck Club*. New York: G.P. Putnam's Sons, 1989.

*_____. *The Kitchen God's Wife*. New York: G.P. Putnam's Sons, 1991.

Tri-State Buddhist Church. *A History of Fifty Years of the Tri-State Buddhist Church, 1916–1966*. Denver, CO: Tri-State Buddhist Church, 1968.

Tsai, Shih-shan Henry. *The Chinese Experience in America*. Bloomington, IN: Indiana University Press, 1986.

Tuck, Donald R. *Buddhist Churches of America: Jodo Shinshu*. Lewiston, New York: Edwin Mellen Press, 1987.

Tweed, Thomas A., and Stephen Prothero (eds.). *Asian Religions in America: A Documentary History*. New York: Oxford University Press, 1999.

Williams, Duncan Ryuken, and Christopher S. Queen (eds.). *American Buddhism: Methods and Findings in Recent Scholarship*. New York: Routledge/Curzon, 1999.

Williams, Raymond B. *Religions of Immigrants from India and Pakistan*. Cambridge, UK: Cambridge University Press, 1988.

Wong, K. Scott, and Sucheng Chan (eds.). *Claiming America: Constructing Chinese American Identities during the Exclusion Era*. Philadelphia: Temple University Press, 1998.

Wu, Jean Yu-wen Shen, and Min Song (eds.). *Asian American Studies: A Reader*. New Brunswick, NJ: Rutgers University Press, 2000.

Yanagisako, Sylvia Junko. *Transforming the Past: Tradition and Kinship among Japanese Americans*. Stanford, CA: Stanford University Press, 1985.

Yang, Fenggang. *Chinese Christians in America: Conversion, Assimilation, and Adhesive Identities*. University Park, PA: Pennsylvania State University Press, 1999.

Yoo, Boo-Woong. *Korean Pentecostalism: Its History and Theology*. New York: Peter Lang, 1988.

Yoo, David K. *Growing Up Nisei: Race, Generation, and Culture Among Japanese Americans of California, 1924–1949*. Urbana, IL: University of Illinois Press, 2000.

Yoo, David K, and Ruth H. Chung (eds.). *Religion and Spirituality in Korean America*. Urbana: University of Illinois Press, 2008.

—— (ed.). *New Spiritual Homes: Religion and Asian Americans*. Honolulu, HI: University of Hawaii Press, 1999.

Yung, Judy, Gordon Chang, and Him Mark Lai (eds.). *Chinese American Voices: From the Gold Rush to the Present*. Berkeley, CA: University of California Press, 2006.

Zhou, Min, and James V. Gatewood (eds.). *Contemporary Asian America: A Multidisciplinary Reader*. New York: New York University Press, 2000.

Some Suggested Questions for Discussion

1. Please compare the differing experiences of the Chinese and Japanese. Besides the anti-Asian discrimination that both of these groups experienced, how similarly or differently did these communities develop in America? What role did or does the observance of traditional cultural and religious practices appear to play in building and uniting these two differing immigrant communities? How do such traditions reinforce ethnic and religious identity more broadly? At the same time, how might ethnic and religious traditions hinder an immigrant community's development and progress in the host country?

2. Generally speaking, there do not appear to be many differences in the experiences of individuals immigrating to the United States. All appear to struggle with maintaining their religious beliefs and observing traditional religious practices. What is it about America's religious and cultural pluralism that makes maintenance of one's particular homeland traditions difficult, if not impossible? Are accommodation and compromise—and eventual assimilation—inevitable?

3. Given the readings by Eve Ma, Lydia Minatoya, and Amy Tan, as well as the brief chapters drawn from *Social Process in Hawaii*, please reflect upon the domestic concerns that religion addresses. What do these concerns tell us about gender roles, both in their customary forms as well as their modern evolving forms?

4. One interesting aspect of the Asian immigration to America has been the cultural and religious *discontinuity* that has informed that experience. Please list and discuss several of these discontinuities between Asian and Western traditions. In what ways have Asian Americans—including the authors and researchers whose works are reprinted in this volume of readings—sought to *reduce* or even to *heighten* these discontinuities?

1. The Chinese in San Francisco 1893

REV. NG POON CHEW.

An address delivered at a Christian Convention in San Francisco, September 1892.

SINCE the passage of the series of anti-Chinese acts by the United States government, the number of Chinese in this country has been steadily and considerably reduced. Once there were from twenty-five to thirty thousand Chinese in this city; now there are somewhat less than fifteen thousand.

They are found in nearly every trade, working industriously and patiently for their livelihood; saving what they can, often very little, to send back home for the support of their dependent relatives. As a class, the Chinese hate to be idle; they must and will work whether they earn much or little.

In their lodgings they are generally dirty, as one will see when he takes a walk through China-town; but in their persons they are comparatively clean. They are living closely together on account of the high rent of rooms in that quarter.

The Chinese are very superstitious. They are so brought up from their childhood. From their standpoint, they are religious, especially their women. There is not a heathen home in China-town which does not contain a number of altars dedicated to the worship of their numerous gods and departed friends. They have about fifteen public temples among them, of different sizes, which are supported by their pious patrons. The temple keeper has to pay a large sum of money into the treasury of the temple before he can take charge of it; and he gets his return by compelling every worshiper to buy offerings from him alone, for which he charges an exorbitant price.

Theoretically, there are two distinct religious sects in China-town, Buddhist and Taoist; the former came from India, the latter is of native origin. But practically there is only one mixed religion. They do not draw any distinction now; one may be at the same time a follower of Confucius, a believer in Buddhism, and an adherent of Taoism.

All the Chinese sincerely believe in the immortality of the soul, and future reward and punishment according to deeds done in this life; but, alas, they do not seem to make any preparation for that life or to make any effort to seek out the way to escape that punishment, while living. They are either ignorant as to the way of preparation or indifferent to their native convictions.

They make offerings to the dead, periodically, both at home and at the grave, in the form of meat, paper clothing, and money, believing that the spirits of the dead need these as well as the living. In accordance with this belief, the Chinese always take the remains of their dead friends with them back to China so they can worship them there.

1

The Chinese are great lovers of games, either for pleasure or money. It is very hard to keep them from gambling. There are many gambling places among them, but not as many as there used to be. If the officers would do their duty, these could be stopped.

The highbinder societies are formed for mutual protection and blackmailing purposes. There are many of them in the Chinese quarter. Nearly all the crimes committed in that quarter are done by the members of these infernal societies, who are enabled to escape justice by the laxness of American laws, and unprincipled lawyers. Such societies could not so openly exist for a day in China; every member would be immediately beheaded when caught, and no mercy would ever be shown to such miserable wretches under the Chinese laws.

The Chinese, as a race, have very little appetite for liquor; very few, if any, ever get drunk. I have never seen a drunken Chinaman in all my life. Though the Chinese do not use liquor to any extent, they have a substitute for it, namely, opium, which is very murderous to the Chinese. It is the devil's curse and device for creating misery. In my humble opinion, it is as bad as whisky in this land; but some say it is not. Well, in one sense, perhaps, it is not so bad, because when a drunken white man comes home, he abuses his children and kicks his wife, but when a Chinese opium fiend comes home, his wife kicks him, which is much better.

This very day there are from eight to ten million human wretches in China, smoking this poisonous drug; and there are more than sixty million living souls suffering directly and indirectly from the use of this infernal extract. It is used among all classes and sexes; you can point them out by their consumptive appearance.

O how many bright and promising young men, the only joy, hope, and comfort of their aged parents, have been wrecked and hastened to an untimely grave by the use of this drug!

After one has acquired the habit of using opium, there is very little hope for his reform; he goes on from bad to worse, until he is unfit for any vocation. He requires more time to smoke and to sleep off its effect, than to work.

But how came opium to be among the Chinese? Did our land first produce it? or did we, the Chinese, invent it?—No, no! ten thousand times, no! It was produced by the Christian English in India, and forced upon us heathen Chinese with powder and balls, killing us by the thousands, and ruining us by the millions with its poison.

Our good and beloved emperor made no resistance but was overcome by the superior forces of the English, and compelled to let his country be overflowed with this death-dealing drug. And then he exclaimed at the close of the opium war, "I know this will kill my poor people by the millions,—my poor people, my poor children!" Poor man! He did fully see its deadly effect before he died; for his own son was among the first victims of opium; and O, what a field of blood and what a world of iniquity will be revealed before the judgment-seat of God, to those men, who, to satisfy their own selfish end, forced this curse upon our country.

The English government opium factories in India are producing a fearful amount of this drug every year. They ship about eleven million pounds to China annually—enough to kill every human being in all Asia and Europe, if taken internally.

If it were not for the devilish actions of the English government, we would be to-day free from this vice, and you would not read in your daily papers about the opium dens and opium fiends among us.

As the time allotted me is limited, I do not wish to go on any longer with this mournful tale of the dire consequences of opium; for they will only shock your feelings, although not half has been told. God only knows all the sad details.

Let us now take a glance at the bright and hopeful side, and see what the Church of Christ has done for the Chinese here.

The Presbyterian, the Methodist, the Baptist, the Congregational, and the Episcopalian churches, are carrying on good and successful work among them. There are schools connected with mission churches, day schools for children and women, where English and Chinese are taught; and evening schools for men, where English alone is taught. There are now about three hundred Christian Chinese in San Francisco who are leading a life consistent with their profession. This number does not represent all that have been converted by these missions since their first operation; for some have gone home to their newly found Saviour, and many have left here for their native land, where they are now preaching the glad tidings of the Gospel to their fellow-men by words and by deeds.

Many things have to be overcome and endured before a Chinaman can be a Christian. He has to discard all the former beliefs and superstitions and ancestral worship which every Chinaman holds dear; and in addition he has to suffer ill-treatment and separation from his former friends and relatives.

The converts here are striving very hard for the conversion of their countrymen in China. They are not only waiting but also working anxiously for the fulfillment of that prophecy in Isaiah, "Behold, these shall come from far; and, lo, these from the north, and from the west; and these from the land of SINIM."

They have founded different missionary societies, and pledged to give so much each month to support the native missionaries employed by them in China, and they have also raised large sums of money to build churches in different districts of Canton Province. Several churches have been already built and supported wholly by the Christian Chinese in this country.

There cannot be more earnestness, pleasure, and self-denial manifested anywhere than at the mission meetings when discussing the building of new churches in China. Every one present would give encouragement, not only with words but also with money. Some would stand up and pledge their help by giving a whole month's wages; some would pledge two months', and some even three months' wages.

The Christian Chinamen, converted in this country, who go back to China, are among the best, the most faithful, patient, consistent, and energetic Christians to be found anywhere.

The conversion of the Chinese in this country is a great factor toward the conversion of China. Therefore the churches should do their duty more earnestly and faithfully in converting these strangers in their midst.

So, friends, come and help us, and the cause of Christ among us, with your fervent prayers, with the wealth God has given you, and with your sympathy, that all of us from the land of Sinim may be instructed in the knowledge of Christ, and with gladness serve the God you adore.

2. The Chinese in America 1909

Intimate Study of Chinese Life in America.
Told in a Series of Short Sketches—An Interpretation
of Chinese Life and Character.

SUI SIN FAR

In these days when the future of China is being discussed by all thinking people, one reads much in the papers and magazines about Chinese diplomats, Chinese persons of high rank, Chinese students, both boys and girls, Chinese visitors of prominence, scholars and others, who by reason of wealth and social standing, are interesting to the American people, but of those Chinese who come to live in this land, to make their homes in America, some permanently, others for many years, we hear practically nothing at all. Yet these Chinese, Chinese-Americans I call them, are not unworthy of a little notice, particularly as they sustain throughout the period of their residence here, a faithful and constant correspondence with relations and friends in the old country, and what they think and what they write about Americans, will surely influence, to a great extent, the conduct of their countrymen towards the people of the United States. For the Chinese on the Pacific Coast are numbered by the thousands. There is scarcely a city that does not have its local Chinatown or a number of Chinese residents. Many of these men are possessed of fine business ability, some are scholars; those of them who are laborers are stalwart, self-respecting countrymen from the district around Canton city and province, or are American-born descendants of the pioneer Chinamen who came to this Coast long before our transcontinental railways were built, and helped the American to mine his ore, build his railways and cause the Pacific Coast to blossom like the rose. In the romantic past of this western country, the figure of the Chinaman stands forth conspicuously, and every true Westerner will admit that the enlarged life in which he is participating today could not have been possible without the Chinese.

Their reasons for exile, apart from the "fortune" question, are individually interesting; the observations of the most intelligent on American life and manners are pertinent and instructive. If the Chinese can learn much from the Americans, the former can also teach a few lessons to the latter. No one, who, without prejudice, goes amongst the Chinese people in America and converses with them in friendly fashion but will find food for thought.

My father, who lived in China for many years, who married a Chinese lady, and who was a personal friend of Li Soon, Li Hung Chang's secretary, is of the opinion that one has a much better opportunity to study Chinese character in this country than in China, for here the Chinese are naturally more communicative than when in their own land. As for me, my

4

interest in them has been keen and perpetual since the day I learned that I was of their race. And I have found them wherever I have wandered. In New York are some of my best Chinese friends; nearly every mail brings me news from Chinese Canadians, both east and west. Down in the West Indies I met a Chinese whose intelligence and active heroism in a moment of danger and distress will cause him and his compatriots to be ever remembered with gratitude and a warm feeling of kinship. In Los Angeles, San Francisco and the Puget Sound cities I know Chinese, both men and women, whose lives, if written, would read like romances, and whose qualities of mind and heart cannot help but win the interest and respect of all who know them understandingly.

It is true that they—these Chinese people—like other nationalities, have their own peculiar customs, manners and characteristics; but in a broad sense they are one with the other peoples of the earth. They think and act just as the white man does, according to the impulses which control them. They love those who love them; they hate those who hate; are kind, affectionate, cruel or selfish, as the case may be. I have not found them to be slow of intellect and alien to all other races in that "they are placed and unfeeling, and so custom-bound that even their tears are mere waters of ceremony and flow forth at stated times and periods." Thus a European traveler some centuries ago described the Chinese people, and travelers ever since, both men and women, have echoed his words and sentiments, while fiction writers seem to be so imbued with the same ideas that you scarcely ever read about a Chinese person who is not a wooden peg. There are a few exceptions, but the majority of writers on things Chinese echo those who enter before, which is a very foolish thing to do in these revolutionary days. The Chinese may be custom-bound—no doubt they are—but they are human beings, nevertheless. In this country they are slow to push their individual claims, and when with strangers, hide the passions of their hearts under quiet and peaceful demeanors; but because a man is indisposed to show his feelings is no proof that he has none. Under a quiet surface the Chinaman conceals a rapid comprehension and an almost morbid sensitiveness; he also possesses considerable inventive power and is more of an initiative spirit than an imitative one, whatever may be said to the contrary by those who know him but superficially. The pleasures of life he takes quietly; there is a melancholy trait in the characters of most Chinamen, as in all people of old civilizations. His mysticism and childlike faith in the marvelous is also an inheritance from his ancestors. Yet we are not without the Chinaman, merry and glad and full of exuberant animal spirits. Indeed, there is no type of white person who cannot find his or her counterpart in some Chinese. Therefore the following sketches of Chinese in America:

The Story of Wah

Wah was a leading member of the Chinese Reform party, whom I met in this city some years ago. He was an alert-minded young fellow, full of enthusiasm for the Reform cause and ambitious to learn the ways of the western people. His father, as he informed me, was a school teacher. "Then," I said, "you, being but a merchant, are not as much in the eyes of your people as your father was." Wah smiled. "We do not think in China as we did in the old days," said he. In Canton we have as much esteem for the clever man of business as we have for the scholar. When my father was a boy it was different." And he went on to compare his father's China with the China of his own remembrance, demonstrating in a surprisingly clear and convincing manner the progress that had been made.

"Why did you come to this country?" I inquired. "To make money and to learn western ways quicker than I could at home," he answered. Picking up an English paper lying on the table and pointing to a picture of an antique book which was advertised for sale, he inquired why it was marked at such a high price as $500. A lady explained that its age made it valuable. He thought for a moment, then said, "Why, then, is the Bible so cheap? It is very old book."

After a while he remarked that it might be a good plan to send to China for some old things for his store. "They will not be so expensive as newly manufactured goods," said he, "and if I can sell them at a higher price, I shall certainly make my fortune in a very little while."

Wah was a practical man of business, but his principles would have done honor to the noblest philanthropist. He had opportunities of making a great deal of money through the smuggling of opium from Canada into the United States. A safe and secret way was open to him through one of his own cousins. But Wah refused to have anything to do with the business. "No," he answered. "I wish for my countrymen to rise, not to fall, and when I speak at the Reform Club I advise that the pipe should be cast out. How, then, can I place it in their hand? Would that not be inconsistent?"

A Chinese Book on Americans

"I think," said Go Ek Ju, "that when I return to China I will write a book about the American people."

"What put such an idea into your head?" I asked.

"The number of books about the Chinese by Americans," answered Go Ek Ju. "I see them in the library; they are very amusing."

"See, then, that when you write your book, it is likewise amusing."

"No," said Go Ek Ju. "My aim, when I write a book about Americans will be to make it not amusing, but interesting and instructive. The poor Americans have to content themselves with writing for amusement only because they have no means of obtaining any true knowledge of the Chinese when in China; but we Chinese in America have fine facilities for learning all about the Americans. *We go into the American houses as servants; we enter the American schools and colleges as students;* we ask questions and we think about what we hear and see. Where is there the American who will go to China and enter into the service of a Chinese family as a domestic? We have yet to hear about a band of American youths, both male and female, being admitted as students into a Chinese university."

Scholar or Cook?

"You seem to enjoy your work," I remarked to Wang Liang, who was making cake in the hotel kitchen, meanwhile crooning a low song.

"It is very pleasant work," was his reply.

"What did you do when you were in China?" I inquired.

"I was a scholar."

"A scholar?"

Wang Liang went on making his cakes.

"Why," I mused aloud, "I thought a scholar in China was not supposed to know anything about work."

"True," answered Wang Liang; "a scholar must be helpless in all ways in spite of his learning. But my mother was ill and needed ginseng and chicken broth, and my father was getting old, and we were poor. All the time my heart was sad, for my parents had always been very good and kind to me and I loved them much. Then one day I read in my Classics, 'Those who labor support those who govern,' and I reasoned that if those who labored supported those who governed, then the laborer must in no wise be inferior to him who governs. So I decided to work with my hands, and in order that my parents might not be made to feel ashamed, I came to America. Since I have come here, with my labor I have supported myself, paid back my passage money to the agent who loaned it to me, kept my father and mother in comfort at home and have placed some part of every month's wages in a bank. When I have enough to live on for the rest of my life I will return to China and again take up my studies and do honor to my parents as a scholar."

Wang Liang rubbed his hands together and laughed softly and gleefully.

—*Westerner,* May 1909

The Chinese in America, Part II
The New and the Old

The following story of youthful business enterprise is told by Lu Seek, a prosperous Chinese merchant and the owner of many shares in a Mexican railway.

"I came to this country at an early age. I first worked for my Uncle who gave me food, lodging and clothing in return for my services. I attended Mission schools of all denominations, Presbyterian, Episcopal, Baptist, Methodist and Roman Catholic. I learned the English language with little difficulty. From the American youth I also learned that a young person's time in America is quite as valuable as any elderly person's, and that eighteen years of age was a far superior age to forty-eight. Imbued with this knowledge I began to assume airs of dignity. When my Uncle bade me do this or that I would answer negligently—sometimes with hauteur. Whereupon my Uncle was one morning led to try the gentle persuasion of a stick. I objected. I said to him, 'Honorable Uncle, you do not respect me as you should nor do you consider that we are living in America, where a man instead of looking backward and admiring one's parents and uncles, fixes his mind on himself, thinks for himself and so acts that his parents and uncles, instead of wishing and requiring him to admire them wonder at and admire him.'

"'Admire you,' exclaimed my Uncle, with an expression of furious contempt and another well aimed blow at my head, which, however, I successfully dodged.

"'That is what they believe in the west,' I persisted, 'and that is why they of the west progress and those of the east stand still.'

"My Uncle's reply conveyed the impression that there was a difference of opinion between us, and as a difference of opinion is a very sad thing to have between those who live under the same roof, I suggested to my Uncle that he hand over to me the sum of money which he held in trust for me from my father, and I would walk my way which was evidently not his way.

"My Uncle considered for fifteen minutes, then he went to his till, took therefrom fifty silver dollars, the amount of my inheritance, and threw them down on the counter. I quickly pocketed them, and with what few personal belongings I possessed rolled up under my arm, started out in the world to seek my fortune.

"I had not gone very far when I met some of my white acquaintances. I informed them that I had been putting into practice the principles they had inculcated, and they cheered me on and told me that I would not take very long for me to become a real American of free and independent spirit. I showed them my fifty dollars and invited them to lunch with me. This invitation they accepted. The fifty dollars soon became ten. Half of that I spent in buying a present for my Sunday school teacher.

"I then tried to earn my own living as a cook or laundryman, but was not successful. I had no experience in the kitchen, neither was I learned in the lore of the laundry, and though I have known many of my countrymen, who as inexperienced as I, have yet made many successes of these callings, it was plain to be seen that as my American friends observed, I had a soul above domestic service. One day, my Sunday school teacher, who was unaware that I had left my Uncle's store, asked me if I knew of a good Chinese boy who could act as a general servant. I mentioned the names of several and she thanked me, remarking that I was better than an Employment Bureau. That put an idea into my head. I would start such an office and provide help for the American ladies. Though I could not secure employment myself I might obtain it for others. I was acquainted with many Mission and Sunday school ladies, whom I knew would bring their friends to me when they needed servants, and for all my estrangement from my Uncle, I was quite popular with the youth of Chinatown.

"But to start a business a little capital is necessary, and that I lacked. I was musing on this fact and a hungry stomach, when I met a second cousin of mine who did business as a fortune teller near the corner of Dupont and Kearney streets. 'Have you eaten your rice?' he exclaimed. That is a simple Chinese greeting but I took it literally and humbled myself to explain that I had no money with which to buy rice. He stroked his chin reflectively, and remarked that it was a pity that my forefathers had not bequeathed to me the spirit of divination; for if such had been the case, he himself would have been glad to adopt me as an assistant in the expounding of mythical lore.

"As we talked together, he in his long silken robes, I in my exceedingly shabby American store clothes, I envied him his prosperity, his calm and affable manners, his pleasing reposeful face. I knew that his elegantly furnished office was quite a resort for the perplexed of Chinatown's four hundred, and moreover, that many unsettled white people also surreptitiously visited him in the hope of having light thrown on certain difficult questions. I knew that through the fortunate reading of her father's horoscope, he had won as wife the prettiest American born Chinese girl in the City of the Golden Gate. Yet, curious fact—for all my envy of his accomplishments and attainments, I had not the slightest desire to be as he—reader of the stars. It was too ancient a business, and though my cousin had found it practical enough for all his purposes, it did not appeal to me in any sense as a business. I wanted a business which would call for a telephone and electric lights; not candles, incense, tortoise shells and diagrams.

"My cousin was both good hearted and good natured. After dining me, he himself proposed that he set me up in a small Chinese drug store. The herbs with which Chinese doctors' prescriptions are usually filled would not cost much; and the dried nuts, lily bulbs, fish eggs, and other stock necessary, could also be obtained without much outlay. In particular, he advised this business, as a Chinese fortune teller often acts as physician, and it would be in his power to occasionally send me customers.

"But I had in mind the Employment Bureau and nothing else would do for me. I said to my cousin: 'Since you are so kind as to propose to set me up in a business to your liking, perhaps you will be a little kinder still and help me to start a business to my liking.' And I told him of my dreams of the Employment Bureau. For a time my cousin scoffed. For one who was unable to find work for himself to seek to make a living by obtaining it for others seemed too absurd. It would be a case of the blind leading the blind.

"Thus he argued. My arguments are unnecessary to relate. Suffice it to say, however, that they won, and when I left my cousin I was furnished with the necessary funds to launch myself on the business career I had chosen.

"I set up my office near the Plaza. From my doorway I could see the drinking fountain which is put up as a memorial to your great writer, Robert Louis Stevenson. Well, to my great satisfaction, it was not long before I found myself standing under an electric light with a green shade answering a call from a society lady on Nob Hill. She was desiring a boy accomplished in the art of cooking. After that the calls came frequently—and I had dozens of Chinese boys ready to answer. Sometimes my customers would interview me several times before deciding on a boy. From their conversations I derived much benefit.

"That was the beginning of my good fortunes. I found that by maintaining a pleasant demeanor and an affable tongue I could manage to get along very well in the finding of employment for my countrymen in America. Because I was reminded of your great writer by the fountain in the Square or Plaza I bought all of his works from a book agent on the installment plan and read them between the hours of business. I admired much his 'Treasure Island,' and the reading thereof furnished me with good conversation whenever the ladies came to my office. Of course I used my discretion. There were some ladies who did not read Robert Louis Stevenson, you understand. There were other ladies who did. I am of opinion that taken all around Robert Louis Stevenson improved much my business.

"When I had made a few thousand dollars I decided to go to live in New York and sell out my business to my third cousin, Lu Wing. He was the adopted brother of the Fortune Teller cousin who had loaned me the money with which to start business and whose debt I had repaid with interest out of what I made my first year. Just before leaving for the big city I called upon my Uncle, and after making a most humble and contrite apology for my past conduct and the improper speeches connected therewith, persuaded him to pay me a visit at my office. There I smoked with him the pipe of peace, and there the old man, after speaking through the phone with some friend in San Jose, acknowledged that it was true—the days were over for young people to wonder at and admire their parents and the time had come for the old people to wonder at and admire them.

"'That is progress,' I replied.

"'When it is not carried to extremes.' supplemented my wife, an American Chinese girl."

—Westerner, June 1909

The Chinese in America, Part III
Like the American

When Tin-a came over the sea to be wife to Sik Ping, there were great rejoicings in Chinatown, for Sik Ping was very popular. Many dinner parties were given, some very brilliant affairs indeed. The one that I attended was on the top floor of a Chinatown building. The dining room was elegantly furnished with black teak wood tables and carved chairs inlaid with mother of pearl; screens adorned the partitions between rooms, and there were couches along the wall where after dining one could lie at ease and smoke; the place was brilliantly illuminated with electric lights and red Chinese candles, and a large incense burner suspended from the ceiling in the middle of the room, filled the air with a truly Oriental fragrance.

Though it is not the custom for Chinese women to sit at meat with men, Sik Ping was Americanized enough to seat his wife by his side. The wife of Go Ek Ju, his friend, gave face to Tin-a as the Chinese say.

The tables were loaded with dishes of chicken, bamboo shoots and confections of all kinds known to the Chinese. Both men and women were attired in gorgeous silk robes, the latter wearing flowers in their hair and in front of their tunics. Each and every one of the Chinese guests presented Sik Ping with a sum of money, as is the custom amongst the Chinese on such occasions.

There was a strange scene at the close of the evening. The little bride, who throughout dinner had sat with downcast eyes, scarcely touching a morsel of food, upon leaving the table was seen to be weeping. Mrs. Go Ek Ju sought to discover the source of her tears, and after a murmured conversation with Tin-a reluctantly informed Sik Ping that his bride had confessed to being afraid that he would be angry with her.

"Afraid that I be angry with her!" exclaimed poor Sik Ping bewilderedly. "Ah No!"

Whereupon Amoy hung her head and shed more tears.

It came out at last that Ping's bride was not the girl whom a cousin had married for him by proxy and for whom he had sent the passage money from China to America. That girl had formed an attachment for her proxy husband, who reciprocated the feeling, they having reaped in the rice fields together. She accordingly prevailed upon Tin-a, her friend, who was an orphan of adventurous spirit, and whose name was the same as her own, to undertake the long ocean journey from which she shrunk and become in reality wife to Sik Ping.

But Tin-a no sooner beheld Ping's kind face when she became conscience stricken, and that feeling so overwhelmed her when he had placed her beside him at the dinner table that she had been unable to restrain her tears.

"Ah!" she cried, falling on the ground at his feet. "You are so good and kind and I so deceitful and evil." But Ping, who had never seen the girl to whom he was married by proxy and who had conceived an affection for the little Tin-a, instead of upbraiding her with hard words, comforted her with loving ones, and the day following bought a marriage license and was married over again by the Chinese missionary.

"I do as the Americans do," said Ping proudly. "I marry the woman I love."

The Story of Forty-Niner

"Why did you come to America?" I asked a Chinaman who was beating a gold ring into shape. He was a manufacturing jeweler.

"Why did I come? Oh, it is so long ago since I came that I am not sure that I can remember the reasons."

And Hom Hing, being a good-natured fellow, began:

"My father had two boys, myself and my brother. I was the eldest, so my father chose me to be the scholar. Therefore, while I was clothed in the best style which the family circumstances would allow, my little queue tied neatly with a string, an embroidered cap on my head, and the whitest of white-soled shoes on my feet, fed on the best which the house afforded and kept in idleness save for study, my brother roamed about the village, bare-footed, bare-headed, and almost bare-bodied. He gathered the wood for fuel, hoed the ground, reaped in the rice fields and grew healthy and handsome. My mother and sisters treated me with respectful politeness, but to my brother they were always careless in manner. As I did nothing but study, naturally my body was weak and I suffered from the slightest exertion or exposure to heat or cold. I was kept at my books from morning till night while I was at home and attended the village school, and when I was old enough to be sent to the university I studied even harder. I was imbued with ambition to become a great scholar and do honor to my parents, but for all that I unconsciously envied my brother, whose lusty arms could fell an ox. When my sisters were given as wives for sons of other families, it became necessary that my brother and myself should marry in order that my mother should have a girl to help her in the house. I was accordingly married by proxy while still in the university. My brother also married, and when I returned home, there was a little son of his crawling about the floor. Our family had become impoverished during my university years, my father was old and unable to do much; almost the whole burden of supporting the family, including myself, fell upon my brother's shoulders.

That year agents of certain Chinese Companies came around our village bribing men to go to America. They offered my father quite a large sum for my brother, Hom Ling, and my father, after talking the matter over with my mother, decided to accept the money and send my brother, Hom Ling, to work in the country across the sea. My parents had no doubt, from what was told them, that Hom Ling's labor would soon repay those who advanced his passage money to America and then he would be free to send his wages home.

"Now, my brother, Hom Ling, loved his wife and child, and the thought of being separated from them filled his heart with sorrow. He spoke to me about it with many sighs, for, though the course of our lives ran in such different channels, we were brothers in affection as well as in blood. While he was lamenting his fate, an inspiration came to me. He was to leave the village at night in company with some other youths. In the darkness it would be impossible to distinguish one lad from another, and though I was weak and he strong, we were of the same build. The cause of this inspiration was the fact that, despite the respect that was paid me, I found home life unbearable. After having lived away from home for several years, my mother, my wife and my sister-in-law's tongues sounded discordantly in my ears. My sedentary life had made me nervous and irritable. Moreover, the wife that had been chosen for me was most repulsive to my taste.

"Why not, then," I suggested to my brother, "that I be the one to go and you be the one to remain?"

"But my parents have placed all their hopes on you," demurred my brother, albeit with brightening eyes.

"Fiddlesticks!" I answered in Chinese, "I shall be doing better by my parents by leaving them you than by remaining with them myself. It will be years before I can earn even my own living as a school teacher and you can help them straight along."

"So I came to America. On this side the change of brothers was never discovered. As for me, the new life brought with renewed health and strength. In the old California days the Chinese lived and worked in the open air, and the work of a laborer in America is easy compared to that of a laborer in China. I had better food and more than I had ever had in my life, and the sunshine and freshness of this western country transformed me both physically and mentally. It is living, not studying that makes a man. Adventures and hairbreadth escapes from death were frequent; hard times, too, but I managed to pull through after fifteen years of it with a nice little bag of gold with which I returned to China. My parents were still living and my brother was surrounded by a large family; my first wife had died. I married a pretty tea picker whom I met while rambling among the hills. She was a slave girl, but I paid her price, and in spite of my parents' opposition, brought her back with me to America. This business I learned after my mining days were over. I have two sons and one daughter, all married and living in this country."

The Story of Tai Yuen and Ku Yum

Tai Yuen was Ku Yum's lover; but whereas Tai Yuen was a See Yup, Ku Yum's father was a Sam Yup. A See Yup is a man from the fourth district of the Province of Kwangtung, a Sam Yup a man from the Third district. Some time before the tale of Tai Yuen and Ku Yum was told, a Sam Yup murdered a See Yup. This was in Southern California. All the See Yups knew that one of their number had been killed by a Sam Yup; but though they thirsted for revenge they could not discover the murderer. It therefore became a case, not of man against man, but of district against district, and as a result a Sam Yup soon went the way of the murdered See Yup. The Sam Yups, however, proved better detectives than their enemies, and traced the crime so that the actual murderer, a man belonging to one of the See Yup's Secret Societies, was convicted and punished by the law of the land. At this the See Yups became so bitterly incensed that notice to boycott all Sam Yups was sent by their chiefs to the See Yups all over the continent. The boycott spread and became a serious matter, for the See Yups are much more numerous than the Sam Yups, the See Yups being chiefly laundrymen and laboring men, and the Sam Yups merchants who depend for the success of their business upon the trade of the See Yups.

Now Tai Yuen was an Americanized Chinaman, having come to this coast at a very early age, and Ku Yum was American born. So when Tai Yuen and Ku Yum met, they fell in love with one another, just as any American boy and girl might have done, and after some more meetings became engaged in true American fashion. It was shortly after they became engaged that the boycott between the Sam Yups and the See Yups became established.

"Do not venture to see me any more," bade poor Ku Yum, fearful for her lover's safety.

But Tai Yuen, being imbued with the American spirit, heeded not her warning, and one night when on his way to see his sweet heart, trusted emissaries of the See Yups' secret society dogged his footsteps. And Ku Yum still looks for her lover.

Wah Lee on Family Life

Wah Lee had left his home when a youth of fifteen with a company of strolling actors who had pitched camp in his home village for a week. From what I learned from a clansman of his, his father's family was a very large one, and home had been full of strife and contention. One day I asked him if he did not wish to return to China. His face sobered at once.

"I love my parents," he answered. "I send to them some part of what I make every month; but when I am at home I am unhappy. Too many tongues in the house interfere with peace." His brothers and sisters numbered fourteen.

"Quite a Rooseveltian family," I observed.

"I think President Roosevelt likes a joke," was his quick reply. "He declares to his people that the best thing for a country is big families, and then he commands them to teach our people to be like them."

Lee had lived for some years in Eastern Canada, and as he had worked in families both there and in the United States, being smuggled backwards and forwards across the line whenever the fancy pleased him, his observations on family life and some of his comparisons were to me quite illuminating. "The French Canadians," he remarked, "are more like the Chinese at home than are the Americans. The parents boss and the children obey; but there is not as much affection of the heart between them as I see in some American families—some not at all. There is also much form of religion with the Canadians and the Chinese. In America it is different. I have been in some families where the religion is not seen at all; but it is felt. That is what makes the heart glad; and to see the father and mother the true friend of the son and daughter, not the boss. The poorer families in Canada have many children, just as in China.

"It makes me sad," said he, "to see a poor little niece of ten years old carrying in her slender arms her uncle or aunt of four or five months. Yet that is what I see very often in Eastern Canada. Some of the little girls never have time to play nor to go to school; there are so many babies to be carried. And if they are not carrying babies, then they must go to work, for the father has too big a family of younger children to support them. And the mother is so cross with so many, and hard words and cruel blows drive the children into the street to steal and do other things for which the priest and the Sunday school teacher scold them. And there is much noise and confusion all the time just like in the big families in China. I think it is better in America, where the family is not so large, but where the children have a happy time and are well brought up. When I was in Montreal I read that more babies die in that city than in any other city in the world. Yet, the men in the black dresses who do not have any children themselves go around to the poor man and advise him all the time, 'Have plenty children, Have plenty children!' The poor little children. I feel so sorry for them!"

The Bonze

I came across Ke Leang in a Joss house. He was a Bonze, or Chinese priest, and a remarkably handsome man. I used to enjoy wandering about the Joss houses, admiring the quaint carvings and images, pondering and wondering over the mysterious hieroglyphics, and now and then confiscating a piece of sandal wood. At that time I had a rage for sandal wood. One day, having possessed myself of a larger piece than usual, I was about to move quietly away from the green bowl or jar from which I had taken it, when a quiet voice just behind me said: "If you like the wood you can take some more." I started guiltily. It was the priest, Ke Leang. He had placed his hand on the bowl and was tipping it towards me. I had the grace to demur, but blunderingly, I said, "Oh, I don't like to take any more. It is sacred, isn't it?" "Not at all," he answered. Then, calmly, and I fancied sarcastically, "Is it so to you?"

I felt ashamed, and feeling ashamed, began to talk of other things. I told him that my mother was Chinese, but because my father was an Englishman and I had been born in England and brought up in Canada, and by choice, lived in America, I was unable to speak my mother tongue. He did not at first pay much attention to my chatter, but when I brought forth a letter of introduction from Chinese friends in my home city to Chinese in other parts of the world, he became more communicative, and I had quite a long chat with him about Chinese religion. He told me that it was error to think that the Chinese bow down in spirit to wood or stone or anything made of such materials. It is true the Chinamen prostrates himself bodily before his ancestral tablets, his images of male and female divinities, but he worships in spirit only the spirit that is supposed to dwell in the image, and not the image itself, which is nothing more to him that what it is—a piece of wood or stone. He declared emphatically that the Chinese worship spirits, not images. "We worship," said he, "in the same way that I have seen American people worshiping in Catholic churches. We kneel before Mother (Ahmah, a Chinese goddess) as the Catholics kneel to the Virgin Mary."

He shook his head gravely when I asked him, in my ignorance, if he were a Confucianist. He admitted, however, that Confucianism, pure and simple, was the religion of most of the learned men of China.

Before I left San Francisco an American friend of mine who occasionally told a true story told me this one of Ke Leang, the Chinese priest.

Ke Leang lived in the province of the Happy River. That was when he was young, happy and not a priest. There also lived Mai Gwi Far. Their parents' houses were close together, the gardens being separated by high stone walls. There was a hole in the separating wall. Mai Gwi Far and Ke Leang looked through the hole. Moreover, they spoke—sighed—smiled. When Ke Leang went to the university in another province he carried within his sleeve one of Mai Gwi Far's little red shoes. Just before the examination for the second literary degree Ke Leang received a letter from Mai Gwi Far. She was in great distress. The leaves of her rose geranium were withering and the night before she had heard the cry of an owl, now near, now far away. These signs meant sorrow and trouble. She feared, she knew not what. Was Ke Leang forgetting her and laughing and jesting with the Sing Song girls—they who sung and danced and painted their faces? Would he be interested to know that her parents had betrothed her to the son of a friend, and that she was to prepare for marriage within five months? The engagement was short because she was beyond the age for betrothing, being seventeen. She was so troubled and sad. What should she do? She awaited his reply with a beating heart. On that same day Ke Leang also received word from his parents that they had betrothed him to the daughter of their neighbor, Mai Gwi Far, she who was called the Pearl of Honan. In the exuberance of his joy at this news Ke Leang lost wisdom and, seeing by Mai Gwi Far's letter that she was as yet in ignorance of the name of her future husband, the spirit of mischief prompted him to sit down and pen the following message to the girl: "Marry the one whom your parents have chosen." When his carrier dove reached Mai Gwi Far it was night. The little bird tapped at her pane as it was wont to do, and she arose and, bringing it in, untied from under its wing her lover's message.

In the morn her parents found her cold in death, the jesting note beside her. It had certainly been her death blow. That is the reason why Ke Leang was a priest in San Francisco's Chinatown. All ambition to attain his literary degree perished with Mai Gwi Far. He entered a monastery and ten years later was ordered by his Abbott to cross the sea to minister to the Chinese people in San Francisco.

—*Westerner*, July 1909

The Chinese in America, Part IV
Yip Ke Duck and the Americans

"I do not like the Americans," quote old Yip Kee Duck. "They do not speak the truth; they are hypocrites; they think only of money; they pretend to be your friends, to admire you, to like you; but for all their smiles and soft words, they mean to swindle you and do you harm. Behind your back they laugh and sneer; they make amusement for themselves out of all the Chinaman says and does. When they come to trade with him, they expect their goods for next to nothing. Around Christmas time, there are always plenty of Sunday School teachers ready to teach the Chinese. They know the Chinese boys never forget to give presents. Whenever a white man does a little business with or throws business into the way of a Chinese, he looks for a bonus bigger than any profits that the Chinaman may gain. I have been fooled by them too often. 'He that hath wine has many friends.' Now they can fool me no more. Moreover, I shall warn all the Chinese boys that believe in the American Sunday school and the American Sunday school teachers. I shall tell my people in China that Americans are not only devils when they call you names and throw stones at you; but they are worse devils still when they come to you and say, 'Oh, Mr. Yip Kee Duck, how quaint and curious and beautiful is your store. What wonderful people you Chinese are! I wish I were one!' and all that fool talk."

Poor old Yip Kee Duck! Like some others of his race in this country, the treatment accorded him by the Americans had made him very bitter and cynical. For, in spite of all the honest endeavors and good work of some of the Christian missionaries and church women there are those amongst them who are wolves in sheep's clothing, and who bring disrepute upon their cause.

It is almost unbelievable the shameless way in which some white people will act towards the Chinese. This was brought to my attention in many very pointed ways when I was in San Francisco. I was very hard up at that time, and in order to obtain bread and butter put in some time canvassing Chinatown for the San Francisco Bulletin. For every subscription that I secured the paper was to pay me thirty cents. When soliciting from the Chinese merchants I simply asked them to sign their name to the voucher setting forth that they agreed to take the paper. Many of these merchants in answer to my request that they subscribe for the paper, would offer me the amount of the subscription for my own use. "Never mind about sending the paper. Just keep the money yourself," said one. I had difficulty indeed in impressing upon them that I was collecting autographs, not money. One fellow, when reluctantly returning the cash asked, "Perhaps you take it next time you come."

It seems that women who would sooner jump into the fire than ask a white man for money or presents will boldly demand such things of a Chinaman, and I have myself seen American women enter a Chinese store, take up some trinket they fancy, and ask the Chinaman to give it to them. He can hardly refuse, and boldly she walks off with her prize. But she has made a mistake. If a woman sinks low in the eyes of a white man by acting that way, she sinks lower still in the eyes of a Chinaman. To retain the respect of the Chinese, both at home and abroad, one must be careful to keep themselves perfectly independent of them. The respect of the Chinese has been worth much more than mere cash or a few trinkets to me.

At the same time the Chinaman is naturally a very kind, generous and open-hearted fellow, slow to think evil, appreciative of goodness, and respectful to every woman who deserves respect. That is why it is such a pity that they do not always see and know the genuine American, the sincere Christian. They are anxious to learn the best that America can teach them, they are so quick to discern truth and goodness to admire it. Very few of them are Yip Kee Ducks. I have known Chinamen to lose faith in person after person, and yet retain his faith in the American people as a whole. Although the scholars and students who come to our shores are properly conservative when pressing themselves concerning things American, the simple yet intelligent Chinamen who are with us gladly acknowledge that many of the ways of the white man are better than the ways of the Chinese.

New Year as Kept by the Chinese in America

Have you ever noticed how very happy looking the American Chinese are from Christmas to the end of their New Year? They are happy because during this topsy turvy season they can indulge their heart's content in the pleasure of giving. Not indiscriminately, of course; but to those who during the year have won, sometimes designedly, sometimes unconsciously, their liking or their gratitude. The Chinese never think of telling you that "it is more blessed to give than to receive." Perhaps their minds have not yet been educated to grasp the meaning of the saying, but they prove its truth. Give a Chinaman a present and he will thank you gratefully, but very calmly. No emotion disturbs his countenance. There is no visible pleasure. But allow him to give you something and watch his face as you receive it from his hand. You will see expressed real, true solid happiness. Never refuse to accept a Christmas present from a Chinaman unless you wish to offend him. You need not feel that you are bound to return the compliment. A Chinaman gives for the sake of giving, not in the hope of receiving. A poor laundryman will sometimes spend a couple of months' hard earned wages and more in a Christmas present for some friend, say a Sunday school teacher. If he has two teachers, he may spend four months' wages, and so on. Such are known facts. But do not blame him for extravagance, do not pity him as a fool for so doing. He is not a fool; he is a wise man, for he receives more than his money's worth of pleasure in believing that he is giving pleasure.

The Chinese New Year is different from the English year; their months being lunar, that is, reckoned by the revolution of the moon around the earth, are consequently shorter. They have twelve, say, instead of January, February, etc., Regular Moon, Second Moon, Third Moon. Each third year is a leap year and has an extra month so as to make each of the lunar years equal to a solar year. Accordingly, the time of their New Year varies between January and February. The week or ten days during which they keep it is a season of relaxation and rest from the cares of business. There is a great deal of mutual giving and receiving and not even the poorest beggar goes hungry. Those of the American Chinamen who have children celebrate with more than ordinary glee. Little Fat One, Little Black One, Tiny Spring Fragrance and Gentle Peach Blossom are all very happy. Red Chinese candles and punk sticks are burning and the quaint little Chinese people are having a good time, eating all manner of good things, dressing in all the colors of the rainbow, having their little hands and pockets filled with all sorts of trinkets, nuts, and sweets, and best of all, watching the fire-flowers. The fire-flowers are called fireworks by the Americans. The fathers and mothers, and all the grown up aunts, uncles and cousins of Little Fat One and Little Black One are also enjoying themselves. They are taking parts in religious ceremonies, listening to Chinese music, dressing, feasting, resting, laughing, enjoying everything. Red, the good luck color, is much in evidence. You see it all over in bright splashes of long narrow strips of paper pasted upon buildings with inscriptions in

Chinese. The restaurants, with their deep balconies ornamented with carved woodwork, brightly colored or gilded, and set off with immense lanterns and big plants in china pots, are distinctively picturesque.

Ceremonies too numerous to be particularized are performed. The name of some of these ceremonies might cause a humorist to smile and the sober-minded to sigh. One is "Keeping company with the gods during the night," a ceremony which consists of making offerings and feasting before a collection of gods or images. The spirits of these gods are supposed to graciously receive the spirit of the food spread before them, while the devotees in order to be sociable with and agreeable to their august company of spirits, represented by the Gods, which, let it be understood, are not themselves worshiped, demolish the substance of the viands.

The Chinese are exceedingly fond of stories and story telling, their favorite themes being magic and enchantment. It is popular also to portray the blessings which fall to the lot of the filial son and the terrible fate of the undutiful. Some of their stories are very pretty. For instance, there is the story of the Storm Dragon, who began life as a snake, but having the misfortune to lose its tail, and, therefore, being unable to enter another world, retired to a mountain spring, whose clear never-failing fountain proved a safe hiding place. There he lived through several centuries, and was the cause of all the storms that came from the southwest. When he became very angry he was said to work fearful destruction through bringing about evil winds and tornadoes. His end, however, was peaceful. In the form of a silkworm's egg, he ventured one day to lie on a palm leaf waving on a tree above the spring. A little girl named Choy found him, and wrapping him in brown paper, placed him within her bosom, hoping by the warmth of her body to hatch him, a silkworm. In that pure and peaceful resting place, the dragon repented of his misdeeds, and when finally he became a silkworm, and from a silkworm to a butterfly, he soared far away on golden wings into the bright heavens, and throughout the region in which he had dwelt there were no more storms.

Another example is the story of the fairy fish. The fairy fish loved a fairy bird, but sacrificed itself for the sake of a poor old woman who had no grandchild to feed her. The fairy fish jumped into a frying pan full of boiling oil and allowed itself to be cooked and eaten by the old lady who was thereby much strengthened. The spirit of the fairy fish, however, entered into a little bird, which little bird became the mate of the fairy bird loved by the fairy fish.

Some Chinamen take advantage of the holiday season to patronize our theatres. I inquired of a well-informed Chinaman if the plays in Chinese theatres resembled those he saw acted on the American stage. He replied that the stories played in Chinese theatres are very much like the stories played here, but nearly all the actors are men, even the female parts being personated by men in the garb of women. He said that a Chinese audience showed its appreciation, not by clapping hands, but by calling out "Good, Good."

Gambling and opium smoking are somewhat indulged in by our black sheep Chinamen during New Year. In some of the gambling places may be found an image made of wood on which is painted a tiger with wings. This image is the God of Gamblers, and is called "The Grasping Cash Tiger." The gamblers light incense and candles before it and cast lots with bamboo sticks.

Chinese-American Sunday Schools

Chinese-American Sunday School festivals are very popular with the exiled Chinamen during the festive season. I was present one time at a gathering of thirteen Chinese Sunday schools, and the crowded room, decorated with Chinese flags and banners, beautifully wrought in various colors, Chinese lanterns, flowers and native plants, presented a very picturesque appearance. The festival was given, not by the teachers, but by the Chinese themselves, and was an expression of the gratitude which Chinamen feel towards those who try to benefit them, and as well, an evidence that these foreign laborers, practical working men for the most part, have buried deep in their hearts, a love and appreciation of the beautiful.

The American preacher who was Chairman said that it gave him great pleasure to see so many of his Chinese brothers, and only regretted that he could not speak to them in their own language and tell them how sorry he was that they had met with experiences which might perhaps cause them to think meanly of the Christian faith. He wished to say that he and all the friends there assembled would endeavor to give them a different impression of Christianity.

The Chinamen who helped in the entertainment betrayed very little embarrassment and acted their parts creditably. One spoke in a very bright direct manner, thanking the American friends for the interest in himself and his fellow countrymen. Another sang the hymn, "Precious Name," and a Chinese orchestra delighted the audience. There was the fiddler with his fiddle, the flutist with his flute, the banjo man with his banjo, and the kettledrummer with his kettledrum. A European gentleman present who could speak Chinese explained that one of the pieces of music was taken from a play in a Chinese theatre. The singer, a man with a falsetto voice, was supposed to be a maiden soliloquizing whilst her lover was in battle. The Chairman remarked with a humorous smile that a piece of such character was not usually chosen for a Sunday school entertainment; but they must "take the will for the deed" and enjoy it in spite of its impropriety. This speech, of course, added to the evening's enjoyment. A little spice is needed, even at Chinese Sunday school festivals.

Chinese Food

Speaking of feasting and festivities brings us to the question of Chinese food. I have partaken of many Chinese dishes, all of which were good and nutritious, many dainty and delectable.

There is, of course, a difference between European and Chinese cooking. For one thing, Chinese use neither milk nor butter in the preparation of food. In their soups they use mostly sundried comestibles and one may observe in their stews various kinds of dried nuts, fruit and vegetables. Their chief article of diet is, as is well known, rice, and the Chinaman cooks it so beautifully that if you will watch him as he manipulates his chopsticks, you will see that nearly every grain rolls separate.

There is nothing on a Chinaman's table to remind us of living animals or birds—no legs, heads, limbs, wings or loins—everything is cut into small pieces. The Chinaman comes to the table to eat, not to work—his carving is done in the kitchen.

At a Chinese banquet, to which I was invited, there were so many fragrant and appetizing dishes passed before me that I thought, even if I could not taste of all, I would take a list of the names. Here it is:

Sin Lip Ap Gang (Duck soup prepared with lotus seeds and flavored with ham)
Foo Yung Dan (Chinese omelette with herbs)
Ham Sun Goey (Sweet and sour fish)
Hung Yan Gaiding (Fried chicken with almonds, bamboo shoots, etc.)
Mo Kwo Bark Gop (Fried mushroom squab)
Jah Tau Goey (Fried fish in fancy)
Mo Kw Gai Tong (Spring chicken soup with mushrooms)
Gai Yong Goey Chee (Fried sharks' fins with chicken and egg)
Choong Taw Chee Yok (Pork with onion)
Foo Yong Har (Lobster omelette with herbs)
Ngow Yok Chop Suey (Chop Suey of beef)
Yin Wah Guy Ga (Chicken chopped with bird's nest)
Gai Yong Wong Ye Taw (Brain of yellow fish with minced chicken)
Hop Howe Gai Nip (Fried walnut and chicken)
Mut Geong (Ginger in syrup)
Mut Kim Ghet (Golden Lime)
Bor Lor (Preserved pineapple)
Mut Ching Moy (Green apricots)
Kwa Ying (Mixed sweet chow chow)
Know Mine Lie Chee Gon (Chinese nuts)
Far Sang Toy (Chinese peanut candy)
Hang Yen Soo (Almond cakes)
Lok Dow Go (Green bean cakes)
Long Sue tea.

A favorite dish is rice flour dumplings filled with mince meat. Another is shark fins boiled to the softest consistency and preserved ducks' tongues—something very gelatinous. Balls of crab and tripe boiled to a tenderness hard to express are also very tempting to the jaded appetite.

A peculiarity of the Chinese table to Europeans and Americans is that although furnished with sauces of every flavor and strength, salt itself is never in evidence.

As a diet for dyspeptics and men of sedentary habits Chinese food is recommended. It is mucilaginous and nutritious.

The Bible Teacher

A lady who had a Chinese pupil in her Bible class lectured him one day for not attending more regularly.

"I am sorry, Miss M—," he replied, "but I myself instruct at that hour two American young men."

"Instruct two American young men! Pray, Sir, in what do you instruct them?"

"In all that you have instructed me."

"From the Bible? Do you mean to say that there are American young men who do not know the Bible?"

Liu Wenti smiled. "There certainly are," he answered. "One day, these two came to my store. I was busy reading a story in the Bible. I told them so. They laughed and asked me if it was a good one. I read it to them. They said they would come again to listen to further stories. They cannot read much themselves and wish me to illuminate them.

Americanizing Not Always Christianizing

It will be seen from the above sketches that some of the Chinamen in our midst are much more Americanized than others, and those who are Americanized are not always those who have been with us the longest. Americanizing does not always mean improving or even civilizing. It ought to, but it does not. Some Chinese are not nearly as fine men after coming in contact with Western civilization as they were before. The majority, however, it is safe to say, benefit by stepping into the Westerner's light, more particularly those who have met with genuine Christian people and have had the privilege of entering into and seeing something of the beauty of the truly Christian American home. I lay great stress on the word "genuine," because an insincere Christian or one to whom religion is but a form, does great harm to the cause of Christianity. This has been repeated over and over again, but there is still reason for its repetition.

The Reform Party

The Chinese of the Reform Party in America are acutely conscious, and have been for many years, of the necessity of a new way of living for the Chinese—and not only a new way of living—a new way of thinking. They are also keenly alive to what is taking place in their own country. Indeed, they may be said to be the only Chinese here who are so. In nearly every city of any importance in America, there are a number of these Reform men, and they are amongst the most influential and enterprising. Not a few of them are graduates from American colleges. Nearly all of the Chinese married to white women in America belong to the Reform party, and they may truly be said to be living revolutionized lives as compared with the lives of their ancestors. Yet their hope and belief in the future of their own country is vital, and nothing causes their eyes to glisten more than to know that China is encouraging educational and industrial reforms, while those of them who have become Christians look forward with bright faith to China's religious reformation.

—*Westerner,* August 1909

3. Chinese Traditional Religion in North America and Hawaii

L. Eve Armentrout Ma

When Chinese first began arriving in North America and Hawaii in the nineteenth century, they brought with them a religious tradition not previously known in America. For reasons of convenience we may call it Chinese traditional religion, or Chinese popular religion. Today few if any native-born Chinese Americans or Chinese Canadians adhere to this religion, but many recent immigrants of Chinese ethnic background do follow it. In fact, in certain of California's cities a decline in the religion's vitality from the 1920s through the 1960s has been followed by a small upsurge.

Few people who are not ethnically Chinese, and not even all Chinese Americans, have a very clear understanding of this religion. Yet it is an essential part of the history of Chinese Americans and therefore also of the history of Hawaii and North America's west coast. In the 1870s and 1880s in California alone there were more than twenty-five Chinese temples, and the religion had thousands of adherents. The first section of this essay characterizes the religion, particularly as it was practiced in southern China (the area from which almost all ethnically Chinese immigrants to North America and Hawaii trace their origins). The second section discusses temples, festivals, and some of the practices of this religion as followed in North America and Hawaii.

A cautionary note: This religion is discussed here as it has actually been practiced. Its more profound philosophical or even religious bases will not be discussed. Nor are the many regional variations to the practice of Chinese religion analyzed here. In spite of these limitations this article will give the reader an idea of the basic characteristics of the religion, along with some particulars concerning its history in North America and Hawaii.

Chinese Traditional Religion

Chinese traditional religion is immediately distinguishable from most religions of the West and the Near East, such as Christianity, Judaism, and Islam, on two grounds. In the first place it is not monotheistic. Second, a follower is not called upon to participate in regular group worship with a temple, a priest, and a set religious service. Not withstanding the above, the religion does have temples, priests (relatively few in number), and written services derived from holy books.[1]

"Chinese Traditional Religion in North America and Hawaii", *Chinese America: History and Perspectives*, 1988, by L. Eve Armentrout Ma. Reprinted by permission of the author.

More to the point, Chinese popular religion is the religion followed (except when the government has intervened) by the average individual in China for the past several hundred years. In the nineteenth century it had more adherents than any other religion in the world. In this century the Communists on mainland China have controlled it, modified it, and at times discouraged its practice. But in places such as, Taiwan and Hong Kong, it continues to be an important force, with tens of thousands of adherents. Many Chinese immigrants, including those to America and to Southeast Asia, have maintained it in their adopted country. The descendants of Chinese immigrants to Southeast Asia have often followed the religion as well, which is of interest here since many of them have recently emigrated from Southeast Asia to the United States and Canada. However, American-born descendants of Chinese immigrants to America rarely adhere to the religion. Many modern Chinese intellectuals shun it as well.

Chinese traditional religion combines Buddhism, Taoism, local cults, and certain elements of Confucianism to form one syncretic whole. It honors a profusion of gods, goddesses, bodhisattvas, and immortals and encourages the belief in fairies, devils, and the like. It makes use of both Buddhist and Taoist clergy, although private religious connotations are just as important as formal services performed in a temple.

The religion's diverse origins, long development, and lack of central hierarchy have meant that its practice varies significantly from region to region. It teaches certain constants, however: Man should follow good and shun evil. There is an afterlife for which we should prepare and which exercises great influence over the mortal world. A large part of virtue consists in maintaining family obligations, including obligations to deceased family members (the latter usually performed by male members of the family group). Fate and chance have a great influence over people's lives. Finally, supernatural beings must be placated, and for the most part, they help to uphold the traditional morality.

Religious Rites Practiced by the Family

Chinese popular religion involves many rites performed in the home. Some are simple daily observances. Others, performed on special occasions such as births, marriages, and death, are much more elaborate. In general these rites serve to define the family unit and bind it together. They also uphold moral tenets and provide an avenue whereby family members can ask for divine assistance.

Worship of deceased ancestors is an essential element of the religion, and a most important aspect of this worship takes place in the home. A small shrine containing an ancestral tablet dedicated to the deceased parents of the male head of the household is set up in the home. Worship at this shrine is supposed to take place daily, although today this is often done only once a week or so. Ordinarily one need only light incense before the shrine, but on special occasions the rites are more elaborate. At festival time, for example, the shrine is presented with offerings of food.

The ancestral tablet is not the only thing in the home that gets an offering of incense. The Kitchen God watches the family all year long to see whether family members behave properly. He is also supposed to receive an incense offering every day, although today this may only be done once a week or even twice a month. Just before Chinese New Year this God, along with several others, is sent up to heaven, where he makes a report to heaven's Jade Emperor. Sometimes the Kitchen God's mouth is sweetened by smearing honey on it right before sending him up so that he will make a "sweeter," better report. (Based on the Kitchen God's report, the Jade Emperor will see to it that family members' good behavior is rewarded and their evil punished.)

Even if an individual behaves properly, he or she cannot completely rule out the possibility of incurring bad luck. In order to find out what lies in store, he or she can purchase an almanac/book of divination that not only predicts the weather and offers little homilies on how to live but also offers astrological calculations and the like to predict one's fortune. A person can also try to influence fate. A charm obtained from a temple, when hung in the home, will give the divine protection of the deity to which it is dedicated. The same charm, if it is burned and the ashes made into a tea, can sometimes cure disease if medical remedies fail. Various paper figures of animals and people can be used in the home to ward off bad luck. Some of these need to be displayed; some should be burned. Mirrors, if surrounded by certain Taoist symbols, are also very effective, as are certain deities.

As might be expected, marriage is considered very important in China. Much of the actual marriage ceremony takes place in the home of the groom and includes worship of heaven and earth, as well as of the groom's ancestors. Certain magical objects are supposed to enhance wedded bliss and harmony; for example, swords made out of old Chinese copper coins ("copper cash") are hung over the connubial bed. Just as Christians may display pictures of Jesus or the Virgin Mary, Chinese often hang pictures of deities, bodhisattvas, Taoist immortals, and the like on their walls. Some of these can help in one of the ultimate aims of marriage—the production of sons.

The family and religious rites carried on by the family are so important in China that several of the most influential types of social organizations act as larger family units. Organization members consider each other to be blood brothers. They establish an "ancestor" (not always in fact a blood relative of members)[2] who is worshiped by the organization. The organizations also worship a variety of other deities, but the principal religious tie among members is the "ancestor" whom the group worships. Organizations of this type include clan, lineage, and surname associations and secret societies.

Festivals with Religious Connotations

Chinese celebrate many festivals throughout the year. Almost all of these festivals have religious connotations, even though most contain important secular elements as well. Among these festivals are Chinese New Year, Ch'ing-Ming, Chung Yuan (Chinese All Souls), Tuan Wu, the Mid-Autumn Festival, and the Mid-Winter Festival (Tung Chin).[3] In addition, annual "birthday" celebrations for the most important deity of a temple provide the occasion for a public celebration that often lasts two or three days.

The Chinese New Year season officially lasts for two weeks—from the first day of New Year until the fifteenth, or Shang-yuan. Even before New Year's Day the devout perform important rites in their homes. The New Year season is a time of natural and cosmic renewal. The house gets a thorough cleaning and family members get new clothes. The family partakes of a feast on New Year's Eve or New Year's Day, while organizations, businesses, and associations offer feasts to members and employees in the days that follow. Children, incidentally, are not to be scolded on New Year's Day, for this portends family disharmony and can bring bad luck.

A visit to a nearby temple for the purpose of worship and fortune telling is another important aspect of the New Year's celebration. It is important to shoot off firecrackers during this season—they frighten away evil spirits. Lion dances perform the same task and bring good fortune, so every organization, association, and business establishment tries to arrange for one before the New Year's season comes to a close. Dragons (who bring water and hence fertility) are often paraded through the streets. Homes, associations, offices, and business establishments paste New Year's couplets next to their doors to bring good fortune and set the tone for the coming year.

The New Year season is also a time for visiting and renewing relationships. First, the family gets together. Later the clan or lineage group will have a feast and meeting. Then even more distant relatives, friends, and business associates are visited. On these visits children are presented with red envelopes containing money for good luck.

The New Year season ends with the lantern festival, at which time a pastry called *yuan-hsiao* (*t'ang-yuan* in Guangdong) is eaten. The lantern festival is not the only one to have its special food; many of the dishes of the family New Year's feast are prescribed to accord with religious practice and bring good fortune. Other festivals, such as the Mid-Autumn Festival and Tuan Wu, require the eating of one particular food: moon cakes in the case of Mid-Autumn Festival, *tsung-tzu* (a rice preparation wrapped in bamboo leaves) for Tuan Wu, *yuan-hsiao* again for the Mid-Winter Festival.

The Tuan Wu festival commemorates the suicide of a Chinese statesman named Ch'u Yuan who lived in the third century B.C. The statesman committed suicide by throwing himself into a river. In the annual celebration religious elements have been added to what was basically a secular historical event. Dragon boat races are an important element of the festival. The dragons—water gods—race to see which can reach the statesman to save his life. *Tsung-tzu*, the food special to this festival, have magical properties that supposedly enable them to float to the body and provide it with nourishment.

The Chung Yuan (Chinese All Souls) festival—brought to China by Buddhist missionaries during the T'ang dynasty (A.D. 618–907)—aims to placate the souls of those who died and did not receive proper burial because they died far from home, left no descendants, or the like. Surely, it is felt, it is both good and appropriate that the believer invite these deceased to come home with his or her family. In addition, elements of the celebration help the souls along the road to the Buddhist heaven. Not surprisingly, much of this celebration involves elaborate ceremonies in Buddhist temples performed by Buddhist monks.

Finally, the annual "birthday" celebration of a local temple's chief deity has been one of the most important events in rural China before the mid-twentieth century. The celebration includes a procession in which the deity is paraded through the streets, a dramatic performance (to please the deity, as well as the mortal audience), and a fair, in which goods from throughout the immediate countryside can be bought and sold. Craftsmen (herbalists, practioners of Chinese medicine, garment workers, porters, even prostitutes) traditionally worshiped a patron deity, and this deity was also given an annual celebration similar to the "birthday celebration" of a temple deity.

Religion in the Temple for the Ordinary Worshiper

Worship in the average Chinese temple is not as organized as that in Christian churches or Moslem or Jewish temples. That is, there are no regular weekly services, professional clergy, or Sunday school classes. Chinese temples are for the most part looked after by temple caretakers. These men often have only slightly better than a layperson's grasp of the essentials of the religious tradition. For special occasions the devout will turn to the trained Buddhist monks or Taoist priests, but for ordinary temple worship the practitioner will rely upon his or her own knowledge of religious practices, as learned from parents and others.

The average Chinese temple houses a variety of deities: Buddha forms, Taoist immortals, gods, goddesses, and figures from Chinese history and legend. The temple will be dedicated to one deity who will be considered the chief god (or goddess) of the temple. In southern coastal China the three most popular deities have been Kuan Kung (Kuan Yu or Kuan-ti, the God of War who values honor, fidelity, valor, and learning), Kuan Yin (a female bodhisattva of great mercy and compassion), and T'ien-hou (the Empress of Heaven, who has special powers to help fishermen and those who travel over the ocean). In addition, many laypersons worship the Buddha.

Ordinary worship in the temple can consist of no more than lighting a stick of incense or a candle and saying a prayer. Rather than relying on one authoritative text, such as the Bible, Talmud, or Koran, Chinese religion draws upon many permissible texts (referred to as "classics," or *ching*), principally either Buddhist or Taoist works. As noted earlier, many of the ideals embodied in these texts come from the Confucian tradition, although Confucius is not considered a god and pure Confucianism is not a religion.

Another common activity in a Chinese temple is the casting of fortunes. The worshiper considers the temple deities to have chosen the fortune obtained. One common method of fortune telling is for the worshiper to kneel and hold one of the temple's large bamboo containers filled with numbered bamboo strips. The worshiper shakes this container until one strip eventually falls out. (If more than one falls out, he or she must start all over again.) The worshiper then takes this strip and gives it to the temple caretaker, who provides a printed fortune that corresponds to the number on the bamboo strip. (The fortunes come from a standard Chinese religious/magical work.)

Death and Burial Practices

As in the case with most of the world's religions, the rites and practices associated with death and burial are of special importance in China. Through these rites and practices the soul of the departed attains its just rewards in the afterlife. The Chinese religious tradition also teaches that the proper observance of burial and postburial rites shows that the living still regard the deceased with respect and love. In addition, the rites help ensure that the dead do not come back to haunt the living. The family of the deceased sees to it that the spirit body of the departed will have better than adequate "material" goods (food, lodging, servants, money) in the spirit world. The living, through prayers, can also atone for many, perhaps all, of the transgressions the departed committed before dying.

The public burial rites are as opulent as financially feasible to bring honor and comfort to the departed as well as to those left behind in the land of the living. Perhaps the most important of these public rites is the funeral procession. As a bare minimum, the procession includes the coffin with the deceased, followed by mourners who travel on foot. The mourners most closely related to the deceased walk closest to the coffin.

If finances permit, the funeral procession will be quite elaborate. The coffin (put on bamboo poles and carried or in more modern days placed in a cart or hearse) is preceded by Buddhist monks chanting sutras, Taoist priests reciting prayers, several musical troupes playing funeral music, and carts with funerary objects: rolls of cloth (given to the immediate relatives by friends of the deceased), paper houses for the deceased to use in the afterlife, and so forth. These days, at least in Taiwan and Hong Kong, elaborate flower arrangements are also much in evidence. Occasionally a family is wealthy enough to hire people to dress as supernatural beings to help the deceased through the different stages of hell and on up into heaven. A painting or photograph of the deceased travels with the coffin or sometimes in a cart or car ahead of it. Behind the coffin comes the family of the deceased, then more distant relatives, then, finally, friends.

For several days preceding the procession and burial, elaborate rites need to be performed. Other rites take place after the burial. Taoist priests perform a large proportion of these rites, including magical incantations on behalf of the deceased to direct him or her to the underworld and prevent him or her from returning to haunt the living. In addition, a paper house is burned to give the departed spirit a home for the afterlife. By the same token much "spirit" money (special paper money) is burned to give the departed enough money to take care of his or her needs. The departed is also provided with food (the odor of real food is enough to satisfy a spirit), a horse to ride on, and perhaps servants. The gods of the underworld are offered gifts so that they will treat the departed well: wine, horses, money, incense, and the like. The departed must pass through all the levels of hell before getting into heaven. ("Hell pictures" hanging in temples show the justice with which sins are punished.)

Religious ceremonies for the deceased do not end with the burial. The official mourning period lasts for days, months, or traditionally even years, depending upon one's family relationship to the deceased. At certain intervals throughout the period, specific religious rites must be performed. As time passes, the individual mourner can perform more and more of these rites without the help of priests or monks. Even later, nothing more is required than that the ancestral tablets be properly honored in the home and that the family visit the grave once a year at the Ch'ing-Ming festival. During this annual visit the family is to sweep and clean the grave site and offer the departed, food, wine, and incense.

Traditional Religion as Practiced in North America and Hawaii

During the nineteenth and the early twentieth centuries, the practice of Chinese popular religion in North America and Hawaii did not vary too much from its practice in southern China. Altars to deities, including the Kitchen God, were set up in the home, as were tablets and altars to ancestors. The Chinese immigrants established Chinese temples, celebrated most of the usual festivals in the usual fashion, and buried the dead with elaborate rites.

The lack of regularly functioning family units and the urban setting in which most Chinese have lived since the 1880s did force some modifications, however, as did the very fact that the immigrants were living far from their native land. Clan and lineage rites could not be established and maintained in the overseas environment, for example, since most members of the clan and lineage groups resided in China. Instead, people of the same surname organized surname ("family") associations. Ancestral rites had to be maintained with the knowledge that in most cases the bones of the deceased ancestors lay across the ocean. In addition, the paucity of wives in this country meant fewer sons to carry on the worship. The urban setting served to undercut the importance of deities associated with agriculture and with location. The lack of Chinese governmental control meant no altars to the City God.

In addition, as early as 1910 the religion began a large-scale decline in both North America and Hawaii. This was due to several factors: the modernization of China, then undergoing a series of revolutionary changes; the Western, rationalistic education that native-born Chinese Americans received; and the low opinion with which the majority (non-Chinese) population regarded Chinese popular religion. This decline has been only partially offset in recent decades by a small revival due to the influx of new immigrants.

We learn from Marianne Kaye Wells, Stewart Culin, and others that from the late 1880s through the turn of the century there were at least thirty functioning Chinese temples in California, several in Nevada, one in Montana, one in Wyoming, and at least three in the eastern part of the United States.[4] There were also at least six Chinese temples in Hawaii during the same period, most of them located in Honolulu. Information about Canada is somewhat harder to come by, but the province of British Columbia, where most of Canada's Chinese population lived, contained at least three Chinese temples (in Vancouver and Victoria). The inland city of Calgary also had at least one temple, and several other locations where Chinese were relatively numerous almost surely did as well. I am including in this list Chinese temples maintained by the Chee Kong Tong Association (also known as Chinese Freemasons), since in many locales (particularly in the continental United States and in Canada) these temples functioned as community-wide religious institutions. In the continental United States, cities that contained Chinese temples included San Francisco (which had about fifteen in the 1890s), Oakland, San Jose, Monterey, Los Angeles, Bakersfield, Marysville, Weaverville, Lewiston, Oroville, Sacramento (all in California), Butte (Montana), Philadelphia, and New York.

In the continental United States some of the temples dated back to the 1850s, including at least three in San Francisco and the one in Weaverville. The greatest period of temple building, however, was in the 1880s and 1890s. Most of the temples in California, as well as those in the eastern part of the United States, were built during those two decades. As for Hawaii, although it is difficult to get any precise information, two of Hawaii's Chinese temples may date from the 1860s or 1870s, when large numbers of Chinese were being brought to the islands as indentured laborers. Certainly all Honolulu's Chinese temples that were still functioning in the 1920s had been built before the turn of the century. The same is true of the three Chinese temples in Canada.

In addition to the regular temples, Chinatown associations ("family" associations, regional associations, and so forth), maintained altars with deities for the protection of members and to give members a place to worship. In this they were simply following the example of their counterparts in China. Even today, when there are probably no more than ten functioning Chinese temples in San Francisco and somewhat fewer in all other North American and Hawaiian communities combined, many of the old-style organizations and associations maintain their altars and deities. For example, in San Francisco and Oakland surname associations for the Lees and Mas, along with multi-surname associations such as the Lung-kong and Soo-yuan, continue to maintain altars.

Not only are there regular temples open to the public and altars in association buildings, but in addition, most businesses in the Chinatowns (and many Chinese-owned businesses in other areas) maintain small altars, a tradition that has existed since the nineteenth century. A favorite deity for this altar is Kuan Kung. Most businesses also post images of the God of Wealth (Ts'ai-shen). In the 1890s the opening of a new business required an elaborate ceremony in the name of this God of Wealth. Today staging a lion dance, setting up the altar, and displaying congratulatory couplets and gifts of fruit are often sufficient.

Judging by numbers, the deities favored by Chinese immigrants to North America and Hawaii have been the Kitchen God (for the home), the God of Wealth (for a place of business), and, in temples, Kuan Kung, Kuan Yin, Hua-t'o (patron God of doctors and pharmacists, and a healer), Pei-ti (who helps protect against floods), Tu-ti (God of the place, the physical location), T'ien-hou, and, in Hawaii, How Wong (a fishermen's God who also protected travelers over the ocean and brought business success). Most of these deities (especially the Kitchen God, the God of Wealth, Kuan Yin, and Kuan Kung) have retained a certain amount of popularity among those Chinese in North America and Hawaii who still practice the traditional religion. In addition, in San Francisco, Oakland, and Honolulu today there are purely Buddhist temples that have been established by Chinese. (In the older Chinese temples, although images of the bodhisattva T'ien-hou were often present, images of the Buddha himself were not common.) All three of these Buddhist temples date from post-1950. The temple in San Francisco does not revere the Buddha as a deity but organizes its functions as a religious institution.

Many Chinese festivals have also been celebrated in North America and Hawaii. From the 1850s through the present, Chinese New Year's has been honored. In the nineteenth century the celebration was quite traditional and included dragon parades, lion dances, feasts, offerings to the deities, firecrackers, the purchase of new clothes, distribution of red envelopes, paper cuttings, the eating of special foods, and the like. Lion dances are still performed in most urban areas that have a large Chinese population, red envelopes are still distributed, and feasts, firecrackers, and the eating of special foods are still important. Many communities, like the one in San Francisco, had dragon parades for the Chinese New Year, and a number also maintained the traditional lantern festival on the last day of the New Year season, in which elaborate lanterns shaped like animals and the like are displayed and taken to temples. Since the 1920s these lanterns are no longer to be seen. In addition, there has been a general decline in some of the more obvious manifestations of the New Year celebration, along with a certain amount of secularization and commercialization of that which is left. As examples of the latter we have the modern version of San Francisco's dragon parade and the Miss Chinatown contest.

Chinese immigrants to North America and Hawaii brought with them other traditional festivals, which were celebrated most noticeably and most traditionally during the last quarter of the nineteenth century and the first decade or two of the twentieth. These included Tuan Wu; in Sacramento Chinese even held dragon boat races in the 1850s, and dragon boat races were also in evidence on San Francisco Bay in the late nineteenth century; *tsung-tzu*, the food special to the festival, are still eaten. Still other festivals celebrated in the New World were Ch'ing-Ming, Chung Yung, and the Mid-Autumn and Mid-Winter festivals.

Some of the "birthday" celebrations held for deities in North American have been quite as elaborate as anything held in China. Theatrical performances of Chinese opera were not uncommon at these celebrations. In San Jose the traditional parade included the giant figures mentioned so often in the literature concerning religion in southern China. A "birthday" celebration for T'ien-hou held in San Francisco in the mid-nineteenth lasted three days. In Watsonville parades were held in the late 1890s. In Monterey, Marysville, San Jose, and San Francisco, "bombs" (hempen rings) were often shot off during the celebration. The Chinese temple at Marysville, one of the few still functioning outside of Honolulu, Vancouver, or San Francisco, still maintains this practice in honor of the "birthday" of Pei-ti. In most other cases, however, by the 1920s the celebration of these festivals had largely fallen into disuse or had been reduced to little more than the eating of special foods associated with the festival.

Worshipers in the Chinese temples of North America and Hawaii today still light incense before the deities and use fortune-telling sticks. For the latter a small fee is required, usually one dollar. Religious texts can be purchased at most temples, and some of the faithful still offer fruit and other foodstuffs on special occasions. In Hawaii as late as the 1930s, the caretaker of one of the temples was also a faith healer.

Probably even more prevalent than temple worship, however, is the honoring of ancestors. Currently all of the surname and most of the district associations in San Francisco maintain altars that contain the tablets of deceased ancestors. These ancestors are honored on special occasions, most notably during the Chinese New Year. In addition, in the Bay Area a significant number of native-born Chinese Americans of the second generation, along with a majority of the China-born, go out to the cemeteries at Ch'ing-Ming, either with their families or with an association. There they clean the graves, bow to the departed, burn incense and "spirit" money, and perhaps offer the three cups of wine, some pork, and some fruit.

Up until the 1950s most Chinese immigrants who died in the continental United States or in Canada had their bones sent back to China for "proper" burial. This did not mean that they had no funeral here. Aside from the fact that close family members were sometimes lacking (in which case, surname association brethren or the like would substitute as family members), Chinese funerals in North America and Hawaii before the middle of this century closely resembled what one would expect in China. The later reinterment in China took place because of the feeling that one's final resting place should be in one's native land (and actually, native county and village).

Due to prejudice against Chinese in North America, during most of the nineteenth and the early part of the twentieth centuries, Chinese were usually forbidden to bury their dead in cemeteries where people of other races were buried. As a result Chinese cemeteries were started. A few major Chinese cemeteries remain in use. In addition, there are many smaller cemeteries in many other communities, particularly but not exclusively in California. There are also Chinese sections of other, larger community cemeteries.

Most of these cemeteries no longer contain any human remains, since the bones have long since been disinterred and sent back to China. Other than the cemeteries in Colma, these cemeteries themselves have pretty much fallen into disuse, and most are overgrown and obviously unkept. However, altars and monuments still remain in most. At the Chinese cemetery in Fresno a fifty-five-gallon oil drum is used to burn "spirit" money. One of the most impressive monuments is the remains of a stone temple with altar located in San Francisco's Lincoln Park, formerly a Chinese cemetery. Athough these cemeteries are for the most part no longer used, in many of them mounted photographs of the deceased still remain at the grave sites, attached to the tombstones. This practice of placing the deceased's photo at the grave site is not unique to the Chinese; other groups in the United States that have followed the same practice include Armenians, Serbians, Jews, Greeks, and Italians.

Chinese traditional religion has been much misunderstood in this part of the world. For many decades its practice in North America and Hawaii differed little from its practice in China in the nineteenth century and in today's Taiwan and Hong Kong. During more recent times to the ranks of the devout have been added those for whom the religion itself no longer has much meaning, but for whom participation in at least some aspects of the festivals has cultural significance. The devout, on the other hand, have shown most interest in maintaining the more private aspects of religious practice. In addition, they have established new temples; one was just opened this year in Vancouver. As noted above, some of these temples are more purely Buddhist than the older temples, but others are not. In their performance of the more private aspects of the religion, Chinese devotees in North America and Hawaii tend to differ little from traditional practice.

Chinese popular religion forms an integral part of the study of the history of this part of the world. After all, Chinese were numerically the largest minority on the west coast of North America and the largest Asian minority in Hawaii for several decades of the nineteenth century. Some of the more public forms of the practice of the religion are interwoven with the broader history of numerous American communities. Reaching its height in the latter part of the nineteenth century, in recent years Chinese traditional religion has enjoyed a partial revival in the United States due to the renewed influx of immigrants from China and ethnically Chinese immigrants from elsewhere in the world (especially Southeast Asia). However, even these immigrants take less interest than did nineteenth century Chinese in deities such as Hua-t'o or Pei-ti, who have been rendered anachronistic by modern science—few Chinese immigrants to the United States would prefer these gods to modern medicine and flood control projects.

Notes

1. The material in this section appeared in substantially the same form in L. Eve Armentrout Ma's "Chinese Popular Religion," a booklet published by the Chinese and Chinese American History Project (now Association). Funded by Chevron, U.S.A., the booklet was written to accompany a museum exhibit of the same name.

2. Clans and lineages kept genealogies that did establish a direct blood tie between the worshipers and most of the ancestors worshiped. Some of the genealogies, however, went back beyond the verifiable ancestors to the dawn of Chinese history and included individuals such as Hsuan-hsiao (a "son" of the mythical Yellow Emperor), who were to be honored as the surname and hence, in a sense, lineage progenitor. In surname associations the tie between association members and the original ancestor worshiped was often quite tenuous. Lao-tsu (putatively surnamed Li, or Lee) is the original ancestor for the Lee Family Association in North America; one ancestor worshiped by the multi-surname Soo Yuan Benevolent Association is a brother-in-law of the Yellow Emperor, and so forth. Secret societies do not pretend to actual blood descent. Instead they become blood brothers through an elaborate initiation ritual. In the Chee Kong Tong and many of the other tongs in America, Kuan-ti is worshiped as if he were an ancestor. In addition, the Chee Kong Tongs worship the five tiger generals and other mythic figures.

3. Other names for these festivals are as follows: Chung Yuan is also called the Yu-lan Festival, or Shao-i; Tuan-Wu can be called Wu-yueh chieh (Festival of the Fifth Moon); and the Mid-Autumn Festival is sometimes called Pa-yueh shih-wu (Fifteenth Day of the Eighth Moon).

4. Marianne Kaye Wells, *Chinese Temples in California* (San Francisco: R and E Research Associates, 1971); Stewart Culin, "Chinese Secret Societies in the United States," *Journal of American Folklore* 3, no. 8 (Jan–March. 1890); Stewart Culin, "Customs of the Chinese in America," *Journal of American Folklore* 3, No. 10 (July–September 1890); and Stewart Culin, "The Practice of Medicine by the Chinese in America," pamphlet, reprinted from *Medical and Surgical Reporter*, March 19, 1887.

   In addition to the above, material for this section of the essay comes principally from the following: Leonard Austin, *Around the World in San Francisco* (San Francisco: Abbey Press, 1955); Hubert Howe Bancroft, *Essays and Miscellany*, vol. 38 of *The Works of Hubert Howe Bancroft* (San Francisco: The History Co., 1890); Rev. Ng Poon Chew, "The Chinese in San Francisco," in *The Pacific Coast Pulpit*, ed. Rev. D. Irwin Hanson (New York: Fleming H. Revell Co., 1893), 49–56; Vyolet Chu, "Folk Religion in Hawaii," paper in the author's collection; Richard F. Hough, "Ethnic and Religious Cemeteries in California, U.S.," paper delivered at the National Council for Geographic Education, Mexico City, Mexico, 1979; Rose Hum Lee, *The Chinese in the United States of America* (Hong Kong: Hong Kong University Press, 1960); Sandy Lydon, *Chinese Gold: The Chinese in the Monterey Bay Region* (Capitola: Capitola Book Co., 1985); Edgar Wickberg et al., *From China to Canada: A History of the Chinese Communities in Canada* (Toronto: McClellan and Stewart, Ltd., 1982); Sau Chun Wong, "Chinese Temples in Honolulu," *Social Process in Hawaii* 3 (May 1937): 27–35; Nancy Foon Young, *The Chinese in Hawaii: An Annotated Bibliography* (Honolulu: Social Science Research Institute of the University of Hawaii, 1973); Harry H. Zeigler and Bernhard Hormann, "A Religious and Cultural Calendar for Hawaii," *Social Process in Hawaii* 16 (1952): 59–67.

4. Preserving Chinese Culture

FENGGANG YANG

According to Will Herberg, immigrants in the United States would give up everything but their traditional religion:

> Sooner or later the immigrant will give up virtually everything he had brought with him from the "old country"—his language, his nationality, his manner of life—and will adopt the ways of his new home. Within broad limits, however, his becoming an American did not involve his abandoning the old religion in favor of some native American substitute. Quite the contrary, not only was he expected to retain his old religion, as he was not expected to retain his old language or nationality, but such was the shape of America that it was largely in and through his religion that he, or rather his children and grandchildren, found an identifiable place in American life. (1960, 27–28)

However, for Chinese immigrants who have even forsaken their traditional religion and converted to Christianity, what is left for them to preserve? This question is especially important for Chinese immigrants because of the historical conflicts between Christianity and Chinese culture and between Christian and Chinese identities (see Chapter 2). For immigrant converts, the Chinese church is not a transplant from the old country but a new invention in American soil. These immigrants are uprooted socially, culturally, and religiously as well. Chinese Christian churches in the United States are self-defined as *Chinese* churches. In what sense do Chinese Christians in America claim their Chinese identity? What Chinese traditions does the church preserve?

Many scholars believe, as reviewed in Chapter 2, that the nature of the Chinese culture was fundamentally defined by Confucian values and notions, or by the Confucian orthodoxy (correct belief); whereas some anthropologists argue that orthopraxy (correct practice) reigned over orthodoxy as the principal means of attaining Chinese identity and maintaining cultural unity among the Chinese. In this chapter I will examine the CCC's preservation of traditional praxes (what people do), including the Chinese language and traditional rituals and symbols, and then analyze the church's different attitudes toward traditional value systems of Confucianism, Daoism, and Buddhism. Generally speaking, when they are able to de-religionize a specific Chinese tradition, these Chinese Christians claim it as compatible with the Christian faith; when it seems impossible to de-religionize a tradition, they reject it; when it looks possible but difficult to separate the religious dimension from the cultural dimension in a tradition, they manifest ambivalent anxiety and tend to avoid it. Overall, the Chinese church helps its members to selectively preserve certain aspects of Chinese culture with transformative reinterpretation.

* * * * *

Chinese Rituals and Symbols

Traditional rituals and cultural symbols are important in defining Chineseness because of the historical orthopraxy that united Chinese people in diverse local cultures and plural religions. Chinese Christians have tried to differentiate traditional symbols and rituals of religious nature from those of secular nature, and have rejected religious ones while accepting secular ones.

Funerals and Weddings

Anthropologists have written intensively about Chinese funerals and weddings (see Watson and Rawski 1988). The argument about Chinese orthopraxy as the core of Chinese identity was largely based on studies of Chinese funerals, which they found quite uniform in structure across the vast land of China. I did not have a chance to observe funerals at the CCC during my field work period, but from interviews and informal conversations I learned that their funerals generally followed Western Christian styles. For example, there would be memorial services both at the church or the funeral parlor and in the cemetery. A pastor would officiate at the funeral. His speeches would honor the dead and comfort the relatives and friends. Following the funeral people would be invited to have a dinner at a Chinese restaurant. Many of the Chinese traditional funeral rites were lacking—no performative wailing, no donning of white mourning attire, no burning of "paper moneys" or other offerings, no setting up ancestral tablets, and so forth. The lack of traditionally Chinese rites is common in Chinese Christian funerals in other churches, as my interviews with Chinese Christians in other metropolitan areas revealed. A study of a Chinese Christian community in Hong Kong finds the same phenomenon (Constable 1994). A Chinese pastor in Houston was willing to conduct a funeral for a non-Christian as long as the family invited him. However, he would use this opportunity to comfort the family *and* to evangelize by explaining the Christian beliefs about the meaning of life. He saw the funeral as an unusual opportunity to challenge non-Christian Chinese who otherwise might never step into a church or talk to a pastor.

The weddings I observed at the CCC and other Chinese churches were all in Western Christian style. At a special wedding service, commonly held on a Saturday at the sanctuary, the bride and the groom would take vows and exchange rings in front of the pastor. Then a reception would follow at the fellowship hall and/or a dinner banquet in a Chinese restaurant. There were no traditionally Chinese wedding rites of kowtowing to the Heaven and the Earth (*bai tiandi*), to the husband's parents, and between the groom and the bride. An interesting comparison was a "Buddhist wedding" that I observed in 1994 at a Chinese Buddhist temple in Chicago. The groom wore a Western style suit and tie, and the bride was in a long white wedding gown. Seeing the Western-style wedding dress, it was surprising for me to watch their kowtowing to the Buddha statue and making three prostrations in front of the monk. The bride seemed to have a hard time because of her high-heeled shoes.

Chinese Christians in America do not follow Chinese traditional ways in weddings and funerals because they do not believe that the traditional orthopraxy in weddings and funerals defines Chineseness. Actually, many non-Christian Chinese have stopped practicing the traditional rites as well. In mainland China those traditional rites have been viewed as feudal superstitions, and the Communist government has made great efforts to abolish them (*yifeng yisu*). In Taiwan and Hong Kong many people have followed similar modernist reasoning against "feudal superstitions" and abandoned them as well. In the construction of Chinese identity, besides the Chinese versus non-Chinese dimension, there is also the premodern versus modern dimension. Many Chinese, both Christian and non-Christian, regard giving up traditional funeral and wedding rites as giving up something backward, rather than as giving up the Chinese identity.

The Chinese New Year and the Mid-Autumn Festival

The Chinese New Year and the Mid-Autumn Festival are the two most important traditional festivals.[1] Both are based on the traditional Chinese calendar system, which is a system of lunar months adjusted to the solar year.[2] This system has been used for many centuries in China and thus has many cultural and religious meanings attached to special holidays, just as the cycles of weeks and seasons in the Western calendar system bear Judeo-Christian meanings. China officially adopted the Western solar calendar after the founding of the Republic in 1911. Some political holidays were set according to the solar calendar, such as the National Day on October 10 (or October 1 for the PRC since 1949). However, Chinese people continue to observe festival days according to the traditional calendar. Consequently, the Chinese today have a bi-calendar system, following the solar calendar (*gongli* or public calendar) in public life—government, school, and work schedules—and the traditional calendar (*nongli* or farm calendar, or *yinli* or lunar calendar) in private life—family, cultural, and religious activities. Chinese calendars are commonly printed with both systems.

Christian Chinese, like other Chinese, maintain the bi-calendar system. The week-cycle and Christian seasons bear significant meanings for their religious faith and practice. At the same time, observing Chinese festivals is habitual and also important for them to assure their Chinese identity. However, Chinese Christians celebrate only certain traditional Chinese festivals that do not have the overtones of traditional religious meanings. With a history of several thousand years, China has many traditional festivals, most having some religious meanings or implications. For example, *Qingming Jie*, which is around the Easter time, is a day to remember dead ancestors by visiting and cleaning their tombs. The Ghost Festival on the fifteenth day of the seventh month, like the Buddhist *Yulan Jie*, is a day to "feed" the vagrant ghosts. Traditional practices on these days include burning "paper moneys" and making other offerings to the dead.[3] Chinese evangelical Christians do not observe these holidays. On the other hand, Chinese Christians in America have no problem in celebrating Chinese New Year and the Mid-Autumn Festival. These days are not religious holidays, although different people may attach various religious meanings to them. The Chinese New Year's Day (*xin nian*), also called Spring Festival (*Chun jie*), marks the beginning of a year and the coming of spring; it usually falls in the early part of February in the Western solar calendar. In Chinese societies Spring Festival is a holiday season that, like Thanksgiving and Christmas in America, extends to many days before the New Year's Day and ends around the *Yuanxiao Jie* on the fifteenth day of the first month (*zhengyue shiwu*). Traditionally, Chinese families have all family members get together on this day, and many community activities are held during this season.

At the CCC the climax of the Chinese New Year celebration is a grand *jiaozi* (boiled dumplings) banquet. *Jiaozi* is *the* traditional New Year's food, as are turkeys for the American Thanksgiving day. The Chinese in America have to adjust their communal celebration day because they do not have paid holidays for celebrating the Chinese New Year. The *jiaozi* party at the CCC is always on a Saturday nearest to the Chinese New Year's Day or the *Yuanxiao Jie*. On that day in the years when I did my research, church members and invited friends would gather at the Fellowship Hall of the church and make lots of *jiaozi* together. Preparing dough and stuffing, making wrappers, wrapping, and boiling, everybody participates in this collective cooking. It provides an opportunity for people to chat and enjoy themselves, and it also creates a jolly family-like atmosphere. The "*jiaozi* banquet" is followed with entertainment programs, including performing Chinese dances, playing musical instruments, and singing gospel songs.

New Year's celebration is a nostalgic time for immigrants to remember the past, a joyfully educational time for the American-born children to learn about Chinese customs and cultural traditions, and a wonderful time to get non-Christian Chinese into the church. Chinese New Year is celebrated as a cultural festival, not a religious holy day. Unlike Christmas, which is celebrated in the sanctuary with special musicals, worship services, and thematic sermons, the entire celebration of Chinese New Year takes place outside the sanctuary. These Protestant Chinese celebrate Chinese New Year in a significantly different way than do other Chinese. I did not see "red-pockets" with lucky money for children. The church did not put up red paper couplets outside the doorways or burn incense or make ritual offerings to dead ancestors, nor did they make dragon and lion dances. Anything with any possible religious implications is omitted on this occasion in this evangelical Protestant church. They exercise great caution to avoid anything non-Christian and deliberately try to distance themselves from the possibility of pagan practices. This practice is common in other Chinese evangelical Protestant churches in the United States and also in a conservative Chinese church in Hong Kong (Constable 1994).

In comparison, I observed a very different celebration of Chinese New Year at a Chinese Catholic church in the Washington area, which adopted more traditional Chinese symbols and practices. At a special ceremony of the New Year's Day, these Chinese Catholics offered sacrificial pig heads and fruits to venerate ancestors, burned incense sticks in front of a memorial tablet labeled for "all Chinese ancestors" (*zhonghua liezu liezong*), and gave out red pockets to small children. These practices would not be acceptable to Chinese evangelical

Protestants. In the past, the Roman Catholic Church forbade practicing ancestral veneration, causing the "rites controversy" in the early eighteenth century. However, it reversed this policy two hundred years later in 1939 (Ching 1993, 192–95), so that Chinese Catholics today integrate many Chinese traditional rites into their Catholic practices. On the Protestant side, the attitudes of mainline Chinese Christians toward Chinese traditional practices may be changing too. In a recent book (Ng 1996), a group of Asian-American ministers and seminary professors of mainline Protestant denominations explore ways to integrate elements of East Asian traditions with their Christian faith. The book shows greater acceptance toward many Chinese (and Korean and Japanese) traditional practices. In sharp contrast to Catholics and mainline Protestants, Chinese evangelical Protestants today deliberately distance themselves as much as possible from any possible "pagan" practices in Chinese traditions. How these evangelical Chinese Christians change (or not change) will be interesting to watch. Nevertheless, the various attitudes among Chinese Christians suggest that the religious (or nonreligious) meanings of many Chinese traditional practices are elastic and are subject to various interpretations from different people in different times.

The Mid-Autumn Festival (*Zhongqiu Jie*) on the fifteenth day of the eighth month (usually in September of the solar calendar) is another important traditional Chinese festival. The moon on this day is said to be at its roundest and brightest. "Roundness" symbolizes the whole family being united together. It is a time for family reunion. The round moon-cake is the special food for this day.

In its early years, the CCC often held a special gathering in the night of the Mid-Autumn Day. The gathering was not purely for preserving the cultural tradition, however. It was transformed and attached with Christian meanings. For instance, the announcement about the celebration of the Mid-Autumn Festival in 1966 reads,

> *Come to our Moonlight Prayer Meeting: During this good festival time when we are missing our family members and relatives, let us come together to pray for our dear family members and relatives, and to pray for our mainland compatriots in the sufferings [under the Communist rule]. After the prayer we will have moon-cakes and fruits, and a time for moon-appreciation.*

In the 1990s, however, the celebration of the Mid-Autumn Festival has become less formal and less regular. It has become more a time for family reunion than for gathering the church community. Sometimes the church combines the celebration of the Mid-Autumn Festival with a welcome party for new students. These evangelical Christians regard it, like the Chinese New Year, as an opportunity to bring non-Christian Chinese into the church, especially lonely students who have just left their families in Asia.

Family Altars, Artworks, and Dragons

Traditionally, many Chinese families had family shrines, either to venerate ancestors or to worship certain gods, or both. However, I did not see any family shrines at CCC members' homes, neither ancestral tablets nor religious altars. In fact, the conversion to Christianity was sometimes marked by an act of removing a family altar. One example is the Zhao family, a couple with three teenage sons, who immigrated from Fujian, China, in the mid-1980s. The Zhao family owned a Chinese restaurant in Washington, D.C., and worked seven days a week, fourteen to fifteen hours a day. They lived in constant fear of black robbers in the neighborhood. The Zhao family used to have a home altar dedicated to *Guanyin*, a popular female Bodhisattva in China, and other gods. In 1994 the family was invited to the church to attend a dinner party for mainland Chinese. After that they attended some Sunday services and other activities. One year later the couple and their three sons were baptized. Mrs. Zhao wrote this testimonial on behalf of her family:

> We used to be very superstitious, like to worship idols and burn incense in front of Guanyin. After we began to come to the church, I stopped worshiping the idols. However, then I sometimes had visions of suddenly stumbling down or my hair burning. One night I had a horrible dream in which I was chased by lots of demons. I was extremely horrified and became almost breathless. Suddenly I remembered the Lord Jesus, so I cried out: "Jesus come to save me!" Immediately, I saw an angel wearing a white robe appearing in the sky, holding a shining cross. The demons were all scared away. In such a wonderful moment I woke up. I prayed to the Lord Jesus and all worked, so I came to know that Jesus Christ is good. He protects me and my family. He is more powerful than ghosts and demons.

Immediately, they got the pastor to their home and demolished the family altar, and soon the whole family was baptized.

Traditional Chinese paintings and sculptures sometimes have religious implications. However, in many cases it is not easy to differentiate the artistic values from religious elements. Many CCC members decorate their houses with Chinese traditional paintings and calligraphic scrolls, often with Christian themes and biblical verses. Most sculptures I saw at members' homes were of a modern artistic nature, and I saw very few Chinese traditional figures. I did see the "triple stars" of good luck (*fu*), officialdom (*lu*) and longevity (*shou*) at the home of a church member who was a restaurant owner. However, whether these statues have religious implications or not depends upon the personal beliefs of the owners. Chinese restaurants often have an altar of certain gods, sometimes including the triple stars; however, these figures can be appreciated solely as artistic works. One young couple had a small china statue of the "Happy Buddha" as an ornament on a table in the living room. The Happy Buddha, a popular legendary figure in China, has a grinning face and a round belly, which signifies lack of worry and broad-mindedness. The wife's parents came to visit them and lived with them. The wife's mother, in her late fifties, had no religion; however, she began to express some revering attitudes toward this statue. Once the young couple noticed this, they removed the statue.

The dragon has been an important Chinese symbol. Chinese people often call themselves "Dragon Descents" (*long de zisun*, or *long de chuanren*). A song written by a young man in Taiwan in the 1970s, "*Long de Chuanren*," became a popular song among many Chinese in Taiwan, Hong Kong, mainland China, and the diaspora. In 1988 a TV commentary series, *The River Elegy*, criticized Chinese traditions and vilified the symbols of the dragon and the Great Wall. This caused emotional rejections by many Chinese people, including overseas Chinese, because they still regard the dragon as a totemic symbol for the Chinese people. The dragon is also a popular decorative image.

However, this sacred Chinese symbol presents some problems for Chinese Christians. In ancient Western cultures, the imaginary dragon is a vicious monster, as depicted in the New Testament book of Revelation and in stories of St. George the dragon slayer. I did not hear CCC people talking about the dragon; I saw no paintings or decorative images of the dragon at members' homes; and no dragon dances were held by these Chinese Protestants to celebrate the Chinese New Year. One lay leader, upon my enquiry, said this:

> *The Chinese dragon and the dragon in the Revelation are totally different things. Their features and their characters are completely different. The Chinese dragon is a cultural symbol, which can be just like the eagle to Americans. Only when someone worships the dragon as an idol it becomes a problem. I once jokingly said to [church] people: if you have a rug with a dragon image, don't throw it away. Give it to me. When someone wears a dragon-shape tie pin, some Christians would say no-no. What is the problem? It should not be a problem.*

However, he acknowledged that some Chinese Christians did not agree with him.

In 1996 a Taiwanese Presbyterian pastor published an article in the newsletter of the Taiwan Christian Church Council of North America in which he distinguished the evil dragon in the Bible from the auspicious dragon of the Orient. He attributed the problem to mistranslation of the Bible and said that the dragon in the Bible should be translated as beast (*guai shou*) instead of dragon (*long*). However, "a group of concerned readers" wrote a letter to the newsletter, which was published in the following issue, in which they insisted that the Oriental dragon was the dragon in the Bible, the image of Satan. No further discussions were published. Apparently the dragon symbol is still problematic for many Chinese Christians. While some people believe that the two dragons are completely different symbols, others insist that they are the same. Most Chinese Christians, however, hold no clear position either for or against the dragon. They simply avoid the image of dragon as much as possible.

Confucianism: Its Compatibility with Christianity

Many scholars hold that Confucianism was the Chinese traditional orthodoxy and that Confucian values still broadly define the nature of Chinese culture and Chinese identity. Understandably, Chinese Christians do not hesitate to claim Confucianism as their cultural heritage. They see most Confucian values as compatible with Christianity and regard them as valuable complements for life in contemporary American society. This positive attitude toward Confucianism is pervasive at the CCC and other Chinese churches.

The Living Water

In 1982 the CCC started a quarterly magazine for publishing testimonials and sharing ideas among church members. They named the magazine *Living Water* (or *Living Spring*) in reference to the biblical verses where Jesus says,

> *Whoever drinks the water I give him will never thirst. Indeed, the water I give him will become in him a spring of water welling up to eternal life. (John 4:14)*

> *If anyone is thirsty, let him come to me and drink. Whoever believes in me, as the Scripture has said, streams of living water will flow from within him. (John 7:37–38)*

Interestingly, the editorial foreword of the very first issue also introduced the magazine with a poem by Zhu Xi (A.D. 1130–1200), the great Neo-Confucian master in the Song Dynasty:

> *A square pond opens up like a mirror*
> *In it glowing light and white clouds are waving together*
> *No wonder this lagoon is so clear*
> *Because from the springhead comes the living water*

The editorial foreword continued,

> *The Word of God is the living water for our hearts. His love is encompassing. Would you open up your heart like the pond to receive the light and reflections of the love of God?*

Quoting a poem by a Neo-Confucian master in the opening remarks of the church magazine is a clear indication of the profound influence of Confucian heritage in the hearts and minds of these Christian Chinese. What is more interesting is that there seems to be a perfect fit between this Confucian poem and the biblical verses. Zhu Xi likens the heart to the water in his philosophical writings, analogically stating that the clearness and cleanness of the heart/mind depend on the living water. What is the living water? It seems unclear in Zhu Xi's poem and other writings. However, when Chinese Christians read the biblical verses quoted above, they find a definite answer—the living water is Jesus Christ. They find not contradiction, but compatibility.

Love and Filial Piety

A core concept of Confucianism is *ren*, which may be translated as humanity, benevolence, or love. Confucianism regards *ren* as the foundation of goodness and all virtues. Following the Confucian phrase *ren zhe ai ren* ('*ren* is to love people'), Chinese Christians equate *ren* to *ren-ai* (love) and regard this *ren-ai* as the quintessence of Confucianism. They see this Confucian core principle as very close to Jesus' new command of love. Jesus said to his disciples, "A new command I give you: Love one another" (John 13:34). Other New Testament passages say, "God is love. Whoever lives in love lives in God, and God in him" (1 John 4:16); and compassion, kindness, humility, gentleness, patience, and forgiveness, "over all these virtues put on love, which binds them all together in perfect unity" (Colossians 3:14). Apparently, both Confucianism and Christianity regard love as the foundation of all virtues. Citing these biblical verses and Confucian texts, these Chinese Christians firmly believe in the compatibility of Confucian *ren* with Christian love.

The foremost virtue in Confucianism is filial piety (*xiao*), which requires children to respect their parents and elders, to take care of them when in need, to honor them in deed by achieving successes, and to venerate them after death. In sermons, lectures, and interviews these Chinese Christians stress the importance of filial piety. They often cite the fifth of the Ten Commandments: "Honor your father and your mother, so that you may live long in the land the Lord your God is giving you" (Exodus 20:12). They like to point out that this is the only commandment that has a promise of worldly blessing, since Paul said, "Children, obey your parents in the Lord, for this is right. Honor your father and mother—which is the first commandment with a promise—that it may go well with you and that you may enjoy long life on the earth" (Ephesians 6:1–3). Several articles on filial piety have appeared in *Living Water*. One article in 1995 clearly manifests the fusion of Christian beliefs and Confucian teachings to justify the necessity of filial piety:

> Some Westerners misinterpret Genesis chapter two verses 23 and 24, and say that "husband and wife are the one bone and flesh; they two are one flesh and the dearest persons. After marriage they are united into one, so they should leave their parents and no longer live together with their parents." The first half of these words is right, but the second half is wrong. We should know that Lord Jesus Christ never said that you should take care of your wife more than your parents. The purpose of husband and wife being united together is to love each other and to learn to live a holy life. "To leave parents" does not mean to dismiss or get rid of the parents, but only means to live not under the same roof. This is reasonable if the wealth allows and if the parents wish to live separately. It is also natural that in American society children often live far away from their parents because of the job. However, if one insists that old parents must live separately, that is a misinterpretation of the teaching of the Bible and forsakes the obligation of children to take care of the parents. We Chinese are a people who highly appreciate filial piety. We must think again and again over this issue. Mark 15:4 says, "For God said, 'Honor your father and mother' and 'Anyone who curses his father or mother must be put to death.'" If you are a Christian, you ought to take care of your parents, because taking care of the parents is one of the three behaviors of filial piety. Furthermore, the Bible also tells us this very clearly. Therefore, we must remember this all the time. . . . When we worship God the Creator we should remember our parents for their grace of giving birth to us and rearing us. . . . We who are parenting should be role models for our children. God is watching us from above. If we can do this every generation, our Chinese traditional principle of filial piety (xiaodao) will be forever preserved.

The "Westerners' misinterpretation" was a target of criticism. This essay also clearly shows the author's conviction of the complete compatibility of biblical teachings and Confucian notions.

The emphasis on filial piety is often accompanied by an emphasis on family life, including harmonious relationships between husband and wife, between parents and children, and among siblings. Living in modern American society and following the biblical traditions, Chinese Christians tend to regard the nuclear family as the basic unit of family life. This is different from the traditional Chinese way in which the family often means the extended family or even the clan. On the other hand, these Chinese Christians disapprove of what they perceive as the "breakdown" of the family in American society. They underscore the need to extend family life beyond the nuclear family. As shown in the above quotation, they regard taking care of old parents as part of the good Chinese tradition that Chinese Christians should preserve.

The Philosophy of Life

Chinese Christians believe that Confucianism and Christianity share many other social and moral values as well. Chapter 4 described several moral values that CCC members cherish and promote, which could be called the "Protestant ethic." Actually, most of these values are Confucian too. Both Protestantism and Confucianism maintain "this-worldly asceticism"—success, thrift, delayed gratification, practical rationalism, and so on. Indeed, Christians at the CCC claim that the Confucian and Christian philosophies of life are very much alike. An article published in *Living Water* in 1989 reads:

> *Learning to be a human person* (xue zuoren) *is the emphasis of Confucianism. To be a human person is to be free and independent. Wealth and rank will not make him wallowing, poverty and lowness will not make him shaking, and coercive forces will not make him bending. He will not give up moral principles no matter in what circumstances. The true freedom is not to be determined by circumstances. This central view of Confucianism is consistent with a biblical principle. Paul said in the Philippians 4:11–13, "I have learned to be content whatever the circumstances. I know what it is to be in need, and I know what it is to have plenty. I have learned the secret of being content in any and every situation, whether well fed or hungry, whether living in plenty or in want. I can do everything through him who gives me strength." . . . Therefore, no matter in what circumstances, we should always strive forward and upward, with full confidence, dynamism and strong will. We should trust the Lord to lead our life and receive His grace and gifts with joy and hope.*

Here the compatibility of Confucianism and Christianity is affirmed with no doubt.

Confucian Deficiency and the Remedy

While pointing out many compatible teachings in Confucianism and Christianity, these Chinese Christians never say that they are the same. In fact, they frequently note various differences between Confucianism and Christianity. The fundamental difference, or the root of other differences, they claim, is the lack of a clear view of God and the spiritual world in Confucianism.

Confucius himself does not deny the existence of God or gods;[4] however, he is agnostic, believing that man cannot know things beyond this world. Confucius talks about no supernatural things and declares that "without knowing life, how can you know death" (*wei zhi sheng, yan zhi si*)! Most Confucian followers in dynastic China moved farther and farther away from acknowledging the existence of God or gods. However, agnosticism is not an essential element in Confucianism, these Chinese Christians argue. They point out that Confucius was fond of ancient classics and that in the classics that Confucius edited, there is no lack of the notion of God. All of the most ancient Chinese classics, including *Shi Jing* (the Book of Songs), *Shu Jing* (the Book of History), *Yi Jing* (the Book of Change), and *Li Ji* (the Book of Rites) have many verses about *Shangdi* or *Tian*. This idea of a supreme ruler who has power and personality is very close to the notion of God in the Judeo-Christian tradition.

Many contemporary Neo-Confucian scholars praise the agnosticism in Confucianism. To Chinese Christians, however, this lack of religious dimension is a fatal deficiency of Confucianism. Although it is true that Confucius cared little about the spiritual world and death, these questions have to be answered. Precisely because Confucianism failed to provide consistent answers concerning God, death, and the spiritual world, these Chinese Christians argue, various human-invented wrong religions have filled China ever since the Han Dynasty (206 B.C.–A.D. 220), when Confucianism became the orthodoxy. Religious Daoists developed a system of gods, spirits, and immortals. Buddhism brought China the doctrine of "soul transmigration." For these Chinese Christians, only Christian beliefs provide the right answer to the questions that Confucianism failed to address. As a member wrote in the church magazine,

> Confucianism did not negate the existence of the spiritual world. Daoist and Buddhist superstitions filled the empty space left by Confucianism, but the [Buddhist] soul transmigration is just absurd. Thank God for giving us a clear answer: after death there will be resurrection for Christians. We trust what the Bible says, that we will be resurrected.

To remedy what they perceive as the deficiency of Confucianism, these Chinese Christians call for a restoration of ancient Chinese culture prior to Confucius. They see that the pragmatic rationalism after Confucius blocked Chinese people from the transcendent or *Shangdi* (God), just like ancient Jews who sometimes betrayed Jehovah, God of their ancestors. Once we are reconnected with God as believed by our ancient ancestors, they say, we can expect the revival and revitalization of Chinese culture in the modern world. These Chinese Christians want to show that God is no alien to Chinese spirituality. Ancient Chinese ancestors believed and worshiped God, who is a universal God and is thus the Chinese God too. By pointing out the verses about God in the most ancient Chinese texts and by arguing that this God is the same God whom Christians believe in and worship, these Chinese Christians want to prove that believing in God is indeed very Chinese, very traditional (in ancient roots), rather than at odds with Chinese identity and Chinese traditions.

Moreover, Confucianism has to be complemented by Christianity in the modern world. These Chinese Christians believe that without believing in the living God many Confucian moral values would be devoid of meaning or impossible to practice. For example, *ren-ai* (love) is an ideal in Confucian morality. But people often fail to love others. This is because of the lack of godly love, these Christians believe. They claim that only if one receives love from God can one love others without utilitarian purposes. "We love because he [God] first loved us" (1 John 4:19) and "since God so loved us, we also ought to love one another" (1 John 4:11). Loving others has to be sustained by the love of God. In this sense, only through Christianity can Confucian moral ideals be fulfilled.

More important, Confucianism has to be complemented with Christianity in the modern world. Modernity has challenged the authority of traditions. In the past the Confucian orthodoxy was maintained by the dynastic state, but the dynastic state has collapsed. Another source of authority for Confucianism is traditionalism—upholding Confucian morals because the ancestors held them. In modern society, however, no traditional values can be preserved intact without passing rational reexamination. Appealing to tradition alone is insufficient to carry on Confucian moral values. In this regard, the absolute notion of God in Christianity can be a powerful source of authority. Because these Chinese Christians find the main Confucian values compatible with conservative Christianity, they find it natural to complement Confucianism with Christian beliefs and to maintain these values through the Christian institution. Christian beliefs provide the absolute foundation for the moral principles of Confucianism in the modern world, and this foundation has well survived various modern or postmodern challenges. Also, living in the United States as a minority, they see that no institution has better resources to implement and pass on Confucian values than the church.

Chinese Christians believe that without the Christian faith, Confucianism alone cannot protect the Chinese people from the rising tide of unhealthy developments in modern society. This is true both to Chinese as a minority in America and to Chinese societies in Asia. The so-called greater China has been in an economic boom. But social anomie and moral chaos are rampant along with the rise of materialism, consumerism, and eroticism. Many Chinese Christians in America share this burning concern about the breakdown of Chinese society and consequently strive hard to evangelize Chinese compatriots. In this process, they do not intend to replace Confucianism with Christianity. Rather, they want to revitalize Confucianism through Christianity.

Confucian Orthodoxy Versus Christian Orthodoxy

The description above shows that these Chinese Christians are integrating Confucianism and Christianity. Their efforts have touched upon many Christian theological questions. To attain the Christian identity, these Chinese Christians adhere to evangelical Christianity. Meanwhile, to retain their Chinese identity, they want to inherit the Confucian orthodoxy. Because syncretism has been regarded as a danger to the Christian faith in the orthodox Christian theology, an unavoidable question is: Is it syncretic to mix Confucianism and Christianity?

How do these Chinese evangelical Christians uphold orthodox Christian beliefs while remaining truthful to the Confucian orthodoxy? Theological judgment is not the purpose of this sociological study. On the other hand, an empirical study of a Christian church cannot avoid asking questions with theological significance. "Syncretism" worries theologians and the subjects of this ethnographic study. The Chinese Christians at the CCC have made great efforts to prove the authenticity of their Christian faith as well as their Chinese identity.

First, for these Chinese Christians, Confucianism is a system of moral values, whereas Christianity provides transcendent beliefs and spiritual guidance. In other words, they regard the core of the Confucian orthodoxy as on the level of moral values or social ethics, whereas the essence of Christianity is on the level of spirituality concerning the transcendent. This is to say that Confucianism and Christianity do not compete on the same level. Therefore, these Chinese evangelical Christians can claim that they remain truthful to both Christianity and Confucianism without being syncretic. A frequent statement in talks and articles at the church is "Worship Jesus Christ as God, revere Confucius as a sage, and honor ancestors as human beings."

An article in *Living Water* tried to clarify proper names for the birthday of Christ and that of Confucius. The conventional Chinese translation of the word *Christmas* is *Shengdan* (*sheng:* sage, saint, holy, sacred; *dan:* birth, birthday). In the 1980s some newspapers in Taiwan adopted a new translation of *Christmas—Yedan* (birthday of Jesus). The article reads:

> *Some Confucian apologists [in Taiwan] even have suggested calling the birthday of Confucius* Shengdan *and claim that only the birthday of Confucius deserves to be called* Shengdan. . . . *Actually, the conventional use of the word "Shengdan" for the birthday of the Lord Jesus Christ has no competition with that of Confucius. The character* sheng *in* Shengdan *is not the* sheng *in* shengren, *but is the* sheng *in the word* shensheng, *which means Holy, Godly, or Divine. The* sheng *in the word* shengren *means sages or saints, who are persons of noble virtues and high prestige. [Chinese] Christians also revere Confucius as a sage, and have the greatest esteem for this great Chinese sage. However, he is a man, not God. He is a sage, but not the Holy Divinity. Jesus Christ differs categorically. He was given birth by the virgin Mary whom the Holy Spirit conceived. Jesus Christ is the incarnation of the Word (Dao), the Son in the triune Persons of God. Although He was a person when he was in the world, He was also God. Therefore, His birthday is and should be called* Shengdan, *the Holy Birth.*

This article may look tedious, but is indicative that assuring the authenticity of both their Chinese identity and their Christian identity is important for these Chinese Christians. For them, calling Confucius a sage, rather than a god, is a restoration of Confucianism to its primary form. Confucius never claimed himself a god, or even a sage. Worshiping Confucius as a god is thus against Confucius himself. The feudal dynasties made Confucius a god for the purpose of social control. Chinese Christians call for going back to the original Confucianism and getting rid of the corrupted practices developed in dynastic times. They assert that only with this restoration can Confucianism be revived in the modern world.

Second, in their attempts to integrate Confucianism and Christianity, these Chinese Christians have simultaneously tried to differentiate primitive or essential Christianity from Western theologies. Western theologies have adopted Greek and Roman philosophies to understand and explain Christian notions. However, the Greek and Roman philosophies are only certain means to approach God and the gospel, not the essence of Christianity. Those theologies have helped Western Christians to understand God; they may be helpful for Chinese Christians; but they are not necessarily essential to the Christian faith. Chinese traditional philosophies are very different from Greek and Roman philosophies. These Chinese Christians hope that Chinese theologians will adopt thoughts of Chinese sages to develop a Christian theology so that Chinese people can easily accept Christian beliefs. In their view, an indigenous Chinese Christian theology should be rooted both in continuity with the historical church and in Chinese culture. They argue that the original Hellenic philosophies are not Christian but pre-Christ.

If Westerners could successfully integrate Greek and Roman philosophies with their Christian faith, the Chinese may do something similar by integrating Chinese philosophies with Christianity. A Chinese Christian thinker, who was a popular speaker at the CCC and other Chinese churches, proposed that Chinese theologians should pay more attention to the Chinese philosophical category of "relation" than the Western philosophical categories of "substance and attribute," pay more attention to the Chinese conviction of the goodness of human nature, and talk less about predestination and eschatology. When such a Chinese theology is established, it will be quite different from existing Christian theologies.

Traditional Chinese Heterodoxies: Daoism and Buddhism

Although Confucianism was the orthodoxy in China, Daoism (Taoism) and Buddhism had pervasive influences among the populace. As two major heterodoxies, Daoism and Buddhism complemented Confucianism and made lasting imprints in Chinese culture. Therefore, Chinese Christians must deal with them and take positions.

Appreciating Philosophical Daoism While Rejecting Religious Daoism

Daoism is a Chinese indigenous tradition with roots in ancient Chinese classics. Whereas philosophical Daoism emphasizes knowing or comprehending the Dao and reaching the Dao through inaction (*wu wei*) and spontaneity (*zi ran*), religious Daoism has a system of gods and spirits, religious rituals and symbols, and monasticism. For Chinese Christians the distinction between philosophical Daoism and religious Daoism is important. Generally speaking, Chinese evangelical Christians reject religious Daoism but selectively accept some notions of Daoist philosophy. They regard the Daoist rituals, spirits, and monastic system as superstitious and wrong, although they appreciate some life wisdom in *Dao De Jing (Tao Te Ching)* and other Daoist classics. A Chinese pastor stated the Christian position clearly:

> *I accept Daoism like I accept Confucianism. I respect Laozi as the founder of Daoism, although I disagree with Daoist religionists who made Laozi the god* Taishang Laojun.

The main link between Daoism and Christianity is the word *Dao*. In *Dao De Jing*, Dao is a mystic force. Many philosophers and religionists have tried to understand and interpret the meaning of this mystic Dao, which seems to be very close to the notion of Logos in Greek philosophy. Interestingly, the word *Logos* also appears in the beginning of the gospel of John in the New Testament. The English Bible translates *Logos* as 'Word,' whereas the most commonly used Chinese Bible translates *Logos* as 'Dao.' Therefore, the first verse of the gospel of John in Chinese reads like this:

In the beginning was the Dao, and the Dao was with God, and the Dao was God.
(Tai chu you Dao. Dao yu Shen tong zai. Dao jiu shi Shen).

To Chinese people who are familiar with *Dao De Jing*, reading these biblical verses can be enlightening. They seem to directly address the important question of Dao and to provide a clear interpretation of the mystic Dao. In light of the Christian scriptures, the Dao is a person of the Triune God. This Dao is God, who later was incarnated as Jesus Christ. The Chinese translation of *incarnation* is "the Dao took up the body of flesh" (*dao cheng rou shen*).

Rev. Moses Chow, the first pastor of the CCC, tells the story of how his Daoist father became Christian (1995, 8–12). After his clandestine conversion to Christianity, Moses brought home a copy of the gospel of John in Chinese, hoping his father, a fervent Daoist follower, would read it. At first his father angrily tossed the book aside because it was a book of a *foreign* religion. Later, when he was alone, he opened the book out of curiosity. Young Moses, hiding from his father's sight, watched closely his father's reactions. Upon reading the first verses, his father murmured, "Why, this book talks about *Taoism*!" "The Holy Spirit began to enlighten his heart as he read on," Chow reported. "I hardly dared breathe while watching father read through the gospel of John at one sitting" (1995, 9–10). Then, the senior Chow called Moses and asked to be taken immediately to the pastor. His father had a long conversation with the Chinese pastor. Chow reported that for the next few months after his father read the gospel of John, "he spent every waking hour intensely studying the Word [Dao] of God" (1995, 10). This was followed by the conversion of the whole family. Not surprisingly, Rev. Moses Chow continues to speak positively about the affinity between Daoism and Christianity.

The Dao as a link to the Christian gospel makes a reinterpretation of *Dao De Jing* possible. Yuan Zhiming, a popular speaker at the CCC and many other Chinese churches, has developed a systematic reinterpretation of *Dao De Jing* in light of Christianity. The manuscript, entitled *The Light of God (Shen Guang)*, was circulated among CCC members before its formal publicatron.[5] To Yuan Zhiming, a Christian convert, God is a universal God of all humankind, and the Dao (Word or Way) of God is the universal Dao. In his book, Yuan comes to the conclusion that more than twenty-six hundred years ago, when God prophesied the coming of Jesus Christ through the prophet Isaiah, God also shed light to ancient China through Laozi. Before the gospel came to China in more recent times, the Dao in *Dao De Jing* had been a myth puzzling generations of people. It was like a gorgeous cloud in the sky. Watching from below, many people have sensed the great superhuman wisdom in it, but they could not see the light above the cloud. The light was from God, Yuan asserts. It has always been there, but people could not see it; therefore, they could not understand Laozi in his own terms. Now with the light of God we can finally understand Laozi.

According to Yuan, Laozi prophesied the Dao of God. The Dao in Laozi is the same as the Dao (Word) in the Bible. Through interpreting various verses in the book, Yuan argues that *Dao De Jing* clearly articulates that the Dao is God, is Who He Is (YHWH), is infinity, eternity, the creator, the transcendent, revelator, and savior. *Dao De Jing* also reveals that the Dao would be incarnated as a *Shengren* (sage), who would be a prophet, a priest, a king, and a savior. Because God's revelation to Laozi was only a "general revelation" (*yiban qishi*), *Dao De Jing* could not prophesy the incarnation of Dao as clearly as Isaiah in the Old Testament, for only Isaiah received God's direct and specific revelation (*zhijie tebie qishi*) at about the same time of Laozi. *Dao De Jing* is not a part of the Holy Scripture. However, reading *Dao De Jing* would help Chinese people to understand God and Christ. Simply put, the Dao of God is not alien to Chinese culture.

This reinterpretation of *Dao De Jing* by Yuan Zhiming is a novel one. It will stimulate debates both among Chinese Christians and among non-Christian scholars of Daoism. Reactions from CCC members during my field work there were positive and accepting, although Yuan has also been challenged at various Chinese Christian meetings. If his reinterpretation can be accepted, this may mark a new era in the development of Chinese Christian theology.

Rejecting Buddhism without Reservation

Buddhism came to China about two thousand years ago. Chinese Christians acknowledge the great impact of Buddhism on Chinese culture and the continuous influence of Buddhism among Chinese people. However, they generally reject Buddhism without reservation. An article in *Living Water* in 1986 listed and articulated ten irreconcilable contrasts between Buddhism and Christianity:

(1) Buddhists worship many gods, whereas Christians worship the "One True God."

(2) Buddhists believe the world is meaningless and has no purpose, whereas Christians believe the world was created by God and it has God's wonderful purpose.

(3) Buddhists hold pessimistic and negative views of life, regard life as sufferings, whereas Christians hold optimistic and positive views of life, regard life as serving the family, the society, the country and the world [note the Confucian tone!] and to glorify God.

(4) Buddhists want to withdraw and escape from the world, whereas Christians affirm and engage in the world.

(5) Buddhists believe in fatalism—causes in the previous life have consequences in this life, whereas Christians seek God's will that can change our fate.

(6) Buddhists regard every and any being as equal, the soul transmigrates [through the forms of god, spirit, human, animal, ghost, and devil] according to cause-consequence

retribution, whereas Christians regard man as the best of all beings who is created in the image of God.

(7) Buddhists advise people to do good for the purpose of escaping from the cause-consequence retribution, whereas Christians advise people to do good for the purpose of breaking away from evil by knowing God.

(8) Buddhists cultivate themselves by relying on their own virtuous work, whereas Christians regard man as unreliable. Just as a strong man cannot lift himself up, every person has to rely on God for salvation.

(9) Buddhists are vegetarians because they fear killing animals may cause retribution in the coming life, whereas Christians eat food to keep health.

(10) Buddhists cultivate themselves for the purpose of entering nirvana, whereas Christians believe in the Lord for the purpose of achieving eternal life. Buddhists cannot explain what nirvana is, which may simply mean nonbeing; whereas Christians have a clear explanation about life after death—eternal life and resurrection.

The writer of this article was not a trained theologian, but a lay believer whose profession was hydraulic engineering. His views on Buddhism are commonly shared by CCC members and other Chinese evangelical Christians. These Chinese Christians feel uncompromising competition with Buddhism. Some church members are adult converts from Buddhist backgrounds. They consistently criticize Buddhist beliefs and practices and try to persuade Chinese people to give up Buddhism for Christianity. In fact, some members even helped to convert a Buddhist abbot. In 1989 six or seven CCC members visited a Chan (Zen) Buddhist Center in the Greater Washington area. A person who had both Christian relatives and Buddhist relatives initiated and arranged this visit. The head monk of the Chan center and several Buddhist nuns welcomed these Christian visitors with a sumptuous vegetarian dinner. At the table they freely exchanged views about life and religion. The monk gave the guests some volumes of Buddhist Sutras and expressed a hope for more conversation in the future. As a reciprocal courtesy the guests later mailed the abbot some books on philosophy, Christianity, and Buddhism written by Christian scholars. Several months later this Buddhist head monk cast off his monastery *jiasha* and was baptized at a Christian church. He gave several testimonies at fellowship group meetings and a Sunday worship service at the CCC before moving to California. This event encouraged many CCC members to further evangelize Chinese Buddhists. Doubtless, the competition with Buddhist religion will continue.

Reflection: Types of "Chinese" Christians

To affirm their Chinese identity, CCC members have been making choices in their inherited Chinese cultural traditions. Overall, they consistently preserve Confucian moral values, selectively accept some Daoist notions, and categorically reject Buddhism. However, this general summary is not applicable to all individuals. First of all, many people change their attitudes toward traditional culture over time. A common pattern for Chinese converts is to at first distance themselves from Chinese cultural traditions as much as possible, and then gradually return to some traditions. Immediately following their conversion, their Christian identity takes priority. Anything that may jeopardize their newly achieved Christian identity is cast off. After they achieve a sense of security in their Christian identity, Chinese cultural traditions become less of a threat to their faith. Then they may look to the traditions for cultural values and religious inspiration. Secondly, Chinese cultural traditions are diverse. Depending on circumstances and personal choices, a Chinese Christian may inherit some Confucianism or some Daoism or some Buddhism or a mixture of elements from all three. I have been able to distinguish three types of "Chinese" Christians.

Most CCC members accept Confucianism, or Confucian moral values. Normally these "Confucian" Christians are conservative in theology, traditionalist in ethics, reserved in behavior, and rationalistic in beliefs. They emphasize family life, moral education of children, and successes in the world. Their religious life is very much family-centered or community-oriented. However, they would object to being called "Confucian" Christians for two reasons. First, Confucianism for them simply means "Chinese." They often refer to certain values as "Chinese" rather than "Confucian." An important reason for this is that the term *Confucianism* is a misnomer coined by Westerners. The Chinese term for Confucianism is the "scholarly tradition" (*rujia*), which is synonymous with Chinese culture. Second, they do not intend to preserve Confucianism per se. Their preservation is selective: preserving Confucian moral values while rejecting Confucian agnosticism. They also reject the ritualistic and state-sanctified version of Confucianism, such as worshiping Confucius and emphasizing imperial loyalty.

Some Chinese Christians at the CCC explicitly accept or appreciate some notions of Daoism. These "Daoist" Christians tend to place emphasis on spiritual cultivation through devotional prayers, direct relationship with God, and personal salvation through grace. Compared with "Confucian" Christians, these people are more pietistic than ethicistic, more individualistic than collectivistic, and more experientialistic than rationalistic. Some may have charismatic tendencies and like to be filled by the Holy Spirit, speak in tongues, conduct spiritual healing, and practice exorcism. "Daoist" Christians are few, less than ten percent at the most. In the Washington area, two of the twenty Chinese churches are obviously charismatic; their members might have more Daoist tendencies.

Buddhism is generally rejected by Chinese evangelical Christians. However, for some converts from Buddhist backgrounds, some habits of the heart may continue to affect their Christian practices. Some "Buddhist" Christians are very otherworldly oriented and like to proclaim the "void" of the world and worldly life. Furthermore, the habits of the heart with Buddhist traditions may have two different manifestations. Chan (Zen) Buddhism emphasizes enlightenment through one's own efforts; Pure Land Buddhism believes in "salvation" through the "other-power" and religious work (*gongde*, including religious observances and moral behaviors). Chan Buddhists prefer simplicity, whereas Pure Land Buddhists like elaborate rituals. At the CCC, very few members like elaborate rituals and observances. One may find more of this type of Christian in Chinese Catholic churches. Meanwhile, I have not seen any Chan-like Christians at the CCC who would favor simple methods (*fangbian famen*) and self-nourished enlightenment. However, some may exist outside the church. For example, since the late 1980s some Chinese intellectuals in China have been called "cultural Christians" (*wenhua jidutu*). These people are scholars of Christian studies who may not join any church or participate in Christian rituals. Nonetheless they accept some Christian notions and beliefs. Some unchurched Chinese in the United States who nevertheless claim the Christian faith may be of this type as well. Overall, "Buddhist" Christians are very few, if any, in the evangelical Chinese churches.

The construction of Chinese identity is a complex process for Chinese immigrants in the United States because of the long history of Chinese civilization and its diverse cultural traditions, because of modern conflicts and divisions in Chinese society, and because of their migrating away from China. This is simultaneously a process of deconstruction and reconstruction.

Notes

1. Bernard Wong provides brief illustrations of festivities in New York Chinatowns (1982, 88–90).

2. It is inaccurate to call the traditional Chinese calendar system a lunar system and the Chinese New Year a Lunar New Year.

3. Francis L. K. Hsu described Qingming activities among the Chinese in Hawaii: "In front of graves both new and old are clusters of Chinese men, women, and children paying homage and making offerings to their dead. The offerings may be slim or abundant, including pigs and chickens roasted whole or simply sliced meats and plates of fruit. But cups of alcohol are poured on the ground in front of the tombs, bundles of burning incense placed before them, and large or small quantities of specially made paper money and papier-mâché life-like figures are burned for the benefit of the dead. The entire assemblage kneels down in twos and threes to kowtow to the dead. There are always offerings of flowers. And finally, in front of many of the tombs, a large string of firecrackers is exploded" (1971, 60). In contrast, these traditional Chinese rituals were not seen in a Chinese Christian cemetery in Hawaii: "Instead there is more of the usual type of observance common among white Christian Americans such as flowers and silent prayers on Easter, Memorial Day, Christmas, birthdays of the dead, Father's Day, Mother's Day, and so on" (1971, 63).

4. "Respect gods and spirits, but keep a distance from them" (*jing guishen er yuan zhi*) is a commonly quoted saying of Confucius.

5. Yuan's book was later published in Taiwan in 1997, entitled *Laozi vs. The Bible: A Meeting Across Time and Space*.

References

Ching, Julia. 1993. *Chinese Religions*. Maryknoll, NY: Orbis Books.

Chow, Moses C. (with Liona Choy). 1995. *Let My People Go!: Autobiography*. Paradise, PA: Ambassadors for Christ, Inc.

Constable, Nicole. 1994. *Christian Souls and Chinese Spirits: A Hakka Community in Hong Kong*. Berkeley and Los Angeles: University of California Press.

Herberg, Will. 1960. *Protestant-Catholic-Jew: An Essay in American Religious Sociology* (2nd ed.). Garden City, NY: Doubleday & Co.

Hsu, Francis L.K. 1971. *The Challenge of the American Dream: The Chinese in the United States*. Belmont, CA: Wadsworth.

Ng, David (ed.). 1996. *People on the Way: Asian North Americans Discovering Christ, Culture, and Community*. Valley Forge, PA: Judson Press.

Watson, James L., and Evelyn S. Rawski (eds.). 1988. *Death Ritual in Late Imperial and Modern China*. Berkeley and Los Angeles: University of California Press.

5. The Kitchen God's Wife

AMY TAN

As I turn down Ross Alley, everything around me immediately becomes muted in tone. It is no longer the glaring afternoon sun and noisy Chinatown sidewalks filled with people doing their Saturday grocery shopping. The alley sounds are softer, quickly absorbed, and the light is hazy, almost greenish in cast.

On the right-hand side of the street is the same old barbershop, run by Al Fook, who I notice still uses electric clippers to shear his customers' sideburns. Across the street are the same trade and family associations, including a place that will send ancestor memorials back to China for a fee. And farther down the street is the shopfront of a fortune-teller. A hand-written sign taped to the window claims to have "the best lucky numbers, the best fortune advice," but the sign taped to the door says: "Out of Business."

As I walk past the door, a yellow pull-shade rustles. And suddenly a little girl appears, her hands pressed to the glass. She stares at me with a somber expression. I wave, but she does not wave back. She looks at me as if I don't belong here, which is how I feel.

And now I'm at Sam Fook Trading Company, a few doors down from the flower shop. It contains shelves full of good-luck charms and porcelain and wooden statues of lucky gods, hundreds of them. I've called this place the Shop of the Gods ever since I can remember. It also sells the kind of stuff people get for Buddhist funerals—spirit money, paper jewelry, incense, and the like.

"Hey, Pearl!" It's Mr. Hong, the owner, waving me to come in. When I first met him, I thought his name was Sam Fook, like the shop. I found out later that *sam fook* means "triple blessing" in old Cantonese, and according to my mother—or rather, her Hong Kong customers—*sam fook* sounds like a joke, like saying "the Three Stooges."

"I told him he should change the name," my mother had said. "Luckier that way. But he says he has too much business already."

"Hey, Pearl," Mr. Hong says when I walk in the door, "I got some things for your mother here, for the funeral tomorrow. You take it to her, okay?"

"Okay." He hands me a soft bundle.

I guess this means Grand Auntie's funeral will be Buddhist. Although she attended the First Chinese Baptist Church for a number of years, both she and my mother stopped going right after my father died. In any case, I don't think Grand Auntie ever gave up her other beliefs, which weren't exactly Buddhist, just all the superstitious rituals concerning attracting good luck and avoiding bad. On those occasions when I did go up to her apartment, I used to play with her altar, a miniature red temple containing a framed picture of a Chinese god. In front of that was an imitation-brass urn filled with burnt incense sticks, and on the side were offerings of oranges, Lucky Strike cigarettes, and an airline mini-bottle of Johnnie Walker Red whiskey. It was like a Chinese version of a Christmas crèche.

And now I come to the flower shop itself. It is the bottom floor of a three-story brick building. The shop is about the size of a one-car garage and looks both sad and familiar. The front has a chipped red-bordered door covered with rusted burglarproof mesh. A plate-glass window says "Ding Ho Flower Shop" in English and Chinese. But it's easy to miss, because the place sits back slightly and always looks dark and closed, as it does today.

So the location my mother and Auntie Helen picked isn't exactly bustling. Yet they seem to have done all right. In a way, it's remarkable. After all these years, they've done almost nothing to keep up with the times or make the place more attractive. I open the door and bells jangle. I'm instantly engulfed in the pungent smell of gardenias, a scent I've always associated with funeral parlors. The place is dimly lit, with only one fluorescent tube hanging over the cash register—and that's where my mother is, standing on a small footstool so she can see out over the counter, with dime-store reading glasses perched on her nose.

She is talking on the telephone in rapid Chinese and waves impatiently for me to come in and wait. Her hair is pulled straight back into a bun, not a strand ever out of place. The bun today has been made to look thicker with the addition of a false swatch of hair, a "horse's tail," she calls it, for wearing only on important occasions.

Actually, now I can tell—by the shrillness of her pitch and the predominance of negative "vuh-vuh-vuh" sounds—that she's arguing in Shanghainese, and not just plain Mandarin. This is serious. Most likely it's with a neighborhood supplier, to judge from the way she's punching in numbers on a portable calculator, then reading aloud the printed results in harsh tones, as if they were penal codes. She pushes the "No Sale" button on the cash register, and when the drawer pops forward, she pulls out a folded receipt, snaps it open with a jerk of her wrist, then reads numbers from that as well.

"Vuh! Vuh! Vuh!" she insists.

The cash register is used to store only odds and ends, or what my mother calls "ends and odds and evens." The register is broken. When my mother and Auntie Helen first bought the store and its fixtures, they found out soon enough that anytime the sales transaction added up to anything with a 9 in it, the whole register froze up. But they decided to keep the cash register anyway, "for stick-'em-up," is how my mother explained it to me. If they were ever robbed, which has yet to happen, the robber would get only four dollars and a pile of pennies, all the money that is kept in the till. The real money is stashed underneath the counter, in a teapot with a spout that's been twice broken and glued back on. And the kettle sits on a hot plate that's missing a plug. I guess the idea is that no one would ever rob the store for a cup of cold tea.

I once told my mother and Auntie Helen that a robber would never believe that the shop had only four dollars to its name. I thought they should put at least twenty in the cash register to make the ruse seem more plausible. But my mother thought twenty dollars was too much to give a robber. And Auntie Helen said she would "worry sick" about losing that much money—so what good would the trick be then?

At the time, I considered giving them the twenty dollars myself to prove my point. But then I thought, What's the point? And as I look around the shop now, I realize maybe they were right. Who would ever consider robbing this place for more than getaway bus fare? No, this place is burglarproof just the way it is.

The shop has the same dull gray concrete floor of twenty-five years ago, now polished shiny with wear. The counter is covered with the same contact paper, green-and-white bamboo lattice on the sides and wood grain on the top. Even the phone my mother is using is the same old black model with a rotary dial and a fabric cord that doesn't coil or stretch. And over the years, the lime-colored walls have become faded and splotched, then cracked from the '89 earthquake. So now the place has the look of spidery decay and leaf mold.

"*Hau, hau,*" I now hear my mother saying. She seems to have reached some sort of agreement with the supplier. Finally she bangs the phone down. Although we have not seen each other since Christmas, almost a month ago, we do none of the casual hugs and kisses Phil and I exchange when we see his parents and friends. Instead, my mother walks out from around the counter, muttering, "Can you imagine? That man is cheating me! Tried to charge me for extra-rush delivery." She points to a box containing supplies of wire, clear cellophane, and sheets of green wax paper. "This is not my fault he forgot to come last week."

"How much extra?" I ask.

"Three dollars!" she exclaims. I never cease to be amazed by the amount of emotional turmoil my mother will go through for a few dollars.

"Why don't you just forget it? It's only three dollars—"

"I'm not concerned about money!" she fumes. "He's cheating me. This is not right. Last month, he tried to add another kind of extra charge too." I can tell she's about to launch into a blow-by-blow of last month's fight, when two well-dressed women with blond hair peer through the door.

"Are you open? Do any of you speak English?" one of them says in a Texas drawl.

My mother's face instantly cheers, and she nods, waving them in. "Come, come," she calls.

"Oh, we don't want to bother y'all," one of the ladies says. "If you might could just tell us where the fortune cookie factory is?"

Before I can answer, my mother tightens her face, shakes her head, and says, "Don't understand. Don't speak English."

"Why did you say that?" I ask when the two ladies retreat back into the alley. "I didn't know you hated tourists that much."

"Not tourists," she says. "That woman with the cookie factory, once she was mean to me. Why should I send her any good business?"

"How's business here?" I say, trying to steer the conversation away from what will surely become a tirade about the cookie woman down the street.

"Awful!" she says, and points to her inventory around the shop. "So busy—busy myself to death with this much business. You look, only this morning I had to make all these myself."

And I look. There are no modern arrangements of bent twigs or baskets of exotica with Latinate-drooping names. My mother opens the glass door to a refrigerator unit that once housed bottles of soda pop and beer.

"You see?" she says, and shows me a shelf with boutonnieres and corsages made out of carnations, neatly lined in rows according to color: white, pink, and red. No doubt we'll have to wear some of these tonight.

"And this," she continues. The second shelf is chock-full of milk-glass vases, each containing only a single rosebud, a fern frond, and a meager sprinkling of baby's breath. This is the type of floral arrangement you give to hospital patients who go in for exploratory surgery, when you don't know yet whether the person will be there for very long. My father received a lot of those when he first went into the hospital and later right before he died. "Very popular," my mother says.

"This, too, I had to make," she says, and points to the bottom shelf, which holds half a dozen small table sprays. "Some for tonight. Some for a retirement dinner," my mother explains, and perhaps because I don't look sufficiently impressed, she adds, "For assistant manager at Wells Fargo."

She walks me around to view her handiwork in other parts of the shop. Lining the walls are large funeral wreaths, propped on easels. "Ah?" my mother says, waiting for my opinion. I've always found wreaths hideously sad, like decorative lifesavers thrown out too late.

"Very pretty," I say.

And now she steers me toward her real pride and joy. At the front of the shop, the only place that gets filtered daylight for a few hours a day, are her "long-lasting bargains," as she calls them—philodendrons, rubber plants, chicken-feet bushes, and miniature tangerine trees. These are festooned with red banners, congratulating this business or that for its new store opening.

My mother has always been very proud of those red banners. She doesn't write the typical congratulatory sayings, like "Good Luck" or "Prosperity and Long Life." All the sayings, written in gold Chinese characters, are of her own inspiration, her thoughts about life and death, luck and hope: "First-Class Life for Your First Baby," "Double-Happiness Wedding Triples Family Fortunes," "Money Smells Good in Your New Restaurant Business," "Health Returns Fast, Always Hoping."

My mother claims these banners are the reasons why Ding Ho Flower Shop has had success flowing through its door all these years. By success, I suppose she means that the same people over the last twenty-five years keep coming back. Only now it's less and less for shy brides and giddy grooms, and more and more for the sick, the old, and the dead.

She smiles mischievously, then tugs my elbow. "Now I show you the wreath I made for you."

I'm alarmed, and then I realize what she's talking about. She opens the door to the back of the shop. It's dark as a vault inside and I can't make out anything except the dense odor of funeral flowers. My mother is groping for the piece of string that snaps on the light. Finally the room is lit by the glare of a naked bulb that swings back and forth on a cord suspended from the high ceiling. And what I now see is horrifyingly beautiful—row after row of gleaming wreaths, all white gardenias and yellow chrysanthemums, red banners hanging down from their easels, looking like identically dressed heavenly attendants.

I am stunned by how much hard work this represents. I imagine my mother's small hands with their parchmentlike skin, furiously pulling out stray leaves, tucking in sharp ends of wire, inserting each flower into its proper place.

"This one." She points to a wreath in the middle of the first row. It looks the same as the others. "This one is yours. I wrote the wishes myself."

"What does it say?" I ask.

Her finger moves slowly down the red banner, as she reads in a formal Chinese I can't understand. And then she translates: "Farewell, Grand Auntie, heaven is lucky. From your favorite niece, Pearl Louie Brandt, and husband."

"Oh, I almost forgot." I hand her the bundle from Sam Fook's. "Mr. Hong said to give you this."

My mother snips the ribbon and opens the package. Inside are a dozen or so bundles of spirit money, money Grand Auntie can supposedly use to bribe her way along to Chinese heaven.

"I didn't know you believed in that stuff," I say.

"What's to believe," my mother says testily. "This is respect." And then she says softly, "I got one hundred million dollars. Ai! She was a good lady."

"Here we go," I say, and take a deep breath as we climb the stairs to the banquet room.

"Pearl! Phil! There you are." It's my cousin Mary. I haven't seen her in the two years since she and Doug moved to Los Angeles. We wait for Mary to move her way through the banquet crowd. She rushes toward us and gives me a kiss, then rubs my cheek and laughs over the extra blush she's added.

"You look terrific!" she tells me, and then she looks at Phil. "Really, both of you. Just sensational."

Mary must now be forty-one, about half a year older than I am. She's wearing heavy makeup and false eyelashes, and her hair is a confusing mass of curls and mousse. A silver-fox stole keeps slipping off her shoulders. As she pushes it up for the third time, she laughs and says, "Doug gave me this old thing for Christmas, what a bother." I wonder why she does bother, now that we're inside the restaurant. But that's Mary, the oldest child of the two families, so it's always seemed important to her to look the most successful.

"Jennifer and Michael," she calls, and snaps her fingers. "Come here and say hello to your auntie and uncle." She pulls her two teenage children over to her side, and gives them each a squeeze. "Come on, what do you say?" They stare at us with sullen faces, and each of them grunts and gives a small nod.

Jennifer has grown plump, while her eyes, lined in black, look small and hard. The top part of her hair is teased up in pointy spikes, with the rest falling limply down to the middle of her back. She looks as if she had been electrocuted. And Michael's face— it's starting to push out into sharp angles and his chin is covered with pimples. They're no longer cute, and I wonder if this will happen to Tessa and Cleo, if I will think this about them as well.

"You see how they are," Mary says apologetically. "Jennifer just got her first nylons and high heels for Christmas. She's so proud, no longer Mommy's little girl."

"Oh, Mother!" Jennifer wails, then struggles away from her mother's grasp and disappears into the crowd. Michael follows her.

"See how Michael's almost as tall as Doug?" Mary says, proudly watching her son as he ambles away. "He's on the junior varsity track team, and his coach says he's their best runner. I don't know where he got his height or his athletic ability—certainly not from me. Whenever I go for a jog, I come back a cripple," Mary says, laughing. And then, realizing what she's just said, she suddenly drops her smile, and searches the crowd: "Oh, there's Doug's parents. I better go say hello."

Phil squeezes my hand, and even though we say nothing, he knows I'm mad. "Just forget it," he says.

"I would," I shoot back, "if she could. She *always* does this."

When Phil and I married, it was Mary and Doug who were our matron of honor and best man, since they had introduced us. They were the first people we confided in when we found out I was pregnant with Tessa. And about seven years ago, Mary was the one who pushed me into aerobics when I complained I felt tired all the time. And later, when I had what seemed like a strange weakness in my right leg, Phil suggested I see Doug, who at the time was an orthopedist at a sports medicine clinic.

Months later, Doug told me the problem seemed to be something else, and right away I panicked and thought he meant bone cancer. He assured me he just meant he wasn't smart enough to figure it out himself. So he sent me to see his old college drinking buddy, the best neurologist at San Francisco Medical Center. After what seemed like a year of tests—after I persuaded myself the fatigue was caused by smoking and the weakness in my leg was sciatica left over from my pregnancy—the drinking buddy told me I had multiple sclerosis.

Mary had cried hysterically, then tried to console me, which made it all seem worse. For a while, she dropped by with casserole dishes from "terrific recipes" she "just happened to find," until I told her to stop. And later, she made a big show of telling me how Doug's friend had assured her that my case was really "quite mild," as if she were talking about the weather, that my life expectancy was not changed, that at age seventy I could be swinging a golf club and still hitting par, although I would have to be careful not to stress myself either physically or emotionally.

"So really, everything's normal," she said a bit too cheerfully, "except that Phil has to treat you nicer. And what could be wrong with that?"

"I don't play golf," was all I told her.

"I'll teach you," she said cheerily.

Of course, Mary was only trying to be kind. I admit that it was more my fault that our friendship became strained. I never told her directly how much her gestures of sympathy offended me. So of course she couldn't have known that I did not need someone to comfort me. I did not want to be coddled by casseroles. Kindness was compensation. Kindness was a reminder that my life had changed, was always changing, that people thought I should just accept all this and become strong or brave, more enlightened, more peaceful. I wanted nothing to do with that. Instead, I wanted to live my life with the same focus as most people—to worry about my children's education, but not whether I would be around to see them graduate, to rejoice that I had lost five pounds, and not be fearful that my muscle mass was eroding away. I wanted what had become impossible: I wanted to forget.

I was furious that Doug and his drinking-buddy friend had discussed my medical condition with Mary. If they had told her that, then they must have also told her this: that with this disease, no prognosis could be made. I could be in remission for ten, twenty, thirty, or forty years. Or the disease could suddenly take off tomorrow and roll downhill, faster and faster, and at the bottom, I would be left sitting in a wheelchair, or worse.

I know Mary was aware of this, because I would often catch her looking at me from the corner of her eye whenever we passed someone who was disabled. One time she laughed nervously when she tried to park her car in a space that turned out to be a handicapped zone. "Oops!" she said, backing out fast. "We certainly don't need that."

In the beginning, Phil and I vowed to lead as normal a life together as possible. "As normal as possible"—it was like a meaningless chant. If I accidentally tripped over a toy left on the floor, I would spend ten minutes apologizing to Tessa for yelling at her, then another hour debating whether a "normal" person would have stumbled over the same thing. Once, when we went to the beach for the express purpose of forgetting about all of this, I was filled with morbid thoughts instead. I watched the waves eating away at the shore, and I wondered aloud to Phil whether I would one day be left as limp as seaweed, or stiff like a crab.

Meanwhile Phil would read his old textbooks and every medical article he could find on the subject. And then he would become depressed that his own medical training offered no better understanding of a disease that could be described only as "without known etiology," "extremely variable," "unpredictable," and "without specific treatment." He attended medical conferences on neurological disorders. He once took me to an MS support group, but we turned right around as soon as we saw the wheelchairs. He would perform what he called "weekly safety checks," testing my reflexes, monitoring the strength of my limbs. We even moved to a house with a swimming pool, so I could do daily muscle training. We did not mention to each other the fact that the house was one-story and had few steps and wide hallways that could someday be made wheelchair-accessible, if necessary.

We talked in code, as though we belonged to a secret cult, searching for a cure, or a pattern of symptoms we could watch for, some kind of salvation from constant worry. And eventually we learned not to talk about the future, either the grim possibilities or the vague hopes. We did not dwell on the past, whether it had been a virus or genetics that had caused this to happen. We concerned ourselves with the here and now, small victories over the mundane irritations of life—getting Tessa potty-trained, correcting a mistake on our charge-card bill, discovering why the car sputtered whenever we put it into third gear. Those became our constants, the things we could isolate and control in a life of unknown variables.

So I can't really blame Phil for pretending that everything is normal. I wanted that more than he did. And now I can't tell him what I really feel, what it's like. All I know is that I wake up each morning in a panic, terrified that something might have changed while I slept. And there are days when I become obsessed if I lose something, a button, thinking my life won't be normal until I find it again. There are days when I think Phil is the most inconsiderate man in the world, simply because he forgot to buy one item on the grocery list. There are days when I organize my underwear drawer by color, as if this might make some kind of difference. Those are the bad days.

On the good days, I remember that I am lucky—lucky by a new standard. In the last seven years, I have had only one major "flare-up," which now means I lose my balance easily, especially when I'm upset or in a hurry. But I can still walk. I still take out the garbage. And sometimes I actually *can* forget, for a few hours, or almost the entire day. Of course, the worst part is when I remember once again—often in unexpected ways—that I am living in a limbo land called remission.

That delicate balance always threatens to go out of kilter when I see my mother. Because that's when it hits me the hardest: I have this terrible disease and I've never told her.

I meant to tell her. There were several times when I planned to do exactly that. When I was first diagnosed, I said, "Ma, you know that slight problem with my leg I told you about. Well, thank God, it turned out not to be cancer, but—"

And right away, she told me about a customer of hers who had just died of cancer, how long he had suffered, how many wreaths the family had ordered. "Long time ago I saw that mole growing on his face," she said. "I told him, Go see a doctor. No problem, he said, age spot—didn't do anything about it. By the time he died, his nose and cheek—all eaten away!" And then she warned me sternly, "That's why you have to be careful."

When Cleo was born, without complications on my part or hers, I again started to tell my mother. But she interrupted me, this time to lament how my father was not there to see his grandchildren. And then she went into her usual endless monologue about my father getting a fate he didn't deserve.

My father had died of stomach cancer when I was fourteen. And for years, my mother would search in her mind for the causes, as if she could still undo the disaster by finding the reason why it had occurred in the first place.

"He was such a good man," my mother would lament. "So why did he die?" And sometimes she cited God's will as the reason, only she gave it a different twist. She said it must have been because my father was a minister. "He listened to everyone else's troubles," she said. "He swallowed them until he made himself sick. Ai! *Ying-gai* find him another job."

Ying-gai was what my mother always said when she meant, I should have. *Ying-gai* meant she should have altered the direction of fate, she should have prevented disaster. To me, *ying-gai* meant my mother lived a life of regrets that never faded with time.

If anything, the regrets grew as she searched for more reasons underlying my father's death. One time she cited her own version of environmental causes—that the electrician had been sick at the time he rewired our kitchen. "He built that sickness right into our house," she declared. "It's true. I just found out the electrician died—of cancer, too. *Ying-gai* pick somebody else."

And there was also this superstition, what I came to think of as her theory of the Nine Bad Fates. She said she had once heard that a person is destined to die if eight bad things happen. If you don't recognize the eight ahead of time and prevent them, the ninth one is always fatal. And then she would ruminate over what the eight bad things might have been, how she should have been sharp enough to detect them in time.

To this day it drives me crazy, listening to her various hypotheses, the way religion, medicine, and superstition all merge with her own beliefs. She puts no faith in other people's logic—to her, logic is a sneaky excuse for tragedies, mistakes, and accidents. And according to my mother, *nothing* is an accident. She's like a Chinese version of Freud, or worse. Everything has a reason. Everything could have been prevented. The last time I was at her house, for example, I knocked over a framed picture of my father and broke the glass. My mother picked up the shards and moaned, "Why did this happen?" I thought it was a rhetorical question at first, but then she said to me, "Do you know?"

"It was an accident," I said. "My elbow bumped into it." And of course, her question had sent my mind racing, wondering if my clumsiness was a symptom of deterioration.

"Why this picture?" she muttered to herself.

So I never told my mother. At first I didn't want to hear her theories on my illness, what caused this to happen, how she should have done this or that to prevent it. I did not want her to remind me.

And now that so much time has gone by, the fact that I still haven't told her makes the illness seem ten times worse. I am always reminded, whenever I see her, whenever I hear her voice.

Mary knows that, and that's why I still get mad at her—not because she trips over herself to avoid talking about my medical condition. I'm mad because she told *her* mother, my Auntie Helen.

"I had to tell her," she explained to me in an offhand sort of way. "She was always saying to me, Tell Pearl to visit her mother more often, only a one-hour drive. Tell Pearl she should ask her mother to move in with her, less lonely for her mother that way. Finally, I told my mother I couldn't tell you those things. And she asked why not." Mary shrugged. "You know my mother. I couldn't lie to her. Of course, I made her *swear* not to tell your mother, that you were going to tell her yourself."

"I can drive," I told Mary. "And that's not the reason why I haven't asked my mother to live with me." And then I glared at her. "How could you do this?"

"She won't say anything," Mary said. "I made her promise." And then she added a bit defiantly, "Besides, you should have told your mother a long time ago."

Mary and I didn't exactly have a fight, but things definitely chilled between us after that. She already knew that was about the worst possible thing she could have done to me. Because she had done it once before, nine years ago, when I confided to her that I was pregnant. My first pregnancy had ended in a miscarriage early on, and my mother had gone on and on about how much coffee I drank, how it was my jogging that did it, how Phil should make sure I ate more. So when I became pregnant again, I decided to wait, to tell my mother when I was in my fourth month or so. But in the third month, I made the mistake of confiding in Mary. And Mary slipped this news to her mother. And Auntie Helen didn't exactly tell my mother. But when my mother proudly announced my pregnancy to the Kwongs, Auntie Helen immediately showed my mother the little yellow sweater she had already hand-knit for the baby.

I didn't stop hearing the laments from my mother, even after Tessa was born. "Why could you tell the Kwongs, not your own mother?" she'd complain. When she stewed over it and became really angry, she accused me of making her look like a fool: "Hnh! Auntie

Helen was pretending to be so surprised, so innocent. 'Oh, I didn't knit the sweater for Pearl's baby,' she said, 'I made it just in case.'"

So far, Auntie Helen had kept the news about my medical condition to herself. But this didn't stop her from treating me like an invalid. When I used to go to her house, she would tell me to sit down right away, while she went to find me a pillow for my back. She would rub her palm up and down my arm, asking me how I was, telling me how she had always thought of me as a daughter. And then she would sigh and confess some bit of bad news, as if to balance out what she already knew about me.

"Your poor Uncle Henry, he almost got laid off last month," she would say. "So many budget cuts now. Who knows what's going to happen? Don't tell your mother. I don't want her to worry over us."

And then *I* would worry that Auntie Helen would think her little confessions were payment in kind, that she would take them as license to accidentally slip and tell my mother: "Oh, Winnie, I thought you knew about your daughter's tragedy."

And so I dreaded the day my mother would call and ask me a hundred different ways, "Why did Auntie Helen know? Why did you never tell me? Why didn't you let me prevent this from happening to you?"

And then what answer could I give?

Grand Auntie Du's Funeral

My mother left the house two hours ago with Auntie Helen so they could decorate the funeral parlor. And now Phil and I are going to be late for Grand Auntie's service, thanks to a spat between Tessa and Cleo that resulted in eggs over easy being flung onto Phil's only good shirt and tie. While we searched for replacements along Clement Street, Phil suggested that we shouldn't bring the girls to the funeral.

"They might be disruptive," he said. "And they might not appreciate seeing someone who is D-E-A-D."

Tessa grinned and said in a singsong voice, "Daddy's saying a naughty word."

"Maybe I could wait with them outside in the car," said Phil.

"They'll be fine," I assured him. "I already asked my mother if it's closed-casket and she said it is. And I've explained to the girls it's like that time we went to Steve and Joanne's wedding—grownup time. Isn't that right, girls?"

"We got cake after," said Cleo.

"All right," said Phil. "But after the service, let's make the usual excuses and go home."

"Of course."

At twenty minutes after two, the four of us walk into the reception area of the funeral parlor. My cousin Frank hands us black armbands to wear. As I put mine on, I feel somewhat guilty, this pretense of grief. I realize now that I knew almost nothing about Grand Auntie Du, except that she smelled like mothballs and was always trying to feed me old Chinese candies and sugared beef jerky, pulled out of dusty tins stored on top of her refrigerator.

Bao-bao is there to greet us as well. He's smiling broadly. "Hey, man, glad to see you guys finally decided to make it." He hands each of us a piece of foil-wrapped candy and a small red envelope of lucky money.

"What are we supposed to do with these?" Phil whispers. "Offer them to Grand Auntie Du?" He pulls out a quarter from the lucky-money envelope.

"How should I know?" I whisper back. "I've never been to a Buddhist funeral, or whatever this is."

"My mom says it's like insurance in case you pick up bad vibes here," says Bao-bao. "You eat the candy for luck. You can buy more luck later with the money."

"I'm gonna eat mine now," announces Tessa.

Cleo waves her candy for me to unwrap. "Mommy, me too, me too!"

Phil flips his quarter. "Say, if I buy chewing gum with this, will my luck last longer?"

We turn toward the main parlor. Suddenly we are blinded by the glare of a spotlight. I'm surprised to see Tessa is now walking down the aisle in the manner of a coquettish bride. And Cleo—she's preening and blowing kisses like a movie star. I can't believe it: Uncle Henry is standing in the middle of the aisle—videotaping the funeral! Who's going to watch this later?

Through the haze of the incense-blurred light, I can barely see my mother. She's gesturing for us to come sit with her in the second row. Phil corrals the girls. As the camera continues to roll, we walk quickly down the aisle, past what must be only a dozen or so mourners— Mary, Doug, and their children, some people from the church, all Chinese. I also see several old ladies I've never met before. They look like recent immigrants, to judge from their undyed cropped hair and old-style brown padded jackets.

As we slide into our seats, Auntie Helen turns around in the front row. She squeezes my hand, and I see she has tears in her eyes. My mother is dry-eyed. "Why so late?" she asks crossly. "I told them to wait until you came."

Suddenly Cleo starts laughing and points. "Daddy, there's a lady sleeping up there! And her dinner's on fire!" Tessa is staring too, only her eyes are big, her mouth dropped open.

And then I see it too—God!—Grand Auntie Du lying in her casket, with glasses perched on her emotionless waxy face. In front of the casket is a long, low table overflowing with food—what looks like a nine-course Chinese dinner, as well as an odd assortment of mangoes, oranges, and a carved watermelon. This must be Grand Auntie's farewell provisions for trudging off to heaven. The smoke of a dozen burning incense sticks overlaps and swirls up around the casket, her ethereal stairway to the next world.

Phil is staring at me, waiting for an explanation. "This has to be a mistake," I whisper to him, and then turn to my mother, trying to keep my voice calm. "I thought you decided on closed-casket," I say slowly.

She nods. "You like? Clothes, I chose for her, all new. Casket, I also helped decide this. Not the best wood, but almost the best. Before she is buried, we take the jewelry off, of course."

"But I thought you said the lid would be down."

My mother frowns. "I didn't say that. How can you see her that way?"

"But—"

"Do we have to eat here?" Tessa asks fearfully. She squirms down low in her seat. "I'm not hungry," she whispers. I squeeze her hand.

"Tell that lady to wake up," Cleo squeals, giggling. "Tell her she can't sleep at the dinner table. It's not nice!"

Tessa slaps Cleo's leg. "Shut up, Cleo, she's not sleeping. She's dead, like Bootie the cat."

And Cleo's bottom lip turns down, dangerously low. "Don't tell me that!" she shouts, and then pushes Tessa's shoulder. I am trying to think of what I can say to comfort the girls, but—too late—they are pushing each other, crying and shouting, "Stop it!" "You stop!" "You started it!" My mother is watching this, waiting to see how I will handle it. But I feel paralyzed, helpless, not knowing what to do.

Phil stands up to lead both of the girls out. "I'll get them some ice cream over on Columbus. I'll be back in an hour."

"Make it forty-five," I whisper. "No more than that. I'll meet you out front."

"Daddy, can I have a chocolate and a rocky road?" asks Cleo.

"And sprinkles on top?" adds Tessa.

I'm relieved to think this may be all the damage that will remain, a ruined appetite and sticky hands. Over on the other side of the pews, Mary's son, Michael, is snickering. As I throw him a scowl, I notice something else: Uncle Henry still has the videocamera going.

After Phil and the girls leave, I try to regain my composure. I look ahead to avoid glaring at my mother or Uncle Henry. No use arguing, I tell myself. What's done is done.

In front of the pews is a large picture of Grand Auntie. It looks like a blown-up version of a passport photo taken fifty years ago. She's not exactly young, but she must have had most of her teeth back then. I look at Grand Auntie in her casket. Her mouth looks caved in, her thin face like that of a wizened bird. She is so still, yet I feel we are all waiting for something to happen, for Grand Auntie suddenly to transform and manifest herself as a ghost.

It reminds me of a time when I was five years old, that age when anything was possible if you could just imagine it. I had stared at the flickering eyes of a carved pumpkin, waiting for goblins to fly out. The longer I waited, the more convinced I became that it would happen. To this day, I can still vividly remember the laughing ghost that finally poured out of the pumpkin's mouth. My mother had come rushing into the room when I screamed. I was babbling tearfully that I had seen a ghost. And instead of comforting me, or pooh-poohing that it was just my imagination, she had said, "Where?" and then searched the room.

Of course, my father later assured me that the only ghost was the Holy Ghost, and He would never try to scare me. And then he demonstrated in a scientific way that what I must have seen were smoky fumes created when the candle inside the pumpkin burned too low and extinguished itself. I was not comforted by his answer, because my mother had then stared at me, as if I had betrayed her and made her look like a fool. That's how things were. She was always trying to suppress certain beliefs that did not coincide with my father's Christian ones, but sometimes they popped out anyway.

"The *jiao-zi*, I made them," my mother is now telling me. "Grand Auntie always said I made the best-tasting." I nod and admire the steamed dumplings on the banquet table. She really does make the best ones, and I think it's a pity that these are just for show.

"Auntie Helen made the chicken and green peppers dish," she says, and after I nod, she adds, "Very dry-looking." And I nod again, wondering if Grand Auntie is appreciating this culinary postmortem in her honor. I scan the other dishes and see they have even added the cake left over from last night.

Above the casket, a white banner made out of ten feet of butcher paper is stuck to the wall with masking tape. The banner is covered with large black characters, and the whole thing ends with an exclamation point, just like political billboard slogans I once saw in magazine photos of China.

"What does that say?" I ask my mother quietly.

" 'Hope that your next life is long and prosperous.' Nothing too special," my mother replies. "I didn't write it. This is from people with the Kwong family association. Maybe Helen gave them a donation."

I see all the wreaths perched on their easels. I search for mine, and I'm about to ask my mother where it is, when Uncle Henry turns the spotlight on again and starts filming Grand Auntie Du, lying at center stage. He waves to someone at stage left.

The next moment, I hear hollow wooden knocking sounds, followed by a persistent *ding-ding-ding*, as if someone were impatiently ringing for the bellhop in a hotel lobby. These sounds are joined by two voices, chanting a tune that seems to consist of the same four notes and syllables. It repeats so many times I'm sure it's a record that has become stuck.

But now, emerging from the left alcove are two Buddhist monks with shaved heads, dressed in saffron-colored robes. The older, larger monk lights a long stick of incense, bows three times to the body, then places the incense in the burner and backs away, bowing again. The younger monk is sounding the wooden clapper. Then they both begin walking down the aisle slowly, chanting, "Ami-, Ami-, Amitaba, Amitaba." As the older monk passes by, I see one cheek is flattened, and the ear on the same side is badly misshapen.

"He must have been in a terrible car accident," I whisper to my mother.

"Cultural Revolution," she says.

The smaller monk, I can see now, is not a monk at all, but a woman, a nun with three or four small scabs on her skull.

"She must have been in the Cultural Revolution too," I tell my mother.

My mother looks. "Too young. Flea bites, maybe," she concludes.

"Amitaba, Amitaba," they drone. And now the old ladies in the old-style jackets begin moaning and wailing, waving their arms up and down, overcome with grief, it seems. Uncle Henry turns the camera toward them.

"Are they Grand Auntie's good friends?" I ask my mother.

She frowns. "Not friends, maybe Chinese people from Vietnam. They came early, later saw we didn't have too many people to mourn Grand Auntie. So they talked to Auntie Helen, she gave them a few dollars. And now they're doing the old custom, crying out loud and acting like they don't want the dead person to leave so fast. This is how you show respect."

I nod. Respect.

"Maybe these ladies can do two or three funerals every day," my mother adds, "earn a few dollars. Good living that way. Better than cleaning house."

"Um," I answer. I don't know if my mother has said this to be disdainful or simply to state a matter of fact.

The wooden clapper and the bell sound again, faster and faster. Suddenly the white paper banner tears away from the wall, and the family association wishes for lucky and long life spiral down and land draped across Grand Auntie's chest like a beauty pageant banner. My mother and several of the older women jump up and cry, "Ai-ya!" Mary's son shouts, "Perfect landing!" and laughs hysterically. The monk and nun continue chanting with no change of expression. But my mother is furious. "How bad!" she mutters. She gets up and walks out of the room.

In a few minutes, she comes back with a young Caucasian man with thinning blond hair. He is wearing a black suit, so he must be with the funeral parlor. I can tell my mother is still scolding him, as she points to the disaster-ridden banner. People are murmuring loudly throughout the room. The old ladies are still wailing and bowing stiffly; the monk and nun keep chanting.

The blond man walks quickly to the front, my mother follows. He bows three times to Grand Auntie Du, then moves her casket, which glides forward easily on wheels. After another bow, the man ceremoniously plucks the banner off Grand Auntie's chest and carries it in both arms as if it were holy vestments. As he tapes the banner back up, my mother is fuming, "That corner, put more tape there! More there, too. How can you let her luck fall down like that!"

Once he has finished, the man pushes the casket back in place and bows three times to the body, once to my mother, who huffs in return, then quickly retreats. Did he bow to show genuine respect, I wonder, or has he learned to do this only for his Chinese customers?

Now Frank is passing out lit sticks of incense to everyone. I look around, trying to figure out what to do. One by one, we each get up and join the monk and nun, everyone chanting, "Amitaba! Amitaba!"

We are circling the coffin 'round and 'round, I don't know how many times. I feel silly, taking part in a ritual that makes no sense to me. It reminds me of that time I went with some friends to the Zen center. I was the only Asian-looking person there. And I was also the only one who kept turning around, wondering impatiently when the monk would come and the sermon would begin, not realizing until I'd been there for twenty minutes that all the others weren't quietly waiting, they were meditating.

My mother is now bowing to Grand Auntie. She puts her incense in the burner, then murmurs softly, "Ai! Ai!" The others follow suit, some crying, the Vietnamese ladies wailing loudly. Now it is my turn to bow. And I feel guilty. It's the same guilt I've felt before—when my father baptized me and I did not believe I was saved forever, when I took Communion and did not believe the grape juice was the blood of Christ, when I prayed along with others that a miracle would cure my father, when I already felt he had died long before.

Suddenly a sob bursts from my chest and surprises everyone, even me. I panic and try to hold back, but everything collapses. My heart is breaking, bitter anger is pouring out and I can't stop it.

My mother's eyes are also wet. She smiles at me through her tears. And she knows this grief is not for Grand Auntie Du but for my father. Because she has been waiting for me to cry for such a long, long time, for more than twenty-five years, ever since the day of my father's funeral.

I was fourteen, full of anger and cynicism. My mother, brother, and I were sitting by ourselves in an alcove, a half-hour before the service was supposed to begin. And my mother was scolding me, because I refused to go up to the casket to see my father's body.

"Samuel said good-bye. Samuel is crying," she said.

I did not want to mourn the man in the casket, this sick person who had been thin and listless, who moaned and became helpless, who in the end searched constantly for my mother with fearful eyes. He was so unlike what my father had once been: charming and lively, strong, kind, always generous with his laughter, the one who knew exactly what to do when things went wrong. And in my father's eyes, I had been perfect, his "perfect Pearl," and not the irritation I always seemed to be with my mother.

My mother blew her nose. "What kind of daughter cannot cry for her own father?"

"That man in there is not my father," I said sullenly.

Right then my mother jumped up and slapped my face. "That bad!" she shouted. I was shocked. It was the first time she had ever struck me.

"Ai-ya! If you can't cry, I make you cry." And she slapped me again and again. "Cry! Cry!" she wailed crazily. But I sat there still as a stone.

Finally, realizing what she had done, my mother bit the back of her hand and mumbled something in Chinese. She took my brother by the hand, and they left me.

So there I sat, angry, of course, and also victorious, although over what, I didn't know. And perhaps because I didn't know, I found myself walking over to the casket. I was breathing hard, telling myself, I'm right, she's wrong. And I was so determined not to cry that I never considered I would feel anything whatsoever.

But then I saw him, colorless and thin. And he was not resting peacefully with God. His face was stern, as if still locked in his last moment of pain.

I took so many small breaths, trying to hold back, trying not to cry, that I began to hyperventilate. I ran out of the room, out into the fresh air, gasping and gulping. I ran down Columbus, toward the bay, ignoring the tourists who stared at my angry, tear-streaked face. And in the end, I missed the funeral.

In a way, this is how it's been with my mother and me ever since. We both won and we both lost, and I'm still not sure what our battle was. My mother speaks constantly of my father and his tragedy, although never of the funeral itself. And until this day, I have never cried in front of my mother or spoken of my feelings for my father.

Instead, I have tried to keep my own private memories of him—a certain smile, a coat he wore, the passion he exuded when he stood at the pulpit. But then I always end up realizing that what I am remembering are just images from photos. And in fact, what I do remember most vividly are those times when he was ill. "Pearl," he would call weakly from his bed, "do you want help with your homework?" And I would shake my head. "Pearl," he would call from the sofa, "come help me sit up." And I would pretend I didn't hear him.

Even to this day I have nightmares about my father. In my dreams, he is always hidden in a hospital, in one of a hundred rooms with a hundred cots filled with sick people. I am wandering down long hallways, looking for him. And to do so, I must look at every face, every illness, every possible horror that can happen to one's body and mind. And each time I see it is not my father, I shake with relief.

I have had many variations of this dream. In fact, I had one just recently. In this version, I have gone to the hospital for a checkup, to see if the multiple sclerosis has advanced. Without explanation, a doctor puts me in a ward with terminally ill patients. And I'm shouting, "You can't treat me this way! You have to explain!" I shout and shout and shout, but nobody comes.

And that's when I see him. He is sitting in front of me, on a dirty cot, in soiled bed-clothes. He is old and pathetically thin, his hair now white and patchy after years of wait-ing and neglect. I sit next to him and whisper, "Daddy?" He looks up with those helpless searching eyes. And when he sees me, he gives a small startled cry—then cries and cries, so happy!—so happy I have finally come to take him home.

Grand Auntie's memorial service is finally over. We are all standing outside and the bay wind has already started to blow, cutting through our thin jackets and causing skirts to whip up. My eyes are stinging and I feel completely drained.

My mother stands quietly next to me, peering at me every now and then. I know she wants to talk about what happened, not about all the disasters at the funeral, but why I cried.

"All right?" my mother asks gently.

"Fine," I say, and try to look as normal as possible. "Phil and the girls should be here any minute." My mother pulls a balled-up Kleenex from her sweater sleeve and hands it to me without a word, pointing to her own eye to indicate I've smudged my mascara.

Right then, Bao-bao comes up. "Boy, that was sure weird," he says. "But I guess that's the kind of funeral the old lady wanted. She always was a bit *you-know*," and he taps his finger twice to the side of his head.

My mother frowns. "What is *you-know*?"

Bao-bao grins sheepishly. "You know, uh, different, unusual—a *great* lady!" He looks at me and shrugs. And then relief springs to his face. "Whoa! There's Mimi with the car. Gotta run. You guys going to the cemetery?"

I shake my head. My mother looks at me, surprised.

Bao-bao walks over to a shiny black Camaro, and Mimi slides over so he can drive. "I don't got a choice. Mom roped me into being one of the pallbearers." He flexes his arm. "Good thing I've been pumping iron." He turns the radio way up and flexes his arm faster in rhythm with the vibrating music. "Well, nice seeing you again, Pearl. Catch you later, Auntie." The car rumbles off.

And now I hear Auntie Helen calling from behind. "Pearl! Pearl!" She waddles over, dabbing a tissue to her eyes at the same time. "You going to the cemetery? Nice buffet afterward, our house. Lots of good food. Your mother made the potstickers. I made a good chicken dish. Mary and Doug will be there. You come."

"We can't. Tomorrow's a work day, and it's a long drive."

"Oh, you kids," she says, and throws her hands up in mock frustration, "always too busy! Well, you come visit me soon. No invitation needed. You come, so we can talk."

"Okay," I lie.

"Winnie-ah!" Auntie Helen now calls loudly to my mother, even though they are standing only five feet apart. "You come with us to the cemetery. Henry is getting the car now."

"Pearl is taking me home," my mother answers, and I stand there, trying to figure out how she manages to catch me every time.

Auntie Helen walks up to my mother, a worried look on her face. She asks her quickly in Chinese: Not coming? Are you feeling sick?

I can't understand all the Mandarin words, only the gist of them. It seems my mother doesn't want anyone to worry, nothing is wrong, only a little discomfort here—and she points to her chest—because something-something has been bothering her. She mentions something-something about the banner falling down, and how her whole body has been aching ever since.

Auntie Helen rubs my mother's back. She tells my mother she can visit Auntie Du when something-something is more quiet, not running around all over the place. And then Auntie Helen laughs and tells my mother that Auntie Du will wait, of course she will wait for her visit, she has no choice. And my mother jokes back that maybe Auntie Du has already become mad-to-death about what happened today and has flown off to something-something place where she doesn't have to do something-something anymore with such a crazy family.

They are laughing hysterically now, laughing so hard that tears sprout from their eyes and they are barely able to catch their breath. My mother covers her mouth with her hand, giggling like a schoolgirl.

Uncle Henry drives the car up, and as Auntie Helen climbs in, she sternly reminds my mother to drink plenty of hot tea. They take off, beeping the horn twice.

"Aren't you feeling well?" I ask my mother.

"Ah?"

"You told Auntie Helen you couldn't go to the cemetery because you were sick."

"I didn't say sick. I only said I didn't want to go. I did my duty. I sent Auntie Du to heaven. Now it's Helen's duty to put her inside the ground."

That's not what they said. And although I'm not sure I understood most of their conversation, apparently there's a lot I don't know about my mother and Auntie Helen.

As we drive across town to my mother's house, Phil drops hints: "I hope we're on the freeway before the weekend rush hour to get back home."

My mother is making small talk. She tells me that Bao-bao may lose his job soon. This gossip she heard at the dinner from Uncle Loy, who heard it from his son. She tells me that Frank is now working the day shift as a security guard, but he is breaking Auntie Helen's heart, spending all his extra time and money at a pool hall on Geary Street.

As we get closer to her house, she points to a place on Clement Street, Happy Super, where she always does her grocery shopping. It's one of the typical Asian markets in the neighborhood, people standing outside, pinching and poking through piles of fruits and vegetables, hundred-pound bags of rice stacked like giant bricks against the window.

"Tofu, how much do you pay?" asks my mother, and I can tell she's eager to outdo me with a better price, to tell me how I can save twenty or thirty cents at her store.

But I can't even oblige her with a guess. "I don't know. I've never bought tofu."

"Oh." She looks disappointed. And then she brightens. "Four rolls of toilet paper, how much?"

"One sixty-nine," I answer right away.

"You see!" she says. "My place, only ninety-nine cents. Good brands, too. Next time, I buy you some. You can pay me back."

We turn left onto Eighth Avenue and head toward Anza. Auntie Helen and Uncle Henry live one block up, on Ninth. The houses in this area all look the same to me, variations of two-story row houses built in the twenties, differing mostly in what color they are painted and whether the front has been modernized in stucco, asbestos shingles, or aluminum siding. Phil pulls into my mother's driveway. The front of her place is Day-Glo pink, the unfortunate result of her being talked into a special deal by a longtime customer, a painting contractor. And because the outside is bumpy stucco, the whole effect looks like Pepto-Bismol poured over cottage cheese. Amazingly enough, of all the things my mother complains about, the color of the house is not one of them. She actually thinks it's pretty.

"When will I see you again?" she asks me as she climbs out of the car.

"Oh, soon," I say.

"Soon like Auntie Helen's soon?" she says.

"No, *soon*. Really."

She pauses, looking as if she doesn't believe me. "Oh, anyway, I will see you at Bao-bao's wedding next month."

"What? The wedding is next month? I didn't hear that."

"Very fast," my mother says, nodding. "Edna Fong from our church said she heard this from her daughter. Mimi washes her hair at that beauty shop. Mimi told Edna Fong's daughter they are in a big hurry to get married. And Edna Fong said to me, Maybe because something else is hurrying to come out. Auntie Helen doesn't know this yet. Don't tell her."

So there goes Auntie Helen's theory about Bao-bao's getting married because she's going to die soon. Something's growing all right, but it's not a tumor in Auntie Helen's head.

My mother climbs out of the car. She turns back and gives Tessa a cheek to kiss, then Cleo. My mother is not the cheek-kissing type, but she knows we have taught the girls to do this with Phil's parents.

"Bye-bye, Ha-bu!" they each say. "We love you."

"Next time you come," my mother says to the girls, "I make potstickers. And you can eat moon cakes for Chinese New Year's." She takes a tissue out of her sleeve and wipes Cleo's nose. She pats Tessa's knee. "Okay?"

"Okay!" they shout.

We all watch my mother walk up the steps to her front door, all of us waving the whole time. Once she's safe inside, we wave once more as she peers out the window, and then we take off.

"Whew!" Phil sighs. "Home." And I too sigh with relief. It's been a difficult weekend, but we survived.

"Mommy?" Tessa says at the first stop sign.

"Yes, sweetie."

"Mommy," she whispers. "I have to go to the bathroom."

"Me too," says Cleo. "I have to go oo-oo *real* bad."

My mother is standing outside the house when we return.

"I tried to chase you, but you were too fast," she says as soon as I get out of the car. "And then I knew you would remember and come back." Tessa and Cleo are already racing up the stairs.

"Remember what?"

"Grand Auntie's farewell gift. Remember? Two three days ago I told you not to forget. Yesterday I said, Don't forget. You forgot?"

"No, no," I say. "Where is it?"

"In back, in the laundry room," she says. "Very heavy, though. Better ask your husband to carry it." I can just imagine what it must be: the old vinyl ottoman Grand Auntie used to rest her feet on, or perhaps the set of chip-proof Melmac dishes. As we wait for Phil to come back with the girls, my mother hands me a cup of tea, waving off my protests. "Already made. If you can't drink it, I only have to throw it away."

I take a few quick sips. "This is really good." And I mean it. I have never tasted tea like this. It is smooth, pungent, and instantly addicting.

"This is from Grand Auntie," my mother explains. "A few years ago she bought it for herself. One hundred dollars a pound."

"You're kidding." I take another sip. It tastes even better.

"She told me, 'If I buy myself the cheap tea, then I am saying my whole life has not been worth something better.' So she decided to buy herself the best tea, so she could drink it and feel like a rich person inside."

I laugh.

My mother looks encouraged by my laughter. "But then she thought, If I buy just a little, then I am saying my lifetime is almost over. So she bought enough tea for another lifetime. Three pounds! Can you imagine?"

"That's three hundred dollars!" I exclaim. Grand Auntie was the most frugal person I knew. "Remember how she used to keep all the boxes of See's candies we gave her for Christmas, telling us they were too good to eat? And then one year, she gave a box back to us for Thanksgiving or something. Only it was so old—"

My mother was nodding, already laughing.

"—all the candies were white with mold!"

"Bugs, too!" my mother adds.

"So she left you the tea in her will?" I say.

"Already gave it to me a few months ago. She was thinking she was going to die soon. She didn't say, but she started to give things away, good things, not just junk. And one time we were visiting, drinking tea. I said, 'Ah, good tea!' same as always. This time, Grand Auntie went to her kitchen, brought back the tea. She told me, '*Syau ning*, you take this tea now.' That's what she called me, *syau ning*, 'little person,' from the old days when we first knew each other.

"I said, 'No, no! I wasn't saying this to hint.' And she said, '*Syau ning*, you take this now so I can see how happy you are to receive it while I am still alive. Some things can't wait until I'm dead.' How could I refuse? Of course, every time I came to visit, I brought back her tea."

Phil returns with Cleo, Tessa is right behind. And now I am actually sorry we have to leave.

"We better hit the road," says Phil. I put the teacup down.

"Don't forget," my mother says to Phil. "Grand Auntie's present in the laundry room."

"A present?" Cleo says. "Do I have a present too?"

Phil throws me a look of surprise.

"Remember?" I lie. "I told you—what Grand Auntie left us in her will."

He shrugs, and we all follow my mother to the back.

"Of course it's just old things," says my mother. She turns on the light, and then I see it, sitting on the clothes dryer. It is the altar for Grand Auntie's good-luck god, the Chinese crèche.

"Wow!" Tessa exclaims. "A Chinese dollhouse."

"I can't see! I can't see!" Cleo says, and Phil lifts the altar off the dryer and carries it into the kitchen.

The altar is about the size of a small upturned drawer, painted in red lacquer. In a way, it resembles a miniature stage for a Chinese play. There are two ornate columns in front, as well as two ceremonial electric candles made out of gold and red plastic and topped by red Christmas tree bulbs for flames. Running down the sides are wooden panels decorated with gold Chinese characters.

"What does that say?" I ask my mother.

She traces her finger down one, then the other. "*Jye shiang ru yi.* This first word is 'luck,' this other is another kind of luck, and these two mean 'all that you wish.' All kinds of luck, all that you wish."

"And who is this on the inside, this man in the picture frame?" The picture is almost cartoonlike. The man is rather large and is seated in regal splendor, holding a quill in one hand, a tablet in the other. He has two long whiskers, shaped like smooth, tapered black whips.

"Oh, this we call Kitchen God. To my way of thinking, he was not too important. Not like Buddha, not like Kwan Yin, goddess of mercy—not that high level, not even the same level as the Money God. Maybe he was like a store manager, important, but still many, many bosses above him."

Phil chuckles at my mother's Americanized explanation of the hierarchy of Chinese deities. I wonder if that's how she really thinks of them, or if she's used this metaphor for our benefit.

"What's a kitchen god?" says Tessa. "Can I have one?"

"He is only a story," answers my mother.

"A story!" exclaims Cleo. "I want one."

My mother's face brightens. She pats Cleo's head. "You want another story from Ha-bu? Last night, you did not get enough stories?"

"When we get home," Phil says to Cleo. "Ha-bu is too tired to tell you a story now."

But my mother acts as if she has not heard Phil's excuses. "It is a very simple story," she says to Cleo in a soothing voice, "how he became Kitchen God. It is this way."

And as my mother begins, I am struck by a familiar feeling, as if I am Cleo, again three years old, still eager to believe everything my mother has to say.

"In China long time ago," I hear my mother say, "there was a rich farmer named Zhang, such a lucky man. Fish jumped in his river, pigs grazed his land, ducks flew around his yard as thick as clouds. And that was because he was blessed with a hardworking wife named Guo. She caught his fish and herded his pigs. She fattened his ducks, doubled all his riches, year after year. Zhang had everything he could ask for—from the water, the earth, and the heavens above.

"But Zhang was not satisfied. He wanted to play with a pretty, carefree woman named Lady Li. One day he brought this pretty woman home to his house, made his good wife cook for her. When Lady Li later chased his wife out of the house, Zhang did not run out and call to her, 'Come back, my good wife, come back.'

"Now he and Lady Li were free to swim in each other's arms. They threw money away like dirty water. They slaughtered ducks just to eat a plate of their tongues. And in two years' time, all of Zhang's land was empty, and so was his heart. His money was gone, and so was pretty Lady Li, run off with another man.

"Zhang became a beggar, so poor he wore more patches than whole cloth on his pants. He crawled from the gate of one household to another, crying, 'Give me your moldy grain!'

"One day, he fell over and faced the sky, ready to die. He fainted, dreaming of eating the winter clouds blowing above him. When he opened his eyes again, he found the clouds had turned to smoke. At first he was afraid he had fallen down into a place far below the earth. But when he sat up, he saw he was in a kitchen, near a warm fireplace. The girl tending the fire explained that the lady of the house had taken pity on him—she always did this, with all kinds of people, poor or old, sick or in trouble.

"'What a good lady!' cried Zhang. 'Where is she, so I can thank her?' The girl pointed to the window, and the man saw a woman walking up the path. Ai-ya! That lady was none other than his good wife Guo!

"Zhang began leaping about the kitchen looking for some place to hide, then jumped into the kitchen fireplace just as his wife walked in the room.

"Good Wife Guo poured out many tears to try to put the fire out. No use! Zhang was burning with shame and, of course, because of the hot roaring fire below. She watched her husband's ashes fly up to heaven in three puffs of smoke. Wah!

"In heaven, the Jade Emperor heard the whole story from his new arrival. 'For having the courage to admit you were wrong,' the Emperor declared, 'I make you Kitchen God, watching over everyone's behavior. Every year, you let me know who deserves good luck, who deserves bad.'

"From then on, people in China knew Kitchen God was watching them. From his corner in every house and every shop, he saw all kinds of good and bad habits spill out: generosity or greediness, a harmonious nature or a complaining one. And once a year, seven days before the new year, Kitchen God flew back up the fireplace to report whose fate deserved to be changed, better for worse, or worse for better."

"The end!" shouts Cleo, completely satisfied.

"Sounds like Santa Claus," says Phil cheerfully.

"Hnh!" my mother huffs in a tone that implies Phil is stupid beyond words. "He is not Santa Claus. More like a spy—FBI agent, CIA, Mafia, worse than IRS, that kind of person! And he does not give *you* gifts, you must give *him* things. All year long you have to show him respect—give him tea and oranges. When Chinese New Year's time comes, you must give him even better things—maybe whiskey to drink, cigarettes to smoke, candy to eat, that kind of thing. You are hoping all the time his tongue will be sweet, his head a little drunk, so when he has his meeting with the big boss, maybe he reports good things about you. This family has been good, you hope he says. Please give them good luck next year."

"Well, that's a pretty inexpensive way to get some luck," I say. "Cheaper than the lottery."

"No!" my mother exclaims, and startles us all. "You never know. Sometimes he is in a bad mood. Sometimes he says, I don't like this family, give them bad luck. Then you're in trouble, nothing you can do about it. Why should I want that kind of person to judge me, a man who cheated his wife? His wife was the good one, not him."

"Then why did Grand Auntie keep him?" I ask.

My mother frowns, considering this. "It is this way, I think. Once you get started, you are afraid to stop. Grand Auntie worshipped him since she was a little girl. Her family started it many generations before, in China."

"Great!" says Phil. "So now she passes along this curse to us. Thanks, Grand Auntie, but no thanks." He looks at his watch and I can tell he's impatient to go.

"It was Grand Auntie's gift to you," my mother says to me in a mournful voice. "How could she know this was not so good? She only wanted to leave you something good, her best things."

"Maybe the girls can use the altar as a dollhouse," I suggest. Tessa nods, Cleo follows suit. My mother stares at the altar, not saying anything.

"I'm thinking about it this way," she finally announces, her mouth set in an expression of thoughtfulness. "You take this altar. I can find you another kind of lucky god to put inside, not this one." She removes the picture of the Kitchen God. "This one, I take it. Grand Auntie will understand. This kind of luck, you don't want. Then you don't have to worry."

"Deal!" Phil says right away. "Let's pack 'er up."

But now I'm worried. "Are you sure?" I ask my mother. She's already stuffing the plastic candlesticks into a used paper bag. I'm not exactly superstitious. I've always been the kind who hates getting chain letters—Mary used to send them to me all the time. And while I never sent the duplicate letters out as instructed, I never threw the originals away either.

Phil is carrying the altar. Tessa has the bag of candlesticks. My mother has taken Cleo back upstairs to find a plastic neon bracelet she left in the bathroom. And now my mother comes back with Cleo and hands me a heavy grocery sack, the usual care package, what feels like oranges and Chinese candy, that sort of thing.

"Grand Auntie's tea, I gave you some," my mother says. "Don't need to use too much. Just keep adding water. The flavor always comes back."

Fifteen minutes after leaving my mother's home, the girls fall asleep. Phil has chosen to take the 280 freeway, which has less traffic and longer stretches between speed traps. We are still thirty-five miles from home.

"We're not really keeping that altar thing?" Phil says. It is more a statement than a question.

"Um."

"It sure is ugly," he adds. "Although I suppose we could let the girls play with it for a while, until they get tired of it."

"Um." I look out the car window, thinking about my mother, what kind of good-luck god she will get for me. We rush past freeway signs and Sunday drivers in the slow lane. I look at the speedometer. We're going nearly eighty miles an hour.

"What's the rush?" I say.

Phil slows down, then asks, "Do we have anything to snack on?"

And now I remember the care package my mother gave us. It is stowed at my feet. I look in the bag. Inside are a few tangerines, a roll of toilet paper, a canister of Grand Auntie's tea, and the picture of my father that I accidentally knocked over last month. The glass has been replaced.

I quickly hand Phil a tangerine, then turn back toward the window so he does not see my tears. I watch the landscape we are drifting by: the reservoir, the rolling foothills, the same houses I've passed a hundred times without ever wondering who lives inside. Mile after mile, all of it familiar, yet not, this distance that separates us, me from my mother.

6. Chinese Temples in Honolulu

SAU CHUN WONG*

The religion of the Chinese combines the beliefs of Buddhism, Taoism and Confucianism. The objects of worship are the forces of nature, ancestors, ancient heroes, and patron deities. Religion, as observed by the uneducated masses, is handed down from generation to generation chiefly through ceremonial practices and tradition and differs greatly from the philosophies and moral systems propounded by the sages.

The Chinese temple in Honolulu, like many other immigrant institutions, arose in response to the need for security and confidence in a strange land. Almost every Chinese mutual aid society had its special altar room for worship of the familiar deities of the homeland, and special temples with sacred idols and priests from China appeared more than fifty years ago. This paper will attempt to describe six of the temples now existing.

The Temples

1. The oldest and most frequented of the various Chinese temples in Honolulu is the **"Goon Yum" (Kwan Yin) Temple** or the Goddess of Mercy temple on Vineyard Street. Established first in the early eighties and later rebuilt several times, it is now situated near the river and stands as a guardian over it. Only a narrow gate with three large characters painted on it informs the visitor of the temple's existence. It is a two story structure, the lower portion of which is used to house the caretaker, and the priest. On the upper floor, reached by an outside stairway, are the four shrines clustered about the central figure of Kwan Yin. Bedecked with paper flowers on either side, with gilded detailed carvings framed about her, and gorgeous embroidered fans on either side, Kwan Yin reposes calm and serene in the center of lesser gods and goddesses. The heaven table is directly in front of her and is laden with copper kettles of sand, drum and gong, incense, candles, *chi-chi*[1] cylinders, and offerings.

As legend tells us, Kwan Yin was the youngest and most beautiful daughter of an ancient king of China. As she grew older she observed the many trials and tribulations that humanity had to endure. In spite of the loud protests of her father, the king, she vowed that she would never marry. In order to escape the punishments threatened by her father, she renounced the world and became a nun. The gods took pity upon her and made her the Goddess of Mercy. Worshippers pray to her for long life, for many sons and children, for fortune, and for strength. Four holidays are celebrated in her name: February 19, her birthday; September 19, her baptismal day; November 19, her ascension to heaven; and June 19, her death. It is believed

"Chinese Temples in Honolulu", by Sau Chun Wong, *Social Process in Hawaii*, Vol. 3, 1937. Reprinted by permission of Social Process in Hawaii.

that Kwan Yin can transform herself into any imaginable form. People call her the woman with a million eyes and hands. Usually her disguises are used to help those in distress.

The shrine situated on the right of Kwan Yin's is the shrine of the Seven Sisters. There are seven figures seated in the shrine, one of which, as legend discloses, returns to her mortal husband on the seventh day of the seventh month, and remains for seventeen days during which time she washes chopsticks and bowls for every day in the year. Girls especially who desire to be skilled in embroidery work come to worship her.

Other shrines in the same temple are the Wah Tow or Doctor's shrine,[2] famed for helpfulness to the sick and diseased, the Quan Dai or war god, worshipped for life and strength, and the shrine of the "king of gods, king and ruler of earth and heaven." Still another in the corner of the room is the shrine of Choy Sun, the god of fortune, worshipped particularly by merchants, housewives, and sons.

Each figure is brightly decorated, and small oil lamps are kept burning before them constantly. Soot-covered lanterns hang humbly down, and strands of crepe paper flowers waver in the heavy air. Worshippers kneel on the badly worn mats and cushions before all the separate shrines, but it is evident that most prayers are made before the image of Kwan Yin.

The caretaker is a middle-aged, wizened-looking man and is usually clad in a pair of soiled woolen trousers, a grimy can, and Chinese shirt and slippers. Several assistants help with the preparation of images and the care of the shrines.

The temple is supported by donations from the Chinese pubic and by the sale of ceremonial papers, candles, and incense. The caretaker and his staff receive their wages from fees given by the worshippers. Other sources of income are few.

2. Another important temple is the **How Wong Temple** on Fort Street opposite the Y.M.B.A. The founder even as a child was considered to be a living god as she healed people with her miraculous power and the potions which she concocted. In all her life, a span of some eighty years, she had never partaken of any solid food. Her diet consisted only of fruit juices, citron water, small lemons, and carambulas. When she left China to come to Hawaii, she brought with her the How Wong god after whom the temple was named. Later, after the temple was built, she had the Bak Sak or White Mountain Temple in China send the other gods. All the money for the temple was earned by this priestess, and today the temple is one of the few that are self-supporting. The present caretaker is unmistakably proud of her mother who, she claims, prayed with such concentration that even the entrance of bandits did not break her trance. She is credited with predicting the Chinatown fire in 1900, even disclosing the number of days of the fire. This increased her popularity tremendously.

There are five different shrines in this temple. Several of them are similar to those of the Kwan Yin Temple. The center shrine is reserved for the How Wong, or the fisherman's god. Legend discloses that once, when a fisherman was fishing out at sea, a white rock kept coming up to him. Sensing some unseen power at work, the fisherman picked up the stone and said that he would take it ashore and erect a shrine for it if it would give him more power and more fish. The shrine, originally for fishermen, has gradually expanded in use, until today people of any profession or trade may petition the god for good fortune, protection, business success, and safety in travel to China. On either side of the god are seated his two assistants still and solemn in their dignity.

To the left of How Wong is hung a piece of white cloth with small black characters of the thirty-six gods, *Jung Sun*. The worshippers must not forget this small shrine, as it represents all of the gods. He must be careful not to invoke the anger of any god through negligence.

Directly in front of the How Wong shrine is a high table with two large copper incense burners, a pair of kidney-shaped wooden blocks and a cylindrical box with *chi-chi* sticks, and oil burners which are kept burning constantly. The copper burners were presents from a rich Chinese merchant and philanthropist.

To the right of the fishermen shrine is the abode of the Zeus of the Chinese gods, *Yuk Wong Dai Dei,* the king and ruler of heaven and earth, while to his right is the doctor's god with a round pill in his outstretched hand. The shrine to Kwan Dei, the war god, has smaller incense burners but no oil burners or *chi-chi* or blocks.

To the left of the fishermen's shrine is the maternity shrine, consisting of three figures. The central figure is of course the mother god with a baby in her arms; on her left is the father who presents the child, and on her right is the nurse who holds a pair of scales to weigh the baby. This shrine is naturally endowed for expectant mothers who pray for a good son, good luck, and happiness.

Each of the side walls has a shrine. *Hin Tan,* the tiger keeper and trainer with tigers by his sides, has control of thunder and lightning.[3] On the other side wall is the life sized figure of *Choy Sun* the god of fortune. He is arrayed in his mourning clothes, as his mother had died, and is leaning on a frilled paper stick which he uses as a cane. He is bowed in grief, and the stick helps him to hold his head bowed, as holding his head up, which signifies happiness, is unfilial. In his left hand, he carries a fan which is supposed to fan away evil. A collection of fans reclines behind him. His ceremonial day is January 26 according to the lunar calendar.

The present caretaker of this How Wong Temple is Hawaiian born and has a fair education in Chinese and a little in English. Her knowledge in ceremonial procedures was received from her mother.

The temple is supported by donations from the public and through the sale of offerings of candle, punk and ceremonial papers. A worshipper pays twenty-five cents for a sheaf of ceremonial papers with two candles, a sheaf of incense, and punk, so the profit is very little. As she has to keep the oil lamps burning day and night she is glad when some one donates a bottle or two of oil.

This temple is popular with mothers who bring their month old babies to the temple to thank the gods for their safe delivery and to celebrate their birthdays which makes them one year old. The mother brings with her some form of meat, usually a succulent roast pig, wine, tea, incense, sweet bread, and rice. The caretaker helps her pray after the mother pays her a fee wrapped in red paper.

3. A very picturesque temple is the **How Wong Temple** on School Street, beyond Liliha Street. It is surrounded by small residential cottages and is itself a rented cottage made over for temple purposes. It is quite colorful with its bright red fence, cement incinerators and shrines. As one enters the gates, he notices a remodeled garage enclosing a large shrine immediately on his left. No idols can be seen, but two large rocks stand imposingly with red paper arrayed about them and incense and candles burning before them. These gods guard the premises of the temple.

The temple is a one-room affair with the gods facing the door and a pair of guardian gods near the door. In the center is the How wong or fishermen's shrine. Two additional shrines, for Wah Tow, or the god of doctors, and Choy Sun, or the god of fortune, are also worshipped at this temple.

The offerings of worshippers are placed on the table in front of the center shrine. These offerings include sweetmeats, to sweeten the god's palate, rice for food, wine and tea for drink, and ceremonial paper as money for the gods. Although ancient in atmosphere, the temple carries a few modern touches as electric lights, electric clock, telephone, doorbell, and a license for operation artistically framed. Even the young caretaker, clothed in American style, is modern and radical in some of his ideas, derived from a western education.

The caretaker states that he came from China to Hawaii, attended the St. Louis College until the seventh grade, then had to return to China. At that time he had no belief in any religion and used to disfigure the idols and the temples. Then suddenly, one day, the spirit entered his body. He could not study, eat, or sleep for seven days and nights. He acquired the power of healing the sick, and his conquests over disease and death were famous. Many came to him for healing. Even the insane and epileptic benefited from his power. He came back to Hawaii with no intention of continuing his healing practice, but his relatives and friends insisted, so he did whatever he could. He became a priest and took charge of the temple. He secured another job but was unable to keep it. Some misfortune always stalked him whenever he was away from the temple. He states that he remained in good health only when he was healing people.

This caretaker laments that because of ignorance, people in China and in the islands are superstitious over small matters. Take the subject of hair washing. Chinese people insist that there are only certain ordained days when they can wash their hair, so they look it up in the *Tung See,* a horoscope-like book. The caretaker shakes his head and laughs. "What difference does it make when you wash your hair. When it's dirty, you know it is, so wash it when necessary, not upon the advice of a book!" He says that as long as the "heart is good", there is no use in offering a huge roast pig to the gods, as the gods do not care. A little incense is as big a thought as roast pig. Only ignorant people do such unnecessary acts. He laughingly says, "If fate determines your life, why do so much unnecessary worship to curb its whims?"

4. **The Quan Dai** or **War God's Temple** is situated in a dark, musty room over a row of grocery stores on Vineyard Street near the river. An old man, about seventy years old, a retired vegetable vendor, is the present caretaker. He bought it from the former owner, and although he did not know much about the procedure, "the gods taught him". In a week's time he learned practically "the whole business." The Quan Dai shrine is black from the fumes of the candles and is shaded in the background by many high tables laden with copper kettles filled with sand and ashes. Quan Dai is worshipped for life and strength.

5. A slightly different temple is located on River Street, near the Japanese produce markets. In the center of the upstairs rooms is the **shrine of Leong Ma**, the goddess of safety, who was a beautiful woman, as one can see from the clear-cut features of the idol. She has bound feet and holds a mirror in her hand. She is surrounded by lesser goddesses, and many have mirrors in their hands which help to light their paths. This temple was built by the

Lum clan and supported by it. Scattered about the walls of the room are pictures of famous Lums and photographs of Lum gatherings. The caretaker, a toothless gentleman clad in an undershirt and a pair of trousers, is also a Lum. He has a small room adjoining the big room and one can spy a tiny sink, dishes, and an iron bed within. This temple is not often frequented by worshippers but is chiefly used for clan meetings and gatherings.

6. Another temple is the **Sing Wong Temple** located on Kukui Street. The temple proper occupies one side and the proprietor's home the other, where ceremonial papers and offerings are sold and where the proprietor sits and gossips with frequent cronies. This temple was founded at Hanapepe, Kauai, by the present caretaker, who is educated in Chinese history and language. The temple houses "guardian gods" who keep watch over the temple, *Choy Sun* or god of fortune. The center shrine holds the "Eight Great Spirits" while on the right are the King of gods, and the *Fut Mu,* the teacher of Kwan Yin. The caretaker is also a spiritual medium and a chanter at funerals, both these occupations being better sources of income than the temple. The temple is not supported by public donations but is supported through sale of ceremonial offerings.

Procedure of Worship

The ceremonials in all of the temples tend to be chiefly of a magical character designed to coerce the gods and spirits to grant the expressed desires of the worshippers. Among the recurrent values sought are: sons, happiness for departed spirits, family happiness, long life, wealth and health, and security against accident and misfortune.

A worshipper usually brings with him on special holidays, and celebrations, a basket of food composed of some form of animal flesh, as pork, chicken, or fish, (or if he is rich, all of the above) wine, tea, and three bowls of cooked rice, and a vegetable dish, as tofu or *jai*.[4] As he enters, he hits a panel and a drum several times to arouse the gods to listen to his supplication and also to chase away the evil spirits that are lurking near. The priest may assist if the worshipper desires. He endeavors to get all the information he can as to the desires of the worshipper. Then he chants in a sing-song manner, all the while kneeling in front of the shrine on the mat or cushion. (If information is sought as to the future of sons and daughters, their names and birthdays are written on a piece of paper.) He picks up the pair of kidney-shaped blocks and answers to questions are secured by the throw of the blocks. If both fall with the curved side up, it is a good sign; if one is flat and the other curved, it is also good, but if both fall on the flat side, the future is not propitious and one should take care. The priest may also secure answers to questions through the *chi-chi* sticks or the *chim.*

This is the procedure followed by a young Chinese who has had an American education, has all the external marks of a westerner, and who is praying for some member of her family who is suffering from a headache. She buys incense from the caretaker, lights it and distributes it among the gods. The caretaker helps her light candles and takes up the tea leaves, after which both kneel down before the shrine and ask the gods for help. Then the caretaker takes up the *chim* and shakes them up and down until one drops out, chanting while he is doing this. He then looks up the predictions for the number in his case book. Gathering up the ceremonial papers he burns them and then dusts the incenseash into the tea leaves and wraps both in red paper. He rings the gong and beats the drum. The girl departs after paying and giving thanks with the thought that after drinking the tea the headache will disappear. If it does not, she will come again to pray.

Caretakers

Every caretaker seems to think of his task as ordained by the gods. As one caretaker said, "I didn't like religion at first; I used to draw mustaches on the gods and mark the temples. But suddenly, I was "*gong*" (the spirit entered my soul) and I became a priest. The gods wanted me to be a priest, so I had to become one or I would he unlucky and have many accidents." This fatalistic viewpoint is rather common.

Pride of position prevents the caretakers from seeking other more remunerative tasks. As one caretaker says, "I tried to look for a job, but after securing one for a while, I would get sick and couldn't go back to work; so I have to stay in the temple." Another caretaker who has been a vegetable vendor says, "I couldn't make much money selling vegetables. Too much competition. When I heard of this chance to take care of the temple, I took it so that when I get old, I can still make a little money without too much effort."

The caretakers and priests, of course, must make a living, and that is one of the chief concerns of some. All lament that too many people come with their own ceremonial papers instead of buying them from the temples, and also do their own praying instead of paying the priest a fee to do it for them. But as the temple is supposedly public, the priests can do nothing.

Each caretaker assumes that his temple is the one truly ordained by the gods and that other temples and priests are fakes. There is not much cooperation among them and no guild to protect and raise their interests.

Worshippers

The worshippers at the temples are chiefly first generation women who most strongly adhere to the traditional religious values and observe the ancient ceremonies, both at home and at the temples. They pin their faith on one or more experiences which have coincided with the priests' predictions.

Most worshippers visit the temples on holidays, as neglect would invite misfortune. Some more devout, however, visit on any good day of the lunar calendar. Some, thrifty, or miserly, bring their own offerings and chant their prayers instead of buying them from the temple or securing the priest's services; others do not visit the temples at all, as they say they can pray to the gods just as effectively at home. The gods, they add, are everywhere.

Some believe in going only to one temple as their faith has strength and security in that certain temple, not because of the sect, but because of the priest who might have a greater influence on the person than would the other priests, and who might have predicted some truth or facts which strengtened the person's faith.

Ceremonies

Altogether there are thirteen definite times for worship. The first and fifteenth of every month are also considered as worship days. Other important days of worship and the items of food usually offered are listed below:

1. New Year's Day—vegetables.

2. Second day of New Year—meat and vegetables.

3. Twelfth day of New Year—pork, chicken, and fish.

4. Tsing Ming—anything.

5. Fifth day of fifth month—pork and sweets.

6. Fourteenth day of seventh month—anything.

7. Fifteenth day of eighth month—pork and moon cakes.

8. Winter of the eleventh month—pork and sweets.

9. Last day of old year—fish, chicken, and pork.

10–13. Birthdays and death days of fathers and ancestors.

Changing Functions

Religious devotion to spirits and natural objects has controlled the life and activities of the Chinese people to a great extent. It was the center about which their life revolved as they believed that the spirits controlled and motivated their activities; in other words, no differentiation was made between fate and the will of the spirits. Ancestor worship was adhered to closely as an example for future generations to follow in respect to the departing generation. Ancestor worship considered the fami

Now, since the advent of Christianity, modern science, and public education, the older type of Chinese worship has ceased to control the life of a large part of the second and third generations of the Chinese community of Honolulu. The first generation go to the temples on feast days, a few consistently, while the younger generations seldom do. The same practices, however, tend to persist, with the exception that ancestor worship has been neglected in the temples but not in the homes. Once a year at about Easter time, *Tsing Ming* is held at the ancestral graves and this is a time when even babies are taken.

Notes

* This was originally a term paper submitted by Chew Young Wong, Florian Wong, Sally Sun, and Sau Chun Wong for an introductory course in Sociology.

1. The *chi-chi* cylinders contain one hundred *chim*. Each of these *chim*, which has a number written on it, refers the worshipper to one of the many printed answers given by the gods—for sickness, he refers to the set of prescriptions, for perplexing problems, he looks up the set which gives him the god's advice.

2. Wah Tow was a famous surgeon living during the time China was divided into three kingdoms under the Tartar king. One day the king received a scalp wound during battle. When Wah Tow recommended that the king be given a head operation, the cowardly king thinking that some treachery was afoot, commanded that the doctor be put to death. The gods took pity upon the unfortunate victim and made him a god.

3. Legend says that long ago there was neither thunder nor lightning. The world was peaceful, and food was plentiful, but people began to waste rice and food, and the gods were angry. So in the dead of the night, the gods came and tried to kill the wasteful people, but in the darkness they killed the wrong people. Feeling very abject, the gods thought of a plan. They appointed the special tiger keeper, gave him the duty of scattering thunder and lightning so that the people would know by the sound of thunder that the gods were angry, and through the lightning the gods might be able to see the people they were punishing.

4. *Jai* is a rich vegetable dish eaten during the New Year fast by some Chinese and it is also the food of monks and nuns who abstain from eating meat all their lives.

7. Changing Rituals in Chinese Births and Deaths

ANONYMOUS

Although I belong to a fourth generation family of the Chinese-Hawaiian ethnic mixture, I can still recall vividly the old customs, traditions, and rituals of folk China as transplanted here to Hawaii. However, within the past twenty years or so, I have also witnessed great changes regarding rituals connected with births and deaths.

Since I am the third oldest in a family of nine children, I can remember the days when my younger brothers and sisters were taken to the Hau Wong* Temple on upper Fort Street on their 'Month-Old-Day' (Gau Yuet). Before leaving for the temple, a venerable woman friend of the family (with tiny bound feet) would rub liquor on the tender head of the month-old baby and proceed with utmost caution to shave the head with a barber's razor. If the baby were a boy she would shave all the hair except a solid round halo-like patch the size of a silver dollar in the middle of the head while in the case of a girl two smaller patches on each side of the back portion of the top of the head were left. (These styles are known as *no sun gai* and *na ja gai* respectively.) Then a very elaborate red silk band decorated with gold charms of an old Santa Claus-like man with a peach (Sau Sing Lo Yeh) in the middle flanked by the Eight Immortals (Bat Dai Sin) was carefully placed about the head.

My grandparents would take a very sumptuous feast suitable for the gods to the temple. This included a whole roast pig complete from head to tail (the tail was even garnished with a fringed piece of red paper for good luck), two high pyramids of buns (*tong bau*), one colored red and the other white. Wine, tea, rice, eggs dyed a cerise red, ginger with sesame seeds etc., completed the lavish foods. After giving thanks for the safe delivery of the baby, we would take all the food home and really have a banquet. The pig would be neatly sliced, and then wrapped and distributed along with eggs, buns, ginger to relatives and friends who had presented gifts to the baby.

Since World War II, I have noticed some marked changes. Nowadays, because most of the Chinese belong to Christian churches of various sects, they neither go to the temple nor shave the heads but they still adhere to the custom of distributing pork, etc. They no longer order a whole pig but have the Chinese grocery store package it individually with the accompanying delicacies. Some may even delay this till the baby is a year old.

---

*All Chinese words have been Romanized to approximate the pronounciation in the Cantonese dialect.

From *Social Process in Hawaii*, Vol. 22 (1958). Copyright © 1958 by Department of Sociology, University of Hawaii. Reprinted by permission.

Inasmuch as death is nothing but birth into the next world in the eyes of the Chinese, I shall attempt to describe portions of my grandfather's funeral. Because he died before World War II, he had a genuine full-length traditional Chinese funeral service which lasted from 7:30 P.M. on Saturday until the actual burial at about 3:00 P.M. on Sunday. Within this span of time some ceremony was constantly going on and no one was allowed to sleep. Because my grandfather was of the middle class, he had only three Taoist priests instead of the usual five had he been rich. The entire funeral was divided into ten parts (*sap nim*).

Before I proceed to describe some of the many complicated rituals, I believe a physical description is in order. The casket was placed in the middle of the funeral parlor with the feet facing the viewer as he entered and paid his respects by kow-towing and slowly walking around the casket. At this end were neatly arranged bowls of rice, wine, tea, etc., and a paper model of a mountain of gold (*gam shan*) and another of silver (*ngaan shan*) on either side accompanied with a slave boy with a towel and pipe for tobacco (*lai jai*) symmetrically arranged.

On the right side seated on straw mats were the male relatives in sack cloth robes and white sashes tied about their foreheads and waists. The female blood relatives were dressed similarly except that they wore white hoods while the daughters-in-law wore checkered blue and white ones. Their hair was disheveled and void of jewelry and their faces without make-up. My grandmother was not allowed to attend except for brief periods as she would wail so hysterically, almost beyond control. The old woman in charge would encourage the women folk to mourn and wail in a classical poetic sing-song fashion each time a visitor came. Since some of my aunts were quite Westernized, they refused to do so and were obliged to pay her to do it for them.

One of the ten ceremonies was the 'keeping the body company' (*chan si*) which occurred at about two o'clock in the morning. Each of us was provided with a white candle and holder in our left hands and we formed a train with the males first according to the degree of kinship followed by the females. The Taoist priest led us in making what seemed like a hundred rounds. Upon the completion of each round at the foot of the casket, we would be given paper money in various forms and sizes to burn with the lighted candles. Meanwhile, the Taoist priests would be blowing the shrill trumpets, beating the gongs and cymbals, and tinkling the brass bell continuously.

When the casket was finally covered prior to leaving for burial, the women would practically scream their heads off. I remember we marched in the middle of the road for a couple of blocks before boarding the automobiles. Each woman would be shaded by a black umbrella and supported by an older woman friend dressed in complete black.

Nowadays the ten ceremonies have been shortened considerably and are completed in about three or four hours. In many cases, the services are a combination of Christian-Taoist. All traces of a Taoist funeral would be hidden and a Christian minister would come and conduct his services. Nevertheless, upon his departure the Taoist priests would bring out all the paraphernalia and resume as though nothing had happened. This is usually the case when a Christian man dies but his widow is still traditionally Chinese. She would not deny him his desired services yet she wants to be sure he gets to heaven. This according to her own beliefs requires the ten ceremonies. The family may now sit in chairs instead of mats and wailing is pretty much out of fashion, much to the regret of the few remaining first generation immigrants.

After the funeral everyone would return to the home of the deceased and have a simple 'cold dinner' (*do pun* or *dung jau*). At the completion of the simple meal, each would take his bowl and chopsticks home. Today instead of porcelain bowls and bamboo chopsticks, people have substituted paper poi bowls and Japanese packaged wooden saimin chopsticks. Close relatives would be given a black and white lantern to light their way home. This has been replaced with flashlights.

All in all these funeral customs have their psychological value as they afford everyone a chance openly to express his grief and sorrow.

In spite of the fact that I am a fourth generation Chinese-Hawaiian, my ties with the ancient folk customs and traditions of China are so strong, I can't avoid them completely. Unless my parents are converted to the Christian faith before their deaths, I will probably be obligated to carry on a modified form of the services described above as I am the eldest son. However, I am sure that it will end with my generation because most of my brothers and sisters are Christian by faith.

8. Some Filipino Traits Transplanted

ROMAN CARIAGA

The important differences of mankind which give rise to group consciousness and group prejudice are not so much biological or racial as they are cultural. After primary contact it is the varying social usages—mores, customs, etiquette,—which set apart the different groups and tend to cause misunderstanding and friction among them.

Transplanted from the simple life of the Philippine country barrio* with its small individual farms, intricate kinship ties and unfailing community spirit into the complex regimented life of Hawaii's agricultural industry with its mechanized competitive system, the Filipino faces many bewildering problems which his training, based on the old Malay community philosophy superimposed with Spanish etiquette and American idealism, has not prepared him to solve. Of the many Philippine traits transplanted to Hawaiian soil, some have withered away under the rigors of the strange environment, some have been crowded out by their hardier and better adapted American counterparts, and some are still flourishing and may perhaps even spread their bloom in the new land.

The first group of Filipinos arrived in Hawaii three decades ago, in December 1906; and immigration continued in rapidly increasing numbers until the recent depression. More than 100,000 Filipinos have sojourned in Hawaii, most of them returning to the homeland after completing their labor agreements on the sugar plantations, and a few of them going on to the mainland of the United States. Today there are 54,668 Filipinos in the territory, and they form the second largest racial element in the varied population. The great bulk of them, about 40,000 laborers, are concentrated in the sugar and pineapple plantations which form the bulwark of the economic structure of the islands; about 6,000 are located in the city of Honolulu supplying domestic, hotel and hospital help and cannery workers; and perhaps 4,000 others may be found in Hilo and the smaller towns in miscellaneous positions. The size of the Filipino group as a whole, and the concentration of its members in distinct areas generally apart from other nationalities has made possible the propagation of many of the homeland habits, customs, culture traits and forms of etiquette—the *Ugaling Filipino.*

Some of these Philippine customs have been considerably altered by certain factors aside from the usual influence of a new environment. Several of the different Filipino dialect groups are represented in Hawaii, chiefly the Ilocano and the Visayan, with smaller numbers

---

*The Philippine *barrio* is a village. Towns are composed of groups of barrios. The great bulk of the Filipino population is distributed among the barrios, and there are few cities of consequence outside of Manila.

From *Social Process in Hawaii,* Vol. 2 (1936). Copyright © 1936 by Department of Sociology, University of Hawaii. Reprinted by permission.

of the Tagalog, Pampangan, Pangasinan, et cetera; each of which has somewhat different customs or variations of the same custom. In Hawaii these customs may fuse; those of the smaller groups may be absorbed or overshadowed by those of the larger group; or they may be rejected in favor of a corresponding American custom, or abandoned entirely. American influence, which has been gaining momentum and scope in the Philippines steadily since 1898, predisposes the Filipinos to adopt and adapt to American ways.

The vast majority of the Filipinos immigrating to Hawaii have been single men or men whose families have remained in the Philippines. The adult sex ratio is about 5 to 1 in favor of the men. The lack of women and the scarcity of families among the Filipinos in Hawaii explain to some degree the constant shifting of the population which tends to disorganize and weaken the force of the old mores. There are, however, in the neighborhood of two thousand families, and among them many of the old traditions are followed, especially those relating to the crises of life.

Ancient customs relating to childbirth still survive and are rigorously practiced by the more superstitious. Those who have come from the more remote rural districts of the Philippines, and who have not yet succumbed to modern American influences due to prolonged isolation among their own people in the rural areas of Hawaii, are following the customs of by-gone generations, which hark back beyond the Spanish era to the days of Malay supremacy.

The prospective mother must be protected from the *anitos,* or evil spirits, which beset her, particularly at the time of delivery. All doors and windows are tightly closed to prevent the entrance of *anitos*; the woman is placed on an improvised bed which stands about three feet above the floor and is inclined so that the head is somewhat higher than the feet; a small stove is kept by the bed constantly burning charcoal, regardless of climate or room temperature, and made to emit smoke by pouring incense on it which is supposed to drive away any *anitos* who may have crept in. This procedure is continued for a week or more. The infant is bathed and rubbed with a concoction of Philippine herbs, and certain boiled herbs are given the mother to drink. A hot compress wrung out of herbal water is placed on the abdomen of the child several times a day irrespective of the temperature or the condition of the child.

In the Philippines where the country houses are built of bamboo and nipa, and there are wide interstices between the bamboo rods which form the wall, and those of the floor, ventilation is assured even when the windows are closed to prevent drafts. But in the wooden plantation houses of Hawaii, whose small glass windows offer the only source of air, the mother and child invariably suffer from over heating and lack of oxygen when the old customs are followed; and the high infant mortality among the Filipinos may in many cases be attributed to them.

Survival of the child under these circumstances seems a blessing of the gods, and is in fact so celebrated. An elaborate christening party is given, usually a *lechon* (barbecued pig), an all day affair in true Philippine style to which all friends are welcome. Social prestige as well as religious observance is a motive, and also the old Malay idea of introducing the child to the village and assuring community interest in his welfare. The baptism occurs at the church the morning or evening before the party in most cases. Filipinos are largely Catholic, Catholicism having been introduced in the 16th century, and the Philippines is the one Christian nation of the East. After the religious ceremony is finished the occasion becomes one of gaiety and abundance, with feasting, speeches, music and dancing. One or two orchestras may be employed. The expense is very great, and a unique method has been evolved to meet the high prices in Hawaii where chickens and pigs are well nigh as much per pound as they are per head in the homeland, and where one must buy at the market instead of depending on generous gifts of the neighbors' produce and livestock. In the Philippines two sponsors are invited to stand with the child at the christening, a godfather and a godmother. In Hawaii this number has been increased to as many as two hundred, and averages perhaps thirty per christening. These numerous godparents of course share in the expense and labor involved in the feast.

At a recent christening party at Ewa plantation attended by the writer, there were sixty sponsors, fifty-four men, and six women. Participation in christenings seems to offer an opportunity for establishing the home and kindred ties so precious in the Philippines, and provides a vicarious parenthood for the large numbers of single men that form the bulk of the Filipino population in Hawaii. After the dinner and program the sponsors gather around the mother of the baby and place money, or envelopes filled with money, in the tray on her lap. Two dollars is the approved amount, although the sum varies from fifty cents to as many dollars on the part of particularly generous or close friends. The priest also reaps a harvest for his church, the usual requirement being fifty cents from each sponsor. Some of the Filipino Protestant churches on the plantations have found it profitable to adopt the same custom.

Marriage rites are celebrated with similar festivities. The service and bridal costumes are usually American, but the celebration is in Philippine style with feasting, dancing, speeches, and music. An interesting folkway still frequently practiced is the solo dance of the bride and groom, who tread their way among the guests to the tune of applause, music, and the clink of coins tossed at their feet. A plate is placed near the center of the floor, and bills as well as change collect there. A couple may receive from forty to fifty dollars in this manner.

Some odd marital situations arise from the keen competition of the many bachelors for wives, and from the conflict between American born and American educated daughters and their strict parents who wish to arrange their marriages for them according to the Philippine tradition. The family with an eligible daughter or two is on its way to prosperity in Hawaii. Presents of all kinds from hopeful suitors pour in: everything from grocery supplies to automobiles, and of course jewelry and personal gifts for the girl. Money is loaned and favors and requests cheerfully carried out by the suitors, and everything goes swimmingly unless the daughter suddenly dives off into the sea of matrimony on her own initiative. Several such cases have been observed by the writer, one of them with amazing results.

A leading family at X plantation had three daughters, each remarkably bright, attractive, and determined. They were very popular and had many suitors. Everything progressed well up to a certain point. As long as it was merely a matter of receiving presents and entertaining callers in the parlour under mother's chaperonage according to Philippine tradition, the girls were amiable. But when marriage came in view and they were ordered to accept prosperous but middle aged and uneducated, unprepossessing husbands, they rebelled. The eldest, a promising student in her sophomore year at an American state university, eloped with a waiter rather than marry her mother's choice. The youngest daughter refused to wed a pockmarked bank roll and left home, despite threats, to go to work as a maid. The other sister, an exceptionally beautiful girl remained the sole hope of her parents. She was kept under rigid surveillance, not allowed to go out alone, and above all never permitted to see or hear from the young man of her own choice. She was pledged perforce to a suitor to whom her family was heavily indebted, and the date set for the wedding. The evening before, she escaped and married her young man, and has now been living happily with him for some five years. The situation for her scheming mother was not so happy. The unfortunate suitor, cheated of his last wifely prospect, lost his patience and his head and threatened to kill himself and the mother for not keeping her promise. As the only solution the mother divorced her husband and married the boy, some 20 years her junior, herself. They now have one child.

Marriage is regarded as sacred in the Philippines and among the old school Filipinos in Hawaii, and there is no divorce, because, according to the old proverb: "Marriage cannot be compared to a morsel of rice which one can spit out when hot!" In Hawaii, where the unbalanced sex ratio gives the woman undue advantage and where the foreign milieu undermines Philippine mores, there is considerable shifting of husbands, and making of matches without legal formalities. One middle aged couple at Y plantation with a 21-year-old son, invited the writer to their house one Saturday night to attend a wedding. Upon arrival at the home with the customary gifts of food and congratulations for the son, the latter was nowhere to be seen. The group proceeded to the church and, lo and behold, it was the solemn parents, dressed in their Sunday best, who had chosen this particular time to be married themselves, as a courteous gesture, no doubt, to their five children.

A christening or a wedding does not measure up to Filipino standards unless there is a lavish celebration. The same is true of their funerals, and the family and friends of the deceased often go deeply into debt to hold services which will evince their respect and affection and assure the departed a safe journey. The deceased is still accorded a vital role in the family functions, especially if he was an elder member. He is considered as a member *in absentia*, his last wishes are executed to the letter, and the moral ties between him and the survivors are sometimes stronger than relationships between the living. Ceremonial rites after death are strictly observed by the Filipinos of Hawaii and are among the most marked of the culture traits transplanted.

Nine-day prayer meetings are held and relatives and friends assemble to do honor to the dead and comfort the living. Meals are served, and on the ninth day a great fiesta is given. Some groups prepare special dishes for the returning soul on the night of the eighth day. The dishes are placed on a special table in the room last occupied by the deceased, and may not be touched until the following day when the final feast takes place. Among some groups another feast is given in honor of the dead on the fortieth day, preceded by nine more evenings of prayer. At the end of the year a huge feast terminates the mourning period. An exceptionally religious family may continue to give an anniversary feast thereafter, usually for not more than three years.

Among the older people these funeral traditions are revered and followed strictly. But the young people enjoy the feast and, forgetting the solemnity of the occasion, make merry and even dance instead of mourning. To the elders this behavior, which they attribute to American freedom and individuality, is immoral and sacrilegious. But it is simply one of many illustrations of the changing attitudes and customs through which the Filipinos of the younger generation are responding to their new environment.

9. Japanese Buddhist Temples in Honolulu[1]

TOSHIMI YOSHINAGA

When the Japanese immigrants came to Hawaii, they brought with them, along with other cultural institutions, several of the principal sects of Japanese Buddhism.[2] Six of these Buddhist sects, Shin, Nichiren, Shingon, Tendai, Jodo, and Zen, are represented by temples or organized groups in Honolulu. When all the sub-sects and branches are included in the enumeration, there are 19 Buddhist temples in Honolulu.

Honpa Hongwanji

All of the sects have been affected more or less by the American setting. Perhaps the most westernized temple in Honolulu is the Honpa Hongwanji,[3] located on upper Fort Street. Here the influence of the west is reflected in the architecture of the temple as well as in the religious rites.

Regular services of the Honpa Hongwanji are held every Sunday at the temple for different age groups, and here also the innovations from the west are apparent. The most obvious innovations are found in the four sections of pews which fill a large portion of the spacious hall, and in the western pipe organ choir, and pulpit located to the right of the highly ornate Buddhist altar. Beginning at 6:00 A.M. on Sundays, there is a sunrise service at the temple for adults. The children's ceremony for grade children begins at 8:40 A.M. for half an hour and serves as a brief gathering in the temple hall of all the Sunday School children prior to an instructional period which is conducted at the Fort Street Japanese Grammar School. The High School group's service which is conducted immediately after the children's service is mainly for young people between the ages of twelve and eighteen years. Student boarders at the high school dormitories are required to attend this service, which consists of several chants, responses, and hymns. The noisy conversations of the boys in the left section and the girls in the right section of the temple quickly subside as the organ begins to play and all bow their heads and press the palms of their hands together in silent meditation. The next hour is devoted to the young people's service. The addition of a sermon makes this service slightly different from the preceding high school service. Occasionally the sermon is delivered in English, but more often it is given in Japanese. Congregational singing, accompanied by the organ, gives these services a distinctly western atmosphere.

"Japanese Buddhist Temples in Hawaii", by Toshimi Yoshinaga, *Social Process in Hawaii*, Vol. 3, 1937. Reprinted by permission of Social Process in Hawaii.

The older people, mainly those between the ages of forty and sixty, gather at 1:30 in the afternoon to worship. This service is conducted entirely in Japanese and retains more of the Oriental flavor. Most of the women are dressed in the traditional ceremonial kimonos and many have their ceremonial *haoris* or coats. The entire congregation averages about seventy-five elderly men and women. Many arrive at the temple before the hour to enjoy a bit of visiting.

The service is begun by the striking of the gong—at first slow and loud with the tempo gradually increased and the volume decreased. This is repeated several times. The congregation sits in silence until the sound from the gong has died away. Then the priests, seated before and to the side of the image of Buddha, begin to chant, followed by the people, some aided by books and some from memory, while still others remain silent. After twenty minutes of chanting, the priests lift to their faces the books from which they have been reading, and then replace them on the small desks in front of them. Then rising, they all leave. Later the head priest or a visiting priest reappears alone, and delivers his sermon from the pulpit.

In addition to the regular services, there are numerous other activities which the Honpa Hongwanji undertakes. One of its major projects is the maintenance of the largest Japanese language school in the territory.[4] Two young people's organizations, the Young Men's Buddhist Association with a membership of 485, and the Young Women's Buddhist Association, are sponsored by the temple. Three dormitories, one for the boys, one for the girls and women, and a third for young men are supervised by the Hongwanji. A priest of the Honpa Hongwanji visits Oahu prison every Sunday morning and conducts a service there. The women of the Y.W.B.A. make regular visits to Leahi Home, a sanitorium for tubercular patients, in order to cheer up the Japanese patients there. Besides these visits, every Monday evening a religious service for the patients is conducted.

The Higashi Hongwanji

This sect is strikingly similar in its activities. The main temple, located on North King Street, is a two story wooden structure—the lower floor consisting of a receiving room and quarters for the priests; the entire second floor comprising a worship hall. As one enters, there is a little room designated as "office" on the left end of a very small porch. On both extremities of this porch are stairways leading to the worship hall. At the head of both of these stairs are small *saisen bako* (offering box) attached to the wall.

Three sections of twelve long benches with backs are found in the main worship hall. An elaborate altar is found on a raised platform in the front. In addition to a large altar house in the center, there are four smaller ones, two on each side of the center altar. The altar is beautifully decorated with fresh flowers contributed by members of the congregation. Within the center altarhouse is a standing image of Amida. Another much larger *saisen bako* is located on the right center of the platform. Just below this raised platform is a speaker's stand where the sermon is delivered.

This temple is maintained mainly through generous donations from its members and by the profits from benefit shows and movies. Donations are received at the office and the name of each donor, his or her address, and the amount donated are written on a long strip of white paper. This paper is then taken upstairs and hung on cords along the walls of the hall during festivals.

This temple sponsors such organizations as the Fujin Kai for the older women, Y.W.B.A. for local-born girls and women, and weekly Sunday schools for little children, in addition to regular Sunday afternoon services.

Kempon Hokke-Shu

Although western ideas are noted in the Hongwanji practices, there is a branch of Japanese Buddhism which, because of its brief contact with the West, is still decidedly eastern in customs and traditions. This temple is the Kempon Hokke-shu, one of the most interesting of the sects represented here. Kempon Hokke-shu belongs to the Nichiren sect,[5] the only Japanese Buddhist sect that bears the name of its founder. Though there are in all nine branches, only two of them are found in Honolulu. They are Kempon Hokke-shu and the Nichiren Mission. Nichiren means "Sun Lotus" and this name was selected in association with the sayings, "nothing is more brilliant and fairer than the sun and the moon," and "nothing is purer than the lotus." The sacred call of this sect is "Namu Myoho-Renge-Kyo", meaning "Adoration to the Lotus of Perfect Truth".[6]

The Hokke-shu temple, located in Nuuanu Valley on Laimi Road, was established in Hawaii very recently (1931), but it has become very popular, with a large following, especially on Oahu. Its congregation of 300 is made up chiefly of Honolulu residents but it also draws from the rural districts such as Wahiawa, Waipahu, and Aiea.

Every worshipper, as he enters the chapel, removes his shoes, or clogs, or slippers and goes to a sink in a concealed corner of the narrow veranda to purify himself. Then, sitting on his knees at the entrance of the main worship hall, each person throws a coin or two into a saisen bako and, with finger tips of both hands touching the floor, bows toward the elaborate gold-plated altar. Each takes his rosary and puts it around the second finger of each hand, presses his palms together, followed by a "vow to carry on the work of this sect." Then lifting his head, he murmurs the sacred call "Namu-Myoho-Renge-Kyo" thrice, bowing after each call. Finally he removes his rosary and claps his hands together five times and ends the ceremonial with another bow. This is a ritual peculiar only to this temple and is practiced nowhere else in Honolulu.

Now every one is free to seek his place in the hall—men usually the left side and the women the right. There are no pews in the temple but *zabuton* or floor cushions are placed at intervals on the mat-covered floor for the use of worshippers.

As the time for the service approaches, the seven members, of the temple staff—a Chief Priest, two nuns, a girl, and three boys who are in training, all with heads closely shaved (*bozu*), and dressed in ceremonial robes, enter the chapel and proceed to their places at the front in a straight line before the congregation. The chief priest strikes a bell and every member in the congregation, even the youngest children, join in a chant. After the chant, the priest sits down on a slightly raised seat, while his assistants sit on either side of him—three boys on his left and three nuns on his right. All face the altar. The service consist almost wholly of chants at various tempos. Sometimes the chant is slow and solemn and at other times it picks up speed and volume to a grand crescendo of chanting and the rapid beating of the gong, drums, and a bell. This continues for about 45 minutes, then the priest and his assistants leave.

For several minutes now the people have time to exchange a few words of greeting with their friends. During this period of intermission, some of the members busy themselves by getting the hall ready for a sermon. They pull a blackboard into the center of the room and also bring in a table. The priest returns and everyone sits attentively for a long sermon averaging about an hour and a half in length. After this seemingly interminable sermon, O-set-tai or refreshments, including hot tea with candies, *manju,* and other Japanese delicacies are often served.

Every day of the week is a "holy day" at this temple, although the service described above occurs typically on Sunday night, but from Monday to Saturday, there are three services daily—at 5 A.M., 9 A.M., and 7 P.M. On Sunday there is a slight change with a 9 A.M. Sunday school service for boys and girls and a single general service at 7 P.M. for the whole congregation, which incidently is open to all visitors. Week day services are open only to members and to others who have formally expressed their desires to join the membership. At these ceremonies, the congregation is usually very small and each person sits on the bare floor near the altar—no mat, no cushion. It is at these services that ceremonies for curing the sick and afflicted are performed.

The people who go to this temple believe staunchly that the priest and the nuns have the power to cure them of their illnesses by praying. There are many miraculous incidents to which the members point as being adequate proofs that faith healing in this temple has been successful. One cannot understand how strongly these people believe in faith healing until he has attended one of the temple's annual sunrise services[7] which are held on the 28th of April at Hanauma Bay. At four in the morning, members from all over the city, as well as from the rural districts gather at the temple and from there drive out to the service on the mountain. The people climb up the rocky mountain sides, and hold the service on some level spot. A small mat is spread on the ground and two large lighted candles are placed on both sides of a bowl of burning incense. This represents the altar in the temple. With this altar in the foreground, all the people stand close together facing the sun and commence to chant. For more than a half hour everyone continues chanting and drumming until the sun has risen. People who have had attacks of paralysis, the blind, the infirm, and the aged, all are present for this service. Those who are unable to climb the mountain due to illness or weakness are carried up on the backs of young men.

According to one of its members the chief aim of the Hokke-shu temple is to offer fellowship and to help and cure those who are weak and sick. All these things, they claim, can be accomplished by vigorous prayer and faith.

The Nichiren Mission

Although it belongs to the same sect as Kempon Hokke-shu, [it] is quite different in its practices. Services are held less frequently, and the congregation is relatively small. The Nichiren-shu of Honolulu is situated on School Street just off Nuuanu Avenue, and, although introduced in Hawaii in 1900, was not established at this spot until 1914. It claims a membership of 300 households in Honolulu and rural Oahu. Services are held on the first and third Sunday afternoons and on the evenings of the 12th and 23rd of each month. The priest also conducts ceremonies every night of the week from Monday to Friday.

An attractive yard surrounds the temple which is built in Japanese style with a verandah extending around the three sides. A few chairs are arranged on the veranda for guests, but most of the members use only the *zabuton*. Within the temple are the altar to Buddha, low lacquered tables for incense, large drums, gongs, containers of holy water, boxes for the Sacred Sutras, and a considerable floor space for worshippers. The Sunday services are largely devoted to chanting, accompanied by the drum, and to sermons by the priest. A language school is maintained by this temple, as well as several semi-religious and social organizations.

The Jodo Sect

This sect, the second largest group of Buddhists in Hawaii,[8] has a new and spacious temple on Makiki Street. As in the Shin shu temples noticeable accommodations to western values have been made. To the left of the temple is a tennis court which is extensively used by the members. The first floor is reserved for social purposes, and the second floor, which houses the figure of Buddha, has chairs for its worshippers, and a pulpit for the priest.

This temple is quite active in the community. Its first girls' school, giving courses in sewing and Japanese morals, was opened in 1910. Two dormitories for school children in Honolulu and a Sunday school for children are maintained by this sect. Regular radio broadcasts are likewise conducted.

Shingon

Among the other sects of Buddhism represented in Honolulu, the Shingon, or True Word sect, is one of the most influential. The doctrine of this sect was introduced into Japan by Kobo Daishi in A.D. 806 and includes a great deal of mystical ritualism, lapsing often into magic. The first Shingon-shu was established in Honolulu in 1914 and at present the main temple is located on Sheridan Street, below King. Another official temple is located in Liliha and there are many small private O-Daishi scattered throughout Honolulu, which are not officially recognized. The main temple claims a membership of 1,000.

Regular services are held three evenings of every month, on the first, tenth, and twenty-first. The bishop, in a brilliant orange robe and his four assistants in black robes chant some of the Buddhist Sutras accompanied at times by the congregation and the music of bells and wood blocks. Certain ceremonies conducted by the bishop, as well as a sermon, are included in these services. The distribution of holy water to the worshippers also occurs afterwards.

Sunday school for children and clubs for young women and men are also provided through the Shingon-shu. But its most spectacular service is in the curing of illness, for which Shingon-shu is noted among its followers. One of the reputed cures involves a student who met with an accident which left her unconscious for several days. The family assembled at the Temple where a special service, called the reading or chanting of *Sengan Shingyo*, was performed for the daughter. This consists chiefly in the repetition of a brief prayer a thousand times. According to the story, when the choir finished the last chant, there was a telephone call from the hospital saying that the patient had just regained consciousness.[9]

The Tendai Sect

With its one temple located on Young Street near Alapai since 1915, this sect is historically older than any of the other Buddhist sects represented in Honolulu. Noted for its eclectic tendencies, this movement in Japan has given birth to the Nichiren, Amida, and Zen sects of Buddhism, and it is not surprising that the small group of Honolulu worshippers at the Tendai temple should also be affiliated with other sects. The chief object of worship in the Honolulu temple is Fudo, god of wisdom, although other deities are also worshipped. The worship is entirely in Japanese and the temple indicates little of western influence. Much emphasis is placed upon healing services.

The Soto Mission

Representing the Zen sect of Buddhism, the Soto Mission was established in Honolulu in 1903 and is located at the corner of School and Nuuanu streets. The temple is an impressive structure of conventional Japanese temple architecture. An elaborate altar is designed to assist in the "silent meditation and abstract contemplation"[10] by which the worshippers seek to penetrate into reality. Chairs are provided for the worshippers and a small organ also is used.

The Soto branch of Zen places considerable emphasis upon "book learning as a subsidiary aid to silent meditation on the truth,"[11] and it supports a Sunday school for children and a vocational school for girls where sewing and embroidery are taught.

Notes

1. Because of limitation of space, this article covers only some of the external features of Buddhist temples in Honolulu. The original study from which this article is extracted, dealt with (1) the history of the sect; (2) a description of the temple; (3) the type of congregation; (4) a description of a service; and (5) the activities of the temple.

2. See Brinkley, *Cap't Frank: A History of the Japanese People*, New York, 1915, pp. 369–372 for short commentaries on the nature and significance of the different sects in the Buddhist thought system.

3. Since its introduction to Honolulu in 1897, this temple has grown steadily both in prestige and membership, until today it has the largest membership (1000) in the Territory of Hawaii.

Honpa Hongwanji is a subdivision of the strong Shin sect founded by Shinran Shonin in 1224 A.D. Of its ten sub-sects in Japan, the Hongwanji branches, Nishi Honpa and Higashi, are the only ones represented in Hawaii. As preaching centres of Shinran Shonin's teachings, the Honpa Hongwanji has a central temple and seven small district branches located throughout the city. The Higashi Hongwanji has two sub-branches in addition to its central temple.

4. The Hongwanji mission maintains three separate language schools in Honolulu, one known as the Fuoto Gakuen or the Fort Grammar School, another as the Palama Gakuen, and the third as the Hawaii Chujokakko or the Hawaii Boys' and Girls' Middle School. The grade schools, covering the first six years of elementary education in reading and writing are pre-paratory schools for the high school which offers a diversified cultural education of four years. A graduate of the high school may complete two more years in the Kotoka or the College Preparatory School. A Kotoka graduate may enter the Shihanka or Teachers College for an extra-year, practicing in the grade schools.

Faculty members, with the aid of a few teaching cadets in the grade schools, teach the students of their respective schools on Sundays.

5. This sect was founded by Nichiren in 1253. The doctrine is based on "the sutra Myoho-renge-kyo, which contains the last instruction of Buddha . . . preached in Japan for the first time by Nichiren. It is the doctrine of the three great secrets; adoration (*honzon*), law (*daimoku*) and moral (*kaidan*), which resume all the discourses of Shaka: It is however so profound that only the Buddha and the highest Bosatsu can comprehend it. The followers of Nichiren have always been the most turbulent and fanatic Buddhists in Japan. Little by little the sect split into nine branches which at present have 5,194 temples, about 3,700 bonzes, chiefs of tera and 1,283,600 adherents." E. Papinot, *Historical and Geographical Dictionary of Japan*, pp. 430–40.

6. Sansom translates it as "Homage to the Scripture of the Lotus of the Good Law" (See Sansom, *Japan, A Short Cultural History*, New York, 1936, p. 326). Members of the Nichiren Sect worship the above revered scripture, the utterance of which they believe brings salvation. The principal book upon which the teachings of the sect is based is the Saddharma-Pundarika-sutra, In Japanese, the Hokkekyo.

7. The origin of this service is explained as follows: "Early on the morning of the 28th of the 4th month in the 5th year of *Kencho-he* (meaning Nichiren) stood on the summit of Kivesumi and gazing intently at the sun which had just begun to rise in all its resplendent majesty above the horizon that united the heaven and the mighty Pacific in the far away distance, sonorously uttered for the first time, the title "'Namu Myoho-Kenge Kyo'" G. Umata, *Foot-steps of Japanese Buddhism*, Part 1, "Life and Teaching of Saint Nichiren'", p. 6.

8. Tajima, *Japanese Buddhism in Hawaii*, p. 24.

9. This student attends a Christian church and her parents are devout members of the Zen sect, yet every month they all attend Shingon-shu.

10. A. K. Reischauer, *Studies in Japanese Buddhism*, p. 116.

11. Ibid.

10. The Second Generation Japanese
and the Hongwanji

KATSUMI ONISHI

The first missionary priest of the Honpa Hongwanji, the largest sect of Buddhism in Japan, arrived in Hawaii in 1897. In spite of early difficulties, this (Shin-shu) sect has grown into the most powerful of the Buddhist sects in the Islands. It numbers among its adherents some 15,000 members, 10,000 Sunday school children and about 3,500 Young Buddhist Association members. Thirty-six temples, some twenty-one language schools, and thirty-nine Y.B.A. organizations scattered throughout the Islands are evidence of the influence of the Hongwanji among the Japanese population of Hawaii. Of the 28,000 odd adherents, more than half are second generation Japanese with American citizenship.

The success achieved by this movement in Hawaii in due in part to the mere persistence of old country values and in part to the sympathetic attitude of the leaders toward Americanization. The first bishop of this sect in Hawaii expressed his attitude as follows:

> *I take here the liberty of announcing in no ambiguous terms that our mission as a whole advocates Americanizing the people of this territory in every possible way. I, more than anybody else, am aware of my incompetency in carrying on this work. Born a Japanese, brought up as a Japanese, I am a Japanese through and through. Whatever honest intention and pure motive I may have, this sense of incompetency has always kept me from pushing to the front as an active participant in this work of Americanization. . . . Our mission in the islands is, in a sense, a cradle of future Americans.*[1]

A similar attitude has been maintained by the leaders of this sect throughout its history in Hawaii.

Youth and Buddhism

The child in the average Buddhist family in Hawaii comes under the influence of the parental religion at an early age. He sees his parents go into the garden to pick the daily *o-hana* (flowers) for the *butsudan* (Buddha's shrine). He watches his mother reverently offer fresh rice to the shrine and soon learns that no rice is to be eaten unless some of it is first offered on the altar. With the flowers and rice before the shrine and two small

---

"The Second Generation Japanese & the Hongwanji", by Katsumi Onishi, *Social Process in Hawaii*, Vol. 3, 1937. Reprinted by permission of Social Process in Hawaii.

candles lighted on either side of the *butsudan*, the mornning worship begins. He may join in the service, imitating his parents as they offer the prayer of thanksgiving (*Namu Amida Butsu*), burn incense, and bow in deep reverence before the altar. He gazes interestedly at the flickering candles, delights in the melodious "ching-ching" of the tiny gong and plays aimlessly with the beads on the rosary. When father lets him light the candles and burn the incense, he is delighted. He asks his father to let him blow out the candles after the worship. Everything is mysterious, an endless wonder to the young child. He does not understand exactly what it is all about, but he sits with the family, watches the candles, hears and repeats the prayer. The service which is held before breakfast is repeated in the evening just before bed time.

Long before the child enters either the public or the language school, he starts attending Sunday school with his elder brother or sister or a neighboring friend. The temple beautifully decorated with flowers, candles and much gold lacquer work, impresses him far more than his own family shrine. He listens to the organ, to the *gathas* (hymns) and learns to sing them in his own childish way. He listens to the tales of Buddha, of Shinran the founder of his sect, to exciting adventure stories, fables and myths. He meets new faces, makes new friends, learns to revere and respect the Buddha. He anxiously looks forward to the *o-sagari-mono*, usually candy distributed to the pupils after it has been offered on the temple altar. Sunday is a day of joy, of fun, and of new and exciting experiences for him.

When the boy approaches junior high school age, Sunday school often loses its charm, and as he gets older, he drifts away more and more. The stories are not interesting enough, or other attractions, usually athletics, demand his time and attention. He may also consider the family worship as something childish and neglect to join in the services. Approximately two thirds of the boys lose touch with the temple when they drop out of Sunday school at adolescence. Only the most conscientious remain with the temple.

On the other hand, the Sunday school has a firmer hold on the average adolescent girl. She continues to attend regularly, often even after she has finished school and may join a girls' club, sponsored by the Sunday school. The more capable of the girls are chosen to help the priest conduct his classes. Later, with increasing duties at home, the girls likewise tend to drop out of Sunday school.

A substantial number of the more interested young people continue their affiliations with the Hongwanji by joining the Y. B. A., an organization similar to the YMCA and the YWCA. They attend the meetings occasionally and participate in the different activities of the organization to their best advantage. At marriage, they may transfer affiliations to the *kyodan*, the active supporting congregation, or may continue as members of the Y. B. A. An eldest son who is fulfilling the obligations of his deceased father, is more likely to cast in his lot with the *kyodan*. Should his father be still living, he remains with the Y. B. A. as long as he sees fit. Only a few are members of both organizations at the same time.

With the gradual decline in the number of first generation Japanese through death and departure to Japan, the active support and the control of the Hongwanji temples with their Y. B. A.'s, language and Sunday schools are passing into the hands of the second generation. The first generation declare that they wish to turn over the temple affairs to the younger set, but they continue to exercise their authority and power. Of the second generation that are elected to the board of directors, only a few take an active interest in the management of affairs. The majority confine their chief activities to the Y. B. A. and postpone joining the older and more conservative *kyodan*. In one community where the first generation have actually retired in favor of the second generation, fears of the elders that the younger set was incapable of continuing the support of the temples have proven groundless. The process is very slow, as those in power are reluctant to relinquish their hold upon the organizations, but the trend is inevitable.

Buddhist Festivals

Among the numerous Buddhist festivals and ceremonies, none has more appeal and glamour than the *Bon* festival, celebrated in Hawaii during the months of July and August, depending upon the use of the solar or the lunar calendar. The approach of this festival, which honors the ancestors and the dead, is eagerly anticipated by all sects and by both young and old. It is a time of gaiety, of dancing, fine clothes, feasts and general merrymaking. With New Year's Day, it is one of the two important days in the year for the Japanese when the scattered members of the family circle reunite to celebrate the occasion.

At *Bon*, the altar of the *butsudan* is decorated more carefully than ordinarily. Instead of the usual offering of rice, special candy, oranges or mochi are substituted. The daily *o-hana* from the back garden is missing and in its place may be a beautiful bouquet from the florist's. A *cho-chin* or lantern, hung before the shine, continues to be lighted a week prior to and for the duration of the *Bon* season.

The most attractive feature of the festival to the second generation is the dance, known as *Bon-odori*. Usually held in the temple yards, these *Bon-odori* attract hundreds of followers who travel long distances to attend them. Even in the strictest of families, the bars of discipline are let down and the children are allowed to participate in the merrymaking. *Bon* without the *Bon-odori* is like Christmas without the Christmas tree.

The most noticeable feature of these *odori* is the almost complete absence of the first generation, especially among the ranks of the dancers. Most of them are content to be merely spectators. The more active and capable ones may help beat the drums or chant in the shed built for the musicians and the drummers. All do their share by contributing towards the dance fund from which must be paid the drummers and the singers. With the retirement of the first generation from active participation in the *Bon-odori*, their places are being rapidly filled by the second generation who today sponsor the majority of these dances through special committees of the Y. B. A. The element of play, the youthful urge for activity, and the fascination of the rhythmic dance can largely explain the eagerness with which the younger group relieve the older generation of the responsibility. It may be noted that in the majority of the cases, the latter are helping behind the scenes in the planning and the preparation of the dance.

Besides the *Bon* festival, *Hanamatsuri*, or the Flower Festival celebrating the birth of Buddha is observed by all Buddhists. Curiously enough, *Hanamatsuri* in Hawaii has never attained the significance of the *Bon* festival. It was not until some ten or twelve years ago when Buddha's birthday was first celebrated as a joint affair under the auspices of all the

Buddhists irrespective of sect, that the second generation Japanese became actively conscious of *Hanamatsuri*.

Like *Hanamatsuri*, Bodhi Day, the day of Buddha's enlightenment, was scarcely known among the second generation a few years ago. After the day was called to the attention of the delegates at a Pan-Pacific Y. B. A. conference some eight years ago, the practice of observing Bodhi Day has become increasingly popular among the second generation Buddhists who observe it more religiously than their parents who are disposed to neglect Buddha for St. Shinran the founder of the sect. This special emphasis on Bodhi Day and *Hanamatsuri* has sharply focused the attention of the second generation on original Buddhism which is more logical and appealing to the American educated Buddhist than the teaching of faith in Amida Buddha by St. Shinran. As the young Buddhist studies original Buddhism, the task of reconciling the teachings of Buddha and the creed of St. Shinran becomes increasingly difficult. It is a problem now facing the Hongwanji priests.

Young Buddhist Associations

Of the many young people's organizations existing among the second generation Japanese in Hawaii, the Y. B. A. is one of the strongest and the most influential. The thirty-nine units scattered throughout the Islands play an important role in the Japanese community. Organized along the lines of the YMCA, they perform a variety of duties and activities in connection with the missions with which they are affiliated. Among the activities engaged in by a typical Y. B. A. unit may be mentioned the following: religious—lectures and classes in Buddhism; educational—night classes in English and Japanese; dramatics and oratorical contests, arts and crafts, etiquette; social—welfare work as cleaning cemeteries, picnics, socials and dances, participation in the Territorial Y. B. A. conventions; athletic—sponsoring and participating in American and Japanese sports.

The Y. B. A. hall affords a convenient place for lectures, educational movies, discussions and parties for the use of the community. Through this organization, the second generation have helped break down some of the traditional customs and prejudices of the older gener-ation. The introduction of social dancing into the Y. B. A. and some slight modifications in the marriage customs, as having a Buddhist instead of a Shinto priest unite a couple, may be mentioned as a possible influence of the Y. B. A. on the first generation. As an active socializing agent in the athletic, educational, religious, and social fields, the Y. B. A. occupies a conspicuous position in the lives of the second generation Buddhists.

Religious Accommodations

Realizing the difference in the background and the education of the rising generation and the inadequacy among them, of the methods that proved so successful in spreading Shinran's teachings among the first generation, the Hongwanji has tried to adapt itself to meet the needs of the young Japanese Americans. The adjustment to the new Hawaiian environ-ment was not begun early enough to cope effectively with the situation today, but a definite beginning has been made to meet changing conditions. In order to spread the gospel of

Buddha more effectively among the Hawaiian-born, publications explaining the fundamental tenets of Buddhism have been issued in English. An English division was established and services in English have been developed to replace the Japanese rituals. This change is particularly welcomed by the rising generation as the services become more meaningful and understandable. Five second generation priests trained in Japan under a special scholarship created by the Hongwanji are now engaged in mission work among the young men and women. Three more studying in Japan will soon return to assist those in active service now.

One of the outstanding features of Japanese Buddhism in contrast with most western religions is the absence of a hymnology. To cope with this deficiency, the Hongwanji has undertaken the task of composing hymns in Japanese and English suitable for the different occasions like *Bon* and *Hanamatsuri*. The result is a repertoire of Buddhist music sufficient to meet the immediate needs of the day. Those actively engaged in the development of new *gathas* and music are pioneering in a field quite foreign to Buddhism.

According to Japanese custom and tradition, wedding rites are properly the function of the Shinto priest, and funerals are properly officiated by the Buddhist minister. In the new environment of Hawaii, Buddhism, especially the Hongwanji sect, has invaded the field of Shintoism and has taken part of its function in the marriage ceremonies. The number of weddings among the second generation that are officiated by a Buddhist priest is increasing year by year. A common practice to-day, it was considered a novelty only a decade ago. This invasion into a field, formerly forbidden by age-long customs, is clearly the influence of the second generation Japanese who, educated in American ideals and practices, wish to have their wedding solemnized in the temples of their faith. Buddhism, flexible and adaptable to new situations, has struck a new note of optimism and happiness in Hawaii and promises to undergo still further changes to meet the conditions and demands of the rising generation.

Language Schools

No discussion of the second generation Japanese in Hawaii is complete without a note on the language schools. The twenty-one language schools[2], a vital factor in the support and maintenance of the Hongwanji temples, are attended by some 8,500 young Japanese Americans. Besides the regular instruction in the Japanese langguage, these schools lay great emphasis on ethics, especially filial piety and respect to elders. The low proportion of personal disorganization among the second generation Japanese in Hawaii has often been credited to the close attention given to the moral and character training of the students by these schools. It is generally conceded among the first generation Japanese that the solidarity of the Japanese family in Hawaii has been maintained in part through the instruction in ethics and language in these schools. The ability to read, speak, and write the language of his parents has been a vital factor in the economic life of many a second generation Japanese. Through his knowledge, he has been able to secure a more lucrative position, a higher social status among his associates and a greater self-respect. Despite the dwindling numbers of first generation Japanese, a poor command of the Japanese language is still an obstacle in getting a good position. The language schools are attempting to meet this situation. The practice among the second generation of going to Japan to continue or round out their education can often be traced to the influence of the language school, although other factors such as parental influence and economic advantage are also involved. Despite the growing reluctance of the local born to attend the language schools, their careers will continue to be influenced by these schools for some time to come.

That the Hongwanji plays a vital and important role in the lives of the second generation Buddhist is evident. In the home, at school, at work, in his social, educational and religious life, through marriage and through death, the Honwanji helps to direct and shape his future. He in turn is breathing new life and vigor into the Hongwanji, freeing it from the shackles of narrow sectarianism, creating and evolving a new Buddhism, peculiar and native to Hawaii.

Notes

1. Y. Imamura, *A Short History of the Hongwanji Buddhist Mission in Hawaii*, p. 7.

2. The language schools maintained by the Hongwanji constitute only a portion of the total. In 1936, 178 Japanese language schools with a total enrollment of 41,173 pupils and teaching staff of 705 were reported to the Department of Public Instruction.

11. Religion in Our Family

MASAKO TANAKA*

Religion has for several generations played an important role in our family. My grandfather and grandmother (my father's parents) had always been devout Buddhists who spent much of their time praying and attending services in temples and in other people's homes. Religious faith had a great influence upon Father from his early youth, and also upon Mother after she got married and came to live with them. And now we in turn are under the strong influence of our parents.

Although my parents do not make a lot of fuss about dances, dates, and acquiring a higher education, like many other Japanese parents, they are very particular when it comes to religious customs and traditions which are ignored in many homes.

Every morning before breakfast, each member of the family is expected to pray before the altar. We must also thank God for the food before and after each meal.

In the morning, each person usually prays individually, since we all rise at different times and are not ready for breakfast at the same time. However, in the evening the whole family gathers before the altar to pray before going to bed. No one is allowed to go to bed before praying, so usually when a member of the family wishes to go to bed early, he lights the candles, burns some incense and taps the little gong that is on the altar. No matter who rings the gong, whether it be Father or the baby of the family, all members of the family will quickly assemble in the room, where our nearly a century old altar is placed.

Then Father sits at the head of the group before the altar and leads the family in prayers. The prayers are difficult and we children do not understand anything we are saying. However, we have been saying them since we were very young, even before we started for school. Everyone in our family knows them so well that we can say them without even thinking.

Every morning Mother places newly cooked rice and fresh flowers on the altar. Also whenever we have anything good to eat, like fruits and candies, or when we make anything special, like mochi or cakes, something is always placed on the shrine. We have been taught since we were very young never to eat anything that is given to the family or that is specially made without first offering some to God. Although pastries, fruits and candies are offered, meat, fish, eggs and other flesh of living things are not offered. It is against our religion to do so.

The offering of food to God isn't such a bad idea after all, for in the evening after the prayers are over, it is taken down from the altar and divided among the members of the

---

*This is a pseudonym used, at the request of the writer, in order to prevent embarrassment to persons involved.

"Religion in Our Family", by Masako Tanaka, *Social Process in Hawaii,* Vol. 12, 1948. Reprinted by permission of Social Process in Hawaii.

family. Therefore the younger children always light the candles and assemble the family early, so that they can enjoy the nice things.

On Sundays, with other children of the neighborhood, my brothers and sisters and I all walk to the Community Sunday school which is located about a mile away. Every child feels it is his duty to go to Sunday school, so fortunately, my parents do not have to coax us, as parents of other families do.

In a recent disaster, I was able to observe the important role of religion in the family. On April 1, 1946, my fourteen-year-old brother Fred was lost in the tidal wave with twenty-five other students and teachers of X school. When the disaster occurred, everyone in the community was upset and there was much disorganization in the community. This was the first time that I could clearly see the difference between one family which had great faith in God and others which had very little faith.

At the time of the disaster, families which were less religious and had very little faith in God cried and cried, blamed their loss upon the waves, the principal of the school, seismologists, and anybody else whom they could possibly accuse. They damned God for making them lose their sons and daughters while other people's children were spared. Of course my parents felt the loss just as keenly and greatly as anyone else. I'm quite sure Fred was just as dear to them as the other children were to their parents, and that the thought must have occurred to them, "Why did our son have to go when the neighbors' children returned safely?" However, they did not blame others for our misfortune, nor did they curse against God for taking away a member of our family. Instead they prayed very hard and tried to make themselves and the rest of the family understand that God wanted it that way, that Brother Fred had only been loaned to us, and that that was the day set for his return to God's land. They shed many, many tears but they were not hysterical like many other parents. It was not because they did not love their child as much as other parents, but because they had such great faith in God. They felt that Fred was safe and that we need not worry for God would take care of the rest. My parents were much more self-possessed than many other parents who had lost their children.

When I first found out that Fred was missing, I was very much afraid to notify my parents for fear that my mother might lose her mind or something dreadful might happen to her from the great shock. But much to my surprise I found that my mother and father acted much more sensibly than many other parents whom I had seen. For the first time I was very grateful that my parents and family had great faith in God, which guided them and gave them great comfort during those dark and grievous moments when we were most in need of help.

Like most true Buddhists, we held an elaborate service for Fred. Since we could not find his body, we only had his picture at his service. We went through all the proper rituals regarding the dead. Our family and close relatives attended the temple the following day and on the seventh day we had another service at our home. On the forty-ninth day, we gave two packages of coffee to all the families who had extended their sympathy during our bereavement. We also had a service at our home that night. When one year passed by, another service was held for Fred. After these services, we always served food, but no meat, fish, or eggs were used. Also, an even number of different kinds of foods were prepared. We held all of the required services, hoping to help the spirit of the dead one to follow the right road to heaven.

Like a majority of the Buddhists, our family has always adhered very closely to the customs of *Bon*.[1] Every *Bon* festival, we decorate our family plot with lanterns, flowers, and food. We also pour some water on the tombstone, meant to soothe the thirst of the dead. Then we light the candles, burn some incense, and all pray together. After our family plot has been taken care of, we place candles, incense, and flowers on our friends' graves, and especially on the graves of those that have no one to decorate them. We also place incense and flowers on a huge tombstone which has an opening at the bottom in which are placed the bones that have been accidently dug up. Then we usually attend a service or the gala *Bon* dance, if any is held. I usually went to a *Bon* dance not with the intention of dancing, but to try to get as many towels as I could to have Mother make an attractive blouse for me. Of course that was not the right spirit to go with to a *Bon* dance.

Another significant thing about Bon, before the war, was that we always gave lanterns to the family who had lost members of their family in the preceding war.

Our family has always participated in the monthly services conducted at one house after another. Each family takes a turn holding the service at their house and all the people go to their home to hear the priest. After the service, food is served and people indulge in gossip and discuss community problems. Food at this type of service includes meat and fish. Also each month, the families take turns in collecting money to pay for the priest.

Most of the community's young children attend these services to enjoy the food. That is how a typical monthly service is held in our community.

As I compare the customs in our home when my grandparents were living with the family customs of our home today, I can clearly see the changes that are gradually taking place. But I do not mean that because we are adhering less and less to the traditions and customs our religious faith is weakening.

One of the first changes which I notice is that our daily prayers are much shorter than they used to be when Grandpa led the family. He always used to chant prayers that took at least one hour and a half to complete. So, we often got bored and would sneak away and go to bed. Of course, Grandpa used to be furious with us. Nowadays, our prayers are only about five minutes long. Only on special occasions are longer prayers chanted.

The practice of offering cooked rice twice a day is reduced to once a day now.

Another change which I notice concerns the fasting on the death days of anyone of our family or a close kin. On those days our grandparents fasted and refrained from meat and fish for the three meals of the day, for forty-nine days. They were very particular about the tradition. However, when Fred died, Dad excused the family from fasting after the seventh day. He felt that with all the worries, shock, and disappointment we would ruin our health. He believes that we should eat everything to bring back our health to normal.

As one of the traditions, our family always fasts on the first, twelfth, and seventeenth of the month in honor of Fred, Grandpa, and Grandma respectively. We used to fast three meals a day but now we refrain from fish and meat only one meal a day. These are some of the changes that have taken place in our traditions and will continue to change from generation to generation.

I believe that religion has a great deal to do with maintaining happiness in the family. As yet, although our family is large, we have very few serious problems concerning the members of the family. Religion seems to help keep the children out of trouble.

Judging from our family, although ours is far from a perfect family, I believe that if more families would worship God and had more faith in Him, there would be fewer conflicts, delinquences, crimes, and broken homes, today. Religion to some people has helped a great deal in times of disaster and sorrow, and to many others it has given hope. It helps make this world a happier and a more comfortable place to live in.

Note

1. The memorial celebration during the seventh month when the spirits of the dead are said to return to earth.

12. Mother and Her Temple

MARGARET MIKI

Mother is a devout Buddhist. It has never occurred to her to doubt the existence of a Supreme Being. That to others this Being is personified in the figure of Christ or Mohammed or any other "one" seems to be of no concern to her. Buddha personifies God for her and that is all that matters.

To one whose faith is centered in the temple, it was a blow to have all communications halted with the coming of the war. December 7th, 1941 not only curtailed many privileges for aliens but it closed the doors of the temple to Mother and many others like her. It was not only a black-out during the evenings but a total black-out of Mother's spiritual life.

For days I remember Mother was too engrossed in other immediate activities to be openly concerned with the question of her temple and the priests residing there. But as the passing of the days brought back a bit of equilibrium, one day I heard her calling her friend. As though she already sensed the deep disapproval of society of anything Japanese, she carried on her conversation in a low pitch. I was openly eavesdropping. Part of it went as follows:

Kinoshita san, what do you think happened to our temple? Do you think that they (the priests) were all taken into internment camps? I wonder if Mrs. M is still there. I want to go so very much but I'm afraid.

The answer from the other end seemed to be one of discouragement for Mother heaved a great sigh and there were signs of tears in her eyes. This brought to me the realization that the prospect of years without the right to pray aloud in the language she understood was to Mother one of the most personal losses from the war. It did not matter to her or to the older generation whether or not they understood all of the prayers they uttered. What mattered was the strong feeling of belonging together that they experienced on Sundays. Mother's we-group was torn apart and she felt lost. Perhaps if the Buddhist temples had remained open during the war years, the older generation could have found some form of relief from their feelings of insecurity.

Week days were not very bad since other activities crowded the day and there was no time to waste in brooding. But on Sundays, when others dressed to attend their church services, the lost look on Mother's face was pitiful. The behavior pattern of twenty-one years so suddenly destroyed could not be replaced by another in such a short while. Often I would

"Mother & Her Temple", by Margaret Miki, *Social Process in Hawaii*, Vol. 12, 1948. Reprinted by permission of Social Process in Hawaii.

see her take out her Japanese prayer book and thumb her way through it, her lips moving to denote that she was praying.

Before the war, funerals of friends had been times when Mother and her friends gathered to express their sympathy together in the form of Buddhist prayers and rituals. Now it was no longer possible to do so. After attending several funeral services for friends, I heard her say to this same friend of hers:

Don't you think it's a pity to die now? One can't even be buried decently.

The friend replied:

It just doesn't seem final without the smell of the incense, the temple gong, and the chanting of the prayers at funerals. These haole services are so incomplete and cold. There almost seems to be no respect for the dead. What is this world coming to?

Mother and her friend obviously missed the elaborate rituals that accompanied Buddhist funerals. To her a person was not really dead and properly buried until there were services of *O-tsu-ya* and the chanting of prayers by black or red robed priests. That perhaps sorrow might be eased and emotions controlled by the calm services of the Christian religion did not seem to occur to them. She ended this phase of her conversation by saying:

I don't want to die until the temples are reopened and the priests return from the internment camps. Then I'll be assured of a decent *funeral.*

With the decrease of the community's suspicion towards the aliens, it was gradually possible for a few of the women to at least help in the upkeep of the physical appearance of the temple. This occasion came once a month. Knowing the resistence we youngsters showed to anything associated with Japan, Mother did not try to share her experience with us. Somehow we, her children, had become an out-group so far as the temple question was concerned. Nothing was said but the barrier was there.

The jubilation of V-J Day was not complete for Mother until the news came that the priests were returning once more and that the temples would be reopened. This was the real end of the war for her.

It has taken months to reconvert the dismantled temple, but the speed with which the older generation organized themselves was amazing. As I saw the effectiveness of the united labor of the members of the temple I could understand the feeling of suspicion, bordering on hostility, that many non-Orientals felt towards the Japanese. I could also understand why politicians still harp on the question of bloc-voting. Granting that in this instance the energy of this group was being used in constructive avenues and for religious goals, nevertheless, the intense we-group feeling the older members nurtured was a thing that gave me food for thought.

With the reopening of the temple, however, I have seen Mother regain many of her values and her purpose of living. What was during the war quite a bleak existence with a strong under-current of insecurity is now once more a more meaningful existence. The days of a week, no matter how burdensome, seem to become a thing of the past when she goes to the temple.

Sometime ago on the way home from school, I was seated in the front of the bus. Next to me was an elderly woman of about fifty-five years. She, evidently, was one of these women who are hired by the day by Caucasians to do the laundering or house cleaning. About two bus stops after she had gotten on the bus, another Japanese woman boarded the bus. I gathered she was a friend of the first woman. After the usual exchange of courtesies in such a loud tone of voice that I felt uncomfortable, I heard the first woman say to the second:

My only pleasure now is to go to the temple on Sunday morning and to the movie after that. All my troubles seem to "fall off my shoulders" on Sunday. The temple, the movies, and perhaps some day a grandson are the only interests in my life.

This woman, my mother, and many others like them have once more been able to pick up the threads of a stable life.

One Sunday afternoon I went to the temple to satisfy my curiosity as to what really happens there to give the aliens this feeling of stability. Contrary to the feeling of restfulness that one receives upon entering some churches, the atmosphere was one of festivity. The worshippers chanted their prayers loudly, Mother not the least among them. I knew that ninety per cent of them did not know the meaning of the prayers they were repeating so enthusiastically after the priest. I doubt if they ever stopped to wonder about the meaning. The thought that prayer is really a way in which one communes with a Supreme Being and tries to face the realities of life, to adjust oneself to the Supreme Being, and to understand oneself, appears to be entirely foreign to them. To chant prayers (difficult words that are just words to them) with their hands together was and is sufficient for them. This they all sum up as being *a-ri-ga-tai*. (In a sense this denotes appreciation or thankfulness.)

After the services were over all the old women clattered downstairs chatting loudly in Japanese. It was the first time in four years that I had heard genuine chuckling that came without any restraint from the throats of the older women. They nudged each other at times, exchanged the latest gossip, and actually let out sounds that we would classify as giggling. These women were actually youthful on Sunday afternoons.

To me it meant more than that. It meant that there in the temple Mother and the older generation are once more able to rebuild their self-respect. The war, among other things, took away much of the authority that they held in the home. Much of what they did and said was brushed aside by the younger generation, namely their own children, as being "Japanesey" or "Bobura-ish". They have had to restrain themselves in the matter of self-expression due to the silent reprimands from the society at large and the general forbidding atmosphere symbolized by the slogan, "Speak American".

At the temple they are in a sense, "free". They may converse, laugh, and think together in Japanese. There are no impatient answers or frowns, but rather congeniality. There, they are not the "old lady" and "old man" of some young citizen but personalities whose ideas are respected. There, they count as human beings.

I am not advocating the indefinite retention of the Buddhist temples. Left alone, and ignored by the younger generation, they gradually will be reduced to a mere skeleton. But at present they do have a vital function in the lives of our older generation. One may add an emotional appeal by saying, "The old folks have worked so hard. Why deny them the satisfaction that their temple worship gives them?" If the temples can continue to rehabilitate many others like Mother, can somehow make them feel comfortable in this new atomic age, then Buddhism has accomplished its greatest good in Hawaii.

I have seen the war cause Mother and her friends to lose their footing in the family and in society. I have sensed their feeling of inadequacy and insecurity. For these reasons I do feel that we can accept the temples and their rituals.

Mother is a devout Buddhist. She accepts the existence of a Supreme Being and is contented with her conception of It in the form of Buddha. Her faith centered in the temple gives her happiness and after all that is the thing that counts, for is not happiness in life the ultimate goal of every human being?

13. My Family

DOROTHY YASHIMA

My family consists of seven persons: Father, Mother, two boys and three girls. Father is 58, Mother is 55, and the children's ages are: Big Sister, 30; Big Brother 25; Second Sister, 24; myself, 20; and Little Brother, 14. No one has married, and all live at home.

Father is head of the house, and his opinions are respected by all. He runs a little grocery store owned by Big Sister. Mother is a housewife, and her functions are feeding, caring for, clothing, and worrying about the family. She is physically weak, and all the members of the family protect her, and try to ease her burden. Big Sister manages the store and dominates the family's business affairs. Big brother works at Hickam Field as a carpenter and contributes his pay check to the family. He is the quiet member of the household, but is an important figure in family affairs because he is the eldest son. Second Sister works at the store. Little Brother and I attend school. We help at home or at the store.

Father and Mother together discipline the family and the older children have a hand in the discipline of the youngsters. If Little Brother and I are scolded by Big Sister, we "talk back" and try to justify our actions, but if Mother scolds us, we seldom do, and if Father is the one doing the scolding, we don't dare "talk back".

Both my parents are Japan-born, and had only a Japanese elementary school education. They respect our opinions for there is much that they can learn through us, just as they can teach us. The three older ones out of school have all graduated from high school. Second Sister has graduated from business school, Big Brother went to vocational school before serving in the Army, and Big Sister has had correspondence courses and taught at an island Japanese school for two years. When Father has difficulty in reading the newspaper, he asks one of us, "What is this word? What does it mean?" Mother neither reads nor writes much English, but since the war we have taught her the alphabet and to write her name in English, and to recognize words like LILIHA, KALIHI and KAIMUKI, so that in going from place to place she wouldn't be too greatly inconvenienced.

Father and Mother consult each other a great deal. For example when Little Brother asks permission to go to a show:

Little Brother: Mama—I can go to movies? (Mother is always asked first).
Mother: See what Oto-san *says.*
Little Brother: Oto-san, I want to go show.
Father: You just went last time. Too often is no good. Did you ask Mama? What she say?

"My Family", by Dorothy Yashima, *Social Process in Hawaii*, Vol. 12, 1948. Reprinted by permission of Social Process in Hawaii.

Little Brother: She said ask you.
Father: If she says all right you may go. But not next week again if you go today.
Little Brother: Mama, Oto-san *said ask you and if you say all right, I can go.*
Mother: All right, but come home early.

Evening mealtime is the only time during the day when the whole family sits at the table together. During the day, Father and the girls eat at home in shifts, the youngsters are in school, and Big Brother at work. The family saves its choicest bits of gossip, anecdotes, and the day's experience to relate to the members at this time. These dinner sessions have helped greatly in maintaining the feeling of group solidarity in our family.

Religion plays an important part in our lives. In those days when we attended language school at Fort Gakuen and at Hongwanji, regular attendance at the Buddhist Sunday School there came naturally to us. When the Buddhist churches were closed as a result of the war, our religious education stopped. During the war years we three sisters visited a Methodist church now and then but somehow we felt we didn't "belong". The director of Christian Education of this church encouraged us to join their groups and sent us cordial letters. We still kept back. Then the letters changed in tone and expressed regret and sorrow in the director's failure to "convert" us. We kept away completely after that. During this irregular "Christian interlude" in our lives, my parents never lifted a finger against our seeming to "change" religions, and we felt that we were free to choose as we wished.

About this time also, Little Brother changed from a public school to a private one. At St. Louis College, he got, and is still getting heavy doses of Catholicism. He wants to become a Catholic, which is the only religion he is familiar with, and to him no other religion exists. In his immature mind, he believes that we are all atheists and will go to purgatory. He is unhappy because we tell him to wait until he is older and knows his own mind before joining the Catholic church. "If I die, I cannot be saved," he says.

Buddhism has been our family religion for many generations. My Issei parents are deeply religious and teach us what they learned from their parents. Through religious stories we have got our lessons in honesty, patience, peace, respecting our elders, and of an awareness of our everlasting obligations (o-n) to them.

Every morning when Father gets up he lights a candle or incense at the family shrine. Then he taps the little bronze bowl that has a clear, ting! ting! sound, and prays to the ancestors. When Mother wakes up she also pays homage. This ritual is gone through every morning, but we children are not forced to do so.

Certain religious days call for special rituals. In our small family shrine, we have three small wooden sticks with the names of my three dead sisters. This morning is the day on which the younger of the three died. Mother said, "Today you must light some *sen ko* (incense) for Yae-san and pray for her." I obediently did as she said. I stood in front of the *hotoke sama* and put the palms of my hands together. I lighted two sticks of incense and said, "*na mu ami da butsu*", three times to myself. I don't understand the meaning of the words, but I know that everybody says them. Today we will eat no meat or fish but only tofu, vegetables, and rice.

Sometime, on a death day the whole family goes to the temple where the bones of two of the girls are kept in small sealed boxes. These boxes are all in a large room where hundreds of such boxes are put. I have the impression that the priests guard them with their lives. The priest on duty brings out the box of the one we have come to pray for, and chants long prayers and hits the gong. At the front of the temple there is a large wooden bowl with burning embers and next to it a small box with fragrant incense which feels and looks like ground tobacco. While the priest is still chanting, Father walks to the front, stops a few feet before the bowl, prays with his palms together, and then steps up to the bowl. He prays again, pinches a bit of the ground incense between his thumb and forefinger, brings it up to his forehead, and drops it in the bowl from which thin smoke is slowly rising. Then he prays again and returns to his seat. After him Mother goes up and then the others one by one do the same.

We observe another ritual every New Year's Day. When the old year draws to a close, it is the busiest time of the year. The whole house must be cleaned. On New Year's Eve, we all wait for 12:00 o'clock, when *so-ba* (black noodles) is served. *So-ba*, unlike noodles and saimin, breaks easily into short bits. This signifies that all the last year's bad luck is broken up and gotten rid of. In the morning a special breakfast of *zo-ni*, a soup made of *mochi* (rice dumpling), abalone or fish, and vegetables, is served. On this day everything has a special touch to it. Mother formally addresses each one individually: "*Oto-san, o me de to go zai masu, Nii-chan, o me de to*," and so on *around* the table. And then she makes a little speech to this effect: "We have again greeted a new year. May we all have good health and happiness. You children will be obedient to *Oto-san* and *Oka-san*. Let us hope that we have a good year." She serves Father a tiny cup of Japanese sake (rice liquor) and the cup is passed around to every one of us. I remember that Mother used to dab a little sake on our forehead when we were young.

Marriage is another institution strongly bound by tradition. When Big Brother marries, his wife must come to live with us. This is an understanding that goes without saying. If Big Sister marries, she would go away to live because Big Brother is home to carry on the family name and to look after Mother and Father. Mother hears much gossip about young brides being mean to their mothers-in-law, and feels distressed about such behavior. "In Japan," she say, "there are many stories about mean mothers-in-law, but here the situation is usually just the reverse."

14. Religion and Resistance in America's Concentration Camps*

GARY Y. OKIHIRO

Religion, imbedded in the psyche, folklore, and identity of immigrants, gave meaning and order to the individual, the family, and community, and helped them survive.[1] Religion has also been both a mobilizer for, and an expression of, resistance to colonialism, slavery, and exploitation.[2] While many authors have written on the resistance function of religion in African, Afro-American, and Native American societies, relatively few have explored that theme among other American ethnic minorities, especially among Asian Americans. That neglect is particularly notable because of the central role of religious belief in the Asian cultural heritage.[3]

This essay examines the role of ethnic religion in resistance among the Japanese confined primarily at Tule Lake concentration camp during World War II. The resurgence of ethnic religious belief is seen as part of a wider network of cultural resistance after the Manzanar model of resistance.[4] Cultural resistance was directed against the camp administrators' efforts to "Americanize" the Japanese, and was effective in preserving Japanese American families from total disintegration and in maintaining ethnic identity and solidarity.

There are two basic historical interpretations of Japanese reaction to life in America's concentration camps. The orthodox view characterizes the Japanese as defenseless, dependent, and abiding victims of circumstance. This image was fostered by the paternalistic War Relocation Authority (WRA) which administered the camps.[5] "The outstanding feature of the evacuation process was the complete absence of disturbance from the evacuees. Accepting without public protest the military orders, the evacuees appeared when called and got themselves on the trains without any compulsion by the public authorities."[6] Consequently, resistance by the "submissive" Japanese was depicted as sporadic and uncharacteristic.[7] The orthodox interpretation dismissed the various mass resistance movements in the camps as mere "incidents," and proposed that resistance was fomented by a small minority of pro-Japan agitators and constituted a necessary release of tension. After the outburst, "normalization" was restored resulting in a peaceful, "happy" camp.

In contrast, revisionist historians regard the concentration camps as the culmination of nearly a century of anti-Asian agitation and racial discrimination in America, the essential thrust of which was exclusionism and cultural hegemony. Resistance for the pre-war Japanese,

*The author gratefully acknowledges the research and editorial assistance rendered by Debra May Ushijima.

"Religion & Resistance in America's Concentration Camps: a Re-evaluation", by Gary Y. Okihiro. Reprinted by permission of the author.

according to that interpretation, was a means of survival to maintain their physical presence and culture in the face of white supremacy. That historical struggle continued in the camps when the Japanese, stripped of their civil liberties and the bulk of their property, resisted manipulation of their lives and the administration's attempt to erase their ethnic identity. Two models of resistance were proposed by a revisionist historian.[8] The Poston model of resistance is protest which results in acceptable responses from the administration. Japanese resisters, in the Poston model, realize their goals and achieve greater camp stability. The Manzanar model, on the other hand, is protest which results in unacceptable responses from the administration. Resistance, in the Manzanar model, did not end with administrative intransigence but continued either in open defiance of the WRA or in "the redirection of resistance into new forms which would be para-administration."[9]

Cultural resistance is seen not as unique to the camp experience but as an intensification and revival of past modes of resistance from the pre-war Japanese experience in America, as Frank Miyamoto put the issue, "to most evacuees but especially to the Issei who frequently reminisced about their experience in America, the evacuation was only the most recent and most outrageous expression of the long history of anti-Japanese agitation on the Pacific Coast." Continuing, Miyamoto noted that, "The historical reaction of the immigrant Japanese to instances of anti-Japanese action has been one of very strong resentment against the attitudes of white supremacy, and one motivation behind their economic struggles in America has been the aim of showing the white majority group that they are a group to contend with as equals and not to be treated slightingly."[10] It appears, thus, that anti-Japanese activity frequently resulted in an upsurge of Japanese American ethnicity.

That phenomenon during World War II paralleled the rise of Buddhism within the Japanese American community during the 1920s and 30s in reaction to the anti-Japanese movement of those decades. Kashima, in his *Buddhism in America*, made that observation, citing a study of the Gardena, California, Buddhist church.

> *After the passage of the Immigration Law of 1924 discriminating against the Japanese, the number of Buddhists increased rapidly, and so did that of the Buddhist churches. Before that event, some of them had been hesitant in declaring themselves Buddhists, considering such an act impudent in a Christian country. But the immigration law made them more defiant and bold in asserting what they believed to be their rights; it made them realize the necessity of cooperation for the sake of their own security and welfare, and naturally sought the centers of their communal activity in their Buddhist churches.[11]*

The WRA program for the camps ostensibly included three principal goals. The first was to provide for the physical upkeep of the internees; the second was a longer range objective to relocate the Japanese out of the camps into "normal" communities; and the third was to deal with hostile anti-Japanese elements, especially in the national press.[12] All three objectives emphasized the importance of the WRA "Americanization" program—to demonstrate the loyalty of the Japanese in acquiescing to camp confinement, to enable assimilation into American life, and to refute the accusations of Japanese disloyalty by a hostile press. The WRA saw the camps as a critical trial period for the Japanese in America. "The entire future of the Japanese in America is dependent on their deeds during the emergency," noted the WRA deputy director. "If the Japanese assist in the war effort and prove by constructive deeds, that they are loyal Americans, the public will recognize this fact."[13] Thus, to the camp administrators, the "Americanization" of the Japanese was an essential element in their program.[14]

However, the concentration camps and the WRA's "Americanization" program were progressions in the anti-Asian movement and attacked the basis of Japanese American ethnicity. "Americanization," noted Berkson, meant Anglo-conformity, and sought to disperse the minority communities and alter their ethnic identities and culture including the family, language, and religious belief.[15] Within that context, then, the maintenance of ethnic culture constituted a form of resistance. "When cultures are whole and vigorous," wrote Blauner, "conquest, penetration, and certain modes of control are more readily resisted."[16] Despite the WRA's "Americanization" program, the Japanese retained ethnic beliefs and values, many rooted in religion, and sought to preserve the ethnic community in the face of cultural hegemony. A camp analyst observed that "the assembly of fairly large numbers of Japanese tended to revive some of the practices which had fallen somewhat into disuse. The emotional upheaval which was the inevitable consequence of the disruption of familiar ways of life manifested itself, for many Issei at least, in a return to religion."[17]

For the majority of Japanese in the camps, that efflorescence of formal religion meant Buddhism along with "informal" Shintoism.[18] "The camp administrators could not suppress the religious needs of the Japanese people by encouraging the growth of Christianity and not of Buddhism," observed Horinouchi. "The masses of the Japanese people still identified with Buddhism in name, if not in practice."[19] A WRA survey in 1942 revealed that 61,719 or 55.5 percent listed themselves as Buddhist, while Protestants numbered 32,131 or 28.9 percent.[20] The designation *Buddhist* was politically significant because Buddhism was viewed as pro-Japanese and subversive and Christianity as American.[21] In the days immediately following Pearl Harbor, Shinto and Buddhist priests, along with Japanese language school teachers, were summarily arrested and interned in detention camps administered by the Justice Department. Christians, both white and Japanese, denounced these religions as "pagan," and many Japanese, fearful of being suspect, destroyed all traces of Shintoism and Buddhism such as the *kamidana* and *butsudan* (Shinto and Buddhist family shrines), scrolls, Japanese flags, and pictures of the emperor and royal family.

While the label *Buddhist* made one vulnerable, *Christian* seemed to offer a measure of security. "Many Nisei Buddhists," wrote Kashima, "apparently were afraid to attend the religious institution of their parents: thousands listed 'no preference' in their religion, and many even became Christians."[22] Remarked a Japanese internee, "Buddhists and Shintoists went to the Christian churches because they felt that there would be more protection for them."[23] Those nominal Christians were ridiculed as "Christians of convenience" by both Buddhists and Christians alike.[24] Still, despite the pressure to conform, the large majority of confined Japanese openly espoused Buddhism, and in some camps, Buddhism gained new adherents. Kitagawa, a Christian minister at Tule Lake concentration camp, reported a "profoundly significant" revival of interest in Buddhism even among those previously disinterested,[25] while Gordon Brown, a community analyst at Gila River concentration camp, reported:

> *It is said that the Christians lost in numbers during life in the center. At the time of registration, a well-known Japanese-American minister spoke publicly supporting volunteering for the Army. He incurred the wrath of many and was labelled a "dog." This opprobrium was extended to all Christians and some extremists even today say that "all Christians are dogs." Many half-hearted Christians ceased to identify themselves as such and would not permit their children to attend Christian Sunday school. They were afraid of the consequences of being considered dogs.[26]*

It would be simplistic, however, to characterize Buddhism as "pro-Japanese" and resistant to assimilation and Christianity as "pro-American" and indicative of Anglo-conformity. While nativistic and "traditional" revivals might clearly be seen as assertions of ethnicity, adaptations and acculturated beliefs could also comprise aspects of an ethnic identity. For example, Buddhism underwent situational changes in America,[27] and a few Japanese Christian ministers advocated the ethnic church in the face of integrationist sentiment among the parent white churches. Further, those ministers linked their support for Japanese Christian churches with the wider struggle for ethnic community survival. "The ministry in the relocation centers," wrote Suzuki,

> *. . . was pregnant with the seed of the theology of pluralism. The emergence of that theology was being pressed down. The articulation and implementation of this concept was still in the future, but there was a feeling for it. The Japanese people had a self-consciousness as an ethnic people. They were trying to demand self-definition but their voices were not heard. They were trying to assert their dignity and humanity in the intrinsic worth of their own traditions and cultural inheritance . . . but they were being pressed down at every turn. The ministry tried to affirm their pride as a people of God, and show fidelity to their peculiar peoplehood as a part of God's intention in a pluralistic community.[28]*

Spencer suggests that this resurgence of religious practice was attributable to the increased amount of leisure time in the camps.[29] In contrast, Horinouchi proposed that a more basic consideration was the psychological stress of the camp situation. "Students of religion," noted Horinouchi, "recognize that religious activity increases in relationship to the stresses of the uncontrollable, the threatening, and the unknown. The Buddhistic rituals of repeating and chanting the *sutras*, the offering of incense, and other ritualistic movements are part of the anxiety release or a reaction formation to the uncertainties of the future. Thus, the increased religious behavior in detention camps may be primarily a psychological behavior response to a unique situation and less attributable to the increased leisure time of the internees.[30] Perhaps even more fundamental, Japanese religious belief permeated the culture which in turn gave meaning to the lives of the internees and which stood in opposition to external hegemony and control. This is not to deny the cathartic function of ritual and belief; it simply proposes that in addition to that role, ethnic religious belief comprised a means to resist "Americanization" and anti-Japanese racism, and formed the basis for a wider network of cultural resistance in the camps. Wrote Brown of Buddhists confined at Gila River:

> *When asked what particular contribution Buddhism has for America the usual answer is "democracy." The Lord Buddha believed all men to be . . . spiritual equals. He attempted to break down the caste system of India. . . . Buddhism disregards race.*
>
> *This pat answer . . . is clearly a response to the particular situation in which Japanese Buddhism finds itself. Many priests are still excluded from California, some are interned. They belong to an "oppressed group." Buddhism is "against discrimination." Hence, both to aid themselves and to meet a hostile world, they must concentrate upon that particular interpretation of their religious teachings. . . .*[31]

Buddhist church membership was simply one indication of ethnic religious belief. Religion in Japanese culture cannot be defined narrowly, but must be broadly defined as a people's beliefs and practices concerning their place in the universe and moral code of conduct. "The difference between the American view of religion and the Japanese view," wrote Hirano, "is that the Japanese did not compartmentalize religion. Religion was a part of and inseparable from life."[32] Thus, although it could be said that most Issei did not concern themselves with formal religion, religious belief, nonetheless, permeated their culture and daily activities. Japanese religious belief was syncretistic, containing elements of Shintoism, Buddhism, Confucianism, and Taoism. The nature of this religious belief was compared by Prince Shotoku to the root, stem and branches, and flowers and fruits of a tree:

> *Shinto is the root embedded in the soil of the people's character and national traditions; Confucianism is seen in the stem and branches of legal institutions, ethical codes, and educational systems; Buddhism made the flowers of religious sentiment bloom and gave the fruits of spiritual life. These three systems were molded and combined by the circumstances of the times and by the genius of the people into a composite whole of the nation's spiritual and moral life.*[33]

There are two fundamental features of Japanese religious belief. The first is filial piety and ancestor worship, and the second is the closeness of man, gods, and nature. Filial piety, as expressed in Confucian status ethics, was the cornerstone of Meiji Japan, and while the family unit may have arisen out of economic or political necessity, filial piety has its origins in religion.[34] This hierarchical system of moral and social conduct was codified in the New Civil Law of 1891 which stressed that (a) the family is the basis of society; (b) the family centers around the father; and (c) Japanese hereditary succession is to be strictly maintained (ancestral spirits dwell in the family house and the head of the household is the living embodiment of those spirits).[35] In that way, ancestor worship was simply an extension of filial piety, and both constituted religious belief and ethical morality. The spiritual basis of ancestor worship was enunciated by Bishop D. Ochi, a Buddhist leader at Gila River concentration camp, in his unpublished manuscript, *The Spiritual Life of the Japanese Evacuees.*

> *By devoting himself to the ancestral cult, a person may appear to be idolatrous. Yet the fact cannot be overlooked that by doing so he is adoring the Buddha in his heart. Buddhist philosophy holds that the Buddha essence melts into the spirit of one's ancestors. . . . On this basis, ancestral worship and the Buddha constitute an inseparable unit. Through sutras and services the ancestor is one with the Buddha. To the Buddhist in America the Buddha and the ancestors exist together as a meaningful part of the life of the individual.*[36]

The other basic feature of Japanese religious belief is the closeness of man, gods, and nature. Neither Shintoism nor Buddhism claimed a monotheistic or transcendent god. In fact, Shintoism stressed a love for the land where the ancestors repose and where gods (*kami*) abound, while Buddhism, especially Zen, emphasized enlightenment and harmony with the cosmos. That view of the natural world and of a person's place within the universe formed the basis for various Japanese cultural expressions such as *bonsai, ikebana* (flower arrangement), landscape gardening, the tea ceremony, and *haiku* poetry.[37]

The WRA's "Americanization" policy threatened one of the most basic Japanese cultural institutions, the family. Filial piety—the respect for elders and the role of the father as head of the household and embodiment of the ancestral spirits—was disregarded by the WRA in its "Americanization" of camp government. The WRA maintained that "since the objective of the WRA was to create a community as nearly American in its outlook and organization as possible, policy should conform with American practice, and only citizens should vote and hold office."[38] Further, the WRA gave the Nisei special privileges and recognition because of their American citizenship. "In addition to making elective offices open only to evacuees who are citizens of the United States," stated the WRA national director, "it is our intention to give them preference in considering application for leave from relocation centers, in assignment of work opportunities, and in other respects. . . ."[39]

Although most studies point to this WRA policy as having caused or at least accelerated the generational breach between Issei and Nisei,[40] there is suggestive evidence which points to Japanese success in resisting such a split. This struggle for the control of the children was poignantly described in a WRA report. "But during their stay at the centers they continued their previous practices of religious worship, tried to achieve some semblance of order and dignity in their broken lives, and frequently showed an almost pathetic eagerness to hold their families together and to work back toward their prewar social and economic status."[41]

Revisionist historians have pointed to countervailing forces which worked against the "Americanization" of the Nisei. Hansen and Hacker, for example, enlarge upon the lead provided by Yatsushiro's thesis which maintains that pre-war Japanese culture contained several basic values and beliefs which governed behavior and promoted ethnic solidarity.[42] These, according to Hansen and Hacker, were "strengthened by the pre-evacuation discriminatory practices, reinforced by the evacuation crisis, and expressed within the concentration camp culture."[43] Filial piety, ancestor worship, and family and ethnic collectivity were cultural values which were emphasized in the home and stressed in the Buddhist churches and Japanese language schools.[44] Those internal values were reinforced by external forces such as anti-Japanese agitation, barriers to Nisei assimilation and restrictive employment opportunities, and the concentration camps themselves which were pointed reminders to the Nisei that they were not considered to be "true Americans."[45]

The dislocation caused by the evacuation and the conditions of camp life reinforced the need for group solidarity and mutual aid. There is evidence to suggest that the traditional family roles were strengthened with the Issei father as the hierarchical head. The Issei, from the beginning, resented the WRA "Americanization," which threatened the group's traditional family structure. Nisei, who were previously drifting away from Japanese culture, were drawn back to the family unit. Discrimination and the denial of their rights disillusioned many Nisei. They now looked more to their families and ethnic community for security and acceptance. Evidence of this was seen in the reasoning of Nisei who answered "No-No" to the loyalty questions, 27 and 28. Two brothers were closely questioned on why they had renounced their American citizenship:

> Board Member: *"You want to be American citizens?"*
> Subject #1:   "Well, there's our parents."
> Board Member: *"You are over 20 years old."*
> Subject #1:   "But the parents come first no matter how old you are."[46]
>   (Emphasis in original)

As time progressed, the block, a camp residential unit consisting of fourteen barracks, emerged as a primary unit of ethnic solidarity. Although many families within the block were from different geographical areas prior to evacuation, living in close quarters resulted in a degree of cohesiveness through group endeavors in improving conditions around their blocks and in self-governance. Solidarity was evident, for example, in boasts of talented chefs or well landscaped grounds within a block. The Issei, respected for their knowledge which comes with age, became the central core of block leadership. That was in direct conflict with the WRA mandate on internal camp government which had disenfranchised the Issei but in harmony with traditional Japanese culture. The success of resistance against that aspect of WRA rule has been documented elsewhere.[47] The block eventually became equated with the extended family in the common camp expression, "My block is like my family."

The block took on the characteristics of the family in stressing conformity of the individual to the collective will. Thus, block residents disciplined children who lacked parental control and brought discredit to the collective. The slogan, "Keep Children Within the Block," was widely circulated. The Young People's Association, a block organization, was initiated and supervised by the Issei as a means of promoting morals and obligations through social activities. With group conformity a policy, members within the block were required to subject their individual wishes to the will of the majority. Rumors and gossip were oftentimes used as tools to maintain conformity and solidarity.[48] Rebels were ostracized from the group and branded *inu*.

The block community merged into a camp-wide group identity by referring to such phrases as the *Japanese spirit* and *We're all Japanese*. On the few special cultic occasions such as New Year's Day and *Obon*, Japanese of all ages observed and participated in the rituals. Traditional speeches extolled the people's Japanese ties. Such occasions were "a means whereby members renewed their solemn allegiance to the group, reaffirmed the established themes in their center culture, and thereby nourished the solidarity of the group."[49] Phrases which exemplified that Japanese spirit were not essentially nationalistic or anti-American. Instead, the phrases sought to remind the internees of the virtues of their cultural ancestry and to enable them to resist the forces of "Americanization" which threatened their existence as a people. The following is a typical exhortation for ethnic solidarity: "It is not possible to be an informer as we are all Japanese. We should have loyalty to our own group. A Japanese cannot kick another Japanese. . . ."[50] The excerpt below exemplifies the use of ethnic cultural values to promote ethnic solidarity, and at the same time illustrates its neutral nationalistic content. *Yamato damashii* or "Japanese spirit" was a patriotic rallying cry for Japanese militarists and an expression of anti-Americanism for the WRA camp authorities; within this context, however, it was employed to depict customary virtues of perserverance, loyalty, forbearance, and sacrifice for the common good. The speaker was a Nisei at Minidoka and the occasion a farewell banquet for the volunteers of the all-Nisei combat team.

> *We have been kicked around and kicked around. We have lost most of what we had. We have been stuck here in these centers. And we don't feel too good about it. But we know our future will depend on what these boy volunteers will do. They have had the courage to risk their lives in spite of this. We know that they will go in there and fight and we know that they will never do anything to dishonor the spirit of* Yamato damashi.[51]

Camp life had achieved a degree of security in the retention of such virtues as filial piety and ancestor worship, in the family unit, and in the ethnic community. In a speech delivered in San Francisco, Dillon Myer, WRA national director, categorically stated: "The bulk of Nisei or second generation groups are wholehearted Americans . . . and have absorbed Americanism almost as naturally as they breathe. To claim otherwise is equivalent to asserting that American institutions exercise a less potent influence over the youthful mind than the transplanted institutions of the Orient. I deny that assertion. I have faith in the strength of American institutions. . . ."[52] In contrast, in a report filed by Myer's own agency, a camp high school principal noted the realities of the "struggle with family institutions for the possession of the future of the child. . . ." The principal wrote of the difficulty in combating the language problems of the students. The Nisei were said to have been greatly influenced by their ties with the ethnic community, thus affording little opportunity to speak English. The report went on to point to "regressive tendencies in the Issei community" as the cause for the decline in the students' English vocabulary "by as much as four full grades since Fall of 1942."[53] In contrast to the languishing English medium schools, the Japanese language schools flourished. For example, at Tule Lake, there were three established Japanese schools with branches dispersed "in all corners of the camp." The schools enrolled 5,355 students and maintained a teaching staff of 160. The English schools, on the other hand, enrolled only a total of 2,529 students from preschool to high school, with a staff of just over fifty-five.[54] Along with the deterioration of English, the Nisei invented a camp jargon called *Evacuese* which reflected the bitterness and irony of camp life. *Evacuese* combined English and Japanese with an underlayer of resistance humor. The term *barracks*, for example, became *buraku* in *Evacuese*; *buraku* to these Nisei implied a primitive, tribal colony. The word *foreman* was substituted for the *Evacuese* term, *foeman*.[55] Suzuki, in his study of the ethnolinguistics of the camps, concludes: "the total camp experience became embedded in a matrix of words used to circumscribe a segment of their lives, of which the images and memories conjured up by some of the slang terms and phrases to account for that experience, although latent for many Nisei, even today evoke powerful emotions that cannot be readily dissociated from a unique phase of Japanese American history."[56]

Besides the revival of formal organized religion in Buddhism, there was a resurgence of Japanese folk beliefs and practices at Tule Lake.[57] Marvin Opler, a community analyst at the camp from 1943 to 1946, observed the rise of a "nativistic cultural revivalism" during that period and documented its swift decline after the closing of that camp in 1946. Following Linton's analysis of nativistic movements,[58] Opler distinguished between perpetuative-magical movements or ones invoked to perpetuate a culture or group, and revivalistic-magical movements or ones in which "revival is a part of a magical formula designed to modify the society's environment in ways which will be favorable to it" and thus take on more intense forms. At Tule Lake, according to Opler, all 19,000 internees participated in this folkloristic revival which took the form of Linton's revivalistic-magical movement. "Folklore which had been remembered by a handful of Issei," wrote Opler, "and perpetuated in a small circle, was seized upon by Issei and Nisei alike in a broadening sphere where it was deemed important to strike back at administrative pressures, programs, and policies with the dignified weapons of Japanese culture."[59]

One of the more prevalent beliefs was the *hidama* or "fireball" which was an omen of bad luck, and the *hinotama* or "ghost seen as a fireball presaging death." These were reportedly seen by Issei and Nisei alike signifying impending death. Two accounts of *hinotama* are excerpted below.

There are ghosts seen over there, hinotama. *Greenish lights, they say, bigger than a fist. Last winter, I heard only one story of light coming out of the camp smoke above the field on a foggy morning, but now all sorts of stories are going around. We wouldn't go near too early in the morning or at night around that barrack. It's the worst place.*

A young girl . . . was walking back to her apartment . . . when something prompted her to look over her shoulder. She glanced up and was chilled by a strange glow hovering over the latrine roof. She shivered violently and hurried home to tell her mother, fully expecting her not to believe it. But her mother look worried, opens the door, looks out, but says nothing. The girl insisted on knowing what it was and her mother told her she must have seen hinotama. *A few days later an elderly bed-ridden block resident died.*[60]

Another folk belief made popular in the camps was of the fox, cat, and badger. These animals were connected with the widespread and important cult of the rice goddess Inari, who descended from heaven to Japan during a time of famine riding on a white fox and holding in her hand sheaths of grain or cereal. Inari was a bearer of food, and thus was not only connected with agriculture and farming but also with commerce. The worship of Inari in Japan, particularly in the agricultural regions from whence most of the Issei derived, was so widespread that it was nearly a distinct cult and religion.[61] The Inari cult was revived in the camps and a number of shrines were maintained by Japanese families in their apartments.[62] The fox on which Inari rode had white hair, denoting age and wisdom, and had the ability to see into the future. Farmers consulted the Inari shrine master before undertaking any important event such as a long journey; thus, many Issei immigrants had in their possession a little image of a fox which had been blessed by the Inari shrine master upon leaving for America. Besides being prescient, the fox, cat, and badger were tricksters and could take possession of a person's mind and body. Although the Inari shrine master could exorcise the victim, the person would nonetheless have a shorter life because fox possession supposedly ate away some of the life force (*ki ga nukeru*, "spirit leaks out").[63] A Tule Lake internee recalled the prevalence of stories of fox, cat, and badger possession.

> *I had never heard much of Fox, Badger, or Cat until this camp. Back in Gilroy, where I was born, I had heard it only once and forgot it until here. Then it was a newcomer had arrived and the old people found he kept several foxes on his farm. They talked about it until it became a choice story among the young that he could set these foxes to bewitch anyone he didn't like. It started when he threatened an oldtime resident. . . .*[64]

The functional usefulness of this revival of ethnic folk belief during the period of camp confinement was evidenced in its rapid decline once the camps had been disbanded. Commented a former Tule Lake internee: "Oh, those fox and badger stories back in the Center; well, people used to believe a lot of things in the Center they never believed before and haven't believed since!"[65]

Other cultural resistance manifestations, rooted in religious belief, included the revival and resurgence of study groups and clubs which promoted such cultural activities as *shibai* and *kabuki* (drama), *utai, shigen,* and *nanaewabushi* (song), *haiku* and *senryu* (poetry), various dance forms and the playing of traditional musical instruments, *ikebana, bonsai,* and rock gardens, and *sumo* and *judo*. Orthodox writers point to the rise of these activities to illustrate internee recreation and the great amount of leisure time available in the camps.[66] Revisionist historians, in contrast, see these not merely as recreation but also as a means of cultural resistance. Like Japanese religious belief itself, however, the ethnic arts, including poetry clubs, did not arise situationally in the concentration camps but flourished in the pre-war Japanese American community.[67] The social and political context of the camps, nonetheless, highlighted their resistance function and meaning to the confined ethnic culture.

Perhaps the most expressive of these cultural resistance forms which we have today and which distills the sensitivity of the people and the bleakness of the camp experience is the *senryu* poetry produced at Tule Lake by members of the Tule Lake *Senryu Kai*.[68] "To understand the poetry," wrote Opler, "one must understand the people. In general, they are all, except the very young, embittered and disaffected by the journey inland."[69] The poetry captures that mood and records the barren landscape of camp life: the barbed wire fence, watchtowers and sentries, the searchlights, fingerprinting and cataloguing, mass feeding, interrogations on loyalty-disloyalty, and a dull, regimented life. Of the 558 *senryu* poems written between January 4 and August 31, 1943, only about seventeen dealt with camp life. That, concluded Opler, pointed to the essentially escapist nature of the poetry. "It may . . . be assumed that they desired to forget the drab existence of the Center, and as a matter of fact sought in Senryu a method of escape from it. Cultural revivalism and folk expression are, then, the prime purposes of Senryu poetry. The cultural form itself provides the refuge, the recreation, and the escape."[70] Nonetheless those poems which did speak to the conditions of camp life were eloquent, reflecting protest, disenchantment, sorrow, and dreams of a better tomorrow. No poem directly attacked the U.S. government or the WRA, but *senryu*, through its techniques of "restraint, suggestiveness, and studied understatement," was clearly an expression of cultural resistance. Examples of such *senryu* follow below.

Original	Literal Translation	Free Translation
Onaji Yane	The uniform roofs,	Here, reminiscence comes
Nagamete shinobu	Looking at, lost in	When looking at
Shyu-yo-sho	reminiscence	The endless rows of
	In the Center	barracks' roofs
Kibana naki	With few natural flowers	Here, where natural flowers
Haru o zoka ni	Spring is seen in the	are rare,
Miru haisho	artificial flowers,	Spring is seen
	In the Center	In artificial ones
Henka naki	Changeless	Here in the exile's
Haisho ni henka	In the place of exile	Monotonous life
Aru kion	Is the temperature	Only the seasons change
Mata shimon ka to	Again, the fingerprints	"So, the finger-printing again!"
Oyaji no	The old man's	See the old man's
Nigai loa	Bitter face	Bitter face
		(We are not criminals)
Chyu, fuchyu	Loyalty, disloyalty	"Loyalty," "disloyalty"
Mojiga men-shimu	The words make eyes sore	Such words to plague us
Kino-o, kyo	Yesterday, today	yesterday, today
		In eyes made red with weeping
Yume dakega	Dreams only	Only in dreams
Jiyu no ten chi	Of freedom and earth	In a world of freedom
Kake meguri	and sky	Earth-bounded, we walk
	Running about	(And here, the fence)

The America of "freedom and earth and sky" was "dreams only"; what was reality was "here, the fence."[71] A satirical wedding song portrays a similar mood. The song deals with the seagulls which fly to Tule Lake in the summer, and the chorus translates as follows.

The sea-birds fly inland to the dry and waterless desert. They stop here, but will not stay. Too dry, too weary here. They fly away. Even the sea-birds find no reason to remain.[72]

Cultural resistance was a reality within the concentration camps and ethnic religious belief provided an ideological basis for that resistance. The pattern of cultural resistance was established even before the creation of the camps largely in reaction to white supremacy. The concentration camps and "Americanization," manifestations of racism and cultural hegemony, reinforced that historical pattern. Before World War II, the various Japanese institutions such as the ethnic church, language schools, and mutual aid and economic associations served to preserve the ethnic identity.[73] Those pre-war institutions were temporarily shattered in the removal and confinement, a process which not only separated family members but also dismantled entire communities. The former means of resistance in the camps were thus lost, though not completely. The ethnic church, language schools, and even unofficial "unions" persisted in the camps; indeed they flourished. The traditional values of filial piety, the primacy of the family, and ethnic solidarity continued to be upheld as cardinal virtues. The family unit merged into the block collective which in turn merged into the wider camp community of the "Japanese spirit" of cooperation, loyalty to the collective, and community participation in cultural activities. Formal religion prospered, as evidenced in the growth of the Buddhist churches and revival of magical and cultic beliefs—perhaps because of the pervasive feeling of insecurity, but also because religious belief constituted the core of Meiji Japanese culture and ethics. The ideals of filial piety and ancestor worship, and of the closeness of man, gods, and nature, were manifested in the wider network of cultural resistance in the various aesthetic expressions through music, drama, and poetry. Resistance was rechanneled away from open rebellion into ethnic beliefs and practices, which, because of the nature of the oppression, themselves constituted resistance. Japanese religious belief, therefore, was both a vehicle for and an expression of the people's resistance.

Notes

1. See e.g., Randall M. Miller and Thomas D. Marzik, eds., *Immigrants and Religion in Urban America* (Philadelphia, 1977).

2. T.O. Ranger and Isaria Kimambo, eds., *The Historical Study of African Religion* (Berkeley, 1972); Vincent Harding, "Religion and Resistance Among Antebellum Negroes, 1800–1860," in: August Meier and Elliott Rudwick, eds., *The Making of Black America*, I (New York, 1969), pp. 179–97; and Anthony F.C. Wallace, *The Death and Rebirth of the Seneca* (New York, 1969).

3. See e.g., Frederick W. Mote, *Intellectual Foundations of China* (New York, 1971); and Masaharu Anesaki, *Religious Life of the Japanese People* (Tokyo, 1970).

4. Gary Y. Okihiro, "Japanese Resistance in America's Concentration Camps: A Re-evaluation," *Amerasia Journal* 2 (Fall 1973): 20–34.

5. Edgar C. McVoy, "Social Processes in the War Relocation Center," *Social Forces* 22 (December 1943): 188–90.

6. Family Welfare Orientation Program, mss. in Barnhart Papers, Box 49, Folder 6, Japanese American Research Project (JARP) Collection 2010, University of California, Los Angeles (hereafter referred to as JARP Collection).

7. See Okihiro, "Japanese Resistance"; and Arthur A. Hansen and David A. Hacker, "The Manzanar Riot: An Ethnic Perspective," *Amerasia Journal* 2 (Fall 1974): 112–57.

8. Okihiro, op. cit.

9. Ibid., 25–6.

10. Frank Miyamoto, "The Structure of Community Relationships," Folder R 20.42, 6–7, in the Bancroft Library collection of material relating to Japanese American evacuation and resettlement, University of California, Berkeley (henceforth referred to as Bancroft Collection). See also, "B.B.," "Caucasian Staff at Tule Lake," Folder R 20.15, 8, Bancroft Collection.

11. Tetsuden Kashima, *Buddhism in America* (Westport, Conn., 1977), p. 37.

12. Dillon S. Myer, *Uprooted Americans* (Tucson, 1971), p. 29. See also, interview with Dillon Myer, May 20, 1968, Oral History Tapes, Box 397, No. 300, JARP Collection.

13. War Relocation Authority, *WRA, A Story of Human Conservation* (Washington, D.C., 1946), p. 76.

14. "Comments by the War Relocation Authority On Remarks of Representative John M. Costello Made in the House of Representatives June 28, 1943," U.S. War Relocation Authority Miscellaneous Publications, vol. 1, Documents Department, Main Library, University of California, Berkeley; and War Relocation Authority, *Community Government in War Relocation Centers* (Washington, D.C., n.d.), p. 10.

15. Isaac B. Berkson, *Theories of Americanization* (New York, 1920).

16. Robert Blauner, *Racial Oppression in America* (New York, 1972), p. 67. See also Michael Hechter, *Internal Colonialism: The Celtic Fringe in British National Development* (Berkeley, 1975), p. 37.

17. Robert Francis Spencer, "Japanese Buddhism in the United States, 1940–1946: A Study on Acculturation" (Ph.D. dissertation, University of California, Berkeley, 1946), p. 164.

18. E.g., the Inari cult, fox, cat, and badger stories, and sumo.

19. Isao Horinouchi, "Americanized Buddhism: A Sociological Analysis of a Protestantized Japanese Religion" (Ph.D. dissertation, University of California, Davis, 1973), p. 210.

20. *War Relocation Authority, The Evacuated People—A Quantitative Description* (Washington, D.C., 1942), p. 79.

21. Spencer, op. cit., pp. 127–8. Official WRA policy, nonetheless, declared religious freedom in the camps.

22. Kashima, op. cit. p. 54.

23. Alexander H. Leighton, *The Governing of Men* (Princeton, 1945), p. 35.

24. Spencer, op. cit., p. 127.

25. Daisuke Kitagawa, *Issei and Nisei: The Internment Years* (New York, 1967), pp. 107–8. At the same time, the Buddhist church itself was undergoing fundamental change in leadership from Issei to Nisei and orientation from Japan to America. Kashima, op. cit., pp. 57–59.

26. G. Gordon Brown, "Final Report on the Gila River Relocation Center as of May 20, 1945," Carr Papers, Box 55, Folder 5, JARP Collection. See also, Kitagawa, op. cit., p. 120; and Lester E. Suzuki, *Ministry in the Assembly and Relocation Centers of World War II* (Berkeley, 1979), pp. 34, 130.

27. Horinouchi, op. cit., Cf. Kashima, op. cit., pp. 217–20.

28. Suzuki, op. cit., pp. 40–1, 345.

29. Spencer, op. cit., pp. 141–2.

30. Horinouchi, op. cit., p. 216. See also Brown, op. cit.

31. Ibid.

32. David Y. Hirano, "Religious Values Among Japanese Americans and Their Relationship to Counseling" (D.M. dissertation, School of Theology at Claremont, 1974), p. 2. See also Anesaki, op. cit.

33. Masaharu Anesaki, *History of Japanese Religion* (London, 1930), p. 8. Sei-cho No Ie, a popular cult in California especially among the Issei during the 1930s, combined Buddhist belief with some of the teachings of Mary Baker Eddy on health and healing. The cult reemerged at Granada concentration camp. Carr Papers, Box 55, Folder 1, JARP Collection; and Suzuki, op. cit., 212.

34. Hirano, op. cit., p. 12.

35. Ibid., p. 13; and Hideo Kishimoto, *Japanese Religion in the Meiji Era* (Tokyo, 1956). Filial piety and Confucian ethics were also taught in the public schools in a course known as Shushin where students learned warrior ethics (*Bushido*), filial piety, and loyalty to Emperor and country. Horinouchi, op. cit., pp. 33–4.

36. Spencer, op. cit., p. 172.

37. Okakura Kakuzo, The Book of Tea (Tokyo, 1956); and Daisetz T. Suzuki, *Zen and Japanese Culture* (Princeton, 1959).

38. WRA, *Community Government*, p. 7.

39. Ibid., p. 27.

40. See e.g., Leonard Broom and John I. Kitsuse, *The Managed Casuality: The Japanese-American Family in World War II*, Berkeley, 1973; Anne Umemoto, "Crisis in the Japanese American Family," *Asian Women*, Berkeley, 1971, 31–34; and Kitagawa, *Issei and Nisei*, 86–88.

41. WRA, WRA, A Story, 95.

42. Toshio Yatsushiro, "Political and Socio-Cultural Issues at Poston and Manzanar Relocation Centers: A Themal Analysis," (Ph.D. dissertation, Cornell University, 1953).

43. "Manzanar Riot," 121.

44. See e.g., Marian Svensrud, "Attitudes of the Japanese Towards Their Language Schools," *Sociology and Social Research*, 17:3 (January-February 1933), 259–64; and Chotoku Toyama, "The Japanese Community in Los Angeles," MA thesis, (Columbia University, 1926).

45. Hansen and Hacker, "Manzanar Riot," 121–22. See also John Modell, "Class or Ethnic Solidarity: The Japanese American Company Union," *Pacific Historical Review*, 38:2 (May 1969), 193–206; and Jere Takahashi, "Japanese American Responses to Race Relations: The Formation of Nisei Perspectives," *Amerasia Journal*, 9:1 (1982): 29–57.

46. Yatsushiro, "Political and Socio-Cultural," 364. See also, Roger Daniels, *Concentration Camp U.S.A.*, New York, 1971, 104–29; Morton Grodzins, *The Loyal and the Disloyal*, Chicago, 1956, 131; and David A. Hacker, "A Culture Resisted, a Culture Revived: The Loyalty Crisis of 1943 at the Manzanar War Relocation Center," MA thesis. (California State University, Fullerton, 1979).

47. Okihiro, "Japanese Resistance"; and Hacker, "Culture Resisted."

48. Toyama, op. cit., p. 29.

49. Yatsushiro, op. cit., pp. 513–14.

50. Yatsushiro, op. cit., p. 529. Kitagawa sees the subordination of the family to the collective will as an indication of the breakdown of Japanese society in the camps, which he termed "primitive tribal community" and an "ostrichlike community." *Issei and Nisei*, p. 106.

51. Quoted in Peter T. Suzuki, "The Ethnolinguistics of Japanese Americans in the Wartime Camps," *Anthropological Linguistics* 18 (December 1976): 422.

52. Dillon Myer, "The Truth About Relocation," mss. in McGovern Papers, Box 119, Folder 1, JARP Collection.

53. Family Welfare Orientation Program, Barnhart Papers, Box 49, Folder 6, JARP Collection. See also Suzuki, op. cit., pp. 416–27.

54. Austin Papers, Box 44, Folder 9, Document 2, JARP Collection. See also, "Letter to friend from a teacher in Tule Lake (Oct. 30, 1944)," Austin Papers, Box 44, Folder 6, Document 7.

55. *The Pen*, mss. in Barnhart Papers, Box 49, Folder 7, JARP Collection. See also Suzuki, op. cit., pp. 416–27.

56. Suzuki, op. cit., p. 423.

57. This was not the only such camp. See e.g., Spencer, op. cit., pp. 173–75.

58. R. Linton, "Nativistic Movements," *American Anthropologist* 45 (April-June 1943): 230–40.

59. Marvin K. Opler, "Japanese Folk Beliefs and Practices, Tule Lake, California," *Journal of American Folklore* 63 (October-December 1950) 385–87.

60. Ibid., pp. 388–89.

61. Morris E. Opler and Robert Seido Hashima, "The Rice Goddess and the Fox in Japanese Religion and Folk Practice," *American Anthropologist* 48 (January-March 1946): 50.

62. Opler, "Japanese Folk Beliefs," pp. 389–90.

63. Opler and Hashima, "Rice Goddess," pp. 43–50.

64. Opler, "Japanese Folk Beliefs," p. 391.

65. Ibid.

66. Myer, op. cit., pp. 56–7; and Michi Weglyn, *Years of Infamy* (New York, 1976), p. 82.

67. Peter T. Suzuki, "Wartime *Tanka*: Issei and Kibei Contributions to a Literature East and West," *Literature East and West: Journal of World and Comparative Literature* 21 (July 1977): 242–54.

68. See Suzuki, op. cit., for similar expressions of the people in other poetic forms such as *haiku* and *waka*.

69. Marvin K. Opler and F. Obayashi, "Senryu Poetry as Folk and Community Expression," *Journal of American Folklore* 58 (January-March, 1945): 2.

70. Ibid., p. 7.

71. Ibid., pp. 8–9.

72. Ibid., p. 11.

73. See e.g., Shotaro Frank Miyamoto, *Social Solidarity Among the Japanese in Seattle* (Seattle, 1939); and Kashima, op. cit.

15. The Role of the Buddhist Church in the Ethnic Adjustment of the Japanese American

TETSUDEN KASHIMA

Not all the Japanese who came to America in the late 1800s espoused Eastern religions; some were Christians. There were obvious differences between the two groups, in terms of cultural continuity and adaptation to the new social environment. The Buddhist missionaries who began arriving in 1899 were able to offer the immigrants a cultural tie to the world they had left behind, in a way the missionary Christian church could not. In any case, social intercourse with the American populace was as limited for the Japanese Christians as for the Japanese Buddhists:

Not only the Buddhist but also the Methodist churches were strictly for Japanese and services were conducted in the Japanese language. Of the two religions, Buddhism provided an important link with Japan in ways Christianity did not. Buddhism was the religion of the ancestors of the Japanese immigrants, and when a man died, his ashes were preserved in the church until ready to be taken back to Japan by one of his relatives or friends.[1]

To offset some of the inevitable "sociological death,"[2] the Japanese created or modified their processes and organizations within the United States. It does not come as a surprise that as the numerically stronger Japanese religious institution, Jodo Shinshu Buddhism was able to retain its Japanese adherents and to attain an importance that far surpassed its original position in Japan. In Japan, the temples in the community are viewed predominantly as religious organizations; in America, the NABM served as a place not only for religious solace, but also for social gatherings that preserved communal ethnic ties.

Life for the early immigrant was full of hardships. Without a surrounding social support to aid and bolster the young men living and working in a foreign environment, such conditions could easily have lead to alienation and loneliness. The following description of the relationship of the church to the immigrants suggests the importance of the social aspects of the religious organization:

Instead of trying to drown out their unhappiness with mere pleasure seeking, they [the young immigrants] turn to the church and religion to afford them comfort and relief from

Abridgement of "The Role of the Buddhist Church in the Ethnic Adjustment of the Japanese American," *Buddhism in America* by Tetsuden Kashima. Copyright © 1997 Greenwood Press. Reproduced with permission of Greenwood Publishing Group, Inc., Westport, CT.

their economic and social misery, and they hold a cheaply optimistic, goody-goody idea that if they stay in their place, work hard and please the Americans and remain happy in the position where God has placed them, surely the Christian Americans, out of the generosity of their hearts, will throw out to them a few more crumbs to ease their condition.[3]

The important point here is that the church was able to offer this necessary spiritual and social solace for those immigrants who desired it.

Most of the elements within the NABM and BCA were brought to America and utilized by the Buddhists, but certain inimical events made it more tactful and judicious to downplay or suppress various constituent parts of the organization that could become controversial or injurious to the Buddhist religion. The story of the Buddhist swastika is one example of a social change within the Buddhist institution in America.

The sauvastika or swastika[4] has long been a traditional Indian symbol for Buddhism. In most Buddhist temples and churches before World War II, the swastika was exhibited ornamentally. The Buddhist church in Seattle, Washington, for example, displayed the symbol on an archway above the front entrance upon a temple building built in 1906.[5]

It is clear today that the sign of the swastika, constructed either in a counterclockwise Buddhist fashion or clockwise as used in Nazi Germany, remains a symbol of Nazism for most Americans. Long before the 1940s, however, the swastika was regarded as a symbol representing a foreign tradition:

One might pass the Buddhist temple in Portland a hundred times a day, and unless one's eyes were quick to spy the modest Swastika 卍 on the door glass, and the neat gold letters BUDDHIST CHURCH on the transom, one would never suspect the square brick house of being other than an old-time domicile, or a present-day rooming house; but there it is, a heathen temple on American soil.[6]

Madden described the swastika as the symbol of Buddhism in America. Her main objection as a non-Buddhist was the presence and threat of this religion to America: "Who shall rule America, Christ or Buddha? Just outside your church door is the sign of the Swastika, what will you do about it?"[7]

Despite anti-Japanese sentiment in America during the 1920s, the swastika did not become as overt an issue at that time as it did in the 1940s. Until the advent of World War II, the Buddhist churches continued to utilize and to display the swastika as a religious emblem. Then, just after the attack on Pearl Harbor, not only things Japanese, but especially Buddhist artifacts and writings, became immediately suspect in the minds of Americans. Some Japanese Americans, cognizant of the suspicions generated by war hysteria, attempted to divest themselves of their Buddhist religious possessions.

Those who had little confidence in their own religious beliefs believed that any association with a Buddhist organization would be to their disadvantage. Possession of Japanese writings became suspect and a source of concern; thus, the fearful ones removed their Buddhist altars, destroyed their sutra books and burned their family albums containing photos of relatives or friends in uniform.[8]

The use of the Buddhist swastika as a symbol was repressed during the war. The attendant meanings that non-Buddhists could attach to the swastika created a crisis for the Buddhists. Hence, from that time, other Buddhist symbols were given more emphasis: the "Wheel of Law," an eight-spoked wheel representing the "eightfold noble path," became, and remained, the accepted logo for the American Buddhists. However, one recently formed Jodo Shinshu Buddhist group in Los Angeles, the Kinnara, now utilizes the swastika as its logo.[9]

The BCA as a Cohesive Force: 1945–1975

To be sure, the swastika is a mere symbol, and the resemblance between the Buddhist and Nazi emblems was ultimately a historical accident. But the repression and degradation inflicted upon all Japanese Americans during World War II was not an accident of history.

The immediate problem after the relocation of the Japanese was the reopening of the dormant temple structures. Most temples were initially used as hostels, with all available space converted to makeshift bedrooms, except the kitchens, which were used to prepare communal food. These hostels also served as job placement offices and community centers for all Japanese and Japanese Americans.

Upon their return, many ministers found that their temples had been vandalized and religious articles destroyed or stolen.[10] Religious services were at first given secondary consideration, since the personal needs of the Japanese Americans were paramount and acute. The ordeal inherent in their return, especially with regard to employment and housing, became another complete dislocation process for the returnees.

Along the West Coast, people of Japanese descent did not return to precisely the places they had left. Before the war, the Bakersfield Buddhist Church had a membership of approximately fifty families, with a resident minister; the only Japanese who returned were those who owned agricultural lands. With only a handful of families to support it, the temple was forced to close. The Guadalupe Buddhist Church also lost many members, although a sufficient number did return eventually to support a resident minister and an active church organization. The Buddhist Church of Salinas lost about a third of its previous membership families, but it retained enough members to continue supporting a resident minister. The Oakland Buddhist Church, an urban temple that had once enjoyed a large membership, also experienced a large decrease. The Placer Buddhist Church and the West Los Angeles Buddhist Church had stable membership numbers only because new families moved in to replace those who did not return.

On the other hand, churches and temples in Berkeley, Palo Alto, Reedley, Gardena, San Diego, Oxnard, and San Jose, and in Denver, Colorado (Tri-State Buddhist Church), experienced a small to large increase in membership. Many new churches or temples were constructed to meet the needs of the new Japanese population; by December 1946, organizations were established in Cleveland, Ohio; Detroit, Michigan; Idaho-Oregon (Ontario, Oregon); Spokane, Washington; Minneapolis, Minnesota (Twin Cities); and Monterey, California. From 1950 to 1971, seven new churches or temples were constructed: at Mountain View, Union City (Southern Alameda County Buddhist Church), Anaheim (Orange County Buddhist Church), Marin, and Fowler, California; Seabrook, New Jersey; and Honeyville, Utah. The last church to become independent was Venice, California, on March 1, 1976.

Since 1945, the Issei population has grown older and fewer in number, while the Nisei and Sansei population has increased. Because the Nisei have continued to move into nonagricultural occupations, rural Buddhist churches have suffered the most from resettlement. Although some ministers who would have returned with their adherents to the West Coast took over the new temples and churches in the Midwest and on the Eastern seaboard, from 1948 onward a continuous flow of new ministers, both Nisei and native Japanese, has entered the BCA.[11]

Conflicts between the Issei and Nisei, within the temples, continued after the war. The Issei and Nisei both desired decision-making powers within the church organization. Most temples had their own constitutions and eventually incorporated under the laws of their respective states whereby the elected board of directors controlled their finances. The Issei ministers with their bishop continued to dominate the BCA, but at the local temples the Nisei continued to gain in ascendancy. Income was difficult to generate since the members were readjusting to life outside the camps. The prewar language schools, which had augmented the salaries of the ministers and temples, were not immediately reestablished to any large extent. Only after the BCA Buddhist adherents started to overcome their financial losses from the evacuation, in the late 1950s, were the churches and temples able to provide substantial increases in the ministers' salaries and other necessary church expenditures. During the readjustment period, large-scale financial projects such as the NABM *Zaidan* (Endowment Fund) were tabled because of insufficient funds; however, two important centers were created to fill the need for more English-speaking ministers.

A Ministerial Training Fund was emphasized through a BCA Special Project Fund in 1966 to further the training of Nisei ministers, through scholarships for prospective ministerial candidates studying here or in Japan, and to aid active ministers desiring to continue their study of English.[12] The BCA established a Ministerial Training Center at the Hompa (Nishi) Hongwanji in Kyoto, Japan. A plan to initiate the training of the priests in the United States resulted in the American Buddhist Academy in 1948 under the Reverend Hozen Seki and the New York Buddhist Church; and the Berkeley Study Center in 1965 under the BCA Bishop Enryo Shigefuji, the Reverend Kanmo Imamura, and the Berkeley Buddhist Church.

The period from 1945 to 1965, with the start of the Institute of Buddhist Studies in Berkeley, can be characterized as a consolidation era, with the BCA reevaluating the Issei priorities and anticipating the changing needs of Buddhists. However, the Buddhist religion remained tied to those of Japanese ancestry, in the Nishi Hongwanji sect as embodied in the BCA.

The Present Crisis

Changes in the BCA in the 1960s have resulted in a more vocal organization than previously existed. An important issue entered into by the BCA concerned the California State Curriculum Committee's approval of a textbook entitled *Japanese Americans: The Untold Story*.[13] The textbook, aimed at the third to fifth grade grammar school level, was written by a team of twelve authors (Nikkei school teachers and citizens) forming the Japanese American Curriculum Project (JACP). The JACP had previously produced a television program in San Francisco on Japanese Americans, which had drawn criticism from some individuals who felt it made "inaccurate representations of the Japanese American Community."[14] After writing the short book in four months, the JACP submitted it to various Japanese organizations for prepublication approval. Instead, the textbook was overwhelmingly denounced by the Japanese American Citizens League, the Southern California Buddhist-Christian Clergy Fellowship, and various Asian American student organizations, as well as parents, educators, and ministers.

On October 7, 1970, in a letter signed by the bishop, the president of the board of directors, and the chairman of the Ministerial Research Committee, the BCA stated that there were "overtones to the book which were racial, consistently anti-Buddhist and pro-Christian biased, and a gross misrepresentation of the true picture of the lives of Japanese Americans. . . . The preface of the book is written as though the authors have acquired the endorsement of the Buddhist Churches of America, but actually the Buddhist Churches of America have not endorsed the book, whatsoever."[15] Through a series of meetings and public presentations, the BCA and other organizations and individuals were able to convince the California State Curriculum Committee to reject the book. The authors now have plans to rewrite some portions of the text and to submit the revised version for reconsideration.

Regardless of the outcome of the television program and textbook controversies, the BCA in 1970 clearly stepped out of what many had considered an insular, conservative community position. The BCA perceived the book to be a threat to the future Buddhists of America. In an unsigned but BCA-sponsored letter distributed to the members of the Buddhist churches to elicit written support of the BCA's position, the concern for the Buddhist child's self-image is very apparent:

> *This book reflects unfavorably upon the Japanese American Buddhists and has a pervading religious bias. We feel that this religious bias could be very detrimental to the Buddhist identity of our children. It can only serve to make our children feel insecure about being Buddhists, but also can serve to make a critical change in their thoughts and minds about their Buddhist identity and heritage. How it will affect the thinking of others about Buddhists and Japanese Americans is an equally disturbing thought.*[16]

The BCA's and their adherents' willingness to come forward to speak in defense of their position had a precedent in Bishop Uchida's testimony at the Immigration Commission meetings in the 1920s. The crisis concerning the textbook was a perceived threat to the image of Buddhism presented to the adherents' children. It was important enough to involve the headquarters and the member churches and temples in a lobbying and letter-writing campaign to help avert the State Education Committee's adoption of the book.

Another issue on which the BCA took an active position concerned the inclusion of the Divine Creation Theory in California public school textbooks.[17] The Reverend Hogen Fujimoto, director of the Bureau of Buddhist Education, BCA, testified before the State Board of Education that this "Divine Creation" represented a religious interpretation; it was therefore a subject for churches—not schools. Reverend Fujimoto quoted from various sources and explained that Buddhists did not subscribe to the ideas inherent in the theory: "According to

Buddhism, human beings and all living things are self created or self creating. The universe is not homocentric, it is a creation of all beings. Buddhism does not believe that all things come from one cause, but holds that everything is inevitably created out of more than two causes."[18]

Thus, by 1972 the BCA was willing to enter into debates in secular areas, utilizing its religious doctrines in defense of its stand on public issues. The YBA has demonstrated a similar initiative by passing an antiwar resolution deploring the destruction of human life in the Vietnam conflict[19] and by giving Buddhists guidelines for becoming more involved in protest against racism and other forms of social oppression.[20]

The BCA and some BCA member churches have also sponsored housing projects to assist the elderly Issei. With the cooperation of the San Francisco Redevelopment Agency and the Japanese community, the Japanese American Religious Federation (JARF) has begun construction of a thirteen-story, 272-unit apartment building for low-income residents.[21] This joint undertaking of the BCA, the Buddhist Church of San Francisco, and nine other Japanese and Japanese American member churches[22] is but one example of the ability of religious organizations to work together on a project of mutual benefit.

The 1970s has been explicitly proclaimed a period for broadening Sansei involvement in the BCA. As the past president of the BCA board of directors has stated, "With the coming of the 75th Anniversary, we must begin the new era of American Buddhism. The area of youth is a challenging area."[23] The Sansei represent the important problems of the present and the future. There is some reason to suppose that some Sansei perceive themselves as outside the mainstream of American life.[24] Many are now, in one sense, returning to their Japanese cultural and associational roots, refusing to forget their Asian past. Of the third generation Marcus Lee Hansen has written that "what the son wishes to forget, the grandson wishes to remember."[25] The creation of Asian American Studies Centers, Yellow Brotherhood, and Asian American Anti-Drug Groups, as well as the Relevant American Buddhists and Kinnara groups within the Buddhists of America, indicates that the Sansei are not only willing to stay in the Buddhist religion, but also to form new organizations tailored to their needs.

To facilitate communication with the Sansei, the BCA board of directors authorized the creation of the Relevant American Buddhists (RAB), with eight youth coordinators' positions within the BCA districts to aid the YBA and their programs and to insure that the youths' needs and demands would be given an official channel of communication to the BCA ruling bodies. Since the older YBA members, parents of the third generation, have now formed the Adult Buddhist Association (ABA), the Sansei have desired to expand their activities to aid the aging Issei, allow other racial groups within the Junior and Senior YBA, become involved in social and political issues, and initiate changes in the presentation of their religion.

The Kinnara, a Southern California-based Buddhist organization, was formed, in the main, by a group of Nisei and Sansei BCA ministers and the Sansei membership to change the format of religious teachings. The Kinnara group, as was mentioned previously, has incorporated traditional Japanese music (gagaku), sutra chanting, and meditation techniques to allow for a diversity of methods in Buddhist services and ceremonies. For instance, the group has instituted Buddhist retreats, daylong celebrations of important Buddhist days of reverence, and interchurch gatherings to sustain and generate new interest in Buddhism among the Nisei's children. It would be premature at this time to estimate the longevity of this new organization. However, it can be stated that the membership is growing. Moreover, since more Nisei and Sansei ministers are entering, while maintaining their particular churches for the Issei and Nisei, there is reason to believe that the Kinnara group represents one vital and important alternative to the existing BCA organization.

There is some evidence too that some of the Sansei are returning to their Buddhist religion.[26] They are still young, in their teens and twenties. The BCA ministers have had difficulty attracting them to existing church organizations[27] primarily because the ministers are still largely Issei, the member churches are controlled by a Nisei board of directors, and the Sansei have not clearly communicated the type of changes they desire.

The Sansei would appreciate a stronger voice in the activities of the church or temple organizations, but they have not yet articulated a positive program that the churches could accept or reject. Most churches have included sports and other social activities, but Buddhist study groups or religious-oriented activities have not met with overwhelming success in attracting the Sansei.[28] The future of the Sansei in the BCA is still uncertain. Programs and activities will continue to be modified to attract the Sansei and non-Japanese; upon their success or failure rests the future of the BCA.

The Continuity of Buddhism and the Problem of Language

The strongest force for continuity in the member temples has, of course, been the Jodo Shinshu Buddhist religion itself. Throughout its history, the basic religious tenets, practices, and ceremonies have constituted the major continuous and unchanging focal point for the membership. An Issei minister was asked in an interview:

INT: What is the difference between Issei Buddhism and Nisei Buddhism, and then Sansei Buddhism?

RESP: That definition would be based on majority membership, and so, of course, [on the] accompanying psychological or other cultural differences.

INT: But they are all Buddhist?

RESP: All Buddhists, yes.

INT: Now, is Jodo Shinshu Buddhism different between the Issei, Nisei and Sansei?

RESP: I don't think so, and the doctrine, of course, never changes. Buddhism you know consists of the triple jewels: [the Buddha], the teaching of the Buddha, and the Sangha [brotherhood of Buddhists]. . . . The Sangha may be changing. Even many of the vocabularies must be carefully used. This is a funny example, but the lady's breast is a symbol of mother's love in Japan. So we often refer to *Ochichi o nomaseru* [literally: to allow someone to drink from the breast], but some Issei ministers came to this country and explained [this concept] pointing [to the breast region] causing laughter among the [non-Japanese speaking] audience. So we have to adapt ourselves to this particular situation even linguistically. So from that stand-point, maybe our way of presentation must be changed.

INT: But not the doctrine.

RESP: Not the doctrine.

INT: What are the purposes of the Buddhist church for the Issei?

RESP: Of course, to retain, to keep the Jodo Shinshu [for] themselves and also through their capacity as the leader of the family to transmit the teaching to the children, the grandchildren. . . .

INT: What is the purpose of the Buddhist Church for the Nisei?

RESP: Niseis of course accept this precious gift of Dharma of Buddha from their parents and transfer [it] to their children. So nowadays, Issei and Nisei are not young anymore. So in spite of linguistic differences, language differences, from their chronological experiences they are becoming closer to the Issei. . . .

INT: Now what is the purpose of the Buddhist church for the Sansei?

RESP: Not very much difference from Issei, Nisei propagation. But if I [could] add a point, it is [that it] makes them missionary agents to all other non-Japanese Americans, because they are at a good position to do that. . . . They have the same language as the American people in general, so they are in a good position to introduce Buddhism, explain Buddhism to others.[29]

This Issei minister, like many others, emphasized the continuity of religious doctrine within a modified form of presentation. The most important modification is the use of English, with the attendant problem of adequately translating Buddhist terminology to make the religious concepts understandable to the membership.

Another minister, a Nisei, seconds the points raised by the Issei *kaikyoshi*:

INT: What do you think are the purposes of the Buddhist Churches in America?

RESP: The first purpose is to keep on propagating the Jodo Shinshu to the Nisei and Sansei and Yonsei and Gosei.[30]

All ministers appear to agree that the roots of the Buddhist tree have been kept healthy in America. They also agree that there are many methods of presentation:

INT: It has been said that the BCA and North American Buddhist Mission stem traditionally from Japan. Can you name some things that are purely Japanese that are still carried on in the 1970's?

RESP: Oh yes, the teaching of the *Nembutsu* (Dharma), the Jodo Shinshu teaching has been the same all the way through, and lately, we have realized that, in some ways, the presentation has to be changed to compromise with our younger youngsters.

INT: What do you mean by compromise?

RESP: Well, in, not to compromise with their wishes all along, but to make them understand, have them enjoy our religion.

INT: Although the Buddhist doctrine comes from Japan, has it changed because we've had to use English as the main language for the Japanese Americans?

RESP: Yes, we have had a language barrier there. The translation of Buddhist teaching into English is very difficult. That is, sometimes we lose the essence of the teaching.

INT: And how is that being counteracted, or is it being counteracted?

RESP: Well it has been brought out by the Sansei and the Nisei. However, I don't think we have found a solution to that yet.[31]

The problem of adequate English translations has yet to be resolved. Thus far, the translations have been handled on a utilitarian or expedient basis—a past course presently undergoing criticism by ministers and lay members alike. There has been no attempt to change the basic doctrines or precepts of Buddhism. Instead, the adaptations have been made to render Buddhism more comprehensible to an English-speaking audience. Transmission and preservation of the tenets of Buddhism has been the paramount goal of the Buddhist institution.

Services and Ceremonies

The most important components of any religious organization are the religious services and ceremonies. From the start of Jodo Shinshu Buddhism in America to the present, important religious observances have continued. Although the format of the religious services may have changed in varying degrees over the years, especially with the prevalent use of English in the services, consistency and continuity in the content of the services are very apparent in the observances of Buddhist religious ceremonial days.

There are eleven important days and ceremonies within the Jodo Shinshu sect. The BCA ritually observes these occasions:

Shusho-E: January 1 (New Year's Service). A dedication service for the start of the new year.

Ho onko: January 16 (Shinran Shonin's Memorial Day). A special service to honor the founder of the Jodo Shinshu sect of Buddhism.

Nehan-E: February 15 (Nirvana Day). A service to memorialize the passing away of Sakyamuni Buddha.

Higan-E: March 21 *and* September 23 (Spring and Autumn Equinox). The equinox day, where the nights and days are of equal length, symbolizes the harmony pervading the universe. "Therefore we gather before the sacred shrine of Amida Buddha and meditate on the harmony of nature and devote ourselves to the realization of this harmony in our inner lives."[32]

Hanamatsuri: April 8 (Wesak Day). A day to commemorate the birth of Sakyamuni Buddha.

Gotan-E: May 21 (Shinran Shonin's Birthday). Commemoration to honor the birth of Shinran Shonin.

Ura Bon-E: July 15 (Obon Festival). A Buddhist memorial day for all who have passed away.

Beikoku Bukkyo Kaiyo Kinenbu: September 1 (BCA Founding Day). September 1, 1899, is accepted by the BCA as the date of its inception, and a service is held to honor the occasion.

Jodo-E: December 8 (Bodhi Day). A special service to commemorate the day that Sakyamuni Buddha finished his meditation under the Bodhi tree and became enlightened.

Joya-E: December 31 (New Year's Eve Service). A service to meditate on the events of the past year.

These eleven special ceremonies (*Higan-E* is observed twice a year) are observed by the member churches of the BCA. Except for the BCA Founding Day, the services have always been a part of Jodo Shinshu services in America. Most temples and churches have taken a very flexible attitude toward the actual date for these observances. Many schedule the ceremonies for the "usual" weekly services or observe them on a more convenient day close to the ritually prescribed date. For instance, the observance of *Ura Bon-E*, or *Obon* for short, usually includes not only a religious service, but also a "dance for the deceased." This celebration is inspired by a legend concerning a disciple of Buddha who performed a dance of joy when his mother was given entrance into Nirvana after her death. The entire congregation, dressed in traditional Japanese attire, enters into the *Obon* dance; it is a time for gaiety and enjoyment. Since *Obon* is very colorful, in many locales the event draws both Buddhists and non-Buddhists as onlookers and as participants. Besides the *Obon* dance, many churches feature booths and counters to sell Japanese foods and other refreshments. For many churches, the revenue generated by the booths augments regular income. In areas where there are many geographically close Buddhist churches, the individual churches will space out the observance of the event over a month's time, so that participants from one church may attend another's celebration. Scheduling also allows for guest speakers in the area to give special sermons at several churches.

At other ceremonies the bishop, as well as other speakers, may be asked to participate. These occasions are reserved for the more important services such as *Shusho-E, Ho onko, Nehan-E*, or *Hanamatsuri*. In order to make his presence available to as many temples as possible, the celebration days are often negotiated with the bishop or other church dignitaries. The spacing of the special services is an example of one form of change within the BCA. Where the special observance days in the Buddhist temples in Japan are more ritually followed, the absence of a large pool of available guest speakers or Buddhist priests outside the BCA has required that the temples accommodate the dates of observances to coincide with the availability of desired speakers. The priests within the BCA often travel to other temples to give guest lectures. This allows each church to hear priests other than the resident minister. However, for the special services, prior coordination must be accomplished with the minister to preclude conflicting engagements.

Aside from these ceremonial occasions, each temple or church conducts funeral, memorial, and wedding services. Among the most important of these services is the *hoji* or memorial service for the departed, which is observed in a very formal manner. For example, just after the death, a *makura-gyo* or bedside service may be held at the home of the deceased. Then an *otsuya* or wake service is held one day prior to the funeral service for the family of the deceased. At the *soshiki* or funeral service, a posthumous Buddhist name (*homyo*) may be given to the deceased if he or she has not previously been granted one. The officiating priest will place the Buddhist name inside the casket, and another copy is given to the family to keep within their family shrine. Family memorial services (*hoji*) are then held on the seventh day after the death, and if the family is very devout, also on the fourteenth, twenty-first, twenty-eighth, thirty-fifth, and forty-ninth day. Ceremonies after the forty-ninth day service are observed on the hundredth day, then on the first anniversary, and thereafter in the seventh, thirteenth, seventeenth, twenty-fifth, thirty-third, and fiftieth year. At most temples and churches, a collective monthly memorial service (*shotsuki hoyo*) is held, and the names of those families with relatives who have passed away during that month are printed in the church bulletin.

Each church or temple also has regularly scheduled services. These include the children's Sunday Schools and the adult services on a weekly, biweekly, or monthly basis, depending upon the number of adherents. The typical adult service may start with an opening address by the chairman. "Meditation" follows, in which the members bow their heads, placing an *ojuzu* (a Buddhist rosary) over their hands with palms together, while the priest gives a Buddhist invocation. The meditation concludes with a thrice-given recitation of an homage to the Buddha, "Namu Amida Butsu." Then a sutra (Buddhist scripture) is chanted by all, followed by the singing of a Buddhist *gatha* or hymn. The minister then gives a sermon, after which another *gatha* may be sung. The conclusion of the service includes another meditation, followed by an "incense offering," where the members may go to the front of the altar to bow, offer incense, recite the homage to the Buddha, and return to their seats. If there are any announcements they are given here; otherwise, the members leave the worship hall (*hondo*) by bowing to the shrine and departing.

The sermons given by the priests are usually of an emotional or analytic type. In the former, the priest starts with a story, usually of a personal nature, introducing an appropriate Buddhist interpretation, and usually concludes with the thought that all human events, be they tragic or comic, can be understood from the Buddhist perspective. The analytic sermon generally starts with a Buddhist concept such as *karma* or *shinjin* (faith). This is exemplified, expounded upon, and interpreted in everyday language. One priest has stated that priests can be typified according to the type of sermon they give. The Issei congregation prefers an emotional appeal, but the sermons given to the Nisei and Sansei vary.[33] For a Sansei audience from a university community, the analytic approach is most common; in an agricultural area, the emotional sermon may be better received. For a regular service, the priest's everyday activities apparently serve as a source for his sermons. The topics may range from mercury poisoning in a village in Japan[34] to the deathbed statements of an eighty-year-old Issei lady.

For special ceremonies, the sermon topic usually revolves around the reasons for the service. For example, *Hanamatsuri* sermons often discuss events surrounding the birth of the Buddha, and *Joya-E* or year-end service may recount the events of the past year as they have affected the temple or its members. For these ceremonies an outside priest or speaker is invited to give a sermon. Having a visiting priest always signals a special event for any temple, for he gives his most effective sermon, having pretested it at his home temple. Thus, there is usually a larger than average attendance during these occasions.

Buddhist Weddings

Another important service conducted by the Buddhist priests in America is the Buddhist wedding ceremony. The wedding ceremony in Japan is traditionally performed by the Shinto priests; however, the Jodo Shinshu sect of Buddhism has had a long history of performing weddings—both in Japan and in America.[35] When a marriage occurred within the family of a Buddhist priest in Japan, the wedding ceremony was almost always performed by another Buddhist official.[36] Reverend Koju Terada stated that the marriage ceremony conducted in front of the Buddhist altar was not an uncommon occurrence, especially if the participating families were strong believers in Buddhism. He also stated that the prevalent view that weddings in Japan are performed solely by Shinto priests is an idea that has developed in America since World War II.[37]

The Buddhist wedding ceremony in Japan is rather uncomplicated. The nuptial couple appears before the family Buddhist shrine, performs a *gassho* (bow) before the shrine, and recites the *Nembutsu*. A sutra may or may not be chanted, although usually there is an exchange *ojuzu* (Buddhist rosary) between the couple. The name of the new bride is then recorded in the groom's family register. Finally, the couple goes to the reception, where part of the ceremony is to sip *sake* three times each (called *sansankudo*).[38]

The American Buddhist wedding ceremony is somewhat more complex. As in Euro-American ceremonies, the American ceremony includes the use of wedding gowns, the playing of a wedding march (Mendelssohn's "Wedding March"), the exchange of rings, and the witnessing of a wedding license. All officiating ministers must be sanctioned by the respective state legal body and empowered to perform a ceremony binding to the laws concerning the rights, privileges, and responsibilities inherent in the marriage contract. The groom wears a formal tuxedo, especially for the picture-taking portion of the wedding ceremony. (This custom, by the way, has been followed in Japan since the Meiji era and was utilized by the Japanese prior to the arrival of the Jodo Shinshu institution in America.) The marriage license is also a part of the Japanese wedding ceremony; the erasure of the bride's name from her family register and the recording of her name in the groom's register is in effect a legal sanction of the marriage ceremony.

Despite all the Western innovations, the American Buddhist wedding ceremony does retain some elements peculiar to the Buddhist faith. The couple offers incense at the Buddhist altar, affirms their faith in the Buddhist religion, and have placed over their hands the *ojuzu*, the string of beads symbolic of the Buddhist faith. The *ojuzu* is given to both participants as an affirmation of their partnership and of their commitment to the Buddhist "way of life."

An important part of the wedding is the postceremony reception. At many of the receptions, a thrice-called salute to the couple ("*Banzai*") is often given by the guests. The reception features the singing of Japanese No songs (*yokyoku* or *utai*) by the guests, along with felicitations in both Japanese and English. There was a time when the nuptial couple would toast each other with *sake*, a custom similar to the *sansankudo*; however, this practice is now less frequently seen at the Sansei weddings.

The social forms of the wedding ceremony in America are now undergoing some changes. For example, some of the young have their ceremonies outside of the temples—in a wooded glen or at home; the guitar is sometimes played instead of the piano; and wedding gowns and tuxedos are becoming optional items of apparel. Such changes will undoubtedly continue in the future.

Sutras and Appurtenances

Other elements besides the religious ceremonies, services, and weddings are intrinsic to Buddhism in America. The most important of these concerns the religious sutras, the sermons of the Buddha. The sutras used by the BCA are in Chinese with Japanese pronunciations. The members chant with the priest. Only a few sutras are used in the Buddhist churches today, although the collection of the original sermons of the Buddha has been estimated at about thirty volumes.[39] The most important for the BCA are: *Shoshin-ge* (the Hymn of Faith), *San Sei-ge* (the Three Sacred Vows), *San Butsu-ge* (the Praises of the Buddha), and *Junirai* (the Twelve Adorations).[40] In a technical sense these four are not sutras since they are not authored by the Buddha. However, the Nikkei Buddhists call them sutras, and we will follow their convention. The sutras are not comprehensible to the American-born Japanese, although they have been translated into English.[41] They are still chanted in the traditional language, however. No service or ceremony is conducted without the chanting of at least one sutra. Although there have been attempts to chant them in English, the cadence and intonations have not been successfully adapted to this idiom.

Besides the sutras, elements that have persisted since the start of Buddhism in America include the shrine (*onaijin*), candles, incense, floral offerings, and gongs, bells, and drums. The shrines are often ornate gold-gilt, elaborate structures. In the center is a statue or picture of the image of the Buddha or a scroll with the sacred writings ("*Namu Amida Butsu*"). The candles are used both to symbolize the impermanence of all material objects and to shed light upon the teachings of Buddha. The incense, which symbolizes a technique of purification, is used to expunge unfavorable odors and to burn and extinguish impure thoughts. The flowers also symbolize the impermanence of living things. The gongs and bells are used to punctuate pauses within the sutras, but the fading tones also symbolize the impermanence of all material beings. All of these appurtenances have been part of the services and ceremonies of the Buddhist churches and temples both in Japan and America. All have continued throughout the years of the NABM and BCA, and have not been altered in content to adapt to a non-Buddhist environment. The Buddhist services, ceremonies, sutras, and appurtenances have remained unchanged for Jodo Shinshu adherents in America.

Problems of Ethnicity

Aside from teaching the precepts and practices of Buddhism, the NABM and BCA have attempted to sustain ethnic community solidarity—for the creation and enjoyment of group cohesiveness through racial, ethnic, and religious ties. Throughout its history, the BCA has been predominantly an organization by and for the Japanese and Japanese Americans.[42] As one Nisei father stated, "The Buddhist church is a place for the Japanese to meet other Japanese." The pressures created by prejudice and oppression during the early 1920s, and especially during the relocation in World War II, drove the Japanese to look to their own group for solace and companionship. The NABM and BCA have been religious institutions, for all Japanese and Japanese Americans, and together with the Japanese Association, the *kenjinkais* (prefectural associations), and the Japanese American Citizens' League, they have offered their members a social haven in a hostile environment.

In 1945, even the Japanese Christians were subjected to anti-Oriental prejudices, the roots of which are traceable to the early 1920s: "The Japanese feel that they are not wanted in the American churches. . . . Some who have attended the Occidental churches have experienced a warm reception, only to find later, as their numbers increased, that they were no longer welcome. Apparently, their presence in white American churches, arouses opposition as soon as there is danger of a Japanese invasion."[43] Thus, since the Japanese Christians also felt the effects of anti-Oriental sentiment, it can be stated that the basis for the prejudice was racial and only partly religious or cultural in origin.

A problem of religious differences between the Japanese and Caucasians occurred even in the 1960s. Situated in an agricultural community near the coast above Los Angeles County, which has a sizable Japanese American population, is a town with both a Nikkei Christian (Methodist) and a Buddhist church. The Methodist organization had a Japanese minister, a predominantly Japanese congregation, and a Japanese-dominated board of directors. A nearby Caucasian Methodist church approached the Japanese Methodist church with a proposal to merge the two churches for their mutual benefit. Part of the benefit involved selling the Japanese church building, making $45,000 available for the downpayment on a new structure. The agreement which was accepted included integration of the membership, combination of the boards of directors, and retention of the Japanese American minister in the combined church. The retention of the Japanese American minister, which later caused some concern, was the result of an informal agreement:

It was an understanding that a Japanese minister would be employed at the merger church. The assumption was [for] forever, I think. Nothing was written on paper. Being a church, I think things were done in "good faith.". . . I think the Japanese never raised this issue [of who would be head minister] but accepted whatever the Caucasians said. There is an interesting followup on this when the confrontation occurred on the head minister position. It was not raised by the Japanese members. It was raised by the second Japanese minister (by second, I mean the one succeeding the first). He was quickly reassigned to a small church in Piru [California], largely a migrant labor community. There were no more ministers of Japanese extraction thereafter. (I suppose that Caucasians here didn't think a Japanese could service their needs.)[44]

A new church building was financed, with substantial monetary contributions from the Japanese and the Nikkei. After the structure was completed in 1963, for a number of years the social relations within the church continued without incident. H. Kajihara explains the nature of the interaction: "I don't feel that there was any harmonious or disharmonious social relationship after the merger. You just went to church. You didn't have in-depth socialization which is common in all-Buddhist or all-Japanese membership church. In fact, the Japanese-Americans formed the Nisei Fellowship. To some Caucasians and Japanese this was strange, because the purpose of the merger was to integrate, so why have a segregated organization?"[45]

A series of events soon disturbed the existing relationship. The initial event was the transfer of the second Japanese American Methodist minister, which was followed by discussions as to his replacement. Although the initial church board had been composed of both Japanese and Caucasians, most decisions were now being made by the Caucasians because the Japanese were outnumbered (by twenty to three)—and apparently because the Japanese were reticent in making their position known. The Asian board members began to skip the board meetings. The general Japanese membership also declined to attend, although they generally never resisted openly, nor did they bring the disagreement into the open. Instead, person by person, they began to drop out of the church. The replacement minister was a Caucasian, and in time the board of directors also became a Caucasian-dominated group.

Subsequent board decisions had further effects on the Japanese and Nisei congregation. For example, the social hall had been reserved for some time, on one Saturday night per month, for meetings or social activities for the Japanese. Suddenly they found that that night was filled with social activities for the Caucasian Methodist Youth Fellowship. A "*shikataganai*" (literally, "cannot be helped") or stoical attitude prevailed among the Japanese Americans, and they expressed few words of protest. One Japanese American board member approached the bishop of the southern district with a plea to improve the situation—but to no avail. The Caucasian church members made no direct attempts to change the deteriorating interracial relationship. The Japanese American congregation gave up and stopped participating in church activities; they perceived the situation as an attempt to give them second-class membership status and to drive them out of the church. Since the Caucasian group had originally introduced the idea of a merger, and since the Japanese had donated funds for the construction of the new structure, the Japanese were troubled. Nonetheless they meekly accepted the situation.

Many Nisei left the church and attended no other religious institution. Others left the church and started to participate in the activities of the nearby Buddhist temple; this group was especially interested in maintaining some institutional ties with a Japanese American religious organization. They apparently believed that the retention of ethnic ties was of paramount importance, since the Caucasians, as a group, had indicated the unacceptability of the Japanese Americans as full members of their religious institution. One member who came from the Methodist church stated: "I started to attend the Buddhist temple for the sake of my children. There, they could meet other Japanese Americans and meet other boys and girls with whom they could play and eventually date. And then I started to learn about Buddhism. It has really been a great help to me and my family."

Racial differences between the Caucasians and Nikkei have not occurred in many other instances, perhaps because the Japanese Americans have been able to retain control over all facets of church organizations, monies, and programs in other churches.

The Buddhist Sunday Schools

The Buddhist Sunday Schools are an important part of the NABM-BCA organization. Along with the Buddhist services, the Sunday Schools have been a strong factor in keeping Japanese American children within the Buddhist religion.

With the start of the Nisei births in the 1920s, the members and ministers of the NABM experienced a crisis that would remain a continuing problem. This crisis concerned the proper education of the Nisei to insure their adherence to Buddhism. The Buddhist Sunday School was thus created, "to make Buddhism an American religion by educating the children of the church members in the ideas and atmosphere of Buddhism; to insure a happy religious life for the individual and the family."[46] The continual problem of perpetuating Buddhism in America was long ago recognized by Ogura: "As the future of Buddhism in the United States depends almost entirely upon the second generation Japanese, the Sunday Schools fill an important position in the work of the Buddhist mission."[47]

Creating and sustaining this educational portion of the NABM was recognized as vitally important to the organization. The Sunday Schools, though, were not without precedent in Japan *prior* to their incorporation within the temples in America. Contrary to other researchers' writings on the BCA, the Buddhist Sunday Schools did not originate in the United States after the arrival of the Japanese immigrants.[48] The Sunday Schools, Young Men's Buddhist Associations, and other such institutions were already in Japan by the late nineteenth and early twentieth centuries. The reasons for the adoption of the Euro-American forms of religious propagation are instructive.

Even before the Jodo Shinshu Buddhist religion was established in America, Japan's Buddhist leaders had sent priests to Europe to study Western religions and their activities. Other Buddhist priests visited the United States to observe religious conditions there through the 1870s, as a result of which changes within the Japanese religious institution occurred.[49] After the Tokugawa era (1601–1868), the Meiji authorities attempted to suppress Buddhism and to make Shintoism the state religion. This move could have resulted in the "complete expulsion of Buddhism from Japan."[50] Aided by reports and observations about the West, the lord abbots of the Nishi and Higashi Hongwanji petitioned the Meiji authorities to allow the Japanese people the right to practice any religion they chose. This petition was accepted in 1876, and as a result the Jodo Shinshu sect, in particular, was able to reassert itself in Japanese national life. Freedom of worship, coupled with the insights brought back from Europe and America, helped revitalize and reorganize Buddhism in Japan.

The Jodo Shinshu Buddhists in Japan adopted certain European and American techniques of religious dissemination. Thus, in the late 1800s and early 1900s, not only the Sunday Schools, but also Buddhist women's societies, orphanages, and Buddhist homes for ex-convicts were instituted. During this phase of Japanese infatuation with Western ideas, some Buddhist sects inaugurated street preaching, "evangelical" campaigns, sermonizing, and hymnals along "Christian" lines.[51] The changes were made primarily to resolve problems that Buddhist organizations were having with the Meiji authorities. For one thing, the government then favored Occidental ideas and practices, and for another, the changes alleviated the problem of membership losses resulting from the apparent complacency of the Buddhist leaders during the Tokugawa era.

The Japanese model was resurrected in the United States with the birth of the Nisei, when the need for some form of educational institution became apparent. As Ogura states, "All the Sunday Schools are modeled after those of Japan, which are conducted by the Shin sect."[52] The first Sunday School in America was established in 1913 by the San Francisco headquarters.[53] The early teachers were the *kaikyoshi* and their wives; later, with more students attending the classes, YMBA and YWBA members were trained and assisted the priests in conducting classes. The various Sunday Schools from the early 1920s to the middle 1930s were affected by conditions at the member temples. The programs and quality of instruction varied according to the talents of resident ministers and interested lay leaders. Mrs. Kiyo Kyogoku gives her impression of the early Sunday Schools: "I was disappointed in the first Sunday School session I attended on my arrival [from Japan] forty years ago [1912]. It consisted of practicing a few secular songs and listening to fairy tales."[54] At that time, the lessons and tales were given in Japanese and were apparently copied from the Jodo Shinshu Sunday Schools of Japan.

For the Buddhist churches in America and for the Buddhists themselves, the designation of Sunday as the day to hold services has no religious significance. Sunday was chosen as a matter of convenience, since in the United States most individuals and families do not work on that day. However, at some churches, the term *Sunday School* is a misnomer. Localities where the members were predominantly agricultural workers often held their services on Saturdays. Sunday was a workday for these people, as they prepared farming produce for distribution to the urban markets for Monday sales.[55]

Aware of the possibility that the Buddhist Sunday Schools might be mistaken for Christian Sunday Schools, some Buddhist churches have changed the old designation to Dharma Schools.[56] Others have instituted monthly Saturday night family services[57] to encourage the children and their parents to attend services together. The Sunday Schools, like many other activities and programs in the Buddhist churches, are best understood as having arisen to meet the demands of the Buddhist members.

The Sunday School was the first organization under the NABM to be directly affected by transplantation to America. The Buddhist education of the Nisei was an immediate challenge to the Issei because the Nisei manifested the immediate influence of their new homeland. As K. Kyogoku states:

> *The strongest reason all of us tried to build up the Sunday School came from a remark my husband overheard at a non-religious function of leaders of the Japanese community. At the meeting, a non-Buddhist minister chanced to say, "Oh, Buddhism will quietly fade away." My husband asked, "Why do you think so?" He replied, "The Issei may be members of your church, but they're sending their children to our Sunday Schools." My husband made a survey right away and was awestruck at the discovery that what the minister said was true.*[58]

The Buddhist institution recognized this possibility in the 1920s with reference to the Nisei. The immediate problem concerned the appropriate method of education to counteract the loss of future members. The initial approach was to examine American religious educational techniques to ascertain those methods most suitable and adaptable for the NABM. One important source of information in the 1920s was a group of four ministers studying at the University of Southern California.[59] A few were majoring in religious education, and all helped the Southern California Buddhist churches on weekends, especially in developing the embryonic Sunday Schools.

Beginning in the middle 1930s, English became the primary means of communication within the Sunday Schools, although the *kaikyoshi* continued to give sermons to the children in Japanese. Sunday School lesson cards, initially printed in Japanese, were later modified for the English-speaking children. The cards, of varying sophistication based on an age-graded system, had religious pictures that the preschool children could color and paste into books. For the advanced children, religious stories were used for instruction and discussion.

An annual NABM summer workshop (*kaki koshukai*) was inaugurated in about 1924 to coordinate and train Sunday School teachers more systematically. The workshops, held throughout California until the outbreak of the war in 1941, were attended by YMBA and YWBA members. The YMWBA teachers were taught by a team of resident area ministers. After the war, the use of picture cards and the more centralized training centers resulted in the development of a BCA Sunday School Department to coordinate most aspects of the religious education of Buddhist children.

By 1959, the training of the young was regarded as important enough to warrant a Bureau of Buddhist Education (BBE). Created by the BCA in 1959, the BBE became an umbrella bureau supervising the Youth Department, Sales Department (e.g., bookstore), Audio-Visual Departments, Boy Scout Committee, and public programs. The Sunday School Department came under the Bureau in 1963; until that time, it had been supervised by the Ministerial Association. This responsibility had been vested in the ministers because the Sunday Schools were primarily viewed as places for religious services. As more sophisticated educational methods were introduced, there was an increasing need to centralize control of the Sunday Schools for more efficient dissemination of materials such as films. Thus, in 1963, a full-time minister-director position was created to oversee the program; this resulted in a cohesive and integrated educational system for preschool to college-aged students.

In interviews, many reverends and lay leaders indicated that the future of the Buddhist churches lies in the children. Despite this view, the Sunday Schools and Junior YBA are often given secondary consideration in the face of economic issues confronting individual temples. For example, the annual food bazaar at one small (198-member) southern California Buddhist church,[60] with a gross receipt of about $5,400 in 1974 and a net gain of about $3,000, is discussed at the board meetings for four months prior to the event, and in the last month before the bazaar is held it almost monopolizes the attention of the temple's leaders and members. The bazaar is important to the financial stability of the church; consequently, the Sunday School, with forty-eight students, is left solely to the Sunday School superintendent, the minister, and the teachers. The future members of the church are often given less consideration than present needs.

The problems of the smaller churches in sustaining an active Sunday School program are different from those of large churches. With fewer members, there are fewer volunteer-teachers, a smaller pool from which new teachers can be recruited, and fewer financial resources to subsidize new methods and techniques of presenting Buddhist materials. If the children are forced to attend Sunday Schools, the atmosphere will hardly be conducive to effective religious training. The first issue that must be resolved is the children's apparent disinclination to attend Sunday services; resolution of this problem will probably necessitate the closer attention of BCA leaders, member ministers, and interested family members. If, as the church leaders state, the future of the church depends upon these youngsters in the Sunday Schools, then the BCA as it is known today faces a bleak and uncertain prospect.

Notes

1. Befu, op. cit., p. 212.

2. The term *sociological death* was used to describe the process whereby blacks attempted to portray themselves as white. "For the negro to pass socially means sociological death and rebirth. It is extremely difficult, as one loses in the process his educational standing (if he has gone to a Negro school), intimate friends, family and work references." St. Clair Drake and Horace Cayton, *Black Metropolis* (New York: Harper and Row, 1945), p. 163.

3. Kazuo Kawai, "Three Roads and None Easy: An American Born Japanese Looks at Life," *Survey Graphics* (May 1, 1926): 165.

4. The Buddhist swastika extends in a counterclockwise fashion 卍, while the symbol associated with Nazi Germany extends clockwise 卐.

5. Munekata, op. cit., p. 166. The swastika is noticeable on the older structures, either embedded within the structure (see Los Angeles Betsuin, constructed in 1925), on the front windows as in San Francisco (Munekata, p. 145), or as a design on the front wall as in Sacramento (Munekata, p. 151).

6. Maude W. Madden, *When the East Is in the West* (New York: Fleming H. Revell Co., 1923; reprint ed., San Francisco: R and E Research Associates, 1971), p. 120.

7. Ibid., p. 128.

8. Reverend Arthur Takemoto, "The War Years," in Munekata, op. cit., p. 61.

9. *Kinnara Newsletter*, Los Angeles, September 1972.

10. "Part of the loss the evacuees suffered during their detention in camps was in communal religious property. Of the twenty-eight temples in Los Angeles, twenty-two were damaged, some almost beyond repair; in Seattle the Navy took over the temple for its use." William Petersen, *Japanese Americans* (New York: Random House, 1971), p. 178.

11. From 1948 to 1971, eighty-five new priests entered the BCA. Of that number, twenty-one have subsequently withdrawn, leaving sixty-four priests still active. There were, in addition, nineteen priests in active service from before 1948. BCA, *Annual Report, 1970*, pp. 1–4; the figures do not reflect changes since 1970.

12. Manimai Ratanamani, op. cit., p. 86.

13. Japanese American Curriculum Project, *Japanese Americans: The Untold Story* (New York: Holt, Rinehart and Winston, 1971).

14. Ethnic Studies Committee, Asian American Alliance, Stanford University, "Critical Reviews of *Japanese Americans: The Untold Story*," mimeographed, March 1971, p. 1; also a letter written to the San Francisco Station (KQED) objecting to the telecast, signed by the bishop of the BCA, the president of the board of directors, and the chairman of the Ministerial Research Committee, dated October 5, 1970, in the personal possession of the author.

15. Ethnic Studies Committee, op. cit., "Documentary Appendices," p. 10. Critiques by the other organizations did not always focus on religious bias, but on the pro-Japanese, anti-Chinese, Anglo-conformity, "model-minority" perspective.

16. Mimeographed letter dated October 6, 1970, in possession of the author.

17. "State Textbook Body Hears Buddhist Viewpoint Concerning 'Divine Creation,'" San Francisco *Hokubei Mainichi*, November 14, 1972, p. 1.

18. Ibid.

19. "Young Buddhists Pass Anti-War Resolution," Los Angeles *Kashu Mainichi*, May 25, 1971, p. 1.

20. The Reverend La Verne Senyo Sasaki, "Buddhism and Social Activism," a lecture presented at the Western Young Buddhist League Conference, March 31, 1973, Los Angeles.

21. "JARF Gets Federal Approval for Apartment Construction," San Francisco *Hokubei Mainichi*, December 2, 1972. The Parlier Buddhist Church has also started a housing project for low-income persons.

22. The other participating churches are: Christ Episcopal Mission, San Francisco Independent Church, Konko Church, Nichiren Church. St. Xavier Mission, Zen Sokoji Mission, Seventh Day Adventist Church, Pine United Methodist Church, and Christ United Presbyterian Church.

23. "New Era of American Buddhism with Youth in Focus Emphasized," San Francisco *Hokubei Mainichi*, February 29, 1972, p. 1.

24. See Amy Tachiki, et al., *Roots: An Asian American Reader* (Los Angeles: UCLA Asian American Studies Center, 1971); and Joe R. Feagan and Nancy Fujitaki, "On the Assimilation of Japanese Americans," *Amerasia Journal* 1, no. 4 (February 1972): 13–31.

25. Marcus Lee Hansen, "The Third Generation in America," *Commentary* 14 (November 1952).

26. Yuki Yanagita, "Familial, Occupational, and Social Characteristics of Three Generations of Japanese Americans," Master's thesis, University of Southern California, Los Angeles, June 1968, pp. 35–37. "On the other hand, among the Sansei generation the percentage of Buddhists has increased, and the percentage of Protestants has decreased."

27. Most conferences on the ministerial and affiliated Buddhist organizational levels have included topics on the problem of the Sansei. Author's personal observation from 1970 to 1974.

28. Personal interview with BCA ministers.

29. Interview with Reverend Masami Fujitani, Oxnard Buddhist Church, Calif., June 14, 1974.

30. Interview with the Reverend Seiko Okahashi, Santa Barbara, June 6, 1974. Reverend Okahashi was formerly with the Seattle Buddhist Church and is one of three active women ministers in the BCA. Yonsei refers to the fourth generation or great-grandchildren of the Issei; Gosei are the fifth-generation Japanese Americans.

31. Ibid.

32. Reverend Osamu Fujimoto, "Nembutsu," in BCA, *Shin Buddhist Handbook*, p. 118.

33. Personal interview with Reverend S. Sakow, Santa Barbara, December 4, 1973.

34. Reverend J. Yanagihara, sermon given at a Buddhist conference, October 21, 1973, Los Angeles.

35. One researcher is in error when he states, "We can conclude that Buddhism as an indigenous religion from Japan had no formal experience with performing weddings in Japan." Isao Horinouchi, "Americanized Buddhism: A Sociological Analysis of a Protestantized Japanese Religion," Ph.D. dissertation, University of California, Davis, 1973, p. 164.

36. Personal interview with Reverends S. Sakow, December 4, 1973, Santa Barbara, and K. Terada, January 1, 1974, San Diego. Both Reverends Sakow and Terada had their marriage ceremonies performed in a Buddhist temple in Japan.

37. Interview with Reverend Terada.

38. Ibid.

39. Eidmann, *Young People's Introduction*, p. 40.

40. BCA., *Shin Buddhist Handbook*, pp. 125–136; and BCA, *Buddhism and Jodo Shinshu* (San Francisco, 1955), pp. 179–186.

41. Ibid., and Shoyu Hanayama, op. cit., pp. 12–29.

42. There have been a few non-Japanese members and ministers. The non-Asian membership has always been very small, however, usually limited to isolated but dedicated individuals and the spouses of Asian members. The non-Asian Buddhist priests have played an important role, especially in influencing the Nisei priests. Within the non-Japanese membership and ministerial group, Caucasians are most widely represented. There are few black, Chicano or native American Buddhists within the BCA, although at the 1972 BCA ministers' conference, three blacks did address the ministers, at least one of whom was singled out as a Buddhist. See "Black Buddhists Speak at BCA Ministers' Seminar," San Francisco *Hokubei Mainichi*, August 28, 1972, p. 1.

43. Forrest E. La Violette, *Americans of Japanese Ancestry: A Study of Assimilation in the American Community* (Toronto: Canadian Institute of International Affairs, 1945), p. 48.

44. Interview with Mr. and Mrs. Harry Kajihara, May 11, 1974; and personal correspondence, June 29, 1974. I am indebted to Mr. and Mrs. Kajihara for this example and for their observations about the Japanese American reactions to the situation.

45. Ibid.

46. Ogura, op. cit., p. 19.

47. Ibid.

48. Both Spencer and Horinouchi appear to be in historical error on this point. Spencer has stated, "As a means of maintaining a Nisei interest in Buddhism, the Sunday School was inaugurated. It is of interest to note that this concept spread back to Japan from America, the Buddhist Sunday Schools or its equivalent now having become part of the organizational program of the Shin sect there." Spencer, op. cit., p. 212.

    Horinouchi states that "Sunday schools were created like the Christian Sunday Schools" and credits a Hawaiian Buddhist adoption of the Christian educational format. Horinouchi, op. cit., p. 100.

49. Hideo Kishimoto, *Japanese Religion in the Meiji Era* (Tokyo: Obusha, 1956), p. 137.

50. Utsuki, op. cit., p. 34.

51. August K. Reischauer, *Studies in Japanese Buddhism* (New York: AMS Press, 1917, 1970), p. 154.

52. Ogura, op. cit., p. 19.

53. Chonen Terakawa (ed.), *Hokubei Kaikyo Enkakushi* [History of the North American Buddhist Mission], (San Francisco: North American Buddhist Mission Publication, 1936), p. 48.

54. Munekata, "BCA Sunday School Department," op. cit., p. 101. 55. Thus, prior to 1942 and after 1946, the Orange County Buddhist Church held its Sunday School on Saturdays, until the population changed from an agricultural occupational base to a suburban housing area in the late 1950s. Munekata, "Orange County Buddhist Church," op. cit., p. 44.

56. The term *Dharma School* is used, for instance, by the Southern Alameda Buddhist Church, Union City, Calif., and the Oxnard Buddhist Church, Oxnard, Calif.

57. Title used by the San Diego Buddhist Church.

58. Munekata, "BCA Sunday School Department," op. cit., p. 101.

59. Reverends Kenjo Kurokawa, Ryugyo Fujimoto, Nishi Utsuji, and Ryuchi Fujii. From Munekata, op. cit.

60. BCA census, 1972.

16. The Adjustments of a Young Immigrant

JOYCE NISHIMURA

I came to Hawaii from Japan in the summer of 1948 at the age of ten. Since my mother is a Hawaii-born Nisei and my father, a Japanese citizen, this makes me sort of a second-and-a-half generation immigrant. Before coming to Hawaii, we lived in Japan for about two years, and we spent the other years in Manchuria. We used to be a part of what the historians now call Japan's excess-population, sent to live in a remote portion of Nippon's once far-flung empire. After the war we went back to Japan, and, when father died, mother brought my three sisters and me to Hawaii.

Coming to Hawaii presented many new adjustment problems to my sisters and me. The first adjustment we had to make concerned the three basic needs: food, clothing and shelter. The struggle to adjust to the Western type of food began as soon as we boarded the ocean liner which was to carry us to Hawaii. My sisters and I were fascinated by the varieties of ice cream that were served in the ship's dining room and we spent the first day eating ice cream until we were quite sick. Then we began craving for the kinds of food we were accustomed to, such as rice, *miso*-soup, *tsukemono* (pickled vegetables), *shoyu*, *ume* (pickled plum), and the like. Of course, these were not available on the American ship. Instead, there was an endless variety of what I now consider superb dishes—steak, fried chicken, leg of lamb, roasts, and so forth. But at that time we could not eat any of them. We, therefore, embarrassed our poor mother by ordering only rice and eating it with nothing but salt on it. I once mistook some pickles for *tsukemono* and some olives for *ume*. I eagerly bit into them, with disappointing results.

After reaching my grandparents' home in Hawaii, things were not so bad, for my aunt was an excellent cook of both Oriental and Haole food. Even then, it took me quite a while to get accustomed to having toast and milk for breakfast instead of rice and miso-soup. It took time, too, to get used to the idea of eating white, polished rice all the time, for in Japan that was a luxury. Rice was usually cooked with whole wheat or even sweet potatoes mixed in it. Now, nine years later, I am quite used to the widely varied food habits in Hawaii. I can now get along without rice for several weeks, whereas, when I first arrived, I had to have rice every day.

Becoming adjusted to the types of clothes was not difficult, for there is not so much difference between the types of clothes worn here and in Japan. There was one thing, however, that shocked me at first. That was the way in which young girls walked around in shorts or in blue jeans and loose Aloha shirts. When I first met one of my cousins, she wore a pair of blue jeans, rolled up several times at the bottom, and an untucked shirt which looked much too big for her. Another cousin wore shorts which exposed a large part of her legs. These greatly embarrassed me, for I had always felt that girls should be more modest in their dress. But after living through the first Hawaiian summer, I learned how comfortable these loose shirts and shorts are, and I soon discarded my earlier feelings against them.

As for houses in Hawaii, one of the things that I had to become adjusted to was having to live on hard wooden floors instead of the soft *tatami* (mat). Seeing some people walk into a house with their shoes on shocked me at first, too. This, however, was not allowed at my grand-parents' house. Sleeping on a bed instead of on the floor, and taking a bath in porcelain tubs instead of in the wooden *furo* were some of the new experiences that I had to face.

In addition to the physical adjustments, there were many new social situations to encounter. The first hurdle was that of learning English. Although mother could speak and write English proficiently, we never used English in Japan. Therefore, my sisters and I had to begin from the very beginning. In school, I was too old to be in the first grade, so I was placed in the third grade. There, with the help of a wonderfully understanding teacher, I slowly advanced from the ABC picture books to the "Dick and Jane" texts, and finally to the third grade readers. Picking up conversational English was less difficult because everyone around me spoke English. I soon found myself translating my Japanese thoughts into English, and then in no time I began thinking, as well as talking, in English. But the force of habit is strong, and I still find some things easier to think out in Japanese. Even now I can work out math problems faster if I do the mental computations in Japanese.

Another adjustment that I had to make, especially in school, was that of associating with people of other nationalities. The dark-skinned Hawaiians and Filipinos, especially, gave me a scare at first. I had not expected anyone to be so "dark." I was not prepared to associate with so many "Haoles" either, although in Osaka, Tokyo, Yokohama, and other big cities in Japan I had glimpses of the tall American G.I.'s. But, as I watched the other children mingle so unconcernedly among each other, I soon lost my self-consciousness and began enjoying associating with all of them.

As I grew older I became acutely conscious of another difference in the way of life here as compared to what I saw in Japan. I noticed that the boy-girl relationship here was more free and open, and that the girls were bolder than those I have seen in Japan. Girls talked nonchalantly about their boyfriends, the boys and girls seemed to think nothing of the public display of affection, and many of the parents, too, did not seem to mind all this. Young people in Hawaii seem to have a freer hand in their own social life than those that I had seen in Japan. Now, I am so accustomed to being my own "boss" in my social affairs, that I think I would resent having any of my relatives telling me what to do. I would most definitely object to being subjected to an arranged marriage like many of my cousins in Japan.

Religion was an area in which I had difficulty in getting well adjusted to. As long as I could remember, I worshipped in the Buddhist temples, not because I had any strong convictions but because that was the general custom in Japan. I had heard about Christianity, and I remember reading Japanese translations of many of the stories from the Bible. But these stories had seemed like fairy tales to me. Then, here in Hawaii I saw Christianity close at hand. I also saw conflict between Christianity and Buddhism. Some of my relatives are strong Christians, others, equally strong Buddhists. I heard my Christian relatives criticized by those who were not. At first, out of habit I attended the local Buddhist temple. But I began to realize that what I did in these Buddhist churches had no meaning for me and that I was merely performing formal rituals. It seemed that the Western way of life was based on Christian beliefs and I could not live long in this way of life and still cling to the old Buddhist beliefs. Thus, I became a Christian. But changing from one religious belief to another involves considerable mental adjustment. I am often made to feel that by becoming a Christian I had turned my back on the memories of my father, grandfather, and the other ancestors and thus am guilty of disloyalty.

Therefore, young as I was when I first came to Hawaii, I had many adjustments to make. I was quite successful in some, not so in others. I am still far from being completely well adjusted. But there is one thing I know: that I will never stop trying to be worthy of this great country which has given me a home and a citizenship.

17. Reflections: An Autobiographical Sketch

ANDREA SAKAI

It is difficult to write about oneself. Everything becomes in time so much a part of oneself that it's hard to know what is worth telling and what is best left unsaid.

I am what in Honolulu is laughingly, and sometimes otherwise, termed a "*kotonk*". You know—the sound the coconut makes as it falls to the ground? The similarity is said to be in the degree of hard-headedness of Mainland-born Nisei as compared with a Hawaii-born Nisei. Well, whatever the reason, I am one of those. My family and I lived in Portland, Oregon, most of our lives. There was a short sojourn in an assembly center, then a longer stay at Minidoka, Idaho, during the "relocation center" days. We also lived for a few years after the war in Salem, Oregon, after which we returned to live permanently in Portland.

Originally my parents came to Oregon from Fukuoka Prefecture, Japan. My mother was 18 years younger than my father, and theirs was an arranged marriage. A none too happy one since there was such an age gap between them as well as the fact that father had a frightful and unreasonable temper which expressed itself more frequently in his declining years as he began to return more and more to the old culture patterns. He had been the first-born son of a shipping firm owner and was raised by a doting grandmother. When his father remarried the son of the second wife became the heir, and my sea-captain father came to America to seek his livelihood. Even to his last days, father retained the characteristic commanding bellow of his seafaring past. After all, in the old days ships had no public address systems and one's voice had to suffice.

My mother had been the eldest daughter of a large farming family. She had played mother since about the second or third year of school to a motherless brood. Mother was quick and clever, but always said she never cared much for school just the same. So along with an age difference there also existed a wide educational gap between my mother and my father, who could read and write the more difficult Japanese. In later years, while in camp, father used to read Buddhist texts, etc., and people who could not read them often came to talk with my father for interpretation and discussion about their religion.

My parents worked in the beginning as cook and housemaid to extremely wealthy families in Oregon. Possibly, this influenced their ability to leave the ghetto in later years. In time they saved enough to open a waffle house and over the years ran one sort of restaurant or another. I'm not able to furnish more than sketchy details about my parents, partly because we children came along after things had settled and we were then in a florist business catering to a Haole trade and partly because my parents almost never talked about themselves or the past with us.

It seems that in my father's younger days he had been an active member of the Japanese community. He had several mementos of his leadership such as gold pens and watches. However, by the time I became acquainted with my family we were living miles from any other Japanese. I was for a long time the only Nisei in school, until my sister joined me three years later. We don't know why or how my parents came to leave the security of "Little Tokyo," but this may have increased in many ways the differences between our family and the typical Japanese families in and around Portland. Also, the fact that my parents lived away from the other Japanese families seems to indicate that as Japanese they may not have been entirely typical in their ways. Yet, my parents were friendly with the Japanese in the area, because as a youngster I can recall seeing friends drop in and have tea and other refreshments with my parents. I was fascinated by their polite responses in greeting and *sayonara,* and wondered with wicked anticipation as children will, if they might not bump heads or even fall forward accidentally as they bowed so deeply and formally to each other. After all, we children never went through these motions and I could never quite understand why our elders did. On rare occasion we went into town and visited some of my parents' friends who still lived and worked in the Japanese settlement.

Our family followed the old pattern with father as head and authority for the family, especially with us children. We were taught to be obedient, never to talk back to our elders, that sex is not to be discussed, and to respect the men in our family as our superiors. My sister and I were taught that young ladies should be quiet and gentle, what in Japanese would be termed a *yasashi musume-san.*

My parents were both Buddhist, but they decided that since we were Americans we should attend Christian churches. Hence, even before my school days began I regularly attended a liberal Congregational church located just a few block away from our home and florist shop. Before the war, my parents did not attend their church. One reason for this may have been the great distance from their church in pre-war days. After my father's death my mother began to attend Buddhist services again. Of course during our stay in the relocation center my parents began to attend services regularly and the habit may have been reinstated at that time. I learned the ways of a Christian faith from the very beginning, although my parents did maintain an altar of sorts for their own worship at home. Nothing was ever said to us of its significance and it never occurred to me that their murmured *Namu amida butsu* and bowed heads had any religious significance. The only vivid recollection I have of the altar is that each New Year's we put *mochi* and other goodies on the altar shelf and father tossed a pair of dice till he obtained the desired lucky combination to place on the shelf with the goodies. So to my mind the altar was mainly just part of the Christmas and New Year's traditional gaiety. We observed Christmas by hanging up our stockings and finding them filled on Christmas morning. We received the usual gifts from Santa Claus and attended Christmas services at church. Mother usually came with us to these functions at church and at school while father tended shop. In recalling this I now realize that mother was always uncomfortable when she attended these functions, but what could she do? We youngsters were forever in the choir, the play, or some part of the school and church programs. New Year's was also the only time that we really had the typical spread of *maki sushi, nishime,* whole fish, etc., but I thought this special food was just synonymous to holiday festivities and never connected it in my mind as part of a Japanese food pattern.

Not only were my parents different in their leaving of the ghetto, but also in their insistence that we be American. They felt that since we were to live in America there was little point in sending us to Japanese school or for our learning all the usual Japanese customs. I can still hear my father saying to me, "You're going to school soon so from now on you must speak English." Yet, I must have spoken a good bit of Japanese prior to my first grade days, but I recall no language embarrassment in school. To this day I can, despite the lack of formal training in Japanese, speak more Japanese than can readily be accounted for. Even when we arrived in the Assembly Centers during the war my understanding of Japanese exceeded my ability to speak. This additional exposure to the Japanese language has helped to reinforce what was earlier acquired at home. In later years even remembering how to say good morning in Japanese was difficult, but if I talked in my sleep at college the students could never, much to their frustration, repeat my comments. It seems that I talked in Japanese in my sleep, but couldn't say much while awake.

This being away from most Japanese influences produced Haole accents in the spoken English of our family. We speak more readily and fluently than many Nisei do and our speech lacks the typical Nisei accents. My sister and brother did begin to associate more closely with the Japanese groups during and after the war and now on occasion have a faint accent in their speech. Their affiliations included activities with the Japanese community groups while mine never have. My thinking and interests were more in line with the Haole group and my closest affiliations have always been so. I left home at seventeen and have more or less continued this same pattern. This was not a matter of decision, merely one of habit. Although my brother was made to feel that other Nisei believed I did this out of snobbishness and a sense of being better than they, to my knowledge this is really not the case. I was more haole-fied during the course of my upbringing and had maintained affiliations which were most comfortable for me. But comfortable is a dubious statement, since in appearance I belonged with the Nisei group, in attitudes with the Haole group, and in actuality felt as though I really did not belong to either group.

The first conscious realization that I contained conflicting cultures within myself and accommodated myself to them unconsciously was brought about by a very simple incident. While visiting a Japanese family, I was offered some refreshments, and suddenly to my horror realized that I had accepted food at its first offering. Haole fashion you say yes or no and mean it. Japanese fashion you politely refuse a few times and are coaxed into acceptance. I pondered this incident and realized that I also had chosen non-slurp eating to polite slurpy Japanese eating. After all it's easier never to slurp than to stop slurping at will. A man without a country or one who forever walks on the borderline, never one thing or another, were my expressions for these feelings.

At home my parents spoke to us in a mixture of Japanese and English. We children spoke to them more in English than in Japanese. This did in later years cause a communication blockage with a limited vocabulary in each other's languages increasing the distance between the older generation and the new. It wasn't till I was sixteen that I felt this loss. We learned American ways in church, school, and in play activities in our neighborhood. Although our parents tried in their own way to help us with this adjustment their capacity to help was limited by their already established culture patterns and by their own adjustment problems created by a foreign culture without the support of ghetto life.

The communication barrier was so high that I often felt as though my parents neither loved me nor were they particularly interested in me. Any attempts at discussion wound up in quarrels due to lack of understanding on both sides and the lack of language with which to accomplish understanding. My brother was away in service at this time so that I could not consult him. He had taught me in his rigorous manner proper behavior, Emily Post style, and coached me on other necessary factors in my early youth. Having no model to follow at home, in many ways we became "super-Americanized." It takes time to find any happy medium. In later years the family ties became almost nonexistent as we children grew up and went about our own business. Out of my parents' encouraging us to be Americanized came two sharply different worlds in which we operated with little or no common meeting ground between the two. Our loss of the old has been compensated for in our being as Americanized in many ways as many third generation Japanese may be, and in our ability to adapt to the American scene, but I sometimes wonder if the gain is worth what we have lost in the process.

Since my family have no relatives outside Japan, with my father's death when I was sixteen, my mother felt extremely lonely. Perhaps for this reason she resumed Buddhist church attendance and became interested again in Japanese community programs and movies. However, mother to this day still does not cultivate the usual close friendships with other people and still does not join any of the Japanese community organizations. I do not know if this is just the old habit of being away from Japanese groups and being so long alone, or if she is characteristically unsociable or a little of both. Mother has turned down opportunities to remarry. Again I do not know if the mentioned traits influence this, if her previous unhappy marriage keeps her from remarrying, or if the possible choice of mates just hasn't met her fancy. My mother has always been strongly distrustful and suspicious of all people and prefers to be entirely self-sufficient. Possibly the strain of being away from her own culture group has encouraged this habit.

We all attended a grammar school which went through the eighth grade. The youngsters attending the school were from families that had been sending their children to the same school for years. The teachers were of long standing in our community. The neighborhood was indeed a very stable one. My conception of myself as being different or Japanese did not begin until the war so that my early school days were lived in a blissful unconsciousness of this fact. It is said that we determine how we look by those around us and I never noticed that my family looked particularly different, nor I from my colleagues.

My parents placed strong emphasis upon good scholarship. Unfortunately for me my brother skipped through school, made mostly "A's," and attained other honors throughout his school years. To shame me into doing well he was held up to me as a constant example of good scholarship. It was a relief to attend a different high school when the war ended. After basking in my brother's reflected glory all through grade school, I had begun to wonder if my own ability or my brother's past record had determined my school progress. In grade school I travelled with the leadership group, and often held lead roles in plays, had special assignments that permitted me to skip classes, and had the honor several times of being school librarian. I was "teacher's pet." As far as I can recall, I was completely accepted at school. There were a very few instances where children did express their parents' prejudices, but this seldom happened, and I recognized them as such only now in retrospect. They meant little to me then. My life up to this point had been extremely sheltered and was composed mainly of school, church, and home, and consequently this gave me a protective naivete.

Pearl Harbor Day changed all this. First we were sent to an Assembly Center in May of 1942. I thought this was quite a lark. My classmates gave me the most marvellous gifts and a wonderful sendoff. We packed up, took shots, had to observe a curfew, and could not travel very far from home. A long bus trip was taken and this was a novel experience for me. However, the arrival at the Assembly Center seemed unreal. We were processed through long lines for housing and medical check-ups, etc., then home suddenly was contained in one room in unpainted barracks with tar paper roofs and partitions between families with openings at the top to keep the circulation of air going between rooms. We had showers and toilet facilities assigned to us depending on what section we were living in. Meals were taken at the mess halls in army fashion. Strangely enough, school was set up immediately. I will never forget my sudden realization—all my classmates look alike! Even when some of them said "hello" to me, I could never be sure if I knew them or if they were just starting up a new friendship with me. Finally—oh successful day—I could identify two of my girlfriends. One had a bad case of acne, a most distinguishing mark, and the other girl had the same first name as I and especially long eyelashes and pigtails. Gradually, I learned to distinguish one from another, and now since my stay in Honolulu I can often distinguish a Chinese, Korean, Japanese, and even mixtures from one another, and I no longer have trouble distinguishing the individual Oriental.

In September of 1942 the Assembly Centers were disassembled and we were sent to Minidoka, Idaho, to what was termed a "relocation center," the idea being that we could relocate from these centers at any time, providing clearance could be obtained, to any of the non-restricted areas in the United States. We arrived in time for the coldest winter that the area had experienced in many a year. Thus, I learned the beauties of crackling cold, drifting snow, and lots of thick ice. We had a marvellous winter ice-skating for the first time on the Gooding Canal. Of course, on the more serious side, we found ourselves living in one room family arrangements again. The size of the family decided the size of the assigned quarters. The block was split up into ten barracks with five barracks on each side. The center portion was occupied by two large buildings, a mess hall and the laundry and bath facilities. School was begun shortly after our arrival. Many of the students knew each other from pre-war days and shared similar attitudes and interests, but I felt out of place and had to begin all over again. Still, I knew that the others noticed that I spoke "lousy" Japanese, didn't know "beans" about the accepted Japanese ways, and even knew very little about common Japanese foods. My family had up to this point eaten American breakfasts, and lunch at school had always been the American institution—a sandwich with soup or milk. At home we sometimes ate Japanese food for lunch or dinner, but this was never a definite matter. Since we were not allowed to eat at other people's houses except on extremely rare occasion, it never occurred to me that we mixed two food patterns under our roof. To my knowledge, other people ate the same things we did.

So as children can and will do, I was made to feel quite stupid because my ignorance of the Japanese ways amused them. Also, after having been with the privileged group in my own school, I now was just another student. This was disconcerting. Especially since I just felt these things and did not possess the necessary insight to think them through. Eventually, I did make a few friends and fell into a somewhat comfortable pattern, playing the usual card games, kick the can, and other such things that youngsters of my age did in "the good old" camp days. There were friends of my own age, but I was closest to people who were a good deal older. My brother and I had more difficulty fitting in than my sister who was only 10 years old and young enough to adapt more readily to the situation.

My parents under contact again with the Japanese community began to become more Japanese in their ways. Father took to playing Goh with the men and mother took to visiting with a few of her Japanese neighbors occasionally and in taking classes for flower arrangement, pattern drafting, etc. My parents felt that the displeasure of the other Japanese for the seeming rudenesses of their children who were much too Americanized by the standards of other Issei. I can remember being scolded often for improper behavior of one sort or another. This was the beginning of being compared unfavorably with other people's children and of being asked why we couldn't be like them. This practice eventually convinced me that I was both unloved and unlovable.

In camp some of the Issei became more "nationalistic" and felt that America would surely lose the war. However, the majority were still for America and wished to remain in their adopted homeland. When the United States' Government announced that the Nisei would now be permitted to volunteer for the service, my brother promptly did so. Well, my parents felt this was as it should be since he was an American. This led to a rather interesting squabble. When New Year's rolled around the army, taking the Japanese customs into consideration, sent enough *mochi* rice into camp for the blocks to make *mochi* for each family. An angry "nationalist" decided that the families of volunteer soldiers ought to be deprived of this treat. Every family did receive their fair share, but mother along with the other parents who also had soldier sons, felt quite unhappy about this. It was difficult enough to wonder if her only son would ever return alive without having to contend with the petty bickering about whether we did or did not deserve any *mochi*.

Camp life was well organized. We had a camp newspaper and a yearly camp annual. The hospital and administrative buildings were on one end of the camp. The schools were located in centralized blocks. We had several recreation halls where students attended free weekly movies by making use of student passes. Three canteens were strategically placed to service the entire camp area. Churches were established by ministers who came into camp or by the few Japanese church men who were present in the camp. We had an annual Christmas contest for the best decorated mess hall, *shibai*, dances, etc., sponsored by various camp groups. Jobs were available at $19.00 per month for top jobs such as doctors, dentists, etc., and at $16.00 per month for ordinary office work, etc. There were outside Haoles who came in and did these same jobs for regular civil service salaries. This used to annoy some of my older friends a little. Especially if the people turned out to be none too competent.

While in camp I began to learn that prejudice existed, and to hear stories from older Nisei about how things were on the "outside." The camp newspaper carried articles on how certain areas did or did not accept Nisei who had relocated from Minidoka into different unrestricted areas, and gave advice on proper and responsible behavior for all Nisei who planned to relocate. People generally seemed to judge what a Japanese is in terms of individual contacts. Gradually out of experiences such as these I became aware that I belonged to a minority group. This was of course in a rather nebulous fashion. I, who had not known about being different, began to fear the outside world which existed beyond the wire fence around my present world.

These realizations left me feeling very inadequate and unsure of myself, almost as though somehow I ought to apologize for being born. After the war I was afraid to be too noticed because it seemed more comfortable not to draw attention to myself. I acquired a sense of responsibility in terms of not doing anything that would bring unfavorable attention upon the Japanese group. But I was caught in the unhappy position of belonging almost entirely by culture, to the Haole group; but by physical appearance and the thought that "I ought to," to the Japanese group, and yet not fitting in with the Japanese group at all, and not entirely belonging because of race to the Haole group either. I knew the bitterness of shame. I was Oriental. The distress of believing myself inferior because I was Japanese overwhelmed me. All these attitudes had become mine by the time I left camp and crystalized as I began to experience prejudice in operation. However, with prejudice it is sometimes difficult to know whether one finds it or invents it.

About August of 1945 we left Minidoka and took up residence in Salem, Oregon. I was terribly self-conscious and painfully bashful. However, my sense of belonging with the Haole group was not entirely lost. I did take a rather quiet part in a few school activities such as sports, drama club, office assistant, etc. I went through the process of being the first girl in the family and had to break the way in regard to clothes, makeup, school activities, and special school expenses which my brother had not required in his school days. My sister because of this had less parental disapproval of her activities and more freedom to do things in the way her schoolmates did. Salem had few Japanese families and so I had just two other Nisei in my graduating class of some two hundred students. My sister had a good many more Nisei in her class and so she continued her activities with the Nisei, but was active with the Haole school group also. My sister has always been able to fit in comfortably with both groups, but her attachment is first with the Japanese element, particularly since she married a Nisei boy, and only secondly, with the Haole group. There is no question in her mind as to where she belongs.

After graduation from high school, I decided to attend a business college in Portland. However, I worried about obtaining a job; recalling the talk during the camp days by my older friends about the problems of being Nisei increased my anxieties. My brother once lost a high school newspaper route when a subscriber objected to having a Japanese boy deliver his papers. His age group had had difficulty prior to the war in obtaining anything except rather menial jobs. However, with the war ended, there are more jobs available for qualified Nisei. Still I feel we need to be better qualified than a Haole competing for the same job in order to obtain it. I feel that we must do well for if we don't the poor impression will be carried over and some other deserving person may be denied a job opportunity. People do stereotype on the basis of a limited experience and this fact is not to be lightly thrust aside. This business of always beign careful, of giving a good impression, and the sense of heavy responsibility to the Japanese group, with whom I hardly associated personally, gave rise to my feeling Japanese first and myself second, if ever. I remember also a phase of scrupulous cleanliness and grooming because the expression a "dirty jap" caused me such distress that I determined never to fit the description.

I was driven further in this uncomfortable direction when I started to date a Haole boy steadily. Then the troubles really began. He was tall, blond, blue-eyed, with a profile like that of King George of England. Bob was also very bright and capable. His Haole friends considered him wasted on me, to put it mildly. People often stared at us because we frequented places seldom visited by Japanese, and because we were such a striking contrast to each other. It seems that he lost a desirable fraternity affiliation during his college days because we dated steadily. In time I began to feel that I would be a detriment to his success, particularly since he yearned to be an industrial relations specialist. Success in this area is often dependent upon social and business contacts and his choice of a mate could make a difference to him. We believed that what we were doing was right, but others believed themselves to be right also, and never the twain could meet. Mother surprised me by her attitude of "marry whomever you please, just be sure he's nice." She would of course prefer a Nisei but there was never any insistence about this point. If father had lived longer, things might have been less liberal. One incident in regard to Bob stands out in my memory. Bob's aunt and uncle came to visit him and I was completely snubbed by his aunt. His uncle was very nice, but his aunt would neither acknowledge our introduction, nor would she speak to me at all. She spent the entire evening discussing at length how well-educated, well-bred and socially acceptable her daughter-in-law was. I could hardly miss the point. I was so angry, yet even then I could not bring myself to be rude. The pacifist attitude for handling these situations, of behaving maturely for long-range results for the Japanese group held me fast. It wasn't easy.

While writing a paper on interracial marriage I had come across an article about the Hawaiian melting pot. Bob and I decided that this might be the solution, so in October 1951 I flew down. This was the end of my engagement to Bob. For the first time in my life I felt part of a crowd. The discovery that being Japanese worked to my advantage at times was a small revelation. This pleased me and at the same time caused a few twinges of conscience. The sense of being just myself and Japanese when and if I "darned" pleased was an enjoyable one. The right to compete for a job and not worry about being Oriental—will they be prejudiced, etc., was refreshing. I knew the headiness of being "superior" in a sense because I was Mainland born and educated and the job opportunities were better for me than for many of my Hawaii-born counterparts. Since pidgin can be an asset, for a while I did use more of it than was necessary. This was much to the annoyance and amusement of my local friends. I also had had my fill of mixed racial dating, and so began dating only Oriental boys. Hindsight has taught me, however, that friends can't be selected by color, so I've gone back to selecting them by mutual compatibility. Out of this experience grew the realizátion that I need not be ashamed of being myself, and that somehow I had secretly down inside resented not being born Haole. For the first time in my life I was glad I was me and not someone else.

Along with the joys of living in Honolulu, however, there were also some painful moments. I stood out because I spoke like a Haole, behaved like a Haole, thought and had interests like a Haole. In Portland this is not extraordinary, but in Honolulu this was a seeming affectation. Once a boy came up from another office to see with his own eyes this Haole who looked like a Japanese, and said so to my face. On the Mainland we use words more freely, and I felt quite verbose when I spoke to my local friends and acquaintances. Our Mainland formalities were awkward in Honolulu unless I happened to be with a Haole group that observed the same formalities. Honolulans have criticized me for being snobbish, aloof, insincere, superior in my attitudes, affected, and many other uncomplimentary things. One reason for this is that there is still strong feeling amongst the local people that speaking well, behaving in certain patterns, etc., are all the earmarks of affecting "Haole-fication." These are the traits which aid local youngsters to obtain and hold jobs, but rather than encouraging such traits this attitude shames many local people into avoiding them in order to belong. It is encouraging that more youngsters are becoming aware of their advantages. This still does not entirely protect me from being regarded as "different and peculiar" by people who do not know me or my background. Prejudice is, after all, much the same in its operation and causes everywhere.

Writing about oneself may be difficult, but there are certain advantages to be found in the process. The systematic examination of some of the factors which shaped me has replaced a tenuous and at times painful comprehension of my personal adjustment with an objective realization that I am part of a large over-all pattern. The orderly picture from unawareness, to disorganization, and the subsequent path toward personality adjustment in terms of my culture, race, family, and other environmental factors has been both therapeutic and educative. The class discussions and subsequent reading have given me a clearer understanding of immirgrant and second-generation problems. In recognizing the significance of culture and personality development in the human being with its ramifications in adapting to a new culture I have enlarged my concepts of marginalism and consequently of myself.

18. Selections from *Talking to High Monks in the Snow*

LYDIA YURI MINATOYA

My Mother's Music

"I believe that the Japanese word for wife literally means honorable person remaining within," says my mother. "During the nineteen twenties, when I was a child in Japan, my seventeen-year-old cousin married into a wealthy family. Before her marriage, I would watch as she tripped gracefully through the village on her way to flower arrangement class. Kimono faintly rustling. Head bent in modesty. She was the most beautiful woman I had ever seen. After her marriage, she disappeared within her husband's house. She was not seen walking through the village again. Instead, she would send the clear, plucked notes of her okoto—her honorable Japanese harp—to scale the high courtyard wall. I used to pause to listen. In late spring, showers of petals from swollen cherry blossoms within her courtyard would rain onto the pavement. I would breathe the fragrant air and imagine her kneeling at her okoto, alone in a serene shadowy room. It seemed so romantic, I could hardly bear it." My mother laughs and shakes her head at her childhood excess. After a moment she speaks. "Courtyard walls, built to keep typhoons out, also marked the boundaries of a well-bred wife. Because of this, in others ways, the Japanese always have taught their daughters to soar."

"And you?"

"When I was eleven years old, my father gave me okoto."

During the 1950s, in our four-room flat on the south side of Albany, New York, my mother would play her okoto. Sometimes on Sunday afternoons when the jubilant gospel singing had faded from the AME Zion Church across the alley, my mother would kneel over a long body of gleaming wood, like a physician intent on reviving a beautiful patient, and pinch eerie evocative chords from the trembling strings of her okoto.

"Misa-chan, Yuri-chan," she would call to my sister and me, "would you like to try?"

"*Hai*, Okaa-chan"—yes sweet honorable mother—we would murmur, as if stirred from a trance.

"I was a motherless child," says Okaa-chan, when I have grown to adolescence. "My father gave me okoto to teach me to cherish my womanhood."

165

"Your womanhood?"

My mother plucks a chord in demonstration. "The notes are delicate yet there is resonance. Listen. You will learn about timelessness and strength. Listen. You will understand how, despite sorrow, heart and spirit can fly."

An American daughter, I cannot understand the teachings of my mother's okoto. Instead, I listen to the music of her words.

A formal, family photograph is the only memento my mother has of her mother. In 1919, an immigrant family poses in a Los Angeles studio and waits for a moment to be captured that will document success and confidence in America; a moment that can be sent to anxious relatives in Japan. A chubby infant, pop-eyed with curiosity, my mother sits squirming on her father's lap. My forty-five-year-old grandfather levels a patrician stare into the camera. By his side, wearing matching sailor suits, his sons aged three and five stand self-conscious with pride and excitement. My grandmother stands behind her husband's chair. In her early twenties, she owns a subdued prettiness and an even gaze.

My seven-year-old aunt is not in the picture. She has been sent to Japan to be raised as a proper ojo-san—the fine daughter of a distinguished family. Within the next year, her mother, brothers, and baby sister will join her. Five years later, my grandmother will be banished from the family. The circumstances of her banishment will remain a family secret for over forty years.

"Your grandmother loved to read," says Okaa-chan. The year is 1969. Okaa-chan and I sit in the kitchen, drinking tea at a table my father has made by attaching legs to a salvaged piece of Formica. It is after midnight; the house lies sleeping. "She was a romantic, an adventurer. In Japan, she caused scandal when she bought a set of encyclopedia."

"A scandal?"

"You must understand these were country people. A young wife wasting her time on reading, spending her money on frivolous facts, people must have thought, What nonsense! My honorable older brothers recall that each day she would read to us from the encyclopedia. She would tell us about science and foreign countries. I think she liked to dream about possibilities." Okaa-chan tilts her head and looks into the distance. "I was too young to remember this but it is a nice memory, neh Yuri-chan?"

"But why was she sent away? Why did your father divorce her?" Direct, assertive, American, I break into my mother's reflection and pull her back to the story I want to hear.

"Saa neh," Okaa-chan wonders. "Ojii-chan—your honorable grandfather—lived in America maybe ten to fifteen years before he went back to Japan and married. Our family is descended from samurai. We thought of ourselves as aristocracy; and Ojii-chan needed a wife from another samurai family."

"And the divorce?" I persist.

"Perhaps my father was naïve about people."

"What do you mean?"

"When he brought my mother to Los Angeles, Ojii-chan owned a pool hall. It was very popular with young Filipino workers. It was against the law for them to bring family to America. They were lonely and restless; and pool halls helped to kill times. My mother worked by Ojii-chan's side, and being young and pretty she was good for business. When work was done, father would leave us alone. My mother had read all the European, great romantic novels. She was much younger than Ojii-chan. She was lonely, and she fell in love with a young Filipino who could read and speak Japanese. He courted her by bringing books."

"She had a love affair!"

"They were very sincere." Okaa-chan is quick to correct any impression that her mother had been a libertine. "The man wanted my father to divorce my mother so she could remarry. Ojii-chan started moving us from house to house, trying to hide Mother, but her lover keeps locating us."

"Why didn't she just take you children and run away with him?"

"You must understand, my mother was from a good family. She would not consider taking her children from a respectable family into a disgraceful situation. She would not think of taking her husband's children from him. Romance is a private peril. Others should not suffer." Okaa-chan pours herself some more green tea. Its aroma is faintly acrid. "Perhaps Ojii-chan finally thought, This is embarrassing nuisance. He sent us all back to Mother's parents in Japan."

"But why did Ojii-chan wait five years to divorce your mother?"

Okaa-chan sighs. "That was a cruel mistake, *neh?* Ojii-chan was a highly honorable man but often he did not understand how his action would affect others. If he had divorced my mother when he first found out, in America, then she could have married her lover." Okaa-chan is silent again. Perhaps she is saddened to recall a flaw in the only parent she clearly can remember. "Ojii-chan divorced as an afterthought. He may have wondered: Why am I supporting this woman? Why is her family raising my children? He broke a promise to my mother's parents."

"A promise?"

"When Ojii-chan sent my mother back to her parents, they begged him not to divorce her. It was a small village. If Ojii-chan and Mother divorced, her parents would have no choice but to send their daughter from their house."

"And so, when they divorced . . ."

"My mother's ancestral home was adjacent to Ojii-chan's ancestral home. There had been warm feelings and intermarriages between the homes for centuries. With the divorce, relations had to be severed."

Okaa-chan is silent for a long time.

"After the divorce, my mother's parents would come to edge of Ojii-chan's ancestral home," she finally says. "My grandmother would be carrying a plate of sweets and she would call to her grandchildren. They only wanted to see us, to give us some candies. We would long to run to them but we knew it was forbidden. Instead, we would turn and run into the house to hide."

I stand and move to the sink and stove, heating more water, helplessly wanting to give Okaa-chan a cup of tea to compensate for losing her grandmother's sweets.

"Did you know beforehand? Did you know the divorce was coming?"

"Oh, no, I was maybe five years old, little more than toddler. But looking back, there are certain memories."

Okaa-chan is quiet as she moves back within her memories. "One day, mother took us to a photographer's studio for a formal portrait. I was excited and I turned to call my mother's attention to something. She was wiping away tears with her kimono sleeve. I never before had seen her cry and thought, Why in the middle of such a grand adventure?" Okaa-chan pauses. "I suppose that happened just before Ojii-chan had us sent from her house."

There is a longer pause.

"How I wish I could have a copy of that picture," she says.

In the quiet, I notice that the sky is lightening outside the kitchen window; birds are beginning to stir. Finally, Okaa-chan resumes her story.

"My clearest memory is this. I am sleeping beneath billowing mosquito netting with my sister and brothers. Suddenly I am awakened. It is a summer night and the rice paper screens are open. In the courtyard are the sounds of crickets and the glows of fireflies. My mother is standing, holding two candles inside white paper lanterns. They make pretty shadows. I am still sleepy as Mother leads us across the courtyard. Our wooden geta scrape along the footpath. It is damp and cool with dew. Mother holds one lantern. Eldest brother holds the other. As we get to Ojii-chan's ancestral home, Mother embraces us. Ojii-chan's sister stands waiting. 'Itte!' Mother commands. Go!"

The second hand sweeps noiselessly around the kitchen clock. From somewhere in the darkened house, my sister coughs and turns in her bed. After a long time, Okaa-chan speaks. "I never saw my mother again."

When my mother is fifty-one, she takes me to the Japanese village where she spent fourteen years of her girlhood.

"I want to tell you about my regret," Okaa-chan says suddenly as we recline on the cool straw mats. In this house where Okaa-chan spent her childhood, the late afternoon air feels sultry and unpredictable. A typhoon has been forecast.

"After I graduated from the Charlotte School of Costume Design in Los Angeles"—my mother always uses the full title of her alma mater; as if the formal labor of carefully pronouncing all those multiple syllables affords her more time to savor her pride—"your Ojii-chan wanted to return to Japan. I accompanied him and became a fashion designer at a large department store. One day I received a letter, from Manchuria, addressed to me through the store. It was from my mother."

"What did you do?"

"I was only twenty years old. It is such a young age. My mother was little older than twenty when she was sent away." Okaa-chan sighs. "I excitedly showed my mother's letter to my father. May I write back? I begged him. I knew nothing of the anger that can be between husband and wife."

"Did Ojii-chan scold you?"

"No. He took my mother's letter from me. He told me not to write back. We never spoke of the letter again." Okaa-chan pauses. "My greatest regret, Yuri-chan, is that I obeyed. I did not write to my poor mother. I do not have her letter. She never wrote to me again."

In the restless, August afternoon, Okaa-chan strokes my hair. I am moved and discomforted by her confession. I am twenty years old.

"Tell us how you and Daddy met!" my sister and I would beg Okaa-chan when we were children. The idea of our parents courting seemed both romantic and silly, and we would become giddy and giggly at the telling.

"During the war, your daddy's daddy and my family were in the same relocation camp—Heart Mountain, Wyoming," Okaa-chan invariably would begin. "Your daddy was in Chicago, at the University of Illinois and your daddy's daddy was very worried about him."

"Why?"

"Because he was thirty-three years old, unmarried, and far from family." Okaa-chan would smile in recollection. "Your daddy's daddy was the sweetest man. Since I am here in camp, Daddy's daddy thought, I will make most of it. I will find my son a good bride."

"You were the good bride!" I would giggle from behind my bands.

"But first there were other steps," Misa would interrupt. Being older and more orderly, Misa's job was to make certain that the whole story was told in the correct sequence.

"Yes," Okaa-chan would oblige us. "Daddy's daddy decided that his son should marry a Kibei—Japanese born in America and raised in Japan. As you know, your daddy has a temper and sometimes can be stubborn."

Misa and I would chortle knowingly.

"Daddy's daddy thought, If Katsuji marries a Nisei—a Japanese born and raised in America—or a non-Japanese, there will be too much commotion in the household. So Daddy's daddy began to ask all his friends."

"Do you know of any nice Kibei girl for my boy, Katsuji, to marry?" Misa and I would chorus. We knew this part by heart.

"Daddy's daddy was a widower in his late sixties. He was separated from all seven of his sons. The bride search made his life in camp more meaningful."

"Tell us about the haiku man."

"Well, Ojii-chan liked to write. He belonged to a haiku poetry group. One of Ojii-chan's haiku poetry friends knew Daddy's daddy. When the haiku friend heard Daddy's daddy ask—"

"Do you know of any nice Kibei girl for my boy, Katsuji, to marry?"

"The haiku friend said, 'Oh, yes. I know the finest Kibei girl. She is an ojo-san—a proper daughter from a fine household—and she even comes from same prefecture in Japan.'"

"And you were that finest Kibei girl!" I triumphantly would shout, overeager for the happy culmination of the story.

"Tell us about Daddy's visit," Misa would urge, savoring the tale.

"When war ended, your daddy came to Heart Mountain to visit his daddy. He planned to stay two weeks. The first week of the visit was agony for Daddy's daddy. He wanted your daddy to agree to meet the Kibei girl, but all your daddy did was eat ravenously and sleep late! Finally, about six days before he was to return to Chicago, your daddy accompanied the haiku man to our barracks and was introduced to my father and me."

"Daddy broke a date for you," Misa reminds Okaa-chan.

"Well, not really, that would have been rude," Okaa-chan explains. "The next evening, your daddy had agreed to play bridge with a young Nisei woman. She had been married to a Hakujin—a white man—but he had divorced her in the midst of wartime hysteria. She was very nice girl."

"But not the girl for Daddy!" Misa and I would gloat at Okaa-chan's victories over shortening time and a nice Nisei woman.

"Instead of playing bridge, your daddy again came to our barracks. This time, the haiku friend did not accompany him. By the end of the week, when Daddy went back to Chicago, our marriage had been arranged. Just before he left, there was an engagement party." Okaa-chan laughs affectionately, "Your daddy and I were still strangers: shy and dazed. The most happiest person at party was your daddy's sweet daddy!"

In the fall of 1945, Okaa-chan and Daddy's Sweet Daddy took a train to Chicago, where my parents were to be married. In formal recognition of the new familial network, Ojii-chan accompanied them to the train station. There in the desert, amidst the howling, whipping winds, Okaa-chan's father stood on the train platform. He held his hat in his right hand; his arms hung straight at his sides. He stood bowing deeply from the waist, long after the other well-wishers had drifted from the platform. He stood bowing, until the train carrying his child and her new father had vanished into the horizon.

In romance, my father's timing was lucky. Until only a few months before she met him, Okaa-chan had been spoken for.

Her engagement had begun on an early autumn morning in 1940. She and Ojii-chan were boarding an ocean liner docked in the busy international harbor of Yokohama. They were returning to Los Angeles after a sojourn of two years in Japan.

Sunlight sliced the crisp sea air. Ships sounded. Everywhere was the commotion of loading. My mother wore high heels and a slim, pinch-waisted suit she had designed herself. My grandfather was regal in pinstripes.

Also boarding was a sophisticated woman in her late twenties, sailing off with her second husband. She and my grandfather began to converse. It seems that, distantly, their great family houses were linked. The woman's brother—a college educated, handsome young baseball idol in the glittering city of Tokyo—was there to bid his sister adieu. He pushed back the brim of his new fedora—the better to see my twenty-year-old Okaa-chan—and immediately fell in love.

And so, in time, a marriage was arranged. Between a bilingual fashion designer, from the city of motion pictures, and a Japanese baseball star. Truly, it was to be a marriage of the twentieth century, of a shining new age at its height. But then came the war and everything changed and wedding plans fell into dust.

When my sister and I were children, we viewed Okaa-chan's wartime Relocation simply as the provident event that enabled her to meet our father. As we grew older, Misa and I began to ask Okaa-chan about the war years themselves.

"Like every American of that era," Okaa-chan says, "I will never forget December seventh, nineteen forty-one. Ojii-chan, my eldest brother, and I were visiting an auntie in San Pedro, California. Ojii-chan had just returned from visiting Japan. It had been the last Kobe-San Francisco sailing, before war. We were laughing and talking when the telephone rang."

Okaa-chan pauses, searching for a way to describe that moment. "Sometimes you catch, out of the corner of your eye, a view of someone's posture suddenly change, just a little," she says, "something so small, and you know that everything has gone terribly wrong."

"Who was it on the telephone?" Misa and I ask.

"Someone from Japanese American community perhaps. My auntie said nothing. She carefully put the receiver back on the telephone, turned like a sleepwalker to the radio, and switched it on. When she faced us, the sight of Auntie's anguished face and the sound of the news came at the same moment."

"Then what happened? What did you do?"

"San Pedro is a harbor." Okaa-chan recalls, "there was immediate panic about Japanese American fishermen. The federal government issued an order blockading all roads leading out of the city. No Japanese were allowed to leave the city and anyone doing anything suspicious was to be arrested and detained indefinitely. Auntie got word from friends that government agents were going from house to house, arresting the leaders of Japanese culture clubs."

"Weren't you terribly frightened?"

"I was paralyzed with fear. Ojii-chan was Issei—born in Japan and not allowed to become American citizen. He had just come from Japan; he was considered a community elder. He was an old man, in his seventies. I was afraid if he was arrested, we never would see him again."

"What did you do?"

"I did nothing. I was too frightened. Onii-san—my honorable older brother—decided that we had to return to Los Angeles. Onii-san wrote to the Los Angeles county clerk's office. He asked for notarized copies of his and my birth certificates. They would be proof of our American citizenship. He selected a time when the military police were likely to be too busy with traffic to search each car. He made our father lie down in the back of car and completely covered him with clothes. It had been one week since that horrible moment when Auntie had turned on the radio. That moment had never ended; it had only grown worse. When we approached the military police station, my brother calmly handed over our identifications paper. The guard looked at us closely; he leaned through the window and stared at the pile of clothes. I wondered if the clothes were moving. I waited for the guard to stiffen, for him to aim his rifle, for him to drag Father from the hiding place. He stepped back and waved us through."

I am a psychologist. People often ask me, "How did wartime Relocation affect Japanese Americans?" Relocation was a wall that my mother's music could not scale.

When asked about her feelings and thoughts during her three years in Relocation Camp, Okaa-chan has little to say. Her memory, usually so rich with character and mood and nuance, becomes oddly unyielding.

"How long did you have to get ready, what did you take?" My sister and I try to encourage her with questions.

"Oh," Okaa-chan stops and thinks. She shakes her head impatiently, as if trying to shake a dormant memory into wakefulness. "Let's see, maybe two weeks? We could bring what we could carry. Everything else had to be sold or given away." Okaa-chan trails off and looks at us with worry. She is disappointed by her memory and afraid that we will be disappointed with her.

When Okaa-chan speaks of her years in Relocation Camp, her voice is hesitant. Often it fades: confused and apologetic. Her recollections are strangely lifeless. In this way, the Wyoming desert, with its cruel extremes, with its aching cold and killing heat, still holds my mother against her will.

My Father's Career

My father is a retired research scientist. He swells and glows when describing the processes of the universe. The laboratory could not contain his enthusiasm. He was a magnet for scientific flotsam. Scraps of litmus and discarded electroencephalograms would spill from the depths of his pockets.

I was six years old when Father showed us mercury. In the slanting sunlight of a summer's eve, we huddled on the back porch, tiptoed and peering. Father poured a heavy silver liquid into the top of a cardboard shoe box. The liquid poured in beads. Scentless, soundless, shimmering beads. They rolled languorously as the box top was tilted this way and that. Father poked the beads with a pencil point and they dented into soft round commas. He told us about atomic weights and mercury poisoning, and the beautiful beads quivered with mystery and power. My mother hovered close and anxious—torn between convictions. Expose children to science. Protect children from hazard.

When Father went away to scientific conferences, he would send me the postcards issued by his hotel. An arrow would be drawn to a tiny hotel window, far above the pavement and the trees. "This is where Daddy is staying," he would write. I would study the postcard for a very long while. In time, the curtains in the tiny window would part and I would feel my father's presence: standing by the window, looking out, and searching for my face.

Once, Father spent a week at a conference with a man named Ponchec. Ponchec was idiosyncratic. Each night, before retiring, Ponchec would drink a bottle of Coca-Cola. He would settle upon his twin bed—stretching his legs along its length, plumping pillows behind his back—and would paw through his battered briefcase with the cheerful anticipation of a child examining his Halloween bag of treats. From his briefcase would emerge a sheaf of papers and a small grocer sack containing two bottles of Coca-Cola. "Shall we review the day's sessions?" he would ask with a shy and shining hopefulness. He would extend a cola across the nightstand.

Each evening, the appearance of those slender, sea green bottles signified the commencement of an academic dialogue, as surely as a gavel's fall convenes a courtroom.

My father laughed and shook his head when he told us about Ponchec. "That old rascal got me into a habit," he said with mock exasperation. For the next two months, while reading his professional journals, my father nightly drank one bottle of Coca-Cola. It was his toast to the spirit of scientific fraternity.

"The first thing I saw in America was a tengu—a treacherous long-nosed demon," says my father. He is recalling the day in 1922 when he immigrated to the United States. "A huge creature with red fur upon its face. It had the pale skin of a ghost and eyes so light they seemed to be transparent."

"What was it?" I shiver. I am ten years old.

"It was a monster posing as an immigration inspector."

"What did you do?"

"I searched for my parents. I expected to meet them at the dock in Seattle. I looked and looked and my fear grew. I had not seen my parents in five years. I began to realize that I could not remember what they looked like."

"Did the tengu trick you with clever speeches?" I inquire. I am familiar with tengu and their dangerous occult arts.

"It could not speak," recalls my father. "Only a strange rumbling came from the depths of its throat. I was confused. I had never encountered a tengu before. Perhaps it was not even a tengu, perhaps it was the unimaginable baku, come to feed upon my dreams!"

I give a little shudder. "Then what?"

"I begged the monster to spare my life. I was carrying a package that contained all the papers I would need. I thrust it at the tengu-baku and started to cry." My father pauses and chuckles. "Actually, the immigration officer was a very nice man."

"What happened? Did your parents recognize you?" But Father's storytelling cannot be rushed.

"As I stood shivering before the giant devil, it smiled and patted me on the head. It rummaged through its clothing and handed me a stick. I sobbed and stared. The tengu-baku pantomimed putting the stick in its mouth. It smiled again. Very gradually, my crying subsided. Very hesitantly, I raised the stick to my mouth and touched it to my tongue." Father's tale pauses tantalizingly.

"And?"

"And immediately I knew I had been tricked. The stick was hot. It singed my mouth; I could taste the sweetness of poison. I hurled the stick to the ground and wept inconsolably." Father tugs gently on my braided hair. "Later," he smiles, "I learned the name of the stick was peppermint."

"And your parents?" I giggle at Father's naïveté.

"Your grandfather had traveled hundreds of miles to meet my boat in Seattle," says Father. "Your grandfather had been born in a tiny fishing village, way back in the 1870s. In America, he worked for the railroad company; but he came from a different world. A smaller, slower world. He was not comfortable living in the industrial age. He never grew to trust the power and speed of trains. Riding them made him weak with anxiety and it took all his courage to meet me."

"Did he bring you presents?" Presents are never far from my mind.

"In a way. The first thing that your grandfather did was to buy me American clothing. It was an immigrant ritual. Near the landing area was a shopping district especially for the new arrivals. In it was a clothing exchange store. Masses of Japanese poured off the boat and into that store. They entered in kimono and exited in Western clothes. I left wearing a navy blue sailor suit with knickers. I had knee-high socks and a little white sailor cap. My father led me down the street and bought me a juicy hot dog. I was bursting with pride. I knew I had become an American."

Braving another train ride, Grandfather took my father home to a little wooden house in the east Washington desert. A wheezing windmill pulled water from deep below the parched soil. Grandmother willed the survival of vegetables, chickens, and flowers. Try as she might, she could never coax them to flourish.

"Where we lived, an odd thing used to happen," says my father, his brow wrinkling in the effort to recapture the image. "Twice a year, a Yakima Indian and his grandson would appear. They would come walking across the desert landscape: two blurred figures growing into an old man and a boy. They would come bearing a gift—an alderwood smoked salmon. To me, it always seemed a miracle, like the kings arriving in Bethlehem or a mirage from some desert delirium. 'Kiku, Kiku, Kikumatsu!' they called in Japanese. 'Chrysanthemum, Chrysanthemum, Chrysanthemum-pine.' From their throats came my father's name: low and singing, like the voices of birds, like the saying of a prayer."

"Where did they come from? Why did they come?"

"They walked from the Columbia River. Each summer the Indians gathered driftwood, timbers washed ashore from overloaded logging barges. But winters were harsh and driftwood limited. Your grandfather gathered railroad ties to keep their babies warm."

"And the fish?"

"The salmons were thanksgiving. When the flickering figures appeared calling, 'Kiku, Kiku, Kikumatsu,' we all would rush outside. Your grandfather was very happy to hear the Kiku call. It was like the first sip of water in the morning of the new year: a sign of Buddha's goodness. It meant the Indians had survived."

Because there were no schools in that part of the desert, my father and his older brother Kaoru moved to a town down the line. They lived in a cabin in an area settled by Mexican railroad workers. There my father learned to speak English and to eat jalapeño peppers. On weekends, Father and Kaoru visited their parents—pumping a flat-bedded cart along the railroad tracks and straining for the distant keening that announced an approaching train. At the first faint lowing, they would scramble to drag their cart from the tracks. Then they would wait, with heads bowed, before a fury of dust and thunder.

My father was a willful boy. He grew sullen working on the track. He withered in the desert sun. Whenever he could, he slipped from the harness of his chores and stole away to read. When Father reached the eighth grade, he decided he would go to college.

And so it happened, that Father moved farther down the line, still farther from his parents' house in the desert. He went to Portland, where public schools fed public colleges. He became a schoolboy, a child servant, in the home of a prosperous automobile distributor. For room and board, Father cooked and cleaned and tended the cool long lawn that sloped away from the big house like a dowager's ample evening skirt.

And slowly, my father began to idolize his employers. A boy who had lived most of his life separated from his parents, he began to imagine a deep well of parental warmth behind the smallest of gestures.

"Early one morning, when I was taking out the trash, I spied a glimpse of supple leather," says my father with nostalgia. "A briefcase lay buried beneath the coffee grinds. Golden letters—the initials of my employer—were embossed on the front. I wanted that briefcase so much, but to take it without asking would be stealing."

My father gazes out the window and sees a distant dawning. He feels the cold and dew-drenched morning, the soft and supple treasure.

"All day, I waited for my employer. I waited for him to return from work, to fix and drink his martini. I served his dinner and my hands shook with impatience. All the time, my mind was on the briefcase. Finally, with a racing heart, I asked if I could use it for my schoolbooks." Father pauses. "My employer was confused, 'Speak clearly, boy!' he cried. I gestured for him to wait. I raced to the end of the long driveway. The briefcase was still there. When I got back to the parlor, my employer was smoking a Havana cigar. The aroma rose rich and woody. I held up the briefcase. I did not say a word. 'Oh, that,' laughed my employer. 'Just take it. It's yours.'"

Fifty years later, recalling this kindness, my father's eyes mist with tears.

My father loved his work. He came home from the lab talking excitedly about his experiments. He paced the kitchen as he spoke, displaying annoyance when my mother could not test him with sufficiently penetrating questions. As he had been a good student and a good servant, my father was a good employee. He developed patents. He was loyal. Late at night and on weekends, he and my mother translated correspondence for his company's international office. From Japanese to English. From English to Japanese. Careful not to lose the nuances within every writer's voice.

Three years before his retirement, my father learned that he was being paid the same salary as his laboratory assistant. His doctorate was earning the wages of a high school diploma.

"Your personnel file has been badly mismanaged by my predecessors," said the supervisor of personnel, "a fact that is most regrettable."

My sister and I were livid. "Sue them blind!" we raged.

But my father refused. He asked the company to base his pension on a more appropriate sum. The company agreed. I imagine they were relieved.

"You let them off too easily. You should have called the American Civil Liberties Union," my sister and I glowered. "You had a case. You could have won. Make the bastards pay."

My father's voice was calm. "For over thirty years, I have awoken each morning with an eagerness to go to my lab," he said. "I am proud to have had an opportunity to do the work I love."

"But they exploited you! It was racial discrimination!"

My father studied his American daughters. He gently smiled. "Before I could sue, I would have to review my life. I would have to doubt the wisdom of loyalty. I would have to call myself a victim and fill myself with bitterness." He searched our faces for signs of comprehension. "I cannot bear so great a loss."

He stood up and walked into the backyard. Through the kitchen window, we watched as he paused to inspect his roses. He stood proud and betrayed—an old man with white hair.

"A lion in winter," murmured my sister.

Ghosts

It was in Okinawa where I first began to feel the presence of ghosts. Oh, maybe not *ghosts* per se, not the white diaphanous things that rise from graveyards in a Halloween's tale. But it was in Okinawa that I first began to believe in things I could not see.

Sometimes, in different places at different times, different spirits, different *moods* if you will, tugged insistently at my awareness. A sense of sorrow here, of gentleness there, of confusion, or tranquility, or vengeance would rise and assume a felt form and a known weight. It was not a scary thing. It was a familiar dimension of daily life.

I lived amidst ancient souls: of people and events, of storms and trees, of lost buttons and broken sewing needles. I would walk into a coral cave and find a wartime agony still cowering. I would enter an old wooden house and be warmed by the faithful glow of generations of household appliances. In Okinawa, the supernatural became a familiar presence, like a stout uncle dozing over the evening papers after a heavy meal.

Perhaps I am overly fanciful. I have been accused of owning a preindustrial mind. To me, it is a mysterious thing that bridges do not crumble atop their spindly legs of steel. To the mathematical formulations that undergird such structures, I grant only my grudging trust. It is far easier for me to believe that a gentle prayer, written and fastened to the branch of a tree, will find its way to heaven.

I am not a religious person. For my father, religion was a practical matter: a need to be educated more than a need to believe.

"Since you live in a Judeo-Christian society," he said when I was six years old, "you will need to understand the assumptions within that society."

"Yes, Daddy," said I.

My father studied the religious choices available to my sister and me. He made the selection of Judaism.

"The family is important to American Jews," I heard him tell my mother, "as is the tradition of education. These beliefs are shared by Japanese Americans."

But although there were advantages of cultural congruency, the deciding factor was practical.

"Besides," said Father as he shifted his gaze to Misa and me, "the Jewish Community Center has a pool. The girls will learn to swim."

When my father shared his decision with his Gentile colleagues, they dissuaded him; and eventually, my sister and I went to Methodist Sunday school. The church was within walking distance from our home.

I was disappointed. The AME Zion Church had been my choice. It too was close to where we lived; its back lot adjoining ours. If proximity was to be the test, surely it fit the bill.

I loved the AME Zion Church. Each Sunday the sounds of the gospel choir would wash across our yard. Rich, soaring voices knowing both joy and pain. Voices that could wrap each note in such transcendent faith, in such perfect reverence, that the purity touched me clear to the bone. "Through many dangers, toils and snares, I have already come. Tis grace that's brought me safe this far. And grace will lead me home." To me, it was the song of angels.

* * *

When I was in Japan and beginning to feel the nudging of things metaphysical, I asked Dr. Kinjo if I could attend his course on Japanese religion. Besides much scholarly reading, the course included field trips to Zen masters, ecstatic healers, and other ascetic beings. During these field trips, some in the class reported sightings of auras and waves of light shooting forth from holy fingertips. I saw nothing. It was fascinating, but I found no answers, no formal faith to embrace. Somehow, I was relieved.

Dr. Kinjo and I were interested in character: cross-cultural, national, individual. Distilling such an interest into a researchable topic was a long process of glorious grieving. It was an exultant, ongoing wake, in which all the ideas we could not pursue were lovingly examined before they were laid to rest.

Once, I dabbled with ideas of grandiose projects.

"Wouldn't it be interesting," I mused, "to gather people's stories? Maybe to videotape them as they recalled some key historical event that had shaped their lives? Collectively, it could illuminate the consequences of history."

"What do you mean?" Dr. Kinjo looked at me strangely.

"Well, for example, the American Wartime Relocation. The survivors are all aging. Soon their stories will be lost. Or, in Japan, what was the Battle of Okinawa like for real people? Most of us depersonalize history. We cannot learn its lessons because it does not seem to have occurred to real people, to people we can care about and suffer with . . ." I was swept away by the boldness of my vision.

"Perhaps that is one of the purposes of art," gently interrupted Dr. Kinjo, "to teach without exploiting."

"Exploiting?"

"A videotape? Of individual people? As they relive the horrors that they knew?"

I flushed.

"My father was an engineer in Taiwan," said Dr. Kinjo. "During the war, I did not live in Okinawa, but my wife did. The war is the only subject that is taboo in our marriage. Once, when our boys were in high school, they casually asked her what it was like. 'Tell us about the Battle of Okinawa, Mom,' they said. 'What was it like for you?' My wife grew still and remote. It is the only time I have ever seen her act with coolness toward her sons."

We sat in silence. Then, Dr. Kinjo spoke.

"My wife lost both her parents. Still in early elementary school, she took her brother and sister by their hands and walked through the battle. She walked and walked, toward the north, toward the mountains where she thought they might be safe."

Dr. Kinjo paused, then gently shook his head. "I cannot imagine what she saw."

When I lived in Boston, I did not like my job. Such a small disappointment, really, but the bitterness made me twisted and shorn. Like a tree that is hit by lightning, I darkened and shrank.

I am not a person of great or specific faith, but I thought of Mrs. Kinjo, of her transcendence and goodness and warmth; and somehow I understood. The lessons I had learned in the backyard of the AME Zion Church came home to me at last. Somewhere, there is a force called Grace.

Karma

When I was in graduate school, the miniseries *Shogun* was aired on television. And for a while things Japanese became the national rage. For days, people arrived at work talking about the characters: the proud noble shogun, the brave beautiful interpreter, the handsome resourceful Englishman. But when the series was over, people felt betrayed. "What kind of ending was that?" they demanded of one another. "The lovers are parted. The woman dies. The man spends his life in futility. After we've invested all this time getting to know and care about them, what the hell kind of ending was that!"

That was what Asians call karma. What Turks call kismet. What we call fate. Often, it is not very satisfying.

Cultures make virtues out of necessities. Americans—immigrants from distant lands, fleeing the past, setting sail from the familiar, from the beloved—built a national ethos based on the future. Based on belief in the goodness of going it alone, on the need for an ultimate happy ending. But Nepalis live in a landlocked country. With mountain avalanches on one end and jungle tigers on the other. From poverty and sadness, they cannot sail away.

On Tuesdays, at Dakshinkali there are blood sacrifices to Kali, the mother goddess. Before dawn, families begin the climb through quiet forested hills, to a natural recess where rivers run between steep jagged mountains, to a place of extraordinary beauty. They carry an animal. Usually it is a chicken. If the family is wealthy enough or the prayer heartfelt enough, the sacrifice might be a goat. After the blood-letting, the carcasses are cleaned in the river. They will be cooked and eaten as a picnic or carried home to feed the family. By 10 A.M., the shallow river is pink. Women sell garlands of holy marigolds. Fallen petals mix with splattered blood forming a mosaic.

The Himalayas are called the abode of the gods and, in Nepal, their presence is potent. Here the sacred mingles with the mundane. But the Hindu gods do not end with lofty creator Brahma—who rides a swan and stays away from worldly affairs. Or with noble naughty Vishnu—whose duty is to preserve the world and whose incarnations include both Rama, the enduring husband, and Krishna, the inventive cowherd who once appeared to a group of girls in as many embodiments as there were women so that he could make love to each in the ways she most secretly desired. No, the Hindu gods also include the destroyer, Shiva, and the bloodthirsty mother, Kali. And in Nepal, it is they who are most revered.

A parking lot overlooks ancient Dakshinkali. It is for tourist minivans. In the thin air of 7,000 feet, skirting the endless line of worshippers and their animals to get to the important spot—the killing spot—feeling the crush of blossoms under your feet while watching one man deftly slash the throat of animal after animal: the colors and sounds and scents begin to hang heavily. Tourists largely come for this experience. It produces a giddiness, a near nausea that many find exhilarating.

It is not death that is being worshipped. Asians do not rejoice in destruction. They believe that life, no matter how joyous, includes pain and loss and sorrow. From endings come beginnings. From separation comes joining. From wrenching pain comes fulfilling pleasure. Think of childbirth and perhaps you will understand.

Beyond the killing spot, down by the banks of the pink river, the atmosphere is very different. Adults clean the carcasses. Children play by their sides. Faced with the quiet dignity of people matter of factly performing their weekly tasks, most tourists hurry past. If you stop and search the scene for too long, you begin to feel intrusive—like a voyeur. The boundaries between which group is engaging in barbaric rituals and which is not begin to blur uncomfortably. The children pause in their play to gaze at the tourists with wonder. Their eyes are rimmed with kohl. Some tourists take pictures; but the parents do not glance up. They know kohl will protect their children from the evil eye.

On Tuesdays, there is a children's pilgrimage to the parking lot of Dakshinkali. The pilgrims are not the kohl-eyed children of the worshippers. They are children with the copper hair of malnutrition. They pertly greet each person disembarking from each van. The cutest, the luckiest, the most tenacious may earn a few rupees, a stick of gum, a cigarette. A man is trying to evade three of these children. He plunges past me on his descent to the shrine. The birdlike children hop by his side. "Hullo, hullo," they chirp. They peer sideways up at him. "Hullo?" they inquire with hope.

The man does not look down at the children. The tension of remaining deliberately unmindful makes him clumsy. He takes the descent in long strides, each stride ending with a downward skid. Small avalanches of dust and stones radiate in his wake. A camera swings wildly from his neck and ricochets against his thorax. Thunk, thunk, thunk, thunk. The sound reminds me of a racing heart.

As the children try to meet his eyes, the man stares desperately ahead. It is painful to meet the gaze of a hungry child.

Then another man begins to lope easily down the trail. "Say," he calls, "what's the rush? We're on vacation!" It must be a friend, for the first man smiles in relief. With one hand, he stills the swinging camera; and in that moment an idea is formed.

Wordlessly, he transfers his camera to his friend. Slowly, he reaches into his coat pocket. Now the children and I are mesmerized. I am aware that it is strangely silent. Then, in a flash, something flicks from the pocket and is brandished in the air.

The man dances a few paces down the trail. Suddenly he is nimble. He holds the object aloft, posing like the Statue of Liberty with her torch. In a common instant, we all recognize it. It is a package of crackers. It is a waxed papered, half-eaten stack of Saltine crackers.

"Hullo!" The children are shrill. "Hullo, hullo!" They leap for the crackers. More children stampede down the trail. They rush the man. "Hullo, Hullo, Hullo!" Again and again, they leap for the crackers. The man laughs. Avoiding the eyes of the children, he beams into the eye of the camera.

"Click."

I think of Venice, of snapshots of feeding the pigeons in Piazza San Marco. The man drops the package and steps unnoticed from the scramble of children.

I board the van. I sit alone. I do not want to chat. Perhaps it is the altitude.

I am an American. I have no patience with fatalism, no regard for the gift of forbearance. Often Asia disconcerts me. She has lured me back. She has willed me into the investment of my time and caring. And again and again, she shows me scenes that I am powerless to change. I sit on the van and rail. What kind of ending is this? What the hell kind of ending is this?

Epilogue

My uncle has spent years tracing the fate of his mother. As eldest son, it is he who travels again and again to Japan, who initiates family reunions, who has traced and located his long lost half-brother. In his seventies, his cancer in remission, my uncle travels to Japan to meet this half-brother. On his return, he flies to Albany. He arrives on my wedding day.

It has been two years since I returned to America. On this day I have married Robert Stone, the man with whom I taught in China and traveled in Nepal.

We have returned from the wedding luncheon and are sitting around the dining room table. The table is honey maple, Early American style. It looks odd against the Japanese shoji screens that separate dining from family room; but my parents are very proud. The table is a recent acquisition, purchased from a mail-order catalog. We sit at this new table, pouring over photographs of the mysterious brother.

"I have learned terrible secret," says my uncle to Okaa-chan. "Our mother tried to kill us."

Okaa-chan says nothing. She picks up a stack of travel snapshots and begins to shuffle them unseeingly.

"Forgive me," says my uncle, "Perhaps you would rather not know. You were only a toddler. Perhaps you have forgotten our mother."

Okaa-chan lays the photos aside. She gazes wistfully at the piles of my uncle's omiyage—specialties from here to take there—which are scattered across the table. Seaweed, forest mushrooms, tiny dried sardines. They smell sharp and salty, like a seaside memory. Strangely, she begins to sing.

"*Miyeko enkara ochite hana utsuna.*" Miyeko do not fall from the veranda, do not fall and bump your nose. She touches her nose and smiles. "Our mother used to sing this to me," she says, "a silly song, to commemorate some childhood mishap of mine. It was a game she played; the whole point was to kiss her baby's nose."

Okaa-chan absentmindedly fans herself with a cellophane bag of dried cuttlefish. "Oh, no," she says. "I have not forgotten."

"You never speak of her. You were close to our father. I was afraid I am asking for feelings you simply could not share," my uncle's voice cracks.

This is my beloved, gentle uncle—the tea master. A sentimental and contemplative man, he is mildly disappointed in himself. He lacks drive, rage, the sublime self-confidence of a samurai. It is his younger brother, Koji—the sword master, the No No Boy—who has inherited all the warrior bushido.

"Once, I recall awakening," muses Okaa-chan, "and I think the house is haunted. Through the cool tatami, echoing under polished wooden floors, comes the scent of incense and the sound of muffled sobbing."

"When Father demanded divorce," my uncle explains, "our mother went to the temple. She spent hours saying sutras. She was longing for some spiritual sign." He hesitates.

"Tell me," my mother's voice is calm and certain.

"On a night selected for auspiciousness," says my uncle, "Mother mixed rodent poisoning in a gruel of tea and rice. She could not bear separation from us and murder-suicide was considered an honorable act. She placed the gruel on the table and gathered us around her. A growing boy, Koji eagerly reached for the bowl."

My uncle pauses. He reaches for his tea. His elegant fingers cup the base. His eyes close. His face disappears behind the earthenware rim as he takes a long draft. I feel a twinge of fear.

"Perhaps the poisoning had a scent, perhaps a not natural aroma. A willful child, Koji thrust the bowl away. He made a face of disgust. In his roughness, the bowl overturned and the gruel spread across the table. Mother sprang up and rushed us from the room. It was as if the spill was fire."

"Do you remember this?" asks Okaa-chan.

"Perhaps a tremble in Mother's fingers, a muffled cry in her throat. Perhaps a confusing rush from an innocent spill in a familiar room. But no, I did not know she intended our deaths."

There is a silence. Misa and I hover like vapors, like forecastings, at the end of the table. We are the future; we are not part of this gathering of ghosts and elders. I look at Okaa-chan with curiosity. I picture her as a little girl, in a summer kimono on an ordinary night. Her singing mother has carefully plotted her murder.

"Our half-brother says that Mother took it as a sign from Buddha," continues my uncle. "She saw the spill as divine intervention. Buddha told her to let us go. From that point on, she busied herself with preparations. She stopped weeping and started to plan for our futures."

We sit in stillness while, somewhere in the past, my grandmother packs her children's belongings.

"Our half-brother had a present for us," my uncle suddenly says. "Something that Mother wanted us to have."

He rises and goes to the guest bedroom. Once, it was Misa's teenaged home. Now, in the family room, Misa's children watch television. Her youngest, her daughter, sits on my sleeping father's lap. My husband sits by his side.

I finger my sleeve, stroking the rich wine-toned silk. I am wearing my mother's kimono. Long ago, it had been a coming-of-age gift from her father. All day, my mother and uncle have been staring at me. They have been seeing her younger self. This gives me pleasure, knowing that I have my mother's face.

I look into my green tea. A stem floats perpendicularly. The Japanese say that this is an omen of luck.

My uncle returns with a gift. "I had copies made for each of us," he explains. The gift is an aging photograph tucked into a silver frame.

Okaa-chan holds the frame in both hands. "Ahhhh," she says. She bows her head.

Misa and I move forward. We peer over her shoulder at the picture. My young kimono-clad grandmother is in a photographer's studio. Around her are her children. Her sons are soldierly in their school uniforms. Her eldest daughter, poised on the brink of womanhood, is astonishingly lovely. Her youngest, my mother, slouches forlorn and pouting.

It is the first time I have seen the photograph but I recognize it immediately. "It's that time, before the parting, when you caught your mother crying into her kimono sleeve!"

Okaa-chan nods her head. "*Saa neh*," she murmurs. A tear slides down her cheek.

From the family room comes a roar of laughter. My father starts from his sleep. "What is it?" he cries, alarmed.

"It is us, Grandpa," reassures Misa's husband.

In the dining room Okaa-chan speaks. "Today is most joyous," she pronounces. "Today, I gain son and find half-brother."

She swallows and looks again at the photograph. "And here is *my* Okaa-chan," she proclaims almost fiercely, "come home to see it all!"

"*Neh, neh, honto neh*," croons my uncle's wife. Yes, yes, truly yes. She scatters soothing little syllables across the table, like a benediction.

19. North Vietnamese Buddhist Nun

from *Hearts of Sorrow*

The first time I saw the Vietnamese nun, in the spring of 1982, she was performing a ceremony at her pagoda, located in a predominantly Hispanic neighborhood in a West Coast American city. The small lawn in front of the pagoda was festooned with brightly colored Buddhist flags; the exterior walls were covered with paintings and decorations, transforming what had once been a modest five-room house into a miniature island of Vietnamese culture. Throughout the day, the transformative image was perpetuated by the hollow, measured beats of the wooden bell; the drone of chanting; the super-sweet smell of burning incense; the subtle flavors of specially prepared rice cakes and other delicacies; and the kaleidoscope of dazzling yellow, green, and blue women's tunics, contrasted with the drab-colored suits of the men. Older women, wearing subdued browns, spoke to each other with animation; they smiled widely, revealing red-and-blackened betel-stained teeth.

Most striking of all was a slight, youthful-looking woman with a shaven head who wore a plain brown robe—the nun. Only later would I learn that she was over 50 years old. Somehow, through simplicity, she projected a commanding presence, at once both lively and dignified, personal yet distant, an individual with whom each follower could identify in his or her own way: the nun was a mother-figure for children, a counselor for troubled adults, a mentor for older women, a ritualist for those celebrating weddings or funerals, a spiritual master for those wishing to enter the monastic life, and a narrator for the anthropologist.

When we met, I told her of my project, and she said she would be happy to tell me about the Buddhist way and her own experiences as a nun in Vietnam and America. Our sessions began around seven in the evening, and lasted from three to five hours. One of my Vietnamese friends helped as an interpreter, but also participated as a third discussant. While talking, we drank tea and occasionally ate oranges, persimmons, or other fruits and snacks donated to the pagoda. I taped the interviews and also wrote notes throughout the evening. On occasion, other persons stopped by to visit the pagoda or the nun. Often she would leave to attend to these persons, but sometimes they joined us and expressed their views of the Buddhist way.

The direction of the interviews was structured, yet flexible; interwoven with the details of her life story is the nun's own exposition of the principles of Buddhism, along with her interpretation of some of the formative events of contemporary Vietnamese history.

The interviews began in October 1982 and continued almost weekly until May 1983. After a three-month break, we met for the final time in September 1983. Earlier I had told her that for our final session I wanted her to discuss how her masters had influenced her life. I figured that this was an appropriate way to culminate our 64 hours of interviews. With vivid anecdotes, the nun described how her master both taught and lived the Buddhist way. Her greatest master was Dam Soan, whom she described as "successful in all respects." Then she concluded, "She was no less than others," a designation which I believe aptly fits the nun herself.

As we were parting, the nun said, "When we began this evening, I had no idea what I would say; not until I heard your questions did I know what to say; it just came out of my unconscious."

I replied, "My questions, too, came from the same source; I had no idea what to ask you until I heard you speak; then I just let it flow. If we do something in a natural way, it is much better."

She nodded, "Yes, much better."

The position of a nun in Vietnamese society is an ambivalent one. Parents often object to and try to dissuade a son or daughter who wishes to choose the monastic life, for it removes them from family ties and commitments. At the same time, Buddhist monks and nuns are given great respect for developing those very traits that enable them to disengage from ordinary society.

In many respects, the life story of the nun highlights the opposition between religious and secular spheres in Vietnamese society. The Buddhist monastic life chosen by the nun is aimed to prepare a person for a new mode of being, achievement of enlightenment. This reverses the principles and life-styles of ordinary, hierarchical, secular society. Ordinary social identities are removed. A monk or nun is known only by the religious names conferred upon them by their religious masters, and later by the names of the pagodas in which they temporarily reside. A novice is shorn of hair, given plain food and garments, and taught to devalue personal attachments. At the same time the novice is enjoined to be compassionate, knowledgeable, and involved for the betterment of other people, all of whom should be treated equally.

In this chapter, the nun describes how she was drawn to the monastic life at the age of five and how the simple lessons she learned while a child remained with her as the foundation of her faith.

I was born in 1932 in a village of about 400 people located in a province of North Vietnam. My father was a farmer and a seller of oriental medicines. My mother took care of my father, my elder sister, and myself.

My earliest memory is that of going to our village pagoda with my parents. I remember that I felt so comfortable there; the pagoda attracted me, I cannot explain why. I now realize that I was predestined for the pagoda. When I was five years old, I told my parents that I wanted to go and live in the pagoda. This was an unusual request from one who was so young, but they did not resent or resist my going there. They figured that I was too young to know what I was doing, and that I'd soon get tired of it. I never returned home again.

When I was young, my daily tasks at the pagoda, which housed six nuns, consisted of house chores such as sweeping and cleaning the house, watering the vegetables, and watching the water buffalo to keep it from eating the rice. At the evening service, I would listen to the nuns reciting the Buddhist prayers. In this way, when I was very young, I learned it by heart.

At the pagoda, we awakened around 4:30 or 5:00 A.M. After breakfast, most of us worked in the rice fields. During the dry season, we cultivated sweet potato and peanuts, while the master remained at the pagoda and cleaned it.

Between the ages of six and twelve, I attended school, where I learned Chinese characters with Vietnamese meanings. While at school, I played with other children, but I had no attachments to them. After school, I'd simply return to the pagoda to do my chores.

One day, when I was still very young, I came from school and found that lunch was unappetizing. A nun said to me, "I'll give you an additional dish; it's a very special one for the master."

I replied, "If I have the right to eat it, give it; if you are doing me a favor, don't." I didn't eat.

Three hours later, the nun took away the special food, saying, "You didn't want the food, so now go hungry." That night I went to bed without food.

That incident taught me a lesson that has stayed with me all my life. I had become angry at first because the nun hadn't served the special dish, then resentful when she brought it as a favor. It was an insignificant event, yet I attached too much importance to it. I failed to keep an even outlook, and the result was that I suffered for it. What I learned from this was never to be angry, nor disappointed; I use that lesson to teach others.

In 1944, when I was 12 years old, I moved with my master to another pagoda. For the next six years we were frequently on the move because of war. I saw the flooding of Hadong city in 1945, and the Japanese invasion of North Vietnam, when they dragged French soldiers through the streets to humiliate them.

But my most vivid memory of that time was the terrible starvation of the people. [See also Chapter 11.] I saw many people die in the villages. The Japanese were losing the war, so they didn't let people cultivate rice, and they threw the rice from storehouses in the river. People streamed into the cities looking for food, stealing whatever they could find, even taking it out of the hands of other people. Ravenous people overate and died of indigestion; the Japanese executed others for stealing, but many simply died of starvation.

When we traveled during these days of turmoil, I was afraid, but my master reassured me, "If something happens, accept fate, but not passively. If there is danger, we should try to escape."

After the defeat of the Japanese in 1945, the Viet Minh and the French fought for control of the country. Again for safety we had to move from one village to another. Finally in 1948, we walked to Hanoi, passing right through the Viet Minh into French-controlled territory. We settled in a large pagoda.

In those troubled days, my master taught me one important lesson. "If you can do something of benefit for others," she said, "try to do your best not only for yourself but for them. Don't be disappointed if you fail; don't be overjoyed if you are successful, for success or failure depends on many circumstances. You may succeed because you are lucky. If you fail, don't feel bad. The main thing is devotion. Failure or success is of no importance."

When I was ten years old, I received my religious name. My master conferred it on me when I participated in the first of three ceremonies that we call "Acceptance of Restraints." At the first or lowest level, we are received as novices. In the ceremony, we commit ourselves to sacrifice things, to follow the rules, to study the Buddha-teachings and canon every day, to wear Buddhist dress, to hold no property, to eat no meat but only vegetables, and to devote our lives for the benefit of others, with an attitude of disinterest, or rather, without self-interest. In other words, we develop less ties for self-attachment, but greater concern for others. For example, if I have a child, I must love it, but since I have no child, I can love my neighbor's child without attachment.

For the same reason, we don't eat meat. The Buddha-teaching is that of cause and effect. If we do harm to somebody, it causes harm to us; we are responsible for our own actions. If we eat meat, we have lost love for the animals. We should show love; the more we eat meat, the more we destroy our love.

So we are taught to consider the seat of love. Our expression has two parts. The first means to bring happiness to somebody other than yourself, while the second refers to the relief of suffering of somebody else. This is a Buddha-expression, the combination of both. If somebody drives me downtown, it makes me happy, since it saves me from walking, so that is happiness and the relief of suffering for the person who offers it.

Before I went through this first-stage ceremony, I was given formal preparation. I had to learn a prayer that I recited when washing my hands, "I use water to wash my hands. I pray for everybody to have clean hands and to understand the Buddha-teachings." When I washed my face, I uttered a different prayer, and so on.

Then I was subjected to a review and tests, not formal tests as in school, but observations through our normal routine. I had to learn the Buddhist canon and rules, but in addition, the master watched my behavior, and tested me to see how I would react. Once, she left a certain amount of money nearby when I was sweeping the floor. She wanted to see if I would keep it or return it, indicating that I was not attracted to desire. She watched to see if I took fruit from the trees in front of the pagoda. Sometimes she would create an incident such as accusing me of making a mistake and would observe my reaction. She also evaluated how I conversed with other people, in a normal way or with flattery to make them happy.

When my master decided I was ready, she announced, "My disciple deserves to be raised to a higher rank. I am responsible for her." The other nuns and monks didn't examine me directly, but they had observed my behavior. They had to approve me unanimously, or I would not be raised to a higher status.

The first-stage ceremony marked my official entrance into the Buddhist religious community. It was a big ceremony presided over by three senior monks.

At the age of 20, I went through the second-stage ceremony, which raised us to a new level. At this stage, monks had to observe 250 rules, while nuns had to follow 348 rules. [Editor's note: Some monks say that the required number of rules for nuns is 290.] Ten senior monks conducted this ceremony for some 15 to 20 other new nuns drawn from many pagodas. It was a big event attended by hundreds of people. The monks, dressed in saffron robes, conducted a ceremony, and the superior monk delivered a sermon on the meaning of the ceremony as well as the ten major rules we had to observe. The description of each rule was ten words long, and consisted of prohibitions such as not to lie, steal, or have lewd ideas. Then we made our vows.

After this ceremony, I was sent to a nun-training school in Hanoi. This was a more formal, detailed, and advanced training than I had received before. In my earlier training, I learned the everyday activities, such as cleaning rooms, prayer, washing hands, and all of the regular services, plus elementary reading and learning of the canon. But at the school we went more in detail, more in depth with the study and explanation of the canon. The first half of the day basically was for myself. I studied for my own improvement, knowledge, and personality. The second half of the day was devoted to economic activities for the self-support of the pagoda. These included handicrafts such as knitting sweaters, making mats, operating hand looms for cotton cloth, all sold to people, and working in the rice fields.

Each year, we also went into a period of retreat for three months. To hold a retreat, at least four nuns or monks agreed to attend. This was an even more intense period for religious activity, with an even stricter regimen than our ordinary routine. On the retreats, we slept only five and a half hours a night. Unlike our ordinary routine, we spent more time in study and prayer, less time in work. Particularly if we went to large pagodas for our retreats, we became involved in a much more intense experience for religion, for we came into contact with people who were much more advanced, and that inspired us to learn more.

From this training, I have learned to distinguish superstitions and obsessions from Buddha-nature. Dreams, for example, reflect our obsessions. If we want to have a car, we dream about that car. This has no significance. I don't believe in the interpretation of dreams. Similarly, a lot of people say that some days are good days, and others are bad, or unlucky. But according to the Buddha, all days are good days, for it depends on us. A lot of people follow the superstition of lucky or unlucky days. Others believe in those ideas which come from Taoism, not Buddhist teaching.

We are responsible for our own deeds; nobody can be responsible for our own deeds but ourselves. The Buddha cannot make us good or bad; he can advise or show us, but then it is our own choice. If a medical doctor gives you a prescription and you throw it away, how can the doctor cure the illness? The Buddha is like a guide; if he shows the way and you don't follow it, the fault is not his, but yours. He cannot make us good, but he can help us. He loves people equally, and gives all people the same opportunity to use, to apply his help. Then it is up to the person, female or male, to develop their Buddha-nature.

That is why in our Buddhist tradition, unlike that of the Catholics, a nun can fulfill all the responsibilities of a monk. I can offer any kind of service, worship, or teaching of the Buddha to people, anything that a monk can do, except for one thing. At the second level of the "Acceptance of Restraints" ceremony, a monk can give exams to other monks, but a nun requires the participation of a monk.

In order simply to preserve harmony, we have eight rules for the social behavior of nuns with monks. These are basically rules of respect and deference, and avoidance of conflict and criticisms of monks.

Feminists in the West have found the teachings of the Buddha easy to criticize, particularly that men should have some control over the behavior of women. But the feminist criticisms greatly misunderstand us. A nun should be restrained simply to avoid disruption. But likewise, the monk must treat the nun with respect. The eight rules are created to assure a harmonious relationship between monks and nuns. This does not mean that monks are superior to nuns. In religious activities, both are equal, just as they are equal in spirit, soul, and capability.

Buddhism Under Communism: 1975–1978

In the view of the Buddhist nun, the Communists proclaim that they allow religious freedom, while in fact they undermine it. She describes how the Communists denounced Buddhist monks, disrupted religious traditions, and constricted religious and social freedoms.

The Closing of the Orphanage

Fifteen days after the fall of Saigon, the Communists sent four people to visit the orphanage that I ran. First they asked me questions about my activities, the financial situation of the orphanage, and about all of the property belonging to the orphanage. They addressed me not with terms of respect, but as "Elder Sister," which was less respectful.

One month later, they sent five men to mix with the children and ask them questions: "Are you satisfied?" They tried to find if the children were unhappy with me, if I had anything to hide, if I had exploited them. They needed evidence to accuse me and evict me. Then the men made an inventory of all the items in the warehouse, and from that time took over control of the orphanage. They let me stay, but would not let me do anything. They kept the key; I became just an employee without any authority. I was not even allowed to speak with the children.

The Communists would not allow me to hold a ceremony on the anniversary of the death of the Buddha, nor to preach at gatherings. Twice they did let me invite a senior monk to give a talk. The first time was about three months after I was relieved of authority; the second was one week later. On a third occasion, the Communist with the key did not show up to unlock the pagoda. The monk and the audience waited outside for a half-hour, and then returned home.

The man with the key appeared long after. I asked him, "Where were you?"

He replied, "I was down over there."

I said, "This is Thursday, and the monk came. Why didn't you open the door?"

He did not respond.

When I complained to the Director of Social Services, who supervises all orphanages, he agreed to let a monk come and preach, provided that he submit his text in advance for approval, that those who attend leave their names and addresses, and other restrictions. People would be afraid to leave their names. It was impossible, so I canceled the talk.

This is typical of how the Communists treated us. They claimed that they respected religious freedom and that they did not forbid religion, but in hidden ways they disrupted and prevented religious gatherings and worship.

Soon after, the Communists separated the children according to age, and moved many of them out gradually to other orphanages in the countryside. They removed the food from our warehouse. Then they moved out the machinery for making bags and ampules. We had used these machines for earning income to make the orphanage economically self-sufficient. The Communists offered to hire me as an employee to continue to run the machines. I refused, saying that the government has few resources, and it should spend its money for others. My actual reason was that I did not want to be ensnared in their trap, under their control, and subject to their orders. I wanted to remain free.

Monks Denounced

One day I was told to attend a ward meeting. When I arrived, a Communist official handed me a piece of paper and said, "We brought you here to denounce the six senior monks we have arrested. Write your opinions!" He did not address me by my title as a Buddhist nun, but in a more familiar, less respectful way.

I hesitated, but a monk near me wrote, "Buddhist monks contribute to the well-being of society."

After reading it, the Communist official said, "No! Write it to accuse the *traitors* who have been arrested!"

The monk wrote another general statement. "Be calm. The government will only punish those who commit crimes and reward those who meet government goals." This monk wouldn't betray his teacher, who was one of the six arrested monks.

Then the Communists brought in their agents who claimed to represent various groups: a woman's association, Catholics, and a Buddhist association. One after another they stood up and said, "Those monks are traitors. They have plotted revolution against the government. Punish them!"

For their third and final step, the Communists handed around a people's petition, prepared in advance, which enumerated all types of wrongdoing the accused traitors were said to have made. Then the officials asked, "Do all the people agree?" Everybody at the meeting automatically raised their hands. "Then sign the petition!"

My heart was beating wildly. I feared that the Communists would insist that the first and most important signature be that of the monk whom they had ordered to write the denunciation. If he signed first, he would betray not only Buddhism, but his own teacher, who was like his father. If he refused to sign, he would break up the meeting and himself be condemned. But the Communists asked an old man to sign first. He was said to represent senior citizens. Next, they asked a representative of veterans. The monk was placed tenth. This is how the petition received its signatures.

In this atmosphere, the Vietnamese Communists declare that they allow freedom of religion, while in fact they discourage it. They encourage sons to denounce fathers, students to accuse teachers, and novices to betray their monks. This is very difficult. If you press the trigger of a gun, at least you kill someone fast. But this other way is a slow death, much more terrible. After three years of living under Communist rule, I realized that they intended to destroy religion. It was then that I decided to escape.

The majority of those who escape do so not to improve their economic or material life but because life in their homeland has become unbearable. They spend a fortune to escape, even though life for most of them is not easier in America. They come here for freedom. They wanted to stay in Vietnam, to help rebuild the country after years of war, but they were not accepted.

Whenever people visited me, they complained about the Communist invasion of their privacy. They were especially upset that nobody could trust anybody, for Communist agents were everywhere in disguise. The agents would say something critical about the government, and if you agreed, they would report you. If they went to your home and saw you talking with another person, they would immediately separate you and ask you both to write on a piece of paper what topic you had discussed, and turn you in if your reports were in disagreement. So whenever we began a conversation, we first agreed on a fictitious subject that we would describe if we were forced to report it. If Communists suddenly appeared, we would switch to that topic. Parents dared not talk to their own children, for the next day the children might involuntarily reveal something to their friends at school. Even husbands and wives became wary of one another.

I had lost all freedom. I could not talk. I could not circulate freely. This was no life at all.

People at Their Worst: 1978–1979

The Communist take-over of South Vietnam in 1975 and the consequent suppression of religious and personal freedoms prompted the nun to flee the country. Under Communism, although her activities were curtailed, her identity remained unchallenged. As a Buddhist nun who could attract followers, she was feared as a potential source of dissent. As a refugee, however, she found herself to be considered powerless and worthless. Her social role changed from respected teacher to displaced boat person.

In Vietnam, the nun's image of herself had been reinforced by prevailing cultural values and practices, and by the society of monks and nuns of which she was a part. While she faced uncertainty regarding her success in spiritual development, the general direction of her quest was clear. As a refugee, she and others faced serious threats to their identities. Their status, the social importance they had had in Vietnam, was denied by fellow refugees as well as by refugee-camp guards. Frequently she heard people say, "All people are equal here; everybody is out for himself." She rightly comments that this was the most trying time of her life, when uncertainty and the potential for disintegration were at their greatest.

Becoming a Refugee

We escaped at twilight on August 19, 1978, with perhaps 150 or 200 people in our small boat. We were so crowded that we were cramped. While I sat on a barrel of water, with my knees bunched up, the girl who accompanied me sat on the floor, with no place to stretch her legs.

As we pulled away from shore, I thought, "Destiny, I have no control over it; what will be will be."

That first night, everybody was very tense. We all worried that the Communist officials, whom we had bribed to let us escape, would now report us. Some people became seasick; others prayed that we would escape. Soon the children fell asleep, while the rest of us sat quietly. No one ate that night, but from time to time people drank water.

Throughout the next day, we remained obsessed with the fear of being caught before we reached international waters. Our minds were not free to think of anything else—except the children: they asked for oranges. People now ate, those who had brought food with them. The others were out of luck. I had not brought food, but the captain of the boat shared his provisions with me and the girl.

Because we slept crowded on the boat for several days, we soon recognized who was good and who was bad. We could not move around the boat, but we could turn around in one place. From time to time, high waves swept over the boat, drenching us if we were outside. Those on the inside were suffocating with insufficient air. People didn't know or care whether the person next to them lived or died. Maybe they were too tired, maybe they concentrated on their prayers, or had a lot of problems on their minds, but the way they sat conveyed the message "Don't bother me."

On the second day, the boat reached international waters; now we worried about not seeing any commercial boats that might pick us up. Since we had no nautical map or compass, we feared that we might be lost.

On the third day, the boat owner and captain told us that for the past day we had been going in the wrong direction, and he didn't know exactly where we were. Now we began to panic. People complained, "We're lost, the boat is lost!" Some people talked of the dreams they had had the night before. Particularly disturbing were the dreams about owls, and those in which one person got others to follow him. Both of these are signs of death. Night birds, especially the owl, are considered inauspicious and are greatly disliked by the Vietnamese people. If someone in a family is seriously ill and at midnight an owl sings, the family says that the person will die. We have an expression, "Wicked like the owl."

On the fourth day, some 30 or 40 ships passed us without stopping. Now we were really scared. Some people made large S.O.S. letters with cloth while others burned cloth to attract attention. Unlike the first day, the people were noisier now. They talked about the boats that passed us by, the fish they saw in the water, or the fact that we were lost and going in the wrong direction.

We felt that our situation was hopeless, that we would die. The passengers blamed the boat owner: "He did not know anything. We trusted him and he is incapable, and now we are lost. He took us to sea and dumped us." Others complained about the boats that passed us by: "They are inhuman." Most of these complaints were from women, but the men also spoke harshly: "I told the captain what to do, but he didn't listen, so look at us now." Whoever spoke tried to show that he was right and the others wrong.

Near the end of this day, a Thai fishing boat approached us. One of their people asked in English what had happened to us. Through an interpreter, our captain explained that we had lost our way. He asked that we be allowed to board their boat. The Thais offered some fuel, along with cigarettes and drinking water.

We took the 5-gallon containers of water. People stood around waiting to drink that water. There was only one cup. I stood next to the container and asked for the cup. A man gave it to a family who were his friends; then they gave it to other friends. Since I did not belong to any group, I was ignored. The container was emptied; then the next. Still, no one gave me water, but passed the cup to others.

In the meantime, after our captain pleaded with them, the Thais let two-thirds of our people transfer to their boat. Now began a mad scramble; those who understood the offer rushed over without consideration of women or children. Families were divided. I lost track of the girl who was traveling with me. It was everybody for himself. I ended up in the Thai boat, where we could circulate freely. The Thais provided food.

A woman of our group washed her handkerchief and put down her bar of soap. I picked it up and asked, "Could I use it?"

She replied angrily, "Why do you use my soap?" I put it down silently.

After another two days and a night, the Thai captain told us that we were close to Malaysia. He told us to return to our boat, and he showed us the direction to the shore. Early the next morning, we arrived, but we were immediately stopped by a patrol boat. We found that we were near Kuching, Borneo. The patrol guards searched us, then forced us to wait all day at the mouth of a river. During the search, my religious vestments and books were found, so people discovered I was a nun. Before that, they had not known; I had disguised myself as a layperson by wearing a wig and ordinary clothes.

That day, the children played, but everybody else became agitated. They talked a lot without making any sense. As they bumped against each other in the cramped quarters, they fell into irritable arguments, "Why did you touch me!" The children ran back and forth, making the boat tip; parents called to them to be quiet.

A Malaysian came by and gave us a message written by Vietnamese refugees in the nearby camp. It warned us that the Malaysians would tow our boat out to sea and send us away unless we destroyed the boat. The owner's brother made a big hole in the boat. When the owner started the engine, water rushed in and the boat collapsed. People jumped into the water, which was only about four feet deep, and waded to shore.

The authorities took us to a stable for cows, and we remained there for four days. The Red Cross provided rice and cooking utensils.

I felt humiliated because they put us in an abandoned stable along the river, a place for cows and animals. The officials were not hospitable. I felt rejected. This was the time of most suffering for me.

Life in a Refugee Camp

One morning, we were taken to a large barge and sent down the river on a journey that lasted about an hour. When we arrived at our destination, we were both surprised and discouraged. We had expected something better. We had left a country in which we had lived in brick houses; now we were put in makeshift huts of palmtree leaves and bamboo. We slept on the floor and in some cases in the open air. The next day, the Red Cross brought some tents.

We were desperate; we never imagined that we would live in such an unbelievable place, surrounded by barbed wire, prevented from leaving or entering by armed guards. Every four days they gave us rice, but it lasted us only three days. We had to adjust to this low ration. Sometimes we received canned fish and meat. I did not eat these, but for others these items were important. Not until four months later did the people of the camp receive fresh meat and vegetables, given twice a week. Probably they changed the contractor.

Once a week a medical doctor visited our small clinic, but for the most part we were not ill, outside of occasional headaches.

But we had to stay too long in one place with no exercise. Life was monotonous. We had nothing to do. We had the same food every day. We had no water for bathing, just for drinking, so we swam in the sea. A lot of people had scabies, and they were bothered a great deal by mosquitoes, since only a few people had mosquito nets. At first, two or three people would crawl under one net together. In order to maximize their use, people threw the nets over tables: one person would sleep on top, the other below. Later, more nets were given out, and as people left the camp, they gave their nets to others.

At first the Red Cross was involved in transmitting mail. After three months, when they refused to do it, the police took over this task, but they told us that for the purposes of control, we would be allowed to write letters only in English or Chinese, not Vietnamese. This was another humiliation for us, but even worse, we had a hard time sending out mail. Sometimes a few guards would take out the mail. In return for this, we hired them to buy things in the market, and we let them overcharge us and make a profit. We knew they were poor and needed the extra income.

I had carried a small address book with me from Vietnam. Immediately upon arriving in the camp, I wrote to the Catholic charity organization that I knew from the time I had lived in West Germany for five years. I told them that I needed a watch and a radio. They promptly sent me about $500. When I received it, I decided not to buy things, but save the money. I wrote also to a family in Washington, D.C., and asked them to forward a message to some monks in the United States. Within three weeks, the monks had sent me $200 and the offer to sponsor me and anyone else who sent them papers.

Before the money and letter arrived, people did not treat me well. I had brought no money with me from Vietnam. After arriving in the camp, I borrowed a small sum from a woman. Later, the girl who had accompanied me from Vietnam asked me for some fruit. I told her, "There is a very good lady who lent me a little money; ask her for a little more."

The woman spoke harshly to the girl, "This is the second time you want to borrow!"

Now that I had money in my hand and a sponsor who would help others, suddenly people came to me for help. The woman who had once refused to give me a piece of soap now was enthusiastic, warm, and friendly to me. Suddenly, too, everybody claimed to be Buddhists, as were their fathers. Whenever they had some vegetables or extra food, they gave it to me. The person who had refused me water and had completely ignored me now gave me warm and polite greetings. She often brought me gifts. "We just offer you," she would say, using respectful words.

When we had transferred to the Thai boat, people had looked down at me in a strange way and said, "Why should she get on the Thai boat? Why her? She should stay with her master." They thought that I was the servant of the boat owner. These same people now inquired about my health with a great show of interest, "Did you sleep well last night? How do you feel today?"

From the ordinary point of view, the behavior of those people was not good. But from the religious, the Buddhist point of view, what they did is normal. People just act or behave according to their interests, what they see as beneficial for themselves. People don't judge a person in their true value or depth, but judge just appearance. If a person is introduced to you as of low status, you may treat him as of less value than if you thought he were of higher status. Not long ago, I was a religious leader with high status in Vietnam, the director of an orphanage. Suddenly, I was brought down to earth, I had nothing. In good times, it is very easy to adjust with the situation; you can gradually move up or down. But when the move is sudden, it becomes very difficult.

In these circumstances, I had to struggle to show my real personality. In the refugee camp, everybody had lost their former positions and their constraints. The refugees said, "All people act alike. Everybody is the same. If you strip the uniform off a colonel and a private, they are the same." But I disagree. It depends on one's true personality. I am different in the quality of my person. I show care to people, all people. I do not run after power. Some people if hungry simply grab food. If you really care, even if you are hungry, you still look and give the food to a person weaker than you.

Experience has taught me a lesson that if someone is in need, we have to share with them. Times may change, but don't act nasty. Be nice, be helpful to everyone in all cases. According to the Buddha, charity should be done according to the following principle: ignore the giver, ignore the receiver, ignore the quality [value] of the gift. If you want to help me, just do it, but without attaching value to the gift.

Each day we would hear an announcement of people who would leave the camp. One day, the Red Cross announced my name as one who had been accepted for the United States. Perhaps if that had happened after only a couple of months in the camp, I would have been excited. But by the time it came, after I had been there for one year, I felt no excitement. I knew it would happen. I left the next day for a transit camp. After a few days for health screening, I boarded a plane for America. When I landed, I was met by the monk who had sponsored me. He took me back to his pagoda, where I remained for nine months.

They Tell Me Their Troubles: 1979–1984

Social, family, and religious patterns that were maintained in Vietnam are rapidly changing in the new American environment. The Buddhist nun's description of this provides insights into the dilemmas faced by Vietnamese people attempting to adjust. Though some Vietnamese Buddhist monks, faced with problems of survival in America, have abandoned their monastic activities, the nun has not. Her solution to this newest, most unpredictable, and most complex change in her life has been to provide a haven of Vietnamese culture where lonely refugees can retreat to rekindle old memories, maintain cultural traditions, and feel comfortable for a while before returning to the pressures of American life. The services provided by the nun are by no means traditional; they are themselves adjustments to a strange new environment. The nun's activities reflect her remarkable flexibility in adjustments that does not diminish her steadfast identity and commitment to seek what she calls "permanence, not the impermanence of this world."

Why Vietnamese Are Not at Ease

In February, around the Vietnamese New Year, the Vietnamese of a midwestern city invited me to visit them. I went there for four days and performed religious ceremonies for them. They had a pagoda, but no full-time religious person, so they were happy to have me there. Most of them had come to America in 1975, and most now had jobs at the automobile plant. At first they had encountered many difficulties in this foreign land, but through much effort they had overcome them. Now they had secure jobs, money, and the ability to provide material needs. Nevertheless, the people who were 30 years and older did not feel satisfied, they did not feel comfortable. They said that if they could return peacefully to their country, they would. Their children do not wish to go back, nor to learn Vietnamese, for they have no attachment, no memories of Vietnam as do the older people.

For the elders, life is unbearable because it is not the way life used to be. Here they just work every day without being "at ease." "In our country," they said, "when we return home from work, we have friends, neighbors, sentimentality, the family, the environment: we feel secure, we feel relaxed physically and emotionally. In Vietnam, you work, but you also can ask to take off a couple of days. If you do that in America, you will be fired. Here you have to work, have to eat, have to run; you must, you have no choice."

We Vietnamese have grown up and lived in a period of continuous war for over a century, ever since the French came to our country. I, too, was uprooted and forced to move many times because of war. That's why I and many others never had long-range plans. We lived day by day. One government after another rose and fell, with no continuity. Family life, too, was not consistent. First it was based on Buddhism, then on Confucianism; when the French arrived, we turned to the French, then the Japanese. When the Americans came, we learned American ways.

Despite all of this, we have an absence of pressure in Vietnam that you do not have here. In America, we are never free of pressure, never free of worrying. There is permanent pressure here because you don't feel "at ease." That's why you cannot enjoy life.

The concept of "at ease" does not mean not doing anything at all. You may work very hard day and night, but you enjoy working, you have an enjoyment of life, and a sense of security. So it means, "free of worry," or rather, we may still worry, but we feel relaxed. If someone tells you how to do something, makes you do it his way, then you do not feel "at ease," but when you do a task freely, when it is not another person's assignment, then it is "at ease." In that sense, the term means "comfortable," and that is what is lacking in America. People frequently say, "Life is not comfortable."

Now you can understand why people have left Vietnam after the Communists took over. What exists there now is not Vietnamese; it is a Russian import. It is inconceivable that "at ease" could exist when people control your life day and night, when your neighbors watch you, and your children spy on you, when you are controlled by the rationing of your food, by restrictions on your travel, and by prohibitions on what you are allowed to say. If we had felt "at ease" in Vietnam, we would not have passed through death as boat people to come here. We came to America not for material gain but for freedom.

We have another important belief, that of suffering. The Buddhists believe that you suffer if you do not have a cause or purpose. But if you believe, as do the Buddhists, that "nothing is permanent," that you are born, grow up, and die, then you see nothing abnormal when someone in your family dies, so why suffer? If something wrong happens, again there is no need to suffer if you believe in the Buddha-teaching of causality. If bad happens to me, I realize that maybe I did a sin in an earlier existence. If good comes my way, I am not overjoyed, because that may just be a reward for my earlier good behavior in another life. So to understand is not to be too happy or unhappy.

There is also no need to feel hopeless. If we suffer, we can correct the cause of that suffering. We can redeem ourselves; we have that chance, for we are solely responsible for our acts. Nobody can save us but ourselves. The Buddha is like a medical doctor who can show us the way but cannot save us if we choose not to take the medicine.

These ideas have been very important for the refugees who have lived under Communism and who are trying to adjust to America. One man whom I know spent three years in a Communist reeducation camp. It just happened, and he had to accept it. Not only did he not feel miserable or suffer, he felt satisfied because he had the opportunity to share suffering with other people. Suffering or enjoyment, it depends on our state of mind, how we conceive it.

Here, too, when refugees arrive in America, they experience a lot of hardship. If they sit down and think about their past, they suffer, they worry, and it does them no good. They destroy themselves after two or three years. Regret destroys the self. If they temporarily forget, not forever, and look forward to the future, they will not feel so bad. For example, unemployment is universal, but it is temporary. If you are unemployed, spend less money, manage, survive, until you can find employment.

Some people are in really dire need. When I find this out, I call on people to help. We do not have any organization to do that. Rather, we do it for each case as it comes up. I just help them personally. I prefer that; I believe that it is not good to have an organization. I do not want to be under the influence of others. If someone is in need, I do not want to have to ask permission of a group to help that person. I decide right there, and if I cannot do it alone, then I ask others.

That's why this pagoda was founded. Three to four months after my trip to the midwestern city, a group of people, mostly women, requested that I establish a pagoda for them in their city. To show respect to the monk who had sponsored me, I told the people to ask him. He agreed to their request.

I rented a house on a corner, next to an elementary school, so only one family lives next to us. When we have large ceremonies, we use the school auditorium next door. Our one neighbor is very friendly. When he saw that I did not have a lawn mower, he came over and mowed my lawn. Later I bought a lawn mower. If I want to plant something in the yard, he offers to help me. From time to time I borrow implements from him. The landlord also is a good person. He is not Vietnamese, but he often brings his friends and relatives to see the pagoda. I pay him the monthly rent in cash which comes from donations.

We have no regulations. Those who worship and wish to give donations do so. Those who wish to help in other ways do so. Everybody is treated the same. Those who come to worship are completely free; nobody asks anybody anything. We have no president or organization, no fighting between factions. Even for big or great ceremonies, we have no organization. People come, they help as they will, spontaneously. Women know in advance what to expect. After talking to each other, they make informal, casual arrangements on what foods to bring.

The pagoda has grown by word of mouth. I did not advertise much because the pagoda is too small. If too many people come to our ceremonies, we will be too crowded, and the neighbors might complain.

I had been in foreign countries, so I knew the importance of retaining one's native language. When I established the pagoda, the first thing I thought of was starting language classes for children. I asked several of the parents to bring children for the classes. At first, only a few did so, but they did not see it as important. They had to drive their children here on the weekends, an additional burden.

The first classes began two weeks after the pagoda opened. Only four or five children attended, sometimes only two. In the summer vacation time, we offered classes from 1:00 to 4:00 P.M. on Monday through Thursday. People gradually learned of the classes, taught by volunteers, heard they were free, and realized the need. Now during the school year we have six classes totaling 75 students ranging in age from five to middle teens. They meet on Sundays from 10:00 to 12:00 A.M., have lunch provided free by the pagoda; then from 1:00 to 3:00 P.M. they participate in activities which we call the Buddhist family. It's like scouts.

In the Buddhist family activities we teach a three-word motto: compassion (to others); knowledge (to determine needs); and involvement (acting courageously based on knowledge). If you have no compassion, you will not treat others well; without knowledge you are blind; but without involvement, your knowledge is useless. Knowledge without action is useless; you cannot just sit.

That is what I taught my children in the orphanage in Saigon. We lived in the spirit of those three words. And I try to teach the same things here. The older children can understand about Buddhism; the younger ones cannot, but they can follow these simple words each day. I want them to help others, to bring a cup of water to a child who is sick, to share a piece of cake, to help with chores, always with this spirit. When they get into arguments, I try to resolve them by reminding the children of those three words. If they have jealousies, I explain that they lack involvement; if they have rancor, I point out that they lack knowledge. In this way, I show them that events of their everyday lives revolve around these three words, all of which are concerned with helping people, sharing.

The children study Buddhist teaching, they play games, and they learn camping skills and handicrafts. At the end of the lunar year, we have a big event for the children. They give musical performances and receive prizes, while their parents prepare a feast. Rather than hire professional singers, I prefer to encourage the children to perform and to make their own costumes and props so that they develop confidence in themselves.

For adults, however, we have the main altar where they can worship. On it we have many images that are designed to remind us of Buddhist teachings. These include representations of the Sleeping Buddha, who reaches Nirvana, and of the Bodhisattva Kuan Yin, who helps those in distress.

Also at the altar, we have fortune sticks. These are of Chinese influence. Some people who are doubtful of their ability to make a decision pray to the Buddha to give them some guidance; they think it helps to select a stick. It has a number. They consult a paper with that number on it. The paper contains a Vietnamese poem, written in Chinese characters, with explanations in Vietnamese, providing guidance on how to behave. The fortune paper might tell you to be satisfied with what you have, or to start new activities on particular days. But the main thing is that it tells you to do good things.

The fortune sticks do not belong in a Buddhist pagoda, but we have to satisfy the needs of people. The sticks are used mainly by women, particularly old women. Whenever they come here, they look for and use the fortune sticks. If we didn't carry them, they'd go to another pagoda. Sometimes young men in distress turn to the sticks. And even some Catholics and other Christians come here to use them.

People in great distress depend not on fortune sticks, but on Kuan Yin. She is part of the Mahayana tradition. Some people say they have received miracles from her.

I have had a miracle of Kuan Yin. Usually I dry my clothes at the laundry, but on this day, for the first time, I decided to dry clothes on a line outside the pagoda. Suddenly, I saw a fire in the house next door. I intended to call the fire department, but the fire was too close, so I put a hose of water on it, called a boy nearby, and he and others put out the fire. If we hadn't, the pagoda would have burned. When the landlord heard of this, he said the pagoda had been saved by the Buddha.

Many people come to the pagoda, where they remain for two to three hours. They have many things in their hearts. They talk to me, and I speak to them about the Buddha teachings, to set their minds at rest. In a sense this is like counseling therapy, and it clarifies and helps them to deal with their problems, marital and economic, as well as those of loneliness.

Buddhists come here for help because they feel at home here. Everything looks like their home in Vietnam, the atmosphere, the furniture. Furthermore, things here are informal and not expensive, so they are not too removed from their own experience.

Some people come here to meet others. When they see old people here, it reminds them of their parents in Vietnam. When they see young people, it reminds them of their younger brothers and sisters in Vietnam. They see the figure that they miss and compare them with the letters from their own people, and that makes them feel better. They eat vegetable dishes like those prepared by their mothers in Vietnam. This relieves them. At the pagoda they don't have to face an actual reality in this country. Some people say that the sound of the bell lightens their sorrow. By coming here, their memories are revived. When they lived in Vietnam, they heard their mothers reciting the canon, but they never paid attention. Now they visit the pagoda and appreciate its value.

Many young adults in the ages of 20 to 25 have no family in this country. They are very lonely. Often they come by themselves to the pagoda. I cook for them. I provide some family for them, like a sister figure. If they need something and I have the possibility, I help to show them that somebody cares about them, pays attention to them.

People visit me with two different types of problems. The first is that of specific crises such as bad news at home, illnesses, or the need for specific services such as dealing with various agencies, or performing ceremonies at funerals or at the anniversaries of deceased family members.

The second kind of problem involves people who want to talk. Usually they do not go directly to the point because their problem cannot be expressed in an explicit way. First they go to the main shrine to worship. Many of them consult the fortune sticks. Then they bring them to me and ask me what it means. I select the paper, read the poem, and explain it to them. When that person sees the relationship between the explanation of the poem and their personal problems, they volunteer more detail.

At first, they don't say anything in particular. Normally they wait until nobody else is here before they volunteer more information. Sometimes they come back two or three times but just talk indirectly, "My family has some problems; I'd like to talk with the master; since she's busy, I'll come back." It is not good manners to go directly to the point. To warm up the conversation, I use all the information people have told me, for example, how much rent people pay. I use all the clichés to encourage them to talk about themselves and their difficulties: the weather; how many relatives are in Vietnam and how many in America; if married, how many children there are; and so on.

I see that people have problems, so I try to give them the time. Most of their problems involve their adjustment in this country. For example, a relative comes to live with a family, but the family does not know how to tell the relative to share costs. Not to tell is bad, but telling directly also is bad. Sometimes children don't want to go to school, or they want to get married, or they want to live separately from the family. Parents worry about this because they fear the children are not mature enough, but also because it involves extra costs. Some of the elderly people complain that they are made to baby-sit over weekends; they do not want to do this, but they do not know how to say no. This is made more difficult because the children never say to their parents that they are going out for fun, only that they need to go out.

The problem for the elderly is that they want to go to the pagoda, but they depend totally on their children, who are reluctant to take them. So the elderly are unhappy. In Vietnam they were not dependent on their children; they used taxis, pedicabs, or they rode with friends, but here that is impossible.

People also complain about the difficulties they have with the English language and their difficulties in getting jobs. They never mention discrimination, but they frequently complain about the stress of living in America, running all the time, with no time to relax physically and mentally. There is too much to do in learning how to survive and not enough time to do it.

They wake up early, work all day, return home tired, then get up early the next day. So do Americans, but Americans do not have to learn a new language at the same time. This is a continual task and a continual strain. People are very insecure. In Vietnam, a person could depend on parents and relatives, and so not go hungry. Here if you do not do everything yourself, you go hungry. People also send much of their earnings back to Vietnam. Two days of average American wages enables a family to live for three months in Vietnam. If one's brother is in a concentration camp and his wife and children are starving, how can a person not send them money? Previously in Vietnam, people didn't have those worries; a person could earn and easily support a family of ten.

On occasion, young men come here who say they want to become monks. Often they are sad and lonely; rarely do they show any strength or determination. If they believe that they want to live the religious life, I explain to them that at the monastery where they will be sent for their training, the path will be very difficult to follow: one meal a day, very isolated, and cold, so they may feel even more lonely. And they will not be able to communicate easily with the monks because most of them are English-speaking Americans. The young men are often too enthusiastic, I think, and also of volatile temperament, showing excessive determination, and then losing heart. Very few people here have the even temper and perseverance to live successfully in the religious life. You cannot be successful if you want to run away from ordinary life because you are lonely.

Sometimes people talk to me about some injustice they have endured. I usually tell them to forget it, not pursue it, or they will simply become more personally involved, but nothing will come of it. Everything is unjust. Instead of using their time for more useful activities, they will be wasting it on a lost cause. Injustice is greater now than it used to be because now that society is modernized, injustice is much wider. Missiles can kill many more people than do spears.

A lot of people complain that they are suffering and that they do not want to live. In one month, for example, ten people told me that they were considering suicide, and three people attempted it. I try to convince people that life is precious, and that others suffer much more. Often the complaints are not really serious, such as when an old lady said to me that she wanted to die because her children didn't treat her as well as in Vietnam.

The quarrels in her family follow a cycle. Her children did not treat her well; now the grandchildren treat the children badly. The grandson says he doesn't want to recognize his parents anymore. The old lady says, "See, the cause and the effect!" She moved to the pagoda for a while and lived here, and her 27-year-old grandson said, "Since you have left, I too have not gone back home."

When they live in American society, the behavior of the children changes. They do not have a connection with their country, and the old teachings and customs disintegrate, for there is nothing to hold them together. Furthermore, every day people work hard under pressure; they are tense, fatigued. They have no time to think of how to act, behave, treat parents. The old woman suffers because she stays home all day long, so has no means of communication outside, no one to take her outside. She is isolated, a recluse, as are most of the older women and men.

One old man told me that fortunately he has one grandchild, so he has the means to communicate. If not, he would become mute, remaining home alone, while his son works all day. When his son returns home at 6:00 P.M., he eats dinner, reads the newspaper, and goes to bed.

Although old people like that are depressed, they are not the ones who attempt to take their lives; mostly it is younger men and women in their middle twenties and early thirties, people who have no family and who have felt lonely; they have had no one with whom to talk. In Vietnam, it was much easier. They mixed with their countrymen. But here people feel isolated. They have no support. Life has no meaning. Whether they die today or later makes no difference. To prolong life is simply to prolong suffering.

In Vietnam, we have had some unhappy and frustrated people, but at least when they came home, they saw their parents and relatives, who made them forget all unhappiness and also made them feel some responsibility to their family. In Vietnam, if a person commits suicide, he hurts his family a great deal. People say that the family is very unfortunate, that they must have committed a sin in the past, so now they are paying that debt. People who commit suicide or have mental health problems are viewed as people guilty of religious sins in the past, so now the family must pay the price. This is a great stigma to the family.

But in America, people do not have any connection, they do not hurt anybody, so they feel free to commit suicide.

A Vietnamese woman married to a Mexican-American came to complain about her long-standing marital and family problems, that her husband acted polite to his work partners, but rude at home.

Because this was a personal family problem, I would not make any comments about what is right and wrong. Instead, I tried to explain to her about the role of women. "As women," I said to her, "we cannot expect to be getting our way all the time. We should show some abnegation, some flexibility. If the husband is angry and will not pay attention to the wife's illness, the wife must accept that. Maybe it is fate, and we cannot escape that."

I advise not only women, but also men to show abnegation. I advised this woman to look at the bright side of her husband, for example, that he brings in a check, gives it to her, lets her handle the financial aspects of the household. If the man shows nice behavior with his co-workers, but not with his wife, perhaps it's her fate that she got that kind of husband. If he does not show love and affection to his child, then the child will follow his mother.

Many Vietnamese complain of headaches. They work very hard in their jobs, then return home to find a peaceful time to relax, but receive a letter from Vietnam, and it's always bad news, followed by a request for money and gifts, or just complaints of the miserable life, arrests, harassment, and jailing of relatives. Often the people cannot solve the problems mentioned, such as requests for $500, or relatives who are stuck for years in refugee camps, or even undisciplined, uncontrollable children. So they get headaches. They are unable to sleep.

Insomnia is widespread among the Vietnamese. If they tell a doctor, he tells them to see a psychiatrist or a counselor. When they go to these people, they find that they receive advice that is not related to their problems.

In some families, husbands have become quite uncontrollable in their anger and hit their children until they bleed. In one case, the husband would refuse to talk to the wife if she tried to interfere or if she would talk back to him. For two weeks or more, he would talk through the children to communicate with her. The more silent he became, the more she talked to him trying to get him to respond. When he could no longer stand it, he left for a friend's house.

In Vietnam, it's much easier. When a woman raises her voice and tries to dominate her husband, he goes out to see friends and they may go to the movies or theater. You might stay with the friend for a few days, until the wife has to go looking for you and beg you to return. The children can go to school by themselves, so the absence of their father does not disrupt their routines.

In America, it's much more difficult; first, because friends are not as close here; second, because housing is much more restricted, and there may be no room for a friend; and finally, because if an angry husband is late for work, he is fired. So there is a lot of pressure in the United States that Vietnamese didn't feel back home. There is no safety valve. In Vietnam, after the husband has stayed away for a few days, his parents and relatives can intervene; they can take his side so he doesn't lose face, and they can mediate for him. A wife's parents would tell her to go to her husband and that helps her to save face. She says to him, "My parents ordered me to ask you to come back."

But in America, there are no parents, and no place to go.

One time, a lady with two small children under three years of age came to the pagoda, worshiped, and threw the fortune sticks. I asked her why.

She said, "I plan to move away."

Again I asked her why.

She replied, "I came here with two children. I live with another family, but they are not helpful. I don't have transportation, a car. I plan to move away."

I asked, "You want to move to another state, but whom will you live with?"

She said, "I know someone."

I said, "Here you have good weather, better than other states. Adjustment will be difficult. With whom will you live?"

"A man. I was engaged to him before 1975. After 1975 he left, and he is married now. After he went, I married another person, and I have two children. In the refugee camp, my husband met another woman and abandoned me and the children. That man in the other state has invited me to come there and be with him, even though he's married to another."

When I heard this, I feared that the woman would be putting on make-up, looking for another man, and she might neglect her children. I felt that she was unstable, and that if she went there, the man would be emotionally divided in two and could not support all of them. There she would have to live alone, with no money, and lots of troubles. She'd have to get a job. Here she has friends. The only thing I advised was, "Don't go; you'll destroy happiness."

The woman replied, "You are like my mother; I listen to you."

She has to baby-sit her two children, so maybe she can baby-sit other children and make some money. When she came to the pagoda and looked at the fortune sticks, I knew she was lonely and isolated. I said, "Now you have a pagoda. You can stay here." She stayed through the afternoon because she had nothing to do at home and she's not happy there, sharing it with other people. Living together with people who are not your relatives has problems, mostly that the children fight or are noisy, or that they have too many visitors, or the children mess up the house and won't clean it. The television may be on all day loudly. The days become long. The old people have a different character. They complain about small things; they are meticulous; they criticize and don't let things go. Living together is quite difficult. All of this is a consequence of the problem of divided families, some in Vietnam, some in America.

Even if families are later united, there may be problems. I heard today about a lady who had come to the United States with her child while her husband remained in Vietnam. He just arrived in America to find that his wife went to work every day, drove the car, took the child to the baby-sitter, and he simply stayed home, feeling neglected that his wife did not pay attention to him. Sometimes she returns home in a bad mood, so he suffers a lot. When she comes home with an unpleasant attitude, he suspects that she has a boyfriend. He lives in hell, and he wants to leave for another country.

A woman came by who complained that her American husband didn't love her. Yet he had learned Vietnamese, sent their children to Vietnamese language lessons, and took them to the pagoda. So I said to her, "Your husband shows he loves you by learning your language and raising your children in your tradition." We see that people always complain, and their complaints range from the truly serious to the banal.

Particularly when people are suffering, they often misunderstand the Buddhist view of events. They expect that an immediate cause will produce an immediate effect, so they wonder, "Why did I receive unfortunate results when I did good?"

Such a view distorts Buddhism. For an orange seed to grow into a tree, you need many causes: soil, sun, rain. The effect may be different at different times. We have to pay attention to different circumstances. When we were boat people, our seat on the boat was considered a good place to sit; when we reached shore, we no longer found the boat seat comfortable. In the refugee camp, we used small sticks with which to eat our rice. They were very precious to us, as were empty cans. But when we arrived in the United States, do we use those things? Life in the refugee camp was better than in Vietnam, but who is satisfied with the camp? We expected to go to another country and have a better life. So too, this life is a false and temporary life, not a true life. If we would like to elevate ourselves to a higher one, we must still depend on our false life, our body.

Buddhism aims at something higher, but people distort that by saying our goal is disinterest. Not so, for our goal is to go for something that is permanent. So if we live here, we cannot do simply nothing. We should do something. The next 20, 30, or 40 years, we act, then we die. If we do nothing, it's just a waste of our life. We should do something, try to help, sacrifice our time because we believe that we can help. If we use our time just to enjoy, that's a waste. If we see a person is hungry, we should give him cake to satisfy his hunger, but it is not good enough if we do not also teach him to avoid sins, not to steal, but to earn the food.

We try to elevate ourselves over and above all the normal passions: anger, selfish stupidity, and greed. If we let our emotions disturb us, we are never happy, never elevated. So according to Buddhism, we must ignore all those passions, get rid of all passion and desire.

The person who achieves this is happy, enlightened. Such a person does not regret this work, is ready to enter another world. This person is very rare, for he is close to being a Buddha.

My master knew in advance that she would die. She told her followers who had come to see her to return in one week to see her die. They did not believe her, did not take her statements literally. One week later, she asked to be cleaned for death. After hot water was boiled and herbs were thrown in to make a scent, she died.

Permanence through Change: Influence of the Master

In earlier Buddhist periods, many people became enlightened, but in our present era, of one million persons, not even one will gain enlightenment. I am not discouraged to see others fail, but am discouraged about myself. If you say something flattering, I am happy; if you criticize, I am sad. I become discouraged when I cannot control my emotions. I try to convince myself like the Buddha had done thousands of years ago that the body is just temporary, that nothing lasts, that nothing is durable, all is temporary. The more we realize that, the more we can neutralize every passion, not become angry, overjoyed, or jealous. It is like food: it's delicious, we appreciate it, but after two or three hours of digesting it, do we dare to touch it? Three hours earlier we took very good care of it. If someone takes some of it, and we have one piece less, we feel bad. But three hours later, who wants it?

One time, I lost $50 I was given for being at a wedding. I was in a hurry; I bought some tofu, and on the way back, I lost the money. I felt bad. But a few hours before, that money belonged to another person; it wasn't mine. When they contributed it, I didn't expect it, and yet one hour later when I lost it, I felt bad. I try to get rid of attachments like this, but this happened. I felt unable to control my feeling. And that is my main concern.

The most important influence on my life was my master, the Reverend Dam Soan. My master always advised me to do everything; she was the best. My master was a woman, but her knowledge was very wide; she knew almost everything. She always said, "Be modest, even though you do something. Don't be pretentious. If you don't keep modest, if you are haughty, people will dislike you, and it will be very difficult to succeed. You will not be able to do anything wisely. If you don't have a correct point of view, if you are no longer impartial, you will think you are superior, and you won't respect the ideas of others. You will feel that your own ideas are better than everybody else's. Then other people will hate you."

We know that sometimes a person has good ideas, sometimes bad. Sometimes an illiterate person has better ideas than a learned person. So my master emphasized that we should not think our ideas are better.

My master also taught that we should not establish close relationships with others because then you begin to depend on them. She stated that we should not depend on anybody, but rather just keep open with everybody, be concerned about everybody. If you develop a close relationship with anyone, then another person hates you and becomes unhappy. I personally am not caught into anything. *I am free.*

When I was about 17, I developed a special friendship with a nun in her early twenties. If a person is just a usual friend, you don't develop deep emotional attachments. Because our friendship became very close, we developed *resentment*. If I don't know you well, I don't care, and I don't develop resentment. But if you are my close friend, I pay special attention to how you react to me. That happened with us.

The master recognized that, saw the backfire of a close friendship, so she told us to stay apart. If we would be distant, we wouldn't develop like this. If you have a special affection, you cannot share with all; if you have $100 and give it to one, you cannot share it with others. If you choose one person as a close friend, you ignore the others, even if they try to treat you nicely.

We treat everybody with the same standard, not too close and not too far. If you are too close one day and too far the next, that person will become jealous and will develop hatred. The next time, he is your enemy. That's why we try to develop equal distance between all.

My master taught us to help people as long as we live, that we live to help others, not to enjoy life, not to drink, not to be involved in the pleasures of the world. "Do something useful," she said. "Don't just let time pass."

Once in Vietnam, after the Communists had taken over, I went to visit a nun. About halfway there, I saw a lot of people collecting wood, splitting it, tying it, and selling it. I thought, "They work very hard to make a living, they suffer, while I go to visit someone." I continued my visit, but I was not happy. I just didn't feel right wasting time.

So in conclusion, don't depend, don't be emotionally attached to others. Do everything the right way; don't be haughty, but modest. I try to follow that, but sometimes it is difficult to control. Even if one tries, it is impossible. But you cannot wait until you are perfectly successful. I follow my master, who said, "Start to do something; don't wait until you have all the necessary means. Just do it."

My master was of medium stature, not thin, not fat. I am very proud of her, that she was of good appearance, not abnormal. Her spiritual, intellectual power, her knowledge and activity were superior to others. I *prefer to say no less than others rather than superior.* That's an example, like a mirror reflected. There are two things, one physical, the other spiritual. She was a mirror-mold [exemplary] person.

Her voice was soft, mild. She was not impulsive, but calm. Her speech was like that. Even though her speech was soft, her rules were very strict. She did not want attachment. I used to think that her way was too strict, but I now realize that hers was the logical way to act.

I thought that my master required us to just work without enjoyment. But from the teaching of my master, now I have achieved something, that people love me and show me consideration and respect. If I led a free life, maybe we would not sit today to talk. I did not tell this story to intend to expose something that is good. It comes naturally. My working spirit, my way of life leads to this.

When I think about my master, I feel very grateful. I benefited a lot from her teaching; she helped my personal growth and my achievement of becoming a *person spiritually successful* in all respects. Parents raise their children with the expectation that they become successful. I am very happy, very lucky to have had a master like that. Had I met another master in a different situation, I might not be here today.

20. Look Tha: A Former Buddhist Monk

USHA WELARATNA

Look Tha and his wife live with their daughter's family in a three-bedroom stucco dwelling situated in a cul-de-sac of unpretentious houses. From the outside, Look Tha's home, with its brown shutters and faded lawn, looks like any other in the neighborhood. But the visitor who peers through the oval glass pane on the front door sees a different world inside. The wall facing the door is lined with a bookshelf, but there are no books on it. Instead, it is adorned with a framed poster of the Buddha placed beside a large painting of the Angkor Wat. A brass container with three sticks of incense stands to the right of the Buddha, and a brass vase with pink and yellow plastic flowers stands on the left. At either end of the painting of the Angkor Wat are deep maroon roses preserved in sealed glass bowls.

I first met Look Tha, which is a polite term for "grandfather," at a Cambodian wat or temple ceremony, where, at 5'2", he was one of the shortest men around. As the day went by, however, I became increasingly aware of his presence; his pleasant, unhurried demeanor projected a certain dignity, and he was treated with much respect by the community who had gathered that day to offer alms to the monks in memory of their dead relatives and friends. I requested the friend who had invited me to the ceremony to introduce me to him. When he discovered I was a fluent English speaker, Look Tha told me of his great desire to learn English. Delighted, I asked him if he would teach me Khmer in exchange for English lessons, and over the next two years we met a couple of times a week at his house to learn languages from each other.

Every time I step across Look Tha's threshold, I leave American culture behind. After greeting me with hands clasped in the traditional manner, Look Tha carries my bag and books to the coffee table, to indicate his respect for me as his teacher, even though I am twenty years younger than he. We begin our lessons only after he serves me a glass of soda, or a cup of coffee prepared by his wife, sometimes accompanied with homemade sweets or tropical fruits. Although I am accustomed to the warm hospitality Cambodians extend to their visitors, I am particularly touched by Look Tha's thoughtfulness and concern for me because he is an elder.

The first time I visited him, Look Tha's actions took me back to my childhood in Sri Lanka, where we stood up when the teachers entered the classroom, greeted them with clasped hands, and carried their books to the teachers' room at the end of the lesson. At the end of my first lesson with Look Tha, I found myself taking his leave as I would from a teacher in Sri Lanka, and I did so almost unconsciously. I bade him farewell first, with my hands clasped, and allowed him to walk to the door ahead of me; I have done that ever since.

I chose Look Tha as a narrator because he appeared to embody many of the characteristics of traditional Khmer culture. But I soon realized that while he agreed enthusiastically to tell me his life history, he was reluctant to recount the Khmer Rouge atrocities in detail, even though he never said so directly. When I asked him about those experiences, he replied that he could not relate them because his English was not good enough. When I asked him to tell me in Khmer, his answer was that my Khmer was not good enough. Despite my knowledge of the regime's atrocities and the immense pain they cause survivors and my firm intention not to probe for information that the narrators did not wish to convey, I was deeply disappointed at his reticence.

Compassion had to come before knowledge, and I did not press him for information on the Khmer Rouge period. Instead, I talked about his culture, traditions, and Buddhism. Recounting these gave him immense pleasure, but Look Tha was by no means a passive narrator. To be sure that I understood Buddhism and his views and experiences, he once tested my knowledge and understanding of Buddhism by asking me to define a list of 30 Buddhist terms.

Because Look Tha displayed such a deep respect for religious teachings and ideals, I was curious to find out if and how he lived a Buddhist way of life; in this way, Look Tha came to mention some events about the Pol Pot era without any coercion from me. Even more important, I discovered he continues to cope with the Pol Pot trauma largely by following Buddhist teachings and practices. He departed from his ideals, however, when it came to his relations with the Vietnamese; here events in his country's history became much more significant.

Since, in the Buddhist outlook, old age and death are as much a part of life as birth and youth, I felt quite at ease talking with Look Tha about his remaining years in this life. His extension of not only his present life but also the lives of the Khmer Rouge soldiers to future rebirths shows how deeply the belief in karma (kamma) and rebirth is ingrained in the Buddhist worldview.

I have presented Look Tha's narrative first in this book for two reasons. First, his explanations of and insights about Cambodian history, society, culture, and Theravada Buddhist doctrines help to clarify information presented in the other narratives. Second, as an elder and a former monk, Look Tha occupies a primary place in his community.

Early Years

I was born a child of a farmer in November 1926, and I am now 62 years old. My father was a strong, handsome man. He was tall and big like an American. My mother was just about five feet tall; that is why I am small. Still, when I was younger, I was strong like my father.

When I was growing up, I lived with my parents, two brothers, and three sisters in a village of about five hundred people, in Battambang province. Many of our relatives, including our grandparents, Mother's older brother, and Father's older sister, lived in our village too. Most of the villagers, including my parents, were good people who went to the Buddhist temple every holy day. We call the Buddhist holy days "*Sila* days."

Almost everybody in my village was a farmer. Rich farmers had big fields all together in one place, and a lot of oxen. Poor farmers had no land, and perhaps just two oxen, so they usually worked for other people.

My father came from a very poor family, but after marriage, he worked very hard and became more prosperous. When I was growing up he was a middle-level farmer, neither rich nor poor. His fields were scattered in different places, and he had only six oxen. But he had a big house, two bicycles, and a motorcycle.

In the village, the only people who were not farmers were the twenty or so Vietnamese families that lived on the riverbank. They were fishermen. They spoke to each other in Vietnamese, but they spoke to us in Cambodian. Since Cambodians were not regular fishermen, we never became close friends with them. We did not like to fish for a living because we did not want to kill, but we fished occasionally when people got together to chat, or when rice fields were far away from the market.

When the rainy season started, Father cultivated about 70 ares of rice fields and orange gardens [100 ares = 1 hectare]. He hired labor only during transplanting and harvesting seasons. After harvesting the rice, he grew beans, peanuts, potatoes, mustard, white pepper, cucumber, chili, corn, and pumpkin in the fields. My father sold some of his harvest to people who came to the farm. Mother and I took the rest to sell in the market.

During the dry season, Father went in his ox cart to distant villages in the countryside to sell clothing, food, and medicines to people who lived there. Those people always looked dirty and ragged, and spoke in a different dialect. They also knew Khmer, so they could deal with us; from them, Father bought tobacco and reeds to make chairs, which he sold in Battambang. Mother helped him in the farm, and also went with him to the countryside whenever possible. Sometimes they hired people to help them, and about thirty ox carts trundled toward the countryside for two weeks or more. My older sisters looked after the family then. After my sisters got married and moved to their houses, I took care of my younger sister and brother. When I grew up and accompanied my parents, somebody from the village took care of them.

My mother never had any free time. When she was not working in the farm, she went to the countryside. During the rainy season she made cakes and sold them at a small stand she built near the river. When she returned home in the evenings, she prepared cakes for the next day. Like other women in the village, Mother cooked on a wood fire, and except for the rice pot, which was made of copper, all her cooking pots were made of clay. Later on, however, people used aluminum pots because the clay ones broke so easily.

When I was a child, I liked to play marbles with my friends.

"Now don't play in the sun, it's too hot. Play in the shade," Mother would say, as I ran out. And, "Don't climb those tall trees, you'll fall and break your legs!"

I also loved to play in the clear, fast-flowing river near my home, and my mother constantly worried that I might drown in it, especially when it was swollen after the rains.

"You are not to go near the river while I am gone," she would tell me whenever she had to go somewhere.

Although I obeyed her much of the time, sometimes when she was gone I could not stop myself from going to the river when friends called me. If I got caught, she or Father caned me for disobeying her.

As I grew older, I had to help Mother cook and take care of younger children, so I did not have much time to play. Still, whenever I could, I went to the river with my friends to swim or fish. Sometimes we brought food to share with each other. In Cambodia we had all kinds of fruits—oranges, grapefruits, papayas, mangosteens, pineapples, bananas, and sugar cane—my favorites were mangoes and young green coconuts, which have delicious water in the center.

My aunt and uncle who lived closest to our house had no children. We visited them often, and looked after them. We also frequently visited other neighbors. In Cambodia, unlike in America, we did not keep our doors closed. They were always left open so we could go to each other's home. If a new person came to the village, people talked to him and introduced him to others. People from my village went to other villages too. Even though our villages did not have paved roads, it was easy to go to other places because many of us had Honda motorcycles.

The happiest time for us in the village was during New Year, which we celebrated in mid-April. In the morning everybody took food to the monks in the temple and made merit. In the night, we played lots of different games in the temple grounds, which would be beautifully lit. Even though New Year came in the dry season, we felt cool and comfortable because we celebrated in the night.

My favorite game was called *chung*. To play chung, we first made a ball with a *kramar* [a large multipurpose scarf]. Then, girls and boys about fifteen to twenty years of age divided into two teams, and they threw the chung to each other, singing:

Boys: *When I throw the chung,*
       The chung will break into four pieces.
       Any girl who gets the chung,
       Can then catch me.
Girls: *When I throw the chung,*
       The chung will break into five pieces.
       Any boy who has my kamma,
       Can wait to wed with me.

Another festival we celebrated was Pchum Ben, in memory of our dead relatives. We believe that when people die, they are born in different places, and that once a year, the spirits of the dead come to visit all the children. So every November, we made floats with banana-tree trunks, and decorated them with 40 or 50 candles, incense, many kinds of foods, cigarettes, and betel leaves, and sent them down the river, saying, "I send all these good things to release you, every spirit, every living thing. So if you are searching for food, take whatever you can eat and be happy!"

Many people gathered on the riverbank to see the floats go down, and we felt very happy as we watched them go. We believed they also made the spirits happy, so that they could go back to their dwellings.

Schooling in the Temple

There were only two government schools in Battambang when I was little, so most villagers taught their children at home until the children could read and write some, after which the boys continued their education at the temple.

When I was about six years old, my father taught me to read and write Khmer, just as he had taught my sisters. Father did not have a high education because he had not gone to school, and after some months had gone by he said, "It is time for you to go and live in the temple and learn from the monks; there is nothing more I can teach you." I was eight or nine years old when my father took me there.

"You must behave well in the temple and not do anything unreasonable or disrespectful," my mother advised me before I left. "Don't speak harshly to the monks, or to the old men and women who come to the temple. Don't steal anything or harm anyone. Listen to the monks and do as they say."

The temple was across from the river, and Father carried my clothes, a blanket, and a pillow, tied up in a bundle. There were 60 or 70 boys of various ages already living there. I was the youngest. Father handed me over to the monks, and before he left, he too advised me to always obey the monks. After he left, I did not want to stay. I missed my parents, brothers, and sisters terribly, and always asked the monks to go back home. They allowed me to go home about seven or eight times the first year, but after that, the monks did not allow me to return home so often.

In the temple, everyone got up at half-past five. The older boys prepared rice gruel for breakfast, plucked ripe fruits from the many fruit trees in the temple yard, and served the monks their breakfast. The younger boys swept the dry leaves off the temple grounds and watered the plants.

When they finished breakfast, some monks walked from house to house with their bowls, and villagers gave them rice to use at lunchtime. After we finished breakfast, those monks who remained in the temple taught us Sanskrit, using long-leaf books. They also told us stories of the Buddha and other great people in our history.

We studied until about nine-thirty, when the villagers started arriving with different kinds of soups, meat and fish, vegetables, fruits, and sweetmeats to offer the monks at lunchtime. We always had enough left over for dinner as well, but the monks had only two meals a day; after the noon hour, they only drank tea or juices. Sometimes, instead of bringing food to the temple, people invited the monks to their houses.

After lunch, the younger monks went to a nearby temple to study because our temple did not have learned monks. The older monks read Dhamma books, studied Pali and Sanskrit, or rested.

We went swimming in the river, and for the next two hours, the river was filled with screaming, yelling children. When we returned we studied Sanskrit again till five o'clock, when we had dinner. In the evening all of us, the monks and students, washed again at the river. Later on the villagers installed a water machine [spigot] in the temple, so the monks did not go to the river to wash. Because we wanted to play, we continued to go to the river, and after we came back we had some free time.

In the night, the monks taught us Dhamma until ten o'clock. At this time they did not give us any books; we had to listen and memorize everything they taught. When it was time to sleep, the monks slept in the bedrooms, and the boys slept outside on the verandah.

Although we were fond of the monks, we were also afraid of them because they were strict disciplinarians. When we misbehaved or did something wrong, the monks first advised us using moral proverbs; if we continued to do wrong things, they beat us two or three times with the switch. However, they did so only to scare us, and to teach us good behavior.

One time a monk beat me too. We went to bathe in the river, and saw some Vietnamese men catching fish. When they finished, the fishermen took with them the big fish, and threw away the little ones, which we picked up and took back to the temple.

"Why did you catch those fish?" asked a monk who saw them.

"We did not catch them, we just picked them up because the Vietnamese threw them out," we told him.

However, the monk did not believe us. Thinking we caught the fish ourselves, he beat us, because in the Buddhist religion we are told not to kill animals.

There were about 30 or 40 monks in my temple, but I liked Sankharaja, the head monk, best. He was 75 years old, and was tall and fair-skinned. Oh, he was handsome! He was also a very good man. When he spoke to the pupils, he always smiled. He never scolded anybody. When he lay down and rested after lunch, he sometimes called me to fan him to keep him cool, or to massage his legs.

When I was fourteen years old, I decided to go back home because I wanted to go to government school. Sankharaja said, "When you go back home, obey your parents just like you did when you were a little boy," and gave me permission to leave. I returned home with my father's approval.

The government school was very different because about 30 percent of the 50 or 60 students in my class were female; but we did not become friends with them. At recess girls played on one side of the schoolyard and boys played on the other side. We talked to each other only if we needed any help with our lessons.

In the classroom, about five students of the same sex sat on a long bench at each table. We learned French as well as Cambodian, but we did not learn English. We used regular books instead of the long-leaf books the monks used in the temple, and since ballpoint pens did not exist in those days we used dip pens for writing. When I came home after school, I continued to help my parents on the farm and with household chores.

When I was about seventeen, my sisters were married, and had left with their husbands to live on their own. Father said to me, "You are a big man and you had your education. Now you must stay at home and look after your younger brother and sister while they go to school."

Although I did not want to stop my schooling I had to obey my father and I remained at home. But whenever I had free time I tried to learn the Thai language from a monk who knew it well, because at that time, Battambang was ruled by the Thai. Two years later I left home again to become a monk.

A Novice Monk

When I was young, it was the tradition for all peasant boys who could do so to become monks. If a boy did not enter monkhood, he would not know the Buddha's teachings and would have wrong thoughts; the villagers did not consider such a person a good man. So when my parents told me to become a monk at age twenty, I returned to the temple in which I had studied, this time to be ordained as a monk, just as my grandfather and father had done.

Five other boys joined the monkhood with me, and this was marked by a big ceremony. A layperson shaved our heads. We were given white kramars to cover our shoulders and special *sarongs* [worn by men and women] to wear, but not the kind that monks wore. When we were ready, musicians, dancers, my parents, and hundreds of other people escorted us into the temple in a procession. There, Sankharaja ordained us as novice monks.

Although I had learned some Dhamma when I lived in the temple before, now I had much more to learn about *dana* [giving], *sila* [disciplinary precepts], and *bhavana* [meditation]. As a monk, I had to strive continually to purify my mind and do good deeds.

The Buddha said:

Sabbha papassa akaranam
Kusalassa Upa Sampada
Sachitta pariyodapanam
Etam Buddhanu Sasanam.

This means:

Avoid all evil,
Do what is good,
Purify your heart,
This is the advice of all the Buddhas.

When monks have *sila*, or are disciplined, they bring happiness to people. The disciplinary precepts taught us how to behave so we could control our thoughts and actions, and not lose our concentration. For instance, when I went to people's houses I could not laugh or speak loudly; and when I walked, I was required to look ahead, and not glance around. If I behaved otherwise, it led to loss of concentration and discipline.

We spent much of our time teaching Dhamma to laypeople, because if people did not know about *dana*, *sila*, and *bhavana*, they would not know about good and bad; then they would be like animals. To teach people about life experiences, we told them Jataka stories, which are about the Buddha's past lives.

In return for our guidance, the people looked after our needs since we had little time to cook, and we lived in the temple without parents or family. They gave us food, robes, bedding, and other items we needed.

In addition to receiving moral guidance, they also received much merit, or good karmic results for their actions. For instance, when someone gave food to us, or to those who were destitute, or to animals, they enabled us to live one more day. We believe that this act of giving to others brings merit to those who gave, and helps them to attain worthy lives in future rebirths. In Buddha's language merit is called *punya*. Even though we believe it is meritorious to give to others and we encouraged people to do so, no one was forced to give anything; it was up to the people to do so if they wished.

In Buddhism, we also believe that we can transfer merit we acquire to those who are deceased, and who may not yet be reborn in a good place. So after lunch, we prayed that those dead relatives of the people who had offered food or other items to us would benefit from those good deeds.

I learned Dhamma at my village temple for three years. There was a great deal to learn, and I wished to study for at least seven years, but after my third year, I was sent to a temple in Phnom Penh to teach for a year. After that I returned to my own temple because it needed a teacher.

I was much happier as a monk than as a layperson, because as a monk, I became a good person. But I was still young and strong, and when I was 26, I decided to return home because I wanted to work. I knew I could return to monkhood when I grew older. I obtained my father's approval to go back home.

Before I left, Sankharaja advised me on how to be a good layperson again. He then blessed me, and sprayed holy water on my head. I removed my robes and put on a normal sarong, and cried as I worshipped Sankharaja and bade him farewell. After returning home, I did what my parents asked me to do, but for a long time, I felt sick in my heart because I wanted to return to the temple.

A few months after I came back, I started working for a Chinese businessman, overseeing about 300 loggers working in the jungles near the Thai-Cambodia border. That work was done in the dry season only. During the rainy season, I supervised coolies building the railway lines in Battambang. Three years later, I got married.

An Arranged Marriage

When I was 16 or 17 I liked a certain girl, but I never told her of my feelings; in those days, boys and girls did not talk about love and romance. She got married when I became a monk, so when I was 29 years old, I got married to a girl chosen for me by my parents, as was our custom.

In Cambodia, when a man's parents found a girl whom they considered a suitable bride for their son, they first asked her neighbors about her character. If those neighbors said, "She never had a boyfriend. She cooks well, and she knows how to look after a house. She will make a good wife!" the groom's parents approached her parents. If the girl's parents found the proposition agreeable, they in turn inquired from the groom's neighbors about his conduct and character. To be considered suitable, a man had to be a good worker who did not drink, gamble, or engage in cockfighting.

When both families were satisfied, the groom's parents came to the girl's house bearing trays with gifts of fruits, a whole head of a pig, two hens, new clothes, and other things. If the young couple agreed to the marriage, a wedding date was set. The night before the wedding monks visited the bride's home and advised the couple to always speak respectfully to each other, not to commit adultery, to take care of one another, and so on, so the two would have a harmonious marriage. Then festivities continued for three days.

I never saw her before my parents arranged my marriage, but everybody who knew the girl that my parents chose for me said she was a very good person. My parents told me she had never had a boyfriend; if it had been otherwise, I would never have married her. I did not worry about how she looked; whether she was beautiful, or whether she was dark or light-skinned, because I trusted my parents' judgment. When I saw her I thought, "That girl is the right person for me."

After the wedding, I went to live with my wife's parents. I had to show my parents-in-law that I would be a good husband to their daughter. I worked with my father-in-law on his farm, and planted mangoes, oranges, grapefruits, coconuts, and many other fruit trees, but because they would not bear fruit for a few years, I also planted vegetables such as cucumber, corn, and eggplant, for faster yields.

After about a year, my wife's parents said, "We see you can do things for yourself, and we think you make a good husband for our daughter. It is time for you to live on your own."

In Cambodia, as people became prosperous, they bought furnishings to decorate the house, or land and other gifts for their children. Parents did not sell things to children as they do in America. When children married, parents gave gold necklaces, earrings, and bracelets to daughters, and rings and necklaces to sons. When newly married couples went to live on their own, their parents gave them land and various household items.

When my wife and I moved from her parents' house, my father-in-law gave me about three ares of land in the countryside and tools for my new farm. It was a very small parcel of land, but sufficient for us to begin our new life. Also, because I had no farm machinery I could not have managed a bigger farm.

Every morning I went to my farm at half-past six, and about an hour later my wife brought me freshly cooked hot rice and grilled fish for breakfast. Sometimes she stayed on and helped me with the work, but I did not think she was strong enough to do farm work. Besides, she had to look after our house and the children. My wife had eleven pregnancies, but she had five miscarriages. Of the other six children, a boy and a girl died just after birth, and a daughter died of disease when she was seven. So we were left with only three children.

After breakfast I worked till about noon, plowing the land with the oxen, or cultivating by hand. Some mornings I drew about 150 buckets of water from the well and watered my plants. When the sun became too hot, I bathed in the river, and went home to eat a full plate of rice, fish, soup, and vegetables my wife cooked for our noon meal.

Then I slept for an hour or two, and returned to my fields and worked until five or six in the evening.

Like my parents, I too worked seven days a week. "You work too hard; why don't you take a rest?" some people would say to me, but I did not like to stop working even for a day because things piled up. Besides, I could see the results of my work. We had nice clothes to wear and good food to eat. My family had a good life, and I had a good marriage.

After we had been married for about seven years, the fruit trees I planted in my father-in-law's land started to produce bountiful harvests. Every year, I earned about six or seven thousand *riel* [Cambodian currency] selling fruit, and I gave that money to my parents for safekeeping. All of us in the village kept our savings in our homes. Only the big people [rich people] in the city kept money in the bank. Later, as I became more experienced, I bought more land in other places, but I was careful to buy only as much land as I could manage.

Peasants in Cambodia were different from government people who were born in Phnom Penh. The city people went to good schools and got a high education; they were rich, high-class people. As a child of a farmer, I knew I could never become rich like the people in Phnom Penh, but I did not feel angry that I was poor, because I knew what I could do for myself. I could plant, sell, and do good things for my family, and for other people in the village.

I never fought with anybody in the village; even if someone made me angry I usually kept quiet, not because I feared others or surrendered to them, but because I did not want to lose control of myself. My village was generally a peaceful place, though, because even if two people disagreed about something, a third person would say gentle words to both and help to resolve their problem.

Although I avoided arguments and physical fights, I knew how to defend myself if someone confronted me, because an elder who liked me taught me martial arts; and once I almost fought with some Vietnamese who tried to steal the food from the floats we had sent downstream to honor our dead relatives. When they heard us shouting and running toward them they turned back, so we never went after them.

Another time, I used my wit to fend off two Laotians who tried to accost me in the countryside. I had gone there with a lot of gold to buy some goods from the villagers when two hefty men closed in on me, asking, "Well, what's your business here?" I knew I was strong, and I carried a knife tucked into my sarong, but I did not want to fight two people. So even though I spoke some Laotian, I pretended not to understand what they said. Instead, I smiled broadly and carried on with my journey, and to my relief, they stopped following me.

In 1970, the year my father died, I was struck with a serious illness. My legs became numb, and at harvesttime I had to hire people to gather my crops. My wife and children too had to work hard. For about six months, I had to crawl on the floor, but finally, some medicine made with tree roots helped me to get better.

About the time I was using a cane and walking a little, Lon Nol soldiers and the Khmer Rouge started fighting close to our village. When bombs started to destroy the houses and farms in my village, we were forced to go to live in the town. There, my wife and daughters earned a living by selling cooked food and sweetmeats in the market.

Life and Death Under the Khmer Rouge

On April 17, 1975, Khmer Rouge came to Battambang. Two days later Pol Pot soldiers came to my brother-in-law's house in the night and said, "We want you to come with us to get something to eat." When they reached the store they shot my brother-in-law, right on the sidewalk. The next day the soldiers came and ordered us to bring his body to the temple for cremation. Since I was still unable to walk, my wife and his wife did so. In the next two or three days they also killed my father-in-law, brother, another brother-in-law, and my wife's uncle. The soldiers did not say why they were killed, but all of the victims had worked in the previous regime.

The Pol Pots also killed the head monk of Battambang, who was my relative. He was a very kindhearted man and everybody loved him. He was also very intelligent; he spoke French, Cambodian, Thai, and Vietnamese, and he also knew Sanskrit and Pali. Later, a woman told me that before he was killed, the Pol Pots ordered the monk to dig a big hole. They then bashed his head with a hoe, and pushed him into it. But, she said, they did not even cover his body properly; after the soldiers left, the monk's legs protruded from the grave.

A week after they came to Battambang, the Pol Pots chased all of us from our houses to the countryside. They talked by the gun: OUT, OUT, OUT. SHOOT.

Like other villagers, my family too kept large supplies of rice and dry fish in our home. When the soldiers ordered us to leave, we wanted to take the food with us, but they said, "Take only enough food for three days. You will come back to your houses after three days, when we have cleaned up the city."

However, we did not believe them, and took as much food as we could carry, and all the money and gold we had collected.

The street was packed with thousands of people. Some even took their pigs, cattle, and chickens with them, and those who had to carry young children as well as their goods could barely walk. But the soldiers did not care. They forced us to hurry, with threats and random shootings.

I brought my family back to my farm in the countryside, only to find that my house and land had been taken over by other people. The Pol Pots gave us a small hut nearby, and that night, I hid my gold inside the bamboo steps leading to that hut, and buried the money in the ground.

A few months after evacuation, the Pol Pots took my older daughter and son to live with other young people in youth camps. For the next several months, we did not know where our children were, or if they were alive. My wife and I felt sick with worry, but there was nothing we could do; the soldiers told us our families belonged to Angka. Finally, after about six months my daughter came to visit us, but only for two days. We did not see our son for a whole year.

My younger daughter who lived with us had to look after small babies because their parents, along with my wife, had to work in the rice fields.

Because I still could not walk without using a cane, the soldiers ordered me to sit on the ground and cut grass, or weave baskets. I worked very slowly because I was old and ill, and the Pol Pots often accused me of pretending to be sick. "We will kill you if you lie to us," they would threaten me often. I knew they would do so; I saw many people who were beaten or killed for such crimes.

We worked all day, under the sun and in the rain, with no medicine and hardly any food. I was so hungry that I caught every snail, lizard, frog, and fish I saw, even though I had stopped fishing after I was about 40 years old, because I did not want to kill living beings anymore. Other people did the same, but we were very careful not to let Pol Pots see us when we foraged for food because they would have punished us severely for "stealing."

Once they killed a handicapped person in my village who ate the stem of a cassava that was left on the ground after the cassava was dug up. Another time I saw a man tied up and beaten with hefty bamboo poles because he had plucked an orange. There was a thundering noise every time they beat him, and blood gushed out of his head and back. Oh, it was terrible! I also saw a soldier return an ax he had borrowed from a boy who lived near my hut, and it was covered with blood. I don't know who was killed. At that time, we all lived with great fear; every moment we expected the soldiers would come to take us away to be killed.

I didn't want to die during the Pol Pot time because the Buddha said that humans who did not purify their minds at the time of death would be born in a bad place. But how could I purify my mind then? I was very angry with the Pol Pots; they did not give us enough clothes or food, and forced us to do hard labor. So because I did not have good thoughts, I did not want to die at that time.

Although I was angry with the Pol Pots, I never said or did anything to get revenge; if I did so, I would also be bad like them. The Buddha said, "If someone does wrong to another person and that person takes revenge, the result will never end."

Whenever I was tempted to take revenge on the soldiers, I thought of those words, and also of my past lives. I believed that if I had acted badly in a previous life, something bad will happen to me in this life. But if in a previous life I had not killed, stolen, or done bad things to other people, I would escape being killed by the Pol Pots.

To help me control my anger, I recited Dhamma in my mind every night, and prayed to the Ratana Thrai [the Three Jewels]. I prayed over and over,

Khadesa, khadesa
Kang karana khadesa
Ahang petthang cha na mi

This means, "Even if anybody does me any wrong, I will never take revenge."

That was all I could do. I had so little food or possessions that I could not give *dana* [alms] to anybody. I had no *sila* because I killed. The only thing I could do was meditate.

I believe my meditation also helped my son. When he was assigned to a youth camp close to our village, he came over to our hut whenever he could, in the night. One night Pol Pot soldiers saw him and arrested him. A man who saw my son being taken away came and told me what had happened. I was terrified that my son would be killed. So while my hands worked, my mind meditated on Buddha, Dhamma, and Sangha on behalf of my son. My son was not killed. Someone had told the Pol Pot leader that my son was a good worker, and the leader had released my son after warning him not to disobey their orders again.

I believe that when people die, they are reborn, and that those who observed *Panchasila* [the Five Precepts] and led good lives will be reborn in the heavens or in the universe. Those who did bad things will be born in hell or as animals. Therefore, in the future, the result of kamma (karma) will not bring Pol Pot soldiers to a good place. Someday they too will suffer and be killed, either in this life or in a future life. Already they have had to suffer in this life; I saw them living in the jungle like animals, after the Vietnamese came.

When the Vietnamese Came

After the Vietnamese liberation, my family and I went back to our farm because the people who lived there in the Pol Pot time had gone back to their own place. We planted sweet potatoes, corn, chili, and other vegetables, and we were in control of our lives when the Vietnamese ordered my eighteen-year-old son and the husband of my older daughter, who married during the Pol Pot regime, to join the army. They did not want to do so, because though it was the Cambodian army, it was controlled by the Vietnamese. We heard that those who did not follow orders were forcibly taken away to the army, and we decided then to leave our country because we knew that whether they were Cambodian or Vietnamese, under Communists we had no freedom.

In November 1979 we left our home for the Thai-Cambodia border. We carried very little food and clothing with us because we did not want to attract the attention of Vietnamese soldiers. Because I walked so slowly, my son and son-in-law helped me by carrying me on their backs, but soon my wife too had problems walking: her soles cracked, became bloody, and caused her severe pain. After five days we had made little progress because we were ill, tired, and had little to eat. We had no choice but to pay some gold and hire a motor trailer [a trailer pulled by a motorcyclist] to take us to the border. When we reached the border, we discovered that it was too dangerous to stay there because the Khmer Rouge and the Vietnamese continued to fight close to our camps, and we left for Khao-I-Dang camp in Thailand on December 8, 1979.

The United Nations gave my family a single room in a long shelter, and rations of bean sauce, fish sauce, salt, and rice. Although we ate sparingly, the rations were not sufficient for our family, and I sold gold for *baht* [Thai currency] and bought food from vendors. Still, I felt happy; even though our living conditions were bad and we did not have enough to eat, things were now much better than in the Pol Pot time.

In the camp I studied English using a Thai-English dictionary because I did not have enough money to pay a teacher. I did not know much Thai, but I could speak and read enough to look up English words in the dictionary. I would then write them in Thai, and memorize them. My son-in-law didn't know Thai, but knew a little English and a lot of French, and we helped each other to learn English, using *English for Today, Book III*.

Thousands of new refugees continued to come to Khao-I-Dang, and I met several people from my village. From them I heard that the Vietnamese soldiers had begun to commit many robberies in my village, although they had not done so before I left. One friend said, "You know what happened to your good friend Prov? He went back and forth between the border and the village selling things, and every time he traveled, the Vietnamese soldiers checked his bags and took whatever they wanted. One time because the soldiers did not find anything they liked, they kicked him so badly that they broke three ribs, and he died."

I decided I would not return to Cambodia until the Vietnamese left.

I had not planned to come to America when I left my country; I knew nothing about America then. I went to the refugee camp only to move far away from the fighting. There, however, I discovered that many people, including my mother, brother, and sister, and their children who had also escaped, had gone to America, and I thought I will also come here. My brother sent a letter saying he would sponsor us, but before I applied to come, I received orders from the camp officials to move with my wife to another camp.

When we first went to Khao-I-Dang, the officials told us that we would not be separated from our children; later, they ordered my wife and me to move. We had no choice in the matter. I do not know why we were moved. After twenty months, with no explanation, they sent us back to live with our children. By then, our children had applied to come to America and they left a few months later. We also applied to come, and finally, in 1982, the Americans called us for an interview. We passed the interview, but we lived in Khao-I-Dang for two more years before being moved to a transit camp in the Philippines. In that camp, we went to school to learn English, and how to live in America. We arrived here in 1984.

An Old Man in America

When we came, my daughter and son-in-law were living in a small apartment, and we too lived with them. My son-in-law showed me how to get to the grocery store, to the International Rescue Committee, which helps refugees, to the hospital, and to various other places. During my first year in America, I went to the hospital often because I still had problems with numbness. In this country, I like the hospital best because the receptionists, nurses, and doctors always speak nicely to me, which makes me feel happy.

Sometimes I think Americans don't like refugees. One time a young American man climbed into the bus ahead of me, but instead of moving forward, he stood still. I waited for a while, and climbed up behind him. Suddenly, he shoved me with his elbow; if I had not been holding the handrail I would have fallen on the street. I did not say or do anything. I kept quiet because I am an old man, and I am not American. The driver and many people in the bus saw what happened, but they didn't say anything. I wonder why that young man did that? America is a capitalist country, not a Communist country, so why do people behave like that?

I miss my homeland. I liked living in my village because I had relatives and friends, and the freedom to go about whenever and wherever I liked. Here, I don't even know my neighbors. During the day they go to work, and in the evening, they keep their doors closed. In America, people wait for Saturday or Sunday to talk to others.

I also miss my rice fields and my big garden with all the fruits and vegetables. There, I worked hard and ate a lot more food than I eat here; in Cambodia we didn't have diets. Now, because I don't do any work, I eat only what I need to keep me from starvation. Otherwise I will get fat, and lose my health.

My biggest problem is that I do not know much English. The first time I heard some white people speak English in Cambodia, I knew it was not French, but I did not know what language it was. When I heard it again in the refugee camp, I remembered the sounds of the unknown language that I had heard before, and realized that it was English!

I wish I could go to school to learn English, but because my children have to go to work they don't have too much time to take us around. My ambition now is to learn to drive, buy an old car, and go to school to learn English. Some people say, "You are an old man. Why do you want to go to school?" I tell them I want to be able to speak to American people.

Sometimes I try to learn English by watching television, but usually the man speaks too fast for me to understand. When I read the English newspaper, I understand only about half of what I read. If I learn more English I will be able to improve my mind because I will have new things to think about, and new people to talk to.

Reflections

When I am lonely I think of Cambodia; but then I think of Pol Pot, and I get so upset. I think, "Why did they kill so many people? They all had the same religion, the same nationality, the same dress; they were all Cambodians!"

I do not cry when I think of what the Pol Pots did to my country and my people, but when I think of those times my head feels very tight, and I feel sick in my chest. At such times, I go to my room, shut the door, and meditate. I concentrate on my breathing, and it helps to relax me. When I breathe in, I concentrate on the cool air that touches the nostril. When I breathe out, I am conscious of the hot air that touches the nostril. I do not think about anything else. When I finish meditating I read newspapers, historical books, or Buddha stories, to forget about Cambodia and my people's troubles.

But when I sleep, I dream of my country. Some nights I dream I am working in my rice fields like I used to, but some nights I dream I am working for Pol Pot, and it is very upsetting. I almost never dream of my life here.

I think Cambodia fell to the Communists because of two major reasons. First, the people in the countryside did not have much education. Most of them went to the temples and became monks, but their temples may not have had highly educated monks who were good teachers. Then, if the people did not go to another temple to study, they would not have learned Dhamma properly, and therefore would not have known what was good and what was bad. When the Khmer Rouge told untruths to such ignorant people, they believed them and became Communists.

Sihanouk's wrong politics was the second reason for Cambodia's fall. I know about Sihanouk's political ideals because when he came to Battambang, soldiers made the people listen to his speeches. Sometimes he spoke for two or three hours.

In 1953, Sihanouk fought for Cambodia's independence and Cambodia became independent in 1954. At that time we all thought Sihanouk was glorious. He kept Cambodia in the middle [politically neutral]. Around 1964–66, however, Sihanouk visited China and his politics changed. He thought that the Communists will triumph over the capitalists, and he formed a friendship with Ho Chi Minh, even though we despised Ho Chi Minh. When Sihanouk left the United Nations in 1966 and started to lean toward socialism, I began to dislike him. Only stupid people in the countryside liked him. The government of Thailand brought progress and peace to their country, but the leader of Cambodia governed the wrong way, and the result he got was Pol Pot.

I had a lot of property in Cambodia. My children would have had good jobs there because we sent them to school and gave them a good education. But we don't think of going back because Cambodia is no longer a peaceful country, and the Khmer Rouge wants to control it again. They have all kinds of weapons they get from China. Even if Pol Pot did not come back, our country is still under Vietnamese Communists, and I don't trust them.

Under Communists, nobody can do what they want. My older sister and her children still live there. She did not escape with us because my nephew wanted to have all our property, but now he has to work as a soldier. His wife works too, in the bank, but their salaries are too small to feed all their children. Since my sister is very old and cannot work, she does not have enough to eat. I wish I had money to spare so I could send some to them every month, but I don't, because I am on welfare. So even though I feel sad about my relatives and I get homesick, I do not think about going back.

Here in America, I have Vietnamese neighbors, but I cannot trust them because I have read the chronicles of Cambodia, and I know that Cambodians and Vietnamese have been enemies through history. Buddha said to treat all people equally, but I cannot become close friends with them. I only say "Hi" to my Vietnamese neighbors, and they say "Hi" to me.

When Cambodian women who live here marry Vietnamese men, I get very angry. I don't know what I would do if my grandchildren married Vietnamese; I don't even want to think about it. I like Chinese people though, they are the same as Cambodians. I would like it if my grandchildren married Chinese people. But I hope my children or grandchildren will not marry American or Spanish people because we have different cultures.

I did not know how different the Cambodian and American cultures were until I came here. When I went to school in the Philippine camp, my teacher was an American Mormon Christian. She told me, "When you come to America, you must not forget your Cambodian culture. Teach your culture to all your children and grandchildren." I could not understand why she said that, because to me it seemed that people will always like the culture of the country they were born in.

I also thought that in America, the government let refugees keep their natural cultures, because in this country there is freedom. Now I know it is not so.

In Cambodian culture, teachers tell the students, "When you go back home, you must never do anything that your parents dislike. You must always obey them." At home, our parents reminded us often to obey our teachers and although we disobeyed them sometimes, we usually did what our parents and teachers told us. However, in America, teachers teach children about their freedom to do what they want, so they don't obey their parents, and many Cambodian refugees have problems with their children.

Some Cambodian youth in this country do not even know about our culture or customs. They grew up in Pol Pot time, and then when they came here, they went to school here; so they know only the American customs. For example, they shout and they jump when they talk to each other, and even if older people tell them not to, they do not listen. Although everybody likes their freedom, it is not good to disturb others by loud and noisy behavior.

I don't dislike everything about American culture, but I dislike people kissing on the road, or on the sidewalk. In Cambodian culture, it is shameful to kiss so all the people can see. I never saw people kiss in public in Thailand, or in the movies we used to get from India. When I wait for the bus, young men and women kiss at the bus stand. I am an old man and I feel ashamed when I see them. If my granddaughters kiss like that I will tell them not to do it, but I do not know if they will listen to me because they grew up here. Also, I can only tell them what is right and wrong. It is up to them to choose what they want to do. Some TV programs have naked people and sex, and then I switch it off. I feel embarrassed to watch them because those stories are for young people.

I want my grandchildren to learn about our history, language, and culture. For instance, when people come to our house, they must greet them respectfully with their palms together, and treat them well. When the people leave, they must again show respect. When we go to another house, they must respect the owner of that house. I am happy to say that my daughter and son-in-law have taught their children these customs.

I would like to teach my grandchildren to read and write our language, but the Cambodian language has many sophisticated words that they don't understand yet because they are too young. Also, the choice is up to their parents. Before I teach Cambodian to my grandchildren, I will ask my daughter and son-in-law if they will allow me to do so. I am their grandfather and I take care of them, but if my daughter and son-in-law do not want them to learn Cambodian, I will not teach them because I do not like to do things that others dislike.

I believe that people must have the freedom to say if they dislike something. For example, if I dislike going to church, nobody should force me to go to church as some people try to do. I think wherever I live, if nobody forces me to do anything, I will have no worries.

Some Cambodians are unhappy here because they came with no education, cannot get jobs, and so cannot have a good life. They do not have enough money to go to Lake Tahoe, Las Vegas, Disneyland, Santa Cruz, Monterey, and other places, like those who came in 1979 with a good education and got good jobs.

As for me, I am neither happy nor unhappy. I am an old man and I am not strong enough to work. The government gives me enough money to get by from month to month, I have a place to live, and I feel contented. I have no desire to go to the cinema or to concerts. I have seen all that in Cambodia. I am happy staying at home, watching TV, reading books. In that respect, I am different from old men in America. They visit places to find ways to happiness. As long as I have the freedom to meditate, to talk about Dhamma, to read, go to the temple, and purify my mind, I will be happy.

All men and women grow old, and I think I am ready to die when the time comes. I do not worry about death because I didn't harm anybody or do anything that others disliked.

After I die, I wish to be reborn in a place where I will know Buddhism because the Buddha's word is true.

The Christian religion says, "If you lie, kill, or commit any other sin, you can wash away the sin," but I don't believe that. If people do wrong, they receive bad results. If they do good, they receive good results. For example, if I say bad words to you, you will get angry with me, but if I say good words to you, you will be happy. If somebody touches the fire, they will be burnt, but if they do not touch the fire, they will not burn.

I don't know where I will be reborn, but I will do good in this life because when people are jealous, greedy, steal, lie, or take intoxicants, the results of kamma will not be very good in another life. My only wish is to be reborn anywhere that has Buddhism, so I can listen to Dhamma, study Dhamma, and purify my mind.

Index